University of Cambridge Oriental Publications No. 32

Interpreting the Hebrew Bible

Dr E.I.J. Rosenthal (Photograph by Ian Fleming)

Interpreting the Hebrew Bible

Essays in honour of E.I.J. Rosenthal

Emeritus Reader in Oriental Studies
in the University of Cambridge
and Emeritus Fellow of Pembroke College, Cambridge

EDITED BY
J.A. EMERTON AND STEFAN C. REIF

CAMBRIDGE UNIVERSITY PRESS

CAMBRIDGE
LONDON NEW YORK NEW ROCHELLE
MELBOURNE SYDNEY

University of Cambridge Oriental Publications
published for the
Faculty of Oriental Studies
see page 319
for the complete list

Published by the Press Syndicate of the University of Cambridge
The Pitt Building, Trumpington Street, Cambridge CB2 1RP
32 East 57th Street, New York, NY 10022, USA
296 Beaconsfield Parade, Middle Park, Melbourne 3206, Australia

Printed in Great Britain at the
University Press, Cambridge

Library of Congress catalogue card number: 81-21668

British Library cataloguing in publication data

Interpreting the Hebrew Bible: essays in honour
of E.I.J. Rosenthal.
1. Bible. *Hebrew*–Addresses, essays, lectures
2. Rosenthal, E.I.J.–Addresses, essays, lectures
I. Emerton, J.A. II. Reif, Stefan C.
III. Rosenthal, E.I.J. IV. Series
220.4'4 BS476

ISBN 0 521 24424 2

קובץ מאמרים בפרשנות המקרא
מוגש בכבוד ובידידות
לד"ר יצחק רוזנטל
במלאות לו שבעים וחמש שנה
ביום ט' לחודש תשרי שנת תש"ם

כל שרוח הבריות נוחה הימנו
רוח המקום נוחה הימנו
מסכת אבות, פרק ג'

קנטבריגיה

CONTENTS

PLATES

Plates 1–6 are printed by kind permission of the Syndics of the Cambridge University Library

PREFACE

Erwin Rosenthal was an active member of the Publications Committee of the Faculty of Oriental Studies in Cambridge from 1957 until his retirement in 1971, and he has continued to help the Committee since then. Moreover, he contributed the first book to the University of Cambridge Oriental Publications series, and, later, the two-volume collection of his more important papers. Over the years the Committee have benefited from his shrewd academic judgement; their meetings have been made pleasant by his good humour, and the sale of his books has contributed materially to the publication of other monographs in the series. When, therefore, the Committee heard that Rosenthal's friends and colleagues intended to present him with a collection of essays to celebrate his seventy-fifth birthday, they were keen to be associated with the proposal and they undertook to publish the volume.

The Committee agreed that the essays should be organized around a single major theme and hence, although this has meant that the papers presented here make a contribution to only one of the fields of scholarship in which Rosenthal has made his mark, the book is limited to studies of interpretations of the Hebrew Bible. The Committee hope that any disappointment occasioned by this decision, felt either by friends who would have liked to contribute an essay, but whose scholarly expertise lies in a different field, or by those who would have liked to see this collection of essays reflect the breadth of Rosenthal's own interests, will be compensated for by having a coherent volume, which seeks to illuminate from different points of view one particularly important subject.

Like all works involving the collaboration of many people, *Interpreting the Hebrew Bible* has been longer in the making than we had originally hoped or intended; but the Committee now lay it before the public as a token of their regard for Rosenthal and as an expression of gratitude for his great contribution to their own work.

On behalf of the Committee I would like to thank Rev. Henry Hart, whose elegant calligraphy forms the dedication; and we are deeply indebted to Professor Emerton and Dr Reif for planning the volume and for bringing it into being.

Cambridge, April 1981

Gordon Johnson
Chairman of the Publications Committee

CONTRIBUTORS

Dr S.P. Brock, *Fellow of Wolfson College and Lecturer in Aramaic and Syriac in the University of Oxford*

Dr R.E. Clements, *Fellow of Fitzwilliam College and Lecturer in Divinity in the University of Cambridge*

Professor David Daube, *Director of the Robbins Hebraic and Roman Law Collections and Professor-in-Residence at the School of Law in the University of California, Berkeley*

Dr N.R.M. de Lange, *Lecturer in Rabbinics in the University of Cambridge*

Professor J.A. Emerton, *Fellow of St. John's College and Regius Professor of Hebrew in the University of Cambridge*

Dr Robert P. Gordon, *Lecturer in Divinity in the University of Cambridge*

Professor R.J. Loewe, *Professor of Hebrew in University College, London*

Professor Shelomo Morag, *Professor of Hebrew Linguistics in the Hebrew University of Jerusalem*

Professor Chaim Rabin, *Professor of Hebrew Language in the Hebrew University of Jerusalem*

Dr Stefan C. Reif, *Director of the Taylor-Schechter Genizah Research Unit and Under-Librarian in the University of Cambridge*

Dr Avihai Shivtiel, *Lecturer in Semitic Studies in the University of Leeds*

The Rev. J.G. Snaith, *Lecturer in Hebrew and Aramaic in the University of Cambridge*

Professor Georges Vajda, *Professeur émérite d'Hébreu à l'Université de la Sorbonne nouvelle, Paris* (*d. 1981*)

Professor J. Weingreen, *Emeritus Fellow of Trinity College and Erasmus Smith's Professor Emeritus of Hebrew in the University of Dublin*

Dr M.P. Weitzman, *Lecturer in the Department of Hebrew and Jewish Studies in University College, London*

ABBREVIATIONS

In addition to standard abbreviations and those separately listed in some of the articles, the following have been employed:

AJR	*AJR Information* (London) issued by the Association of Jewish Refugees in Great Britain.
AP	*The Aryan Path* (Bombay).
AV	Authorized Version.
BDB	F. Brown, S.R. Driver and C.A. Briggs, *Hebrew and English Lexicon of the Old Testament* (Oxford, 1907).
BJRL	*Bulletin of the John Rylands Library* (Manchester).
BSOAS	*Bulletin of the School of Oriental and African Studies* (London).
ByZ	*Byzantinische Zeitschrift* (Leipzig)
BZ	*Biblische Zeitschrift* (Paderborn).
BZAW	Beihefte zur Zeitschrift für die Alttestamentliche Wissenschaft.
CBQ	*Catholic Biblical Quarterly* (Washington).
CSCO	Corpus Scriptorum Christianorum Orientalium (Louvain).
DNB	*Dictionary of National Biography* (Oxford).
EJ	*Encyclopaedia Judaica* (Jerusalem, 1971).
EvTh	*Evangelische Theologie* (Munich).
GK	A.E. Cowley (ed.), *Gesenius' Hebrew Grammar as edited and enlarged by the late E. Kautzsch*, 2nd edn (Oxford, 1910 = 28th German edn).
HTR	*Harvard Theological Review* (Cambridge, Massachusetts).
HUCA	*Hebrew Union College Annual* (Cincinnati).
HZ	*Historische Zeitschrift* (Berlin–Munich).
I	*Der Islam* (Berlin–New York).
IA	*International Affairs* (London).
IC	*Islamic Culture* (Hyderabad–Deccan).
JA	*Journal Asiatique* (Paris).
JAOS	*Journal of the American Oriental Society* (New Haven, Connecticut).
JB	Jerusalem Bible.
JBL	*Journal of Biblical Literature* (Boston).

JC	*The Jewish Chronicle* (London).
JE	*The Jewish Encyclopedia* (New York–London, 1906–7).
JJS	*Journal of Jewish Studies* (London).
JM	*Jewish Monthly* (London).
JMUEOS	*Journal of the Manchester University Egyptian and Oriental Society* (Manchester).
JNES	*Journal of Near Eastern Studies* (Chicago).
JQ	*Jewish Quarterly* (London).
JQR	*Jewish Quarterly Review* (London – later Philadelphia).
JRAS	*Journal of the Royal Asiatic Society* (London).
JSS	*Journal of Semitic Studies* (Manchester).
JTS	*Journal of Theological Studies* (Oxford).
LJM	*The Liberal Jewish Monthly* (London).
MAS	*Modern Asian Studies.*
MEJ	*Middle East Journal* (Washington).
MGWJ	*Monatsschrift für Geschichte und Wissenschaft des Judentums* (Breslau).
MR	*The Maghreb Review* (London).
NEB	New English Bible.
N.F.	Neue Folge.
N.S.	New Series.
RB	*Revue Biblique* (Paris).
REG	*Revue des études grecques* (Paris).
REJ	*Revue des études juives* (Paris).
RS	*Religious Studies* (Cambridge).
RSV	Revised Standard Version.
RV	Revised Version.
SR	*The Synagogue Review* (London).
Stud. Sem.	E.I.J. Rosenthal, *Studia Semitica* (Cambridge, 1971).
SVT	Supplements to *Vetus Testamentum.*
Theol.	*Theology* (London).
TLS	*The Times Literary Supplement* (London).
VT	*Vetus Testamentum* (Leiden).
WJ	*World Jewry* (London).
ZAW	*Zeitschrift für die Alttestamentliche Wissenschaft* (Giessen – later Berlin).
ZDMG	*Zeitschrift der Deutschen morgenländischen Gesellschaft* (Leipzig).
ZNW	*Zeitschrift für die Neutestamentliche Wissenschaft* (Giessen – later Berlin).

QUMRAN AND RELATED TEXTS

1Q, 2Q etc. – the number refers to the cave at Qumran in which the relevant scroll was found.

CD	the Damascus Document.
1QH	*Hōdāyōt*, the Hymns of Thanksgiving.
1QIsa[a] or [b]	the first or second Isaiah scroll from Qumran Cave 1.
1QM	*Milḥāmā*, the War Scroll.
1QpHab	the Habakkuk Commentary.
1QS	the Rule of the Community.
1QS*a* or *b*	Appendix *a* or *b* to the Rule.
4QarP	Aramaic papyrus fragment.
4QFlor	*Florilegium*.
4QMess ar	the Aramaic messianic text.
4QPrNab	the Prayer of Nabonidus.
4QpNah	Pesher on Nahum

MISHNAIC AND RELATED TEXTS

Prefixed M. – Mishna; BT – Babylonian Talmud; PT – Palestinian Talmud; Tos. – Tosephta.

ʿAbod. Zar.	ʿAboda Zara
B. Bat.	Baba Batra
Bek.	Bekorot
B. Meṣ.	Baba Meṣiʿa
Ber.	Berakot
ʿErub.	ʿErubin
Ket.	Ketubot
Mak.	Makkot
Makš.	Makširin
Meg.	Megilla
Menaḥ.	Menaḥot
Ned.	Nedarim
Nid.	Nidda
Ohol.	Oholot
Pesaḥ.	Pesaḥim
Qidd.	Qiddušin
Roš. Haš.	Roš Haššana
Šabb.	Šabbat
Sanh.	Sanhedrin
Šeb.	Šebiʿit
Šebu.	Šebuʿot
Šeqal.	Šeqalim
Sukk.	Sukka
Taʿan.	Taʿanit
Ṭohar.	Ṭoharot
Yebam.	Yebamot

Erwin I.J. Rosenthal: A Biographical Appreciation

STEFAN C. REIF

Erwin Isak Jakob, the last child of a family of two sons and four daughters, was born on 18 September 1904 to Moses and Amalie Rosenthal (née Levis) of Heilbronn, a Jewish couple both of whose ancestors had been domiciled in Germany for many generations. In spite of its long exposure to the prevailing culture, and the predominantly German liberal middle-class life-style that it had adopted, the Rosenthal family still adhered to traditional Jewish practice. One of the many charming memories that Erwin delights to share with his close friends is of his father, wrapped in the *ṭallit* and wearing his *tefillin*, reciting his morning prayers at the window facing the garden. Moses Rosenthal would certainly not have approved of rearing a child ignorant of the background to his faith, and along with the general education customary at that time Erwin received an adequate, if by no means intensive, grounding in the Bible and Jewish religion, as they were traditionally understood. This father was not, however, destined to witness the intellectual development of his younger son; nor was the latter to enjoy further paternal guidance in his formative teenage years, since Herr Rosenthal died of diabetes in 1915 at the early age of fifty-two. Though never affluent, Erwin's father had, as a wine merchant, provided reasonably well for his family, but with his loss and the subsequent toll taken of all such families by the ravages of the First World War and the fearful inflation that followed it, the family's economic fortunes sank low. On matriculating in 1923 Erwin, anxious not to become a financial burden to his mother, took a temporary post in a Heilbronn bank.

Young Rosenthal's academic potential was not, however, to be denied realization, and he took advantage of the bank's generous policy of permitting its trainees to acquire a sound academic basis for their commercial prowess by enrolling in courses at the University of Heidelberg in 1924. It is true that the lectures attended were expected to be those given in economics and that Erwin's active interest in Hebrew and Arabic, as well as English and History, contributed little to his knowledge of the world of high finance. Nevertheless, the bank was sufficiently pleased with their young protégé's development in areas of learning that concerned commerce to ask no questions, and the newly registered student was thus called upon to tell no lies. Among his teachers during his year at Heidelberg were Artur Weiser, later to win fame as a biblical scholar, and his professor, Georg Beer, one of the editors of a critical edition of the Mishnah and the scion of a family of Jewish origin. Although their approach was that of the nineteenth-century German Bible critic, and therefore something of a revelation for Erwin, they apparently still believed that every Jew must have imbibed something from the vast fount of Jewish knowledge, since they often invited their two Jewish students to offer solutions for difficult biblical passages. This introduction to *alttestamentliche Wissenschaft* was, however, balanced by a sound training in Semitics that has, on his own testimony, proved invaluable to him throughout his life. The mentor here was no less than the brilliant Gotthelf Bergsträsser, and his efforts were complemented by those of the Assyriologist, Albrecht Goetze. The communist convictions of Goetze, which soon forced him to flee Germany, were not the only aspect of political ideology destined to touch the life of the budding Semitist over the next few years.

The degree of influence wielded by Bergsträsser over his student is apparent from the fact that when this outstanding scholar moved to Munich, the erstwhile bank-trainee abandoned all expectations of a life of financial security and followed him there to pursue a full-time academic career. Although Erwin's special interests were becoming clearer and his primary subjects were now in the Arabic and Islamic areas, no opportunity yet presented itself for settling down in one adopted home. Contemporary legislation necessitated a transfer of his studies to Berlin, since the acquisition of a schoolmaster's diploma enabling him to practise anywhere in Germany was possible only in the capital. The move was not without its academic, intellectual and social advantages. For three years Erwin pursued a course in Modern and Medieval History, with Arabic and Aramaic as subsidiaries and, of course, the History of Philosophy as an obligatory subject. The most distinguished of his teachers of Arabic and the one who clearly exercised the strongest influence on his development was the German Jewish orientalist Eugen Mittwoch, whose sound rabbinic training and commitment to modern spoken Hebrew ensured that his students enjoyed the opportunity of becoming competent Semitists in the widest sense of the term. Encouraged by Mittwoch, Erwin continued to take the private lessons with Zalman Rabinkov that he had begun in Heidelberg, studying Talmud with this unfortunate *melammed*, who had come from Russia to improve his lot but was apparently still forced by economic circumstances to subsist on a diet of herrings. The culmination of his pre-doctoral studies came in 1929 with the submission of a Dr. phil. dissertation on Ibn Khaldun's Political Thought. The tone had now been set for his later work as an Arabist and Islamicist particularly interested in Islam as a political philosophy, and the first substantial indication that the name of Rosenthal was to figure in publications in the area of Semitics for the next half-century came with the appearance of his dissertation as Beiheft 25 of *Historische Zeitschrift* in 1932, printed at the expense of the Prussian Kultusministerium.

Further recognition of the young doctor's academic ability took the form of a post-doctoral research award made by the Förderungsgemeinschaft der Deutschen Wissenschaft which enabled Erwin to devote three years to the topic 'Averroes' Commentary on Plato's "Republic"'. This work was intended to serve as his Habilitationsschrift as Privatdozent at the University of Berlin but Hitler's rise to power thwarted this intention; and the upheavals of the next twenty years, both in his personal career and in Western Europe as a whole, were among the factors that delayed its publication until 1956. Unlike those of today, young scholars of that generation did not expect to obtain a university post without some delay and often taught at school during the intermediate period. Erwin thus followed his original plan of obtaining a schoolmaster's diploma and, since his chosen field was Hebrew, spent the winter semester of 1932–3 at that outstanding institution of *Wissenschaft des Judentums*, the Berlin *Hochschule*, where the teachers then included Ismar Elbogen, Leo Baeck, Julius Guttmann, Ḥanokh Albeck and Harry Torczyner, names that constitute a microcosm of modern Jewish scholarship and commitment.

It must not be imagined, nor would those who know the lighter, even jovial, side of his character ever be prepared to believe, that Erwin's preoccupations at this time were fully orientated towards

Semitic scholarship. As well as all the usual cultural pursuits, he enjoyed taking part in amateur dramatics, being particularly fond of improvised playing, and it was this love that led to another, which not only shaped the remainder of his life but probably ensured that he retained a life to be shaped. In 1932 the friend with whom he shared his theatrical interest took Erwin to meet Ann-Marie Marx and her sister Elizabeth, daughters of Hugo, a pathologist (a distant relative of the famous Karl), who had held a post as prison doctor in Berlin and conducted the autopsy on Rosa Luxembourg, and whose wife's family, the Münsterbergs, had been active in Jewish and general politics in Danzig for many years. After Hugo's death in 1920 the family had returned to the Free Port for a few years but they were now again resident in Berlin, where Elizabeth was continuing the family's association with medicine and practising as a medical technician.

Elizabeth's artistic and musical talents were even more impressive than Erwin's dramatic talents and the young couple took only a week to decide that they would make ideal partners. Sadly, their sunny days of courtship were soon darkened by the Nazi storm, especially after Hitler came to power and his anti-Jewish legislation was enacted. Forced out of the University and denied access to the libraries, Erwin foresaw, even then, that the Nazis would be true to their promises and do violence to the thousand-year-old German Jewry, but his instinct was not to emigrate but to share the fate of his co-religionists however tragic it might be. Elizabeth's family saw things differently and persuaded the young couple to make good their escape while it was still possible. Erwin left for England in April 1933 and was joined by his fiancée two months later. In July that year they were married and they both still chuckle at the welcome that they received at a Westcliffe boarding-house when looking for an inexpensive abode at which to spend their honeymoon, which clearly demonstrated to them that England, however depressed, was not Hitler's Germany. 'Sorry, we only take Jews', they were told – and they proudly claimed admission.

Armed with his academic qualifications and a recommendation from Ismar Elbogen, Erwin set about the task of finding employment and, through the good offices of C.G. Montefiore, who had the experience of half-a-century's involvement with Jewish scholars and scholarship, and Herbert Loewe, who enjoyed considerable prestige in the Universities of Oxford, Cambridge and London, he was appointed as Lecturer in Hebrew and North

Semitic Epigraphy and Head of the Hebrew Department at University College, London. The post was not full-time and the income of £100 per annum had to be supplemented by the amount of £125 by the Academic Assistance Council for Refugees, but at least he had a position and he was grateful for it. Within a matter of months his life had been drastically changed. The single, Berlin student of Arabic had become the married, London lecturer in Hebrew.

Transformations such as these are not of course made overnight, as Erwin must often have reflected in the course of his three years at University College. Before him lay a welter of daunting challenges. He had to master a foreign language, acquaint himself with a different university system, advance his academic career in all the usual ways and, in spite of the obvious economic difficulties, set up a home with his young bride. English friendships were not easy to cultivate but some assistance was forthcoming in meeting these challenges. His students breathed some colloquial life into the stiff frame of his correct but unidiomatic English, distinguished academic groups such as the Society for Old Testament Study and the Jewish Historical Society of England welcomed him into membership, while the Royal Asiatic Society invited him to review for its *Journal*, and H.A.R. Gibb, Professor of Arabic at the School of Oriental and African Studies, and W.O.E. Oesterley, Professor of Hebrew at King's College, arranged participation in seminars and public lectures for him. Among the topics with which he concerned himself were the Aramaisms in Ezekiel, Pope Gregory VII's political theory and Maimonides' concept of state and society. At that time Jews' College dominated the processes of teaching and examination for the University of London's B.A. honours course and he found himself a fellow-examiner with its then Principal, Adolf Büchler, and the lecturer who was later to succeed him, Isidore Epstein. For one to whom the whole concept of 'proses', translations from English into Classical Hebrew, was a strange and novel one, Büchler provided a further shock by setting for such translation one of the German Crown Prince's orders of the day addressed to his troops during the First World War.

No less of a shock was the realization that a considerable degree of mathematical ingenuity would be required to convert an annual resource of £225 into a prescription for financial liquidity. It was not enough to avoid indulging in luxuries. When, after a year, the Rosenthals exchanged Lewisham for Welwyn Garden City, Erwin found that he could make a substantial saving on fares by travelling into College each day on the 6.21 a.m., which entitled him to purchase a workman's return ticket at the reduced price of 1*s* 3*d* per day. Further economies were effected by purchasing groceries in the market off Tottenham Court Road, which was within reasonable walking distance of University College. These and other means were devised to ensure that expenditure did not exceed income and, as Mr Micawber had once declared it would be, the result was indeed happiness. Before that happiness made itself manifest in the arrival of baby Thomas, the fees earned through some public lectures made possible a belated honeymoon abroad to compensate for the *ersatz* version previously enjoyed at Westcliffe, though it has to be acknowledged that bed and breakfast in Antwerp at 5*s* a night does not today sound like the height of luxury. Among the vivid impressions left on Elizabeth and Erwin by this trip are their feelings when they participated with many Jewish refugees in a Passover *seder* meal in a Jewish boarding-house in Antwerp, and the paradox of being shunned by Belgians because of the German passports they both had no choice but still to carry.

The part-time nature of the London post and its unsatisfactory financial structure made it inevitable that Erwin would move on within a short time. The final impetus for him to do so was created by the need to make such a post, and the kind of financial support provided for it, available for more recently arrived academic refugees. The possibility of his being able to respond positively to the impetus was brought about by the offer of an alternative post sponsored by Nathan Laski, 'the uncrowned king of Manchester Jewry', at the university of that city. Laski and the Jewish community provided the financial backing and Edward Robertson, Professor of Semitic Languages and Literatures, the academic support for the creation of a post concerned with post-biblical Jewish studies and, since Erwin had given a course of lectures in this area during the session of 1935–6, the institution and its prospective teaching officer were already acquainted. In October 1936 he was appointed Special Lecturer in Semitic Languages and Literatures and he joined a strong team of experts in the ancient Near East, which included Mahdi Allam in Arabic, T. Fish in Assyriology and A.M. Blackman in Egyptology, as well as Robertson himself, with his Samaritan interests. Those familiar with Erwin's sociability, as well as his commitment to sound scholarship, will readily understand that he soon became a popular and productive member of the Department, and this situation remained substantially unchanged until the latter part of the war years. The way in which he successfully straddled the Hebrew and Arabic sides of the same Semitic fence is clearly exemplified by the range of his publications. He contributed an article on Islam to the second volume of *Judaism and Christianity* edited by Herbert Loewe and entitled *The Contact of Pharisaism and other Cultures*, he edited and contributed to the third volume of that series, *Law and Religion* and he edited, with no small degree of heartache for his efforts, the *Saadya Studies* commemorating the thousandth anniversary of the great Gaon's death. Never a scholar to deny the public the fruits of his researches in their wider ramifications, he lectured on International Affairs in the university's extra-mural department and had his first contact with the British Army when he gave a course for the Central Advisory Council for Education in His Majesty's Forces. On the social side, a close relationship was developed with the Unitarian scholar Robert Travers Herford who was a friend of the Jewish people and free of the religious prejudice of many Christian scholars of Judaism. The Rosenthals paid many pleasant visits to the Herford home in Kelsall, near Chester, and were later evacuated there during the War.

Erwin's interests in public affairs also found expression in the contribution he made to Jewish communal, educational and political activities. He even made what must be for any serious scholar the ultimate sacrifice and taught in a voluntary capacity at the part-time synagogue classes of the Manchester Sephardi community while the rabbi was away on sick-leave. Like many a young scholar before and since he found that the attention and enthusiasm of pupils whose attendance is not the result of their own choice but of parental insistence leave much to be desired. On one occasion, at a given signal from one who was obviously made of the stuff of which communal leaders are formed, the whole class donned their gas-masks during a lesson. No doubt their teacher found this and similar experiences an invaluable asset in developing the ability to cope with the various pedagogical situations with which undergraduates might confront him. Thankfully his own children, Thomas and Miriam, who had by now joined the family, did not demonstrate such revolutionary tendencies but made good progress at primary school in Manchester, laying the first foundations of what were later to become impressive scholastic attainments. Their British citizenship was something that their father was unable to share until February 1940 when he swore the oath of allegiance before Nathan Laski. The unpleasantness of having German nationality had often been experienced, but never more obviously than when his passport had been stamped with a *J* when renewed just before the War and the German Foreign Office had insisted on following domestic procedure and had added the name Israel to his forenames. Erwin was content with Isak and Jakob as demonstrations of his religious allegiance and declined to make use of the additional name. Whether it was at this time that he was classified by the German government as an undesirable element, or not, is not clear, but his name certainly appears on the Nazi Central Security Agency's list of those to be arrested as soon as 'Operation Sea Lion' had been successful and Britain occupied. Once war was declared some British citizens seemed incapable of distinguishing between Germans and victims of Nazi oppression who had German nationality. Erwin's naturalization came too late to save him from the unpleasantness of having to report weekly to the police, but just soon enough to ensure that he did not have to suffer internment and other such indignities during the remainder of the War.

Fate was not, however, to allow him to pass the whole of this period on the educational reserve list with war duties limited to fire-watching, though the latter occupation could be rather a busy one in the north-west conurbation. In 1944 certain Manchester interests, both communal and academic, conspired to use the financial provisions of the Nathan Laski Memorial Fund to establish a post in post-biblical Jewish studies, in the filling of which preference would be given to a trained talmudist. Erwin did not claim such competence and consequently did not apply. Once this new post was filled, his own lapsed and, now de-reserved, he found himself called up for army service at the age of almost forty. After basic training he was posted to the R.A.S.C. and believing, surely with some justification, that his talents could better be employed in a more specialist unit he applied for transfer to the Army Education Corps. Needless to say he soon discovered that such moves are not calculated to promote friendly relations with one's superiors. There was even one encounter in which an officer, jokingly one hopes, absurdly one knows, referred to him as a Nazi and threatened to shoot him. By the time that he was seconded to the Foreign Office for work in the Middle East mission of its Political Intelligence Department in February 1945, he could almost have been said to welcome the sea-journey to Egypt even if it did involve German naval attentions, which were rather too close for comfort. Although now reverting to civilian status, he enjoyed a close relationship with G.H.Q. in Cairo and a position equivalent to that of a Lieutenant-Colonel, with educational responsibilities involving German prisoners-of-war. After twenty years of studying the Middle East he now found himself, not by choice, in a position to obtain first-hand experience of the area. The exposure was not without its value especially since he also took the opportunity of acquiring some modern spoken Arabic at the American University. By the same token, editing a newspaper for the prisoners challenged him to produce the kind of balance between scholarly writing and popular presentation that would not come amiss if achieved by many a fellow-orientalist. The challenge was to last no more than a year since Erwin contracted infective hepatitis in 1946 and returned to London to spend three weeks in the Hospital for Tropical Diseases. Remarkably, to those without direct experience of those years, his work with the prisoner-of-war division of the Foreign Office continued in London for two more years, so that Elizabeth and the children were soon reunited with him in a new residence in the north-west of the city, and something like a normal family life, including the barmitzvah ceremony for Thomas, was restored. This normalization was a particular relief to Elizabeth, who had borne the responsibility of managing the family budget during Erwin's absence. With a grand total of £3 a week contributed by the Army this had been a challenging task, and she had successfully tackled it by undertaking crocheting, with string at that, for five hours each day at a rate of £5 per week. She even organized a group of thirteen refugee ladies to do work beyond what she could cope with, but the quality did not always satisfy the high standards of handicraft that she had consistently set herself and she sometimes had herself to do it again.

In addition to his Foreign Office duties Erwin returned to more academic pursuits by lecturing on International Affairs at the University of London's Extension Courses. By the middle of 1948 it was obvious to him that there was little choice but to resign from his post or await the closing of the department a few months later. With some trepidation and with no real prospect of academic employment he severed the link of the previous three years and accepted a six-month grant from the Society for Jewish Study to complete the work on Averroes that he had had to abandon in Berlin fifteen years previously. What he would have done then is not clear, but he never had to face the problem nor indeed was he yet permitted to return to Averroes since a new post in Hebrew was created at Cambridge as a result of the Scarbrough Report's recommendation for the expansion of Oriental Studies, and Erwin was appointed to the Lectureship. He had had connections with Cambridge ten years earlier when he had often been both a personal and academic guest of Herbert Loewe, but this was his first formal link with the University. He joined a Faculty of Oriental Languages in which the Regius Chair of Hebrew was occupied by David Winton Thomas, and Arthur Arberry was Sir Thomas Adams's Professor of Arabic, and the Rosenthals moved into 199 Chesterton Road, where they still reside, in early October 1948.

There is little room for doubt that Erwin's scholarly interests and the intensely academic environment of Cambridge were made for each other and that his years at his sixth, and final, university have been his most professionally productive and rewarding. From the start he was well nurtured by the tranquil atmosphere, the rich library resources and the availability of specialist colleagues with whom to exchange ideas, and the first fruits of the intellectual growth that ensued were not long delayed. *Averroes' Commentary on Plato's Republic*, for so long forcibly confined in its chrysalis, emerged in 1956 and set a standard of sound scholarship that augured well for the success of the University's Oriental Publications, at the head of which it stands. The ill-fortune that had for so long dogged the work remained with it even in its final stages since it was originally to have been included in the *Corpus Platonicum Medii Aevi* of the Warburg Institute but serious disagreement between author and general editor necessitated a change of plan. Once published, however, the book was soon recognized to be a basic reference work in the field, as attested by the need for second and third editions. If, as Erwin has always claimed, this book represents his single most important contribution to specialized scholarship, the next volume he produced, *Political Thought in Mediaeval Islam*, has certainly attracted the widest academic interest since its publication by the University Press in 1958. In this case, the demand went beyond what the publication of three editions could satisfy and the book received the finest accolade known to the modern publisher, the issue of a paperback version. Even distinguished university presses are no longer averse to judging books as much by the degree to which they are marketable as by the brilliance of their content, and the sales achieved by the Rosenthal volumes helped to build a comfortable and positive relationship between author and publisher. When Erwin used his expert knowledge of Islamic political philosophy for an examination of the degree to which contemporary Muslim nations have applied their religious traditions to modern government, he found the University Press a willing partner in publication. Recent events in the troubled Middle East seem to have lent a new relevance to those topics covered fourteen years ago in *Islam in the Modern National State*, and many would be grateful if the Press could prevail upon the author to prepare a revised, up-to-date edition. Although these important volumes all demonstrate Erwin's primary research interests, he never neglected the medieval Jewish scene or lost his fascination with the intellectual developments in nineteenth-century German Jewry. The collection of his articles published in 1971, with a volume devoted to Jewish themes as well as one on Islamic themes, amply testifies to this, and the way in which he dealt with the cultural interplay between the Jewish and Muslim traditions in his popular paperback *Judaism and Islam* demonstrates clearly that the two areas of interest were never artificially compartmentalized in his mind.

Paradoxically, scholars sometimes find themselves giving few university lectures in the specific fields in which they are authorities, and Erwin's duties in the Faculty of Oriental Languages (later Oriental Studies) required him to teach Hebrew and not Arabic. Strangely enough, his specialist knowledge of Islamic Philosophy and Political Institutions was used by the Arabists only for graduate students until 1968, when he gave a course of undergraduate lectures on that theme. Those reading Hebrew, however, welcomed the opportunity of studying with such a conscientious teacher. Not only did he consistently give students, postgraduate Islamic as well as undergraduate Hebrew, much more of his time than duty demanded but, at once sympathetic and firm, he also played the role of 'father-figure' for a number of them. Among his former students there are those for whom he is still called upon to provide references over a quarter of a century after they have gone down. Although he always taught the Hebrew Bible in a scientific and critical manner his Jewish commitments prevented him from approaching it in a cold, clinical fashion and this was much appreciated by his students. He has always been especially fond of Rosenzweig's oft-cited remark that for him the 'R' of the critics was not 'Redactor' but rather 'Rabbenu'. Particularly in his early years at Cambridge he also complemented his routine teaching with involvement in a wide variety of lectures, seminars and symposia, both in Cambridge and beyond. When a symposium to mark the thousandth anniversary of the birth of Avicenna was conceived by Professor Arberry and organized by G.M. Wickens, University Lecturer in Arabic, in 1951, he and his colleague, Dr J.L. Teicher, University Lecturer in Rabbinics, covered Avicenna's influence on Jewish thought and his importance as a general philosopher respectively. In 1956, when Leo Baeck College was opened as the seminary to serve the Reform movement in Anglo-Jewry, Erwin was the first to teach Jewish philosophy. He often made the point that the college would never establish itself as an important academic institution while it remained dependent on part-time teachers, and the truth of this diagnosis was recognized years later when the Reform and Liberal communities joined forces to strengthen the College and a marked improvement in standards ensued. Another academic body that enjoyed his support was the Institute of Jewish Studies, both while it was directed by his close friend Rabbi Dr Alexander Altmann, Communal Rabbi in Manchester from 1938 (when he escaped from Nazi Europe), and later when it came under the aegis of University College, London, and another good friend, Professor Siegfried Stein. In spite of these wide scholarly commitments, Erwin did not shirk responsibility on the administrative side of Faculty business at Cambridge. He was a member of various committees, where he could be relied upon to express his views sensibly and frankly even in those instances when others might have preferred to maintain their personal popularity at the price of silence, and in 1962–3 he shouldered the burden of the chairmanship of the Faculty Board of Oriental Studies. He was Chairman of the Committee of Management of the Middle East Centre from 1969 until 1978 and was also honoured by being elected President of the Society for Near Eastern Studies for 1957–9, 1972–4 and 1979–80 and of the British Association for Jewish Studies for 1977.

Recognition of his scholarly accomplishments by his peers was not restricted to Cambridge or the British academic community but was given an international dimension during this latter part of his career. Following visits to Israel in 1955, when he spent two months studying Israeli methods of teaching the Bible, and again in 1957, when he attended the Second World Congress of Jewish Studies as the official Cambridge delegate, he paid a number of visits to his native Germany during 1958 to deliver various lectures including the Franz Delitzsch Vorlesungen at Münster and the Loeb lectures in Frankfurt-am-Main, both series carrying considerable academic prestige and the former later published as a short book entitled *Griechisches Erbe in der jüdischen Religionsphilosophie des Mittelalters.* Try as he might to remain cool and unemotional this return to the country that had once driven him out was bound to create some sort of tension between him and those who had unconcernedly advanced their academic careers while their Jewish colleagues were systematically liquidated, and, paradoxically enough, breaking-point came when he was being pressed to consider a distinguished post in one of his old universities. Driven to anger by his German colleagues' inability to understand his reticence in this matter, Erwin finally exploded. 'How do I know that one of the men with whom I may have to shake hands did not murder my sister in Theresienstadt?' he exclaimed, and the subject was swiftly dropped. The visits to Pakistan, India, Malaya, Iran, Turkey, Tunisia and Morocco, made possible by a research grant from the Rockefeller Foundation between 1960 and 1963 and ultimately resulting in *Islam in the Modern National State*, were thankfully less traumatic, although questions were inevitably asked in certain quarters about Erwin's precise degree of commitment to the Jewish national homeland. Happily, former students were sometimes present to repay the debt they owed their teacher from their Cambridge days and to smooth his path. In some cases the visiting Cambridge scholar was even given access to the highest level of leadership, as for instance when he obtained interviews with Ayub Khan, President of Pakistan, Dr Zakir Husain, Governor of Behar and later President of India, and the Minister of Education in Iran. The sabbatical year that the Rosenthals spent at Columbia University in 1967–8 was marked by neither tension nor excitement but offered the opportunity of making the acquaintance of important American colleagues and contrasting the bustle of New York with the tranquillity of Cambridge. Having completed his two semesters as Visiting Professor of Advanced Arabic Studies at Columbia, Erwin then gave a course of ten lectures in a similar capacity at El Colegio de Mexico. Wherever they went Erwin and Elizabeth not only had an eye for the general cultural offerings of the place but would also visit centres of Jewish interest about which Erwin would then write pieces for the Jewish press. Thus it is that descriptions of the treasures of the Jewish Museum in Prague and the Royal Library in Copenhagen appear in his bibliography.

Although he had of course had the degree of M.A. conferred upon him following his appointment in 1948, in accordance with the

University's statute relating to those appointed to tenured posts who are not Cambridge graduates, it was not for ten years that there was any formal advancement of his status within the University. In 1958 he was awarded the degree of Litt. D. for the important contribution made to scholarship by his published work, and a year later came a Readership in Oriental Studies. The award of this distinguished doctoral degree was a particularly exciting event for the Rosenthal family, and Erwin very much coveted the academic robes reserved for this level of graduation. In view of his financial situation, however, he limited himself to the purchase of only the hood and cap. Unknown to him, Elizabeth approached the same robemaker and was informed that only the gown remained, a gentleman having earlier acquired the hood and cap. She promptly completed the transaction, though the cost had to be met by the sale of a piece of her jewellery.

Whatever their academic status within the University and their distinction as scholars, orientalists are not easily absorbed into the college system as at present constituted, since the number of students reading Oriental Studies is small, and it is therefore rare for colleges to elect Fellows solely with responsibilities in this field. A fair proportion of orientalists therefore remain without fellowships, though it should be said that the University as a whole is aware of the inequitable nature of the situation and proposals are from time to time put forward to ease it. Erwin was granted dining privileges by both King's and Pembroke after a few years at Cambridge but it was not until 1962 that he was offered a college non-stipendiary fellowship in Humanities. It was Pembroke that was generous enough to make the offer and it has never had reason to regret its decision. Erwin quickly established himself as a keen College man whose engaging conversation, ready ear and wise advice were much prized, no less by younger men than by his contemporaries, and whose regular attendance and frank but considered expressions of opinion were appreciated on the governing body. For his part Erwin has greatly enjoyed the camaraderie, the intellectual stimulation and the culinary attractions of college life, and if he still recalls the reference he made at his acceptance speech to the fourteen years that Jacob had to serve to win his heart's desire it is only to stress how much sweeter the relationship was when finally consummated.

In his earlier years at Cambridge Erwin's personal life was no less active than his professional one. He contributed to the development of Jewish–Christian relations on the new basis of mutual respect, was a vigorous member of the Association of Jewish Refugees and a member of the board of the Leo Baeck Institute. Liberal in outlook but traditional in various aspects of observance, he played his part in providing the necessary religious facilities for the local Jewish Residents' Association and on one occasion found himself called upon to conduct the burial service for Sir Hersch Lauterpacht, one of this century's most distinguished jurists and Professor of International Law, before a congregation that had come from far and wide to pay its respects. It is typical of Erwin that he should have chosen a text dealing with the attributes of a judge as laid down by Maimonides in his classical code of Jewish law, and those present felt that the choice was a most apt one for the occasion. Jewish students, too, enjoyed the hospitality and warmth of the Rosenthal home, particularly on Sabbaths and festivals and when examinations had to be deferred for religious reasons and invigilation was required at Chesterton Road until the paper could be written. His own children also graduated, married and made successful careers in publishing, and before Erwin's retirement he was enjoying the pleasure of entertaining visiting grandchildren, taking particular delight in conducting the Passover *seder* service for them as his father had once done for him.

That retirement came in 1971. The financial difficulties which had been the bugbear of earlier years had disappeared a decade earlier but were replaced by problems of ill-health, particularly in the case of Elizabeth. In spite of these, their small circle of close friends know that they can still spend delightful hours in the Rosenthals' company, entertaining or being entertained, and both College and Faculty can rely on Erwin's regular participation in their activities. Fortunately, the couple can still indulge in the great pleasure of concert-going, and Erwin makes special efforts to attend synagogue not only on special occasions but also whenever he feels that his presence may be needed for the quorum. In spite of the domestic chores now laid upon him his pen is not idle, and a Leverhulme Emeritus Fellowship in 1974–6 permitted him to start work on an important new topic, *The Political Thought of the Muʿtazila: Abd al-Jabbar's Treatise on the Imamate*. The list of contributors to the present volume, drawn from only one area of Erwin's scholarly activity, provides ample testimony to the good wishes that Erwin and Elizabeth carry with them into their mature years. It is the wish of all their friends that they may be spared to enjoy together many years of health, contentment and satisfaction.

Bibliography of the Publications of E.I.J. Rosenthal

* denotes inclusion in *Studia Semitica* (see under 1971)

1930

'Der Plan eines Bündnisses zwischen Karl d. Grossen und Abdul Rahman III', *Neues Archiv der Gesellschaft für ältere deutsche Geschichtskunde* 48 (Berlin), pp. 441–5.

1931

'Muawija', in P.R. Rohden and G. Ostrogorski (eds.), *Menschen die Geschichte machten. Viertausend Jahre Weltgeschichte in Zeit- und Lebensbildern*, vol. I (Vienna), pp. 271–5.

Review of T.W. Arnold and A. Guillaume (eds.), *The Legacy of Islam*, in *HZ* 145, p. 630.

Review of F.W. Buckler, *Harunu'l Rashid and Charles the Great*, in *HZ* 145, pp. 630–1.

1933

'Carl Heinrich Becker. Nachruf', *HZ* 148, pp. 445–6.

Review of H.A.R. Gibb, *The Damascus Chronicle of the Crusades. Extracted and translated from the Chronicle of Al-Qalânisî*, in *HZ* 148, p. 170.

1932

Ibn Khaldûns Gedanken über den Staat. Ein Beitrag zur mittelalterlichen Staatslehre, *HZ*, Beiheft 25.

Review of E. Patzelt, *Die fränkische Kultur und der Islam*, in *HZ* 147, p. 642.

1934

'Averroes' Paraphrase on Plato's "Politeia"', *JRAS*, pp. 737–44.

'Speyer' (in part), in I. Elbogen, A. Freimann and H. Tykocinski (eds.), *Germania Judaica* (Breslau), pp. 326–35, 346–51.

Review of R. Kittel, *Gestalten und Gedanken in Israel. Geschichte eines Volkes in Charakterbildern*, 2nd rev. edn, in *HZ* 149, pp. 311–12.

Review of M. Gaudefroy-Demombynes and S.F. Platonov, *Le*

monde musulman et byzantin jusqu'aux croisades, vol. VII, 1 of E. Cavaignac (ed.), *Histoire du monde*, in *HZ* 150, pp. 326–30.

Review of A.S. Atiya, *The Crusade of Nicopolis*, in *Zeitschrift der Deutschen Morgenländischen Gesellschaft* (Berlin–Zürich–Vienna) 88 = N.F. 13, pp. 350–2.

1935

* 'Maimonides' Conception of State and Society', in I. Epstein (ed.), *Moses Maimonides* (London), pp. 189–206: one of the Public Lectures at Cambridge University during its celebration of the octocentenary of Maimonides' birth.

1936

Review of J. Schacht (ed.), *Kitāb Iḫtilāf Al-Fuqahā'. Das Konstantinopler Fragment*, in *JRAS*, pp. 107–8.

Review of William Popper (ed.), *Abū'l Maḥāsin ibn Taghrī Birdī's Annals*, v. 2, *A.H. 778–792*, in *JRAS*, p. 108.

1937

'Politische Gedanken bei Ibn Bâǧǧa', *MGWJ* 81, 1 (special issue in honour of Eugen Mittwoch), pp. 153–68, 185–6.

* 'Don Isaac Abravanel: Financier, Statesman and Scholar', *BJRL* 21, pp. 445–78: Manchester University Lecture on the occasion of the quincentenary of Abravanel's birth.

'Notes on Some Arabic Manuscripts in the John Rylands Library I: Averroes' Middle Commentary on Aristotle's *Analytica Priora et Posteriora*', *BJRL* 21, pp. 479–83.

'Don Isaac Abravanel', *LJM* 8, pp. 3–4.

'Islam', in H. Loewe (ed.), *Judaism and Christianity* vol. II, 'The Contact of Pharisaism with Other Cultures' (London), pp. 145–85.

1938

Editor of *Judaism and Christianity*, vol. III, 'Law and Religion' (London).

'Medieval Judaism and the Law', *ibid.* pp. 169–208.

1940

* 'Rashi and the English Bible', *BJRL* 24, pp. 138–67.

* 'Ibn Khaldūn: A North African Muslim Thinker of the XIVth Century', *BJRL* 24, pp. 307–20.

Review of A.S. Atiya, *The Crusade in the Later Middle Ages*, in *JRAS*, pp. 76–9.

1942

* 'Saadya Gaon: An Appreciation of his Biblical Exegesis'. *BJRL* 27, pp. 168–78.

'An Aramaic Root נדע?', *JMUEOS* 23, p. 120.

1943

Editor of *Saadya Studies: In Commemoration of the one thousandth anniversary of the death of R. Saadya Gaon* (Manchester).

* 'Saadya's Exegesis of the Book of Job', *ibid.* pp. 177–205.

* 'Sebastian Muenster's Knowledge and Use of Jewish Exegesis', in I. Epstein, E. Levine and C. Roth (eds.), *Essays in Honour of the Very Rev. Dr. J.H. Hertz* (London), pp. 351–69.

1948

* 'Some Aspects of Islamic Political Thought', *IC* 22, pp. 1–17.

Review of H.A.R. Gibb, *Modern Trends in Islam*, in *World Affairs* (London) N.S. 2, pp. 440–2.

Review of C. Delisle Burns, *The First Europe. A Study of the Establishment of Medieval Christendom, A.D. 400–800*, in *Adult Education* 20, pp. 208–10.

1950

* 'Edward Lively: Cambridge Hebraist', in D.W. Thomas (ed.), *Essays and Studies Presented to Stanley Arthur Cook* (London), pp. 95–112.

'Judaism and Islam', *SR* 24, pp. 281–2, 309–12.

'A Famous Library in Copenhagen', *JC* (6 October).

Review of Charles Issawi, *An Arab Philosophy of History: Selections from the Prolegomena of Ibn Khaldun of Tunis*, in *JC* (1 September).

Review of Theodor H. Gaster, *Purim and Hanukkah in Custom and Tradition*, in *JC* (1 December).

1951

* 'The Place of Politics in the Philosophy of Ibn Bājja', *IC* 25 (Jubilee Volume), pp. 187–211.

'State and Society in Medieval and Later Judaism', *LJM* 22, pp. 71–3.

'Prophecy and Philosophy', *SR* 25, pp. 295–7.

Review of I. Maybaum, *The Jewish Mission*, in *SR* 25, pp. 167–70.

Reviews of *Saadya Gaon, The Book of Beliefs and Opinions*, trans. Samuel Rosenblatt; *The Code of Maimonides, Book Thirteen, The Book of Civil Laws*, trans. Jacob J. Rabinowitz; *Book Fourteen, The Book of Judges*, trans. A.M. Hershman; *Book Nine, The Book of Offerings*, trans. Herbert Danby (Yale Judaica Series), in *JC* (15 June).

Review of A. Marmorstein (ed. J. Rabbinowitz and M.S. Lew), *Studies in Jewish Theology. The Arthur Marmorstein Memorial Volume*, in *JM* 5, pp. 244–6.

1952

* 'Avicenna's Influence on Jewish Thought', in G.M. Wickens (ed.), *Avicenna: Scientist and Philosopher. A Millennary Symposium* (London), pp. 66–83.

'The Concept of Torah in Medieval Jewish Philosophy', *Chayenu* 20 (London), pp. 1–4.

'Jewish Exegesis in the English Bible', *SR* 26, pp. 193–201.

Review of Walter J. Fischel (ed.), *Semitic and Oriental Studies Presented to William Popper*, in *JC* (9 May).

1953

* 'The Place of Politics in the Philosophy of Ibn Rushd', *BSOAS* 15, pp. 246–78.

'Interpretation of Judaism. Reflections on the Occasion of Rabbi Dr. Baeck's 80th Birthday', *SR* 27, 9 (dedicated to Dr L. Baeck), pp. 259–63, 271.

'Saadya Gaon: Philosopher of Judaism' *SR* 27, pp. 357–60.

'A Note on the Samaritans', *SR* 27, pp. 75–6.

'Maimonides and Jewish Law', *SR* 28, pp. 33–9.

Review of Robert Graves and Joshua Podro, *The Nazarene Gospel Restored*, in *SR* 28, pp. 109–12.

1954

'Revelation and Reason in Islam', *AP* 25, pp. 105–9.

'Pillars of Jewish Life', *SR* 28, pp. 211–14.

'The Bible and its interpretation through the ages', *SR* 28, pp. 276–8, 302–9, 376–80.

Review of Will Herberg, *Judaism and Modern Man*, in *SR* 28, pp. 145–9, 153.

Review of Leon Roth, *Jewish Thought as a Factor in Civilization*, in *SR* 29, pp. 102–3, 112.

1955

* 'Ibn Jaldūn's Attitude to the *Falāsifa*', *Al-Andalus* 20 (Madrid), pp. 75–85.

* 'The Place of Politics in the Philosophy of Alfārābī', *IC* 29, pp. 157–78.

'The Language of the Bible', *SR* 29, pp. 193–8, 257–61, 272.

Review of D.M. Dunlop, *The History of the Jewish Khazars*, in *SR* 29, pp. 342–3.

Review of Gotthold Weil, *Maimonides: Über die Lebensdauer*, in *The Islamic Quarterly* 2 (London), pp. 150–1.

Review of Louis Gardet, *La cité musulmane: vie sociale et politique*, in *The Islamic Quarterly* 3, pp. 236–9.

1956

Averroes' Commentary on Plato's 'Republic', edited with introduction, English translation, notes and glossaries (Cambridge).

'Religion and Education', *JQ* 3, pp. 8–10, reprinted as 'Judaism in the Jewish State' in Jacob Sonntag (ed.), *Jewish Perspectives* (London, 1980), pp. 172–8.

'The Bible in Israel today', *SR* 30, pp. 161–9.

Review of Edmund Wilson, *The Dead Sea Scrolls*, in *AJR* 11 (May).

Review of Humayun Kabir, *Science, Democracy and Islam and Other Essays*, in *AP* 27, pp. 75–6.

Review of Raffaele Pettazzoni, *The All-Knowing God. Researches into Early Religion and Culture*, trans. H.J. Rose, in *AP* 27, pp. 270–1.

Review of *Essential Unity of All Religions*, compiled by 'Bharata Ratna' Bagvan Das, in *AP* 27, pp. 319–21.

1957

'Religion in the State of Israel', *Quarterly* 3 (of the Anglo-Jewish Association, London), pp. 1–9.

Review of M. Zucker, *A Critique against the writings of R. Saadya Gaon by R. Mubashshir Halevi. With Introduction, Translation and Notes*, in *JSS* 2, pp. 306–7.

Review of J.J. Petuchowski, *The Theology of Haham David Nieto: An Eighteenth Century Defense of the Jewish Tradition*, in *JSS* 2, pp. 408–9.

Review of I.F. Baer, *Israel Among the Nations*, in *SR* 31, pp. 312–13.

Review of Solomon Goldman (ed. Maurice Samuel), *The Ten Commandments*, in *JC* (31 May).

Reviews of Adele Bildersee, *The Hidden Books*, and Bruce M. Metzger, *An Introduction to the Apocrypha*, in *JC* (20 December).

Review of S.D. Goitein, *Jews and Arabs*, in *AJR* 12 (May).

1958

Political Thought in Medieval Islam: An Introductory Outline (Cambridge).

* 'Some Aspects of the Hebrew Monarchy', *JJS* 9, pp. 1–18.

'Father of modern political science. E. Rosenthal on Ibn Khaldun', *The Listener* (17 April).

'Der Kommentar des Averroes zur Politeia Platons', *Zeitschrift für Politik* (Berlin–Zürich–Vienna), N.F. 5, pp. 38–51.

Review of Soheil Afnan, *Avicenna: His Life and Works*, in *Theol.* 61, pp. 514–16.

Review of Muhsin Mahdi, *Ibn Khaldūn's Philosophy of History. A Study in the Philosophic Foundation of the Science of Culture*, in *TLS* (2 May).

Review of E. Jenni, *Die politischen Voraussagen der Propheten*, in *JJS* 9, pp. 199–201.

Review of N. Glatzer (ed.), *Leopold and Adelheid Zunz: An Account in Letters*, in *JC* (28 November).

Reviews of Frederic Kenyon (rev. A.W. Adams), *Our Bible and the Ancient Manuscripts;* and *The Apocrypha of the Old Testament (RSV)*, in *JC* (12 December).

1959

Review of *Ibn Khaldun: The Muqaddimah*, trans. Franz Rosenthal, *TLS* (18 December).

1960

Griechisches Erbe in der jüdischen Religionsphilosophie des Mittelalters (Stuttgart): the Franz Delitzsch Vorlesungen for 1957.

'Anti-Christian Polemic in medieval Bible Commentaries', *JJS* 11, pp. 115–35.

'Averroes', 'Avicenna' in J.O. Urmson (ed.), *The Concise Encyclopaedia of Western Philosophy* (London).

'The Concept of "Eudaimonia" in medieval Islamic and Jewish Philosophy', in *Atti del XII congresso internazionale di filosofia*, vol. XI, 'Storia della Filosofia antica e medievale' (Florence), pp. 145–52.

Review of A. Altmann and S.M. Stern, *Isaac Israeli, a Neoplatonic Philosopher of the Early Tenth Century: his works translated with comments and an outline of his philosophy*, in *BSOAS* 23, pp. 393–4.

Review of Salo W. Baron, *A Social and Religious History of the Jews*, vols. III–VIII, 'High Middle Ages (500–1200)', 2nd edn, in *JSS* 5, pp. 196–204.

Review of A. Altmann (ed.), *Between East and West. Essays Dedicated to the Memory of Bela Horovitz*, in *JSS* 5, pp. 310–11.

Review of S. Löwinger, A. Scheiber and J. Somogyi (eds.), *Ignaz Goldziher Memorial Volume*, Part II, in *JSS* 5, pp. 311–16.

Review of Moses Cordovero, *The Palm Tree of Deborah, trans.*

from the Hebrew with an introduction and notes by Louis Jacobs, in *Theol.* 63, p. 349.

Review of Norman Bentwich, *The Religious Foundations of Internationalism: A Study in International Relations through the Ages*, in *AP* 31, pp. 508–9.

1961

Judaism and Islam (London).

Review of Heinrich Simon, *Ibn Khaldūns Wissenschaft von der menschlichen Kultur*, in *BSOAS* 29, pp. 145–6.

1962

Political Thought in Medieval Islam – re-issue, also as a paperback.

* 'The Role of Islam in the modern national state', *The Year Book of World Affairs* 16 (London), pp. 98–121.

'*Arā' Ibn Rushd al-siyāsīya*', *Al-Bayyina* 1 (Rabat), pp. 94–103.

'Whither Jewry in Tunisia and Morocco?', *AJR* 17 (August).

Review article on Sayyid Abul A'lā Maududi, *The Islamic Law and Constitution*, in *IA* 38, pp. 365–8.

Review of Donald Harden, *The Phoenicians*, in *JC* (19 October).

1963

* 'Ismar Elbogen and the New Jewish Learning', *Year Book 8* (of the Leo Baeck Institute, London), pp. 3–28.

* 'Some Observations on the philosophical Theory of Prophecy in Islam', in A.A. Siassi (ed.), *Mélanges d'Orientalisme offerts à Henri Massé* (Teheran), pp. 343–52.

Review of Kemal A. Faruki, *Islamic Jurisprudence*, in *IA* 39, pp. 579–80.

1964

'Medieval Jewish Exegesis: its character and significance', *JSS* 9, pp. 265–81.

'Some Reflections on the separation of Religion and Politics in modern Islam', *Islamic Studies* 3 (Karachi), pp. 249–84.

Review of Osman Chahine, *Ontologie et théologie chez Avicenne*, in *BSOAS* 27, pp. 496–7.

Review of Ralph Lerner and Muhsin Mahdi, *Medieval Political Philosophy. A Sourcebook*, in *MEJ* 18, pp. 256–9.

Review of Solomon ibn Gabirol, *The Fountain of Life*, trans. from the Latin by H.E. Wedeck, in *Theol.* 67, pp. 39–40.

Review of Hans Franke, *Geschichte und Schicksal der Juden in Heilbronn*, in *AJR* 19 (April).

1965

Islam in the Modern National State (Cambridge).

Review of Robert Weltsch (ed.), *Year Book 10* (of the Leo Baeck Institute), in *AJR* 20 (September).

1966

Averroes' Commentary on Plato's 'Republic' – re-issue.

'Torah and Nomos in medieval Jewish Philosophy', in Raphael Loewe (ed.), *Studies in Rationalism, Judaism and Universalism in Memory of Leon Roth* (London), pp. 215–30.

'Judaism in the Museum – Czech Monuments to a once famous Jewry', *AJR* 21 (November).

1967

Political Thought in Medieval Islam, trans. into Spanish by Carmen Castro as *El Pensiamento Político en el Islam medieval*, Biblioteca de Politica y Sociologia (Madrid).

* 'Politics in Islam', *The Muslim World* 57 (Hartford), pp. 3–10.

Review of W.P. Eckert and E.L. Ehrlich, *Judenhass – Schuld der Christen? Versuch eines Gesprächs*, in *AJR* 22 (April).

1968

Political Thought in Medieval Islam – second re-issue.

* 'Jüdische Antwort', in K.H. Rengstorf and S. von Kortzfleisch (eds.), *Kirche und Synagoge* (Stuttgart), pp. 307–62.

'Political Philosophy in Islam and Judaism', *Judaism* 17 (New York), pp. 430–40.

1969

Averroes' Commentary on Plato's 'Republic' – second re-issue.

'La filosofía política en la España musulmana', *Revista de Occidente* 78 (Madrid), pp. 259–80.

* 'The Study of the Bible in Medieval Judaism', in G.W.H. Lampe (ed.), *The Cambridge History of the Bible*, vol. II, *The West from the Fathers to the Reformation* (Cambridge), pp. 252–79.

Editor of 'Judaism', Part I of *Religion in the Middle East*, general ed. A.J. Arberry (Cambridge).

Review of W. Montgomery Watt, *Islamic Political Thought. The Basic Concepts*, in *MEJ* 23, pp. 551–2.

Review of *Maimonides Regimen Sanitatis*, German trans. and intro. by Süssmann Muntner (Basel), in *AJR* 24 (June).

1970

'Religion and Politics in Muslim States', *Islam in the Modern Age 1* (New Delhi) pp. 50–64.

'Arthur J. Arberry – A Tribute', *RS* 6, pp. 297–302.

Review of M.H. Kerr, *Islamic Reform. The Political and Legal Theories of Muḥammad 'Abduh and Rashīd Riḍā*, in *JSS* 15, pp. 115–25.

1971

Political Thought in Medieval Islam – Japanese trans. by Yasuo Fukushima, published by Misuzu Shobo.

Studia Semitica, vol. I, 'Jewish Themes'; vol. II, 'Islamic Themes' (Cambridge) – containing articles marked with * in the list of publications above.

'Vom geschichtlichen Fortleben des Judentums', in W. Strolz (ed.), *Jüdische Hoffnungskraft und christlicher Glaube* (Freiburg), pp. 17–79.

Review of Majid Fakhir, *A History of Islamic Philosophy*, in *MEJ* 25, pp. 425–6.

1972

'Politisches Denken im Islam I: Kalifatstheorie und politische Philosophie', *Saeculum. Jahrbuch für Universalgeschichte* 23 (Freiburg–Munich), pp. 148–71; II: 'Die Entwicklung von Averroes bis Ibn Khaldun', *ibid.*, pp. 295–318.

Review of W. Strolz (ed.), *Jüdische Hoffnungskraft und christlicher Glaube*, in *AJR* 27 (April).

Review of Muhsin Mahdi (ed.), *Alfarabi's Book of Religion and Related Texts. Arabic Texts*, in *Orientalistische Literaturzeitung* 67 (Leipzig), cols. 565–7.

1973

'The Role of the State in Islam', *I* 50, pp. 1–28.

'Jüdisches Erbe im Islam', *Emuna/Horizonte* 8 (Frankfurt), pp. 263–9.

Review of P.H. Holt, Ann K.S. Lambton and B. Lewis (eds.), *The Cambridge History of Islam*, in *MAS* 7, pp. 128–33.

Review of Kenneth Cragg, *The Mind of the Qur'an: Chapters in Reflection*, in *WJ* 16, p. 26.

1974

'The Notion of Revelation in Medieval Judaism', *S. Bonaventura, 1274–1974*, vol. IV (Grottaferrata), pp. 57–69.

'Averroes', *Encyclopaedia Britannica*, vol. XV, *Macropaedia*, vol. II, pp. 538–40.

'Some Observations on Al-Farabi's "Kitab Al-Milla"', in O. Amine (ed.), *Etudes Philosophiques présentées au Dr. Ibrahim*

Madkour (Cairo), pp. 65–74.

'Hermann Cohen and Heinrich Graetz', in *Salo Wittmayer Baron Jubilee Volume on the occasion of his Eightieth Birthday*, English Section, vol. II (Jerusalem), pp. 725–43.

Review of K.A. Fariq, *History of Arabic Literature*, in *WJ* 17, p. 18.

Review of Ignaz Maybaum, *Trialogue between Jew, Christian and Muslim*, in *AJR* 29 (April).

Review of G. Scholem, *Sabbatai Ṣevi. The Mystical Messiah 1626–1676* (London), in *AJR* 29 (October).

1975

Review of Menahem Mansoor, *Baḥya Ben Joseph Ibn Paquda. The Book of Direction to the Duties of the Heart. Introduction, translation from the Arabic original, notes*, in *RS* 11, pp. 117–20.

1977

'Yoḥanan Alemanno and Occult Science', in Y. Maeyama and W.G. Saltzer (eds.), *Prismata. Naturwissenschaftsgeschichtliche Studien. Festschrift für Willy Hartner* (Wiesbaden), pp. 349–61.

1978

Review of Hans Liebeschütz and Arnold Paucker (ed.), *Das Judentum in der deutschen Umwelt. Studien zur Frühgeschichte der Emanzipation*, in *AJR* 33 (December).

1979

'Some Observations on Yoḥanan Alemanno's Political Ideas', in S. Stein and R. Loewe (eds.), *Studies in Jewish Religious and Intellectual History Presented to Alexander Altmann* (University, Alabama), pp. 247–61.

'Political Ideas in Moshe Narboni's Commentary on Ibn Ṭufail's *Ḥayy b. Yaqẓan*', in G. Nahon and Ch. Touati (eds.), *Hommage à Georges Vajda, études d'histoire et de pensée juive* (Paris), pp. 227–34.

'Ibn Khaldūn as a Political Thinker', *MR* 4, pp. 1–5.

Review of Werner Ende, *Arabische Nation und islamische Geschichte. Die Umayyaden im Urteil arabischer Autoren des 20. Jahrhunderts*, in *I* 56, pp. 326–30.

1980 and forthcoming

'Constitutional Law and Political Philosophy in Islam', *MR* 5, pp. 1–7.

'Plato and Political Thought in Islam', *Paideia*, Special Middle Ages Issue, 'The Cultural and Intellectual Life of the Middle Ages'.

'A Remarkable Friendship: L. Zunz and A. Geiger', in *I.O. Lehman Jubilee Volume*.

'Die Wissenschaft des Judentums. Vortrag' in *Martin Buber. Leben, Werk, Wirkung* (Heilbronner Vorträge 11, Heilbronn), pp. 52–80.

'Jewish and Islamic traditions', being a review of H.A. Wolfson, *Repercussions of the Kalam in Jewish Philosophy*, in *JQ* 28, p. 69.

Review of Alex Carmel, *Palästina Chronik 1853 bis 1882*, in *I* 58.

Review of Norman A. Stillman, *Jews of Arab Lands*, in *I* 59.

Addenda

1953

Review of I.I. Mattuck, *The Thought of the Prophets*, in *AP* 24, pp. 462–3.

1954

Review of E.B. Ceadel, *Literatures of the East: An Appreciation*, in *JC* (9 April).

1959

Review of K.M. Walker, *So Great a Mystery*, in *AP* 30, pp. 75–6.

An Early Interpretation of *pāsaḥ:'aggēn* in the Palestinian Targum [1]

S.P. BROCK

The verb *pāsaḥ* occurs three times in the Passover narrative of Exod. xii.13, 23 and 27, and it can come as something of a surprise to discover that at least six different interpretations of its meaning were already current in antiquity:[2]

(1) The most widespread understanding, which lives on in the very term 'Passover', probably takes Exod. xii.23, *wĕʿābar yhwh*, as its basis; thus the LXX translates both *ʿābar* and *pāsaḥ* in this verse by παρελεύσεται (whereas in verses 13 and 27 it employs σκεπάζει, on which see (6) below). This interpretation is already adopted by Ezekiel Tragicus[3] and Jubilees xlix.3; it also underlies διάβασις/διαβατήριον in Philo, ὑπερβασία in Josephus and ὑπέρβασις in Aquila. Jerome's *transire/transitus* led to this interpretation becoming standard in the vast majority of modern translations.[4]

(2) The *Mekilta*,[5] commenting on Exod. xii.13, states *'al tiqrē* "*ūpāsaḥtī*" *'ellā* "*ūpāsaʿtī*", which is understood as 'step, leap over', and in illustration Song of Songs ii.8–9 is cited (surprisingly

1 The following abbreviations are employed here in addition to those listed at the beginning of the volume: FT = Fragment Targum, Nf = Targum Neofiti, P = Peshitta, PsJ = Targum Pseudo-Jonathan, ST = Samaritan Targum, TJ = Targum Jonathan, TO = Targum Onqelos.

2 I am not here concerned with modern discussions of *psḥ*; for these, surveys will be found in J.B. Segal, *The Hebrew Passover* (London, 1963), pp. 95–101, and P. Laaf, *Die Pascha-Feier Israels* (Bonn, 1970), pp. 142–7.

3 In A.M. Denis, *Pseudepigrapha Veteris Testamenti Graece*, vol. III (Leiden, 1970), p. 213, line 1.

4 For early Christian interpretations see C. Mohrmann, '*Pascha, passio, transitus*' in *Études sur le latin des chrétiens*, vol. I (Rome, 1958), pp. 205–22. The relevant passage from Origen's *Peri Pascha* is given by P. Nautin in *Sources chrétiennes* 36 (Paris, 1953), pp. 34–6.

5 Ed. J.Z. Lauterbach (Philadelphia, 1933–5), vol. I, p. 57.

not Isa. xxxv.6, where *psḥ* and *dlg* occur together). This interpretation, which occurs in *Midraš haggādōl*, Rashi, Qimḥi and elsewhere, was evidently a standard one among Jews in the Middle Ages, and is reflected in the medieval Greek translation known as Graecus Venetus (which employs ἅλλομαι); it also turns up in the sixth-century Greek writer, Procopius, who states καλεῖται δὲ Φασε, ὅπερ ἐστὶ πλατέσι τοῖς βῆμασι χρῆσθαι, 'it is called "Phase", that is, to use broad steps'.[6]

(3) At the only other comparable occurrence of *pāsaḥ* in the Hebrew Bible, Isa. xxxi.5, both the LXX and TJ render it by 'save', 'deliver'. It is quite possible that this understanding of *pāsaḥ* in Isa. xxxi was also applied to Exod. xii; this would then give meaning to Theodoret's statement[7] σημαίνει δὲ τὸ ὄνομα τῶν Ἑβραίων πρωτοτόκων τὴν σωτηρίαν, 'the word [Phasech] means the saving of the first-born of the Hebrews'. Support for this suggestion surprisingly comes from PsJ Exod. xii.42: 'and his right hand saves (*měšēzěbā*) the first-born of Israel' (Nf has a similar phrase, but uses instead the verb *'aggēn* (cp. p. 32 below), which, as we shall see, it also employs to render *pāsaḥ* (see (6) below)). The same interpretation is probably also presupposed by the entry Πασεκ·λύτρωσις, 'Pasek: deliverance', in some of the *Onomastica*.[8]

(4) In P the Hebrew verb is taken over as *'apṣaḥ*. It is, however, unclear why the causative was used and what the original translator meant by this; later on in Syriac tradition *'apṣaḥ* was linked by popular etymology with *pṣīḥūtā*, 'joy'.[9] A straight transcription is also found in ST, Nf (as the first part of a doublet), and in the Aramaic introduction to the Passover Haggadah: *kol diṣěrīk yētē wěyipsaḥ*, where, however, the meaning is 'let everyone who is in need come and *keep passover*'.

(5) The *Mekilta*[10] offers a second interpretation of Exod. xii.13,

6 *Patrologia Graeca*, vol. LXXXVII, col. 561B.

7 *Patrologia Graeca*, vol. LXXX, col. 252A. (He is referring to Theodotion's transliteration.)

8 F. Wutz, *Onomastica Sacra*, vol. I (Berlin, 1915), pp. 472–3. Wutz was probably wrong to suppose that *pesaḥ* was here linked with *ḥopšī*. Note that P combines *'aggēn* with *praq* at Ecclus. xxxi(xxxiv).19.

9 E.g. Isho'dad of Merv (ninth century), *Commentary on Exodus*, *CSCO* Scriptores Syri 80, p. 23. Possibly the statement in *Pěsiqtā děrab Kāhănā*, *Pěsīqtā 'Aḥărītā děsukkōt*, ed. S. Buber (Wilna, 1925), p. 338 (or ed. B. Mandelbaum, New York, 1962, vol. II, p. 458), Eng. eds. W.G. Braude and I.J. Kapstein (London, 1975), supplement, 2, 8, p. 472, that there is '*no* commandment to rejoice at Passover' is a polemic against this Christian interpretation; *Exodus Rabba* 12. 5, however, says in connection with Exod. xii.5: *šěhū' lākem śimḥā gědōlā*.

10 Ed. Lauterbach, vol. I, p. 57.

attributing it to R. Jonathan: *ʿălēkem 'ănī ḥās*. Possibly *ḥws*, 'spare', 'protect', was chosen on the grounds that it shared two radicals with *psḥ* and because it was thought that *w* and *p* might be interchanged.[11] This particular interpretation is the one adopted in TO, and it is also found in PsJ at verses 13 and 27 (but not 23), and in the margin of Nf for all three verses. TO and PsJ also render the substantive *pesaḥ* by *ḥăyās(ā)*.[12] In the Palestinian Targum tradition this interpretation is closely associated with (6).

(6) Nf, both text and margin, contains a series of doublets for all three occurrences of *pāsaḥ* in Exod. xii; in every case the second element consists of the *'aphʿel* of *gnn*:

verse 13 text	אפסח ואגן במימרי עליכון
margin	ויחוס ויגן ממרי
verse 23 text[13]	ויפסח ויגן מימריה דייי על
margin	ויחוס
verse 27 text	דיפסח ויגן על
margin	חס ואגן מימריה דיי על

This rendering of *pāsaḥ* by *'aggēn* clearly takes Isa. xxxi.5 as its base:

כן יגן יהוה צבאות על ירושלם גנון והציל פסוח והמליט

where *psḥ* is balanced by *gnn*. As will shortly become apparent, this interpretation of *pāsaḥ* in Exod. xii is already presupposed by the LXX rendering of the verb by σκεπάζω in verses 13 and 27;[14] it also features, along with interpretations (2) and (5), in the *Mekilta*, where, after quoting Gen. xviii.8 (*wĕhū' ʿōmēd ʿălēhem*), we have the comment:[15]

והקב״ה הגין על בתי בניו במצרים . . . שנאמר ופסחתי על הפתח

(Exod. xii.23)

11 I am indebted to Dr S.C. Reif for this suggestion.

12 Cp. *Mekilta*, ed. Lauterbach, vol. I, p. 56: *'ēn pĕsīḥā 'ellā ḥăyās*. This interpretation also lies behind the delightful explanation of *ḥăzeret* (one of the bitter herbs that qualify as *mārōr*, M. Pesaḥ. 2.6) in BT Pesaḥ. 39*a*: 'Rabba said, What is *ḥăzeret*? Lettuce (*ḥassā*). What does *ḥassā* signify? That the Merciful One spared (*ḥās*) us.'

13 The 'glory of the Shekhinah' is subject. Cp. also Targum Song of Songs ii.9.

14 This was rightly seen by W. Riedel, 'Miscellen 5', *ZAW* 20 (1900), 319–29, and by T.F. Glasson, 'The "Passover", a misnomer: the meaning of the verb *pasach*' *JTS*, N.S. 10 (1959), 79–84. S. Lieberman, *Hellenism in Jewish Palestine* (New York, 1950), pp. 50–1, in contrast held that LXX here was closer to *ḥās*.

15 Ed. Lauterbach, vol. I, p. 185.

What precisely did the Aramaic translators understand by *'aggēn* when they opted for it as a rendering of *pāsaḥ*? Are the verb's connotations more of Hebrew *māgēn*, i.e. 'shield, protect',[16] or do they verge more upon Aramaic *gěnūnā*, 'bridal couch', i.e. 'overspread', 'overshadow'? A glance at the various translations of *'aggēn* in, for example, J.W. Etheridge's translation of PsJ will indicate the uncertainty surrounding this point.

It is with the background, then, to Nf's rendering of *pāsaḥ* in Exod. xii by *'aggēn* that the remainder of this study will be concerned. The matter can be approached from two different angles: first, the treatment of the Hebrew cognate *gānan* in the ancient versions and, secondly, the use of *'aggēn* in the Targumim and Peshitta outside passages where it represents Hebrew *psḥ* or *gnn*.

(*a*) Hebrew *gnn* in the ancient versions

For the verb (where God is always subject) the LXX consistently has ὑπερασπίζω (2 Kgs. xix.34, xx.6; Isa. xxxi.5, xxxvii.35, xxxviii.6; Zech. ix.15, xii.8; likewise Hos. xi.8 and Prov. iv.9), while at Isa. xxxi.5 and xxxviii.6 θυρεόω is recorded for Aquila. Jerome consistently opts for *protego*. In 2 Kings and Isaiah both TJ and P employ *'aggēn*, and this is also found in P in the two Zechariah passages, whereas TJ there renders Hebrew *gnn* by *rḥm*, 'have pity on'. This interpretation of TJ (which remarkably, is also found in the Akhmimic translation[17] of the LXX at Hos. xi.8 and Zech. xii.8) is of interest in connection with passages later to be considered (under (*b*)) where *'aggēn* in the Targum tradition is associated especially with the idea of 'mercy'.

Turning to passages where God is described in the Hebrew Bible as *māgēn*,[18] 'a shield', we meet considerable variety:

(i) For the most part the LXX employs ὑπερασπιστής/-ισμός (ἀντιλήμπτωρ/-λημψις also occurs three times in the Psalter),[19] and in this they are followed by Symmachus and

16 This seems to be the case with Hebrew *higgīn*.
17 That the Akhmimic version of the Minor Prophets contains traces of a Hebraizing recension not otherwise preserved in the LXX tradition is well known.
18 Outside the Psalms only Gen. xv.1; Deut. xxxiii.29; 2 Sam. xxii and Prov. ii.7, xxx.5.
19 In the Pentateuch and Proverbs passages the translators analysed *mgn* as a participle.

Theodotion. The Peshitta Psalter goes a stage further and simply renders by 'helper' (usually *msayy ʿānā*).

(ii) Aquila, not surprisingly, prefers to translate literally, and θυρεός is recorded as his regular translation (in the LXX only non-metaphorical); this finds a parallel in *tĕrīs*, the rendering of Nf (as a doublet) and PsJ in the two Pentateuch occurrences of *māgēn*, and of the Targum to the Psalms. Jerome, too, prefers a literal rendering (*scutum* or *clypeus*). In this connection it will be recalled that in the thanksgiving benediction of the ʿAmidah God is described as *māgēn yišʿēnū*.

(iii) In contrast to Aquila and the Palestinian Targum tradition, both TO and/TJ avoid a literal rendering and employ *tĕqōp*, 'strength' (similarly ST at Gen. xv.1).

Two further renderings of *māgēn* are of particular interest in the context of our main theme:

(iv) At Psalm lxxxiii.12 σκεπαστής is recorded as the rendering of Quinta. This confirms that LXX σκεπάζω at Exod. xii.13 and 27 represents the same exegetical tradition as Nf's *'aggēn*,[20] and suggests that the 'covering' aspect of the verb figured fairly prominently in the background.

(v) We have a pointer to yet a further aspect of *'aggēn* as an interpretation of *pāsaḥ* if we compare the literalist rendering of *māgēn* (referring to God) by ὅπλον in the Lucianic manuscripts of LXX 2 Sam. xxii.3 and 36 with a translation of *māgēn* at Gen. xv.1 to be found in the margin of the LXX manuscript j: ὑπερμάχομαι καθάπερ ὅπλον. Evidently we have here a doublet, where the first element analyses *mgn* as a *hiphʿil* participle (as do the LXX, P and the Tosephta Targum here), but gives the verb a rather different meaning from any we have met so far. Furthermore, it would appear that we have in this rendering of *mgn* by ὑπερμάχομαι at Gen. xv.1 the clue to Symmachus' puzzling translation of *pesaḥ* at Exod. xii.11 by ὑπερμάχησις;[21] behind this we must evidently suppose that *psḥ* has again been linked with *gnn* (even though our extant sources attest this equation only for *pāsaḥ* and not *pesaḥ*).

20 Note that σκέπη, as a rendering of *māgēn* in its literal meaning, is attested as a variant in the LXX tradition at Judg. v.8 and 2 Sam. i.21 (*bis*).

21 Theodoret wrongly gives ὑπέρβασις as his reading.

(*b*) *'aggēn* in the Aramaic Bible

We may now turn to the use of *'aggēn* in the Aramaic versions of the Bible, both Targumim and Peshitta, where it renders Hebrew verbs other than *pāsaḥ* and *gānan*. The comparatively large number of instances in both Palestinian and Babylonian Targum traditions and in the Peshitta suggests that the term *'aggēn* has become a technical one for divine activity of a protective or saving character.

First of all it will be helpful to give a conspectus of occurrences in the Pentateuch and Latter Prophets:[22]

		Hebrew	*Nf*	*N*^mg^	*PsJ*	*TO*	*P*	*context*
Gen.	vii.16	*sgr*	*gnn*	*ḥws + gnn*	*gnn*	*gnn*	*'ḥd*	'in his mercy'
	xv.11		*šyzb*	*gnn*	*gnn*			'merits'
	xxxiii.5	*ḥnn*	*ḥnn*	*ḥws + gnn*	*ḥws*	*ḥnn* var. *ḥws*	*yhb*	
Exod.	xii.42		*gnn*		*šyzb*			'right hand of God'
	xxxiii.22	*skk*	*prś*[23]	*ṭll*	*gnn*	*gnn*	*gnn*	
Num.	x.34		*gnn*		*ṭll*	*ṭll*		'divine cloud'
	xxiii.21		*gnn*		*ybb*			
Deut.	xxviii.15 (*bis*)				*gnn*			'merits'
Deut.	xxxii.10	*sbb*	*gnn*		*gnn*	*šr'* (*'aph'el*)	*nqp*	'clouds of glory' (object)
	xxxii.38	*str*	(*gnn*)		*gnn*	*gnn*	*str*	
	xxxiii.12	*ḥpp*	*gnn*		*gnn*	*gnn*	*rḥp*	

		Hebrew	*TJ*	*P*	*context*
Isa.	i.6		*gnn*		'merits'
	iv.5	~	*gnn*	~	'his Shekhinah will *'aggēn* him like a bridal chamber (*gĕnūnā*)'
	xxvii.3	*nṣr*	*gnn*	*nṭr*	
Jer.	xvii.17	*ḥs'*	*rḥṣ*	*gnn*	
	xxxvi.26	*str*	*gnn*	*ṭšy*	
Jonah	iv.6	*nṣl* (*hiṣṣīl*)	*gnn*	*rwḥ*	

22 My list is not quite complete since, for reasons of space, I have not included FT (Num. xxi.1 appears to be the only passage where FT alone attests *'aggēn*). I take the opportunity to thank the Rev. J.C. Okoye for drawing my attention to some additional examples in PsJ.

23 Cp. FT (and Nf^mg^?) at Gen. xv.1, and *Mekilta* (ed. Lauterbach), vol. I, p. 184, with Nf and PsJ Deut. xxxii.10.

Outside the Prophets, P employs *'aggēn* to render *skk* at Job i.10, iii.23, and *gmr* at Psalm cxxxviii.8; in books translated from Greek *'aggēn* represents ὑπερασπίζω at Wisd. v.16 (parallel with σκεπάζω/*'aṭṭel*) and σκεπάζομαι at Wisd. xix.8 (Exodus context).[24] In the Apocalypse of Baruch *'aggēn* occurs twice, at xlviii.18 and lxxi.1, both times in the context of 'mercy'; in 4 Esdras vii.122 the verb is used of the action of 'the glory of the Most High' upon those who have lived chastely.

This rapid survey sufficiently indicates something of the wide range of connotations that Aramaic *'aggēn* has, extending from the more military associations of Hebrew *māgēn*, through the straightforward idea of protection, to a very positive concept of divine overshadowing. In connection with our main concern, the use of *'aggēn* to represent *pāsaḥ*, the following features in particular may be singled out:

(i) The verb is especially associated with theophanies, and the Shekhinah is specifically introduced in the Targum tradition at Num. x.34, Deut. xxxii.10 and Isa. iv.5, as well as at Exod. xii.23. It is interesting to find that this usage is developed in subsequent Syriac liturgical tradition, where *'aggēn* is frequently employed as a technical term for the advent of the holy spirit at the epiclesis in the liturgy.[25]

(ii) The close connection between *'aggēn* and *ḥās*, which we have already found in the Palestinian Targum renderings of *pāsaḥ*, is again in evidence (Gen. vii.16, xxxiii.5).

(iii) At Gen. xv.11 and Exod. xii.42 *'aggēn* and *šēzēb* are variants, a point of significance for interpretation (3) of *psḥ*.

(iv) In several passages *'aggēn* has clearly shifted in meaning from 'protect' to 'cover over', but nowhere more dramatically than in Isa. iv.5, where *'aggēn* is associated in TJ with *gĕnūnā*.[26]

(v) Although it is normally God (or his hand) who is subject of the verb, in four passages (Gen. xv.11; Deut. xxviii.15 (*bis*) and Isa. i.6) it is 'merits' (*zĕkūtā*) that afford protection.

24 In the light of (*a*)(i) above it is interesting that at Judith v.21 and vi.2 P has *sayya* 'corresponding to ὑπερασπίζω.

25 See my 'The Epiklesis in the Antiochene baptismal *ordines*', *Orientalia Christiana Analecta* 197 (1974), 202–3. The mysterious *'gn* on Palmyrene tesserae is probably unconnected (see J.T. Milik, *Dédicaces faites par des Dieux* (Paris, 1972), pp. 108–11).

26 Compare Aquila's παστόω to render *ḥpp* at Deut. xxxiii.12.

(vi) A number of passages specifically associate *'aggēn* with the idea of mercy (Gen. vii.16; Apocalypse of Baruch).[27]

(vii) In two verses, Exod. xxxiii.22 and Num. x.34, *'aggēn* and *'aṭṭēl*, 'overshadow', are variants. That the two words were considered to have overlapping semantic fields is further shown by TJ's use of *'aggēn* to render *hiṣṣīl* at Jonah iv.6, deriving it from *ṣll* (cp. LXX σκιάζω), and by P's 'shade covers (*maggen*) me' at Ecclus. xxiii.18. This particular association is of interest in connection with the choice of *'aggēn* to render ἐπισκιάζομαι in all the Syriac versions of Luke i.35, the angel's annunciation to Mary.[28] Here, in view of the Palestinian Targum's choice of *'aggēn* to render *pāsaḥ* in Exod. xii, it is fascinating to discover that Ephrem (died A.D. 373) actually links the annunciation, which took place according to him on 10 Nisan, with the selecting of the Passover lamb on the same day.[29]

Conclusion

From this summary survey it is evident not only that Aramaic *'aggēn* was richer in overtones than Hebrew *higgīn*, but that it was also in itself a technical term for divine activity of a salvific character. Although it remains unclear what precise associations were intended by the choice of *'aggēn* to render *pāsaḥ*, its use in Exod. xii nevertheless brings the very specialized *pāsaḥ* of the Hebrew into the wider context of the covenantal theophanies of Gen. xv and Exod. xxxiii.

27 Compare also a poem by Marqah, in Z. Ben-Ḥayyim, *The Literary and Oral Tradition of Hebrew and Aramaic among the Samaritans* (Hebrew), III, vol. 2 (Jerusalem, 1967), p. 153 (stanza R).

28 In the Syriac New Testament *'aggēn* has already become a technical term for the activity of the logos and the holy spirit (e.g. John i.14; Acts x.44); see my *The Holy Spirit in the Syrian Baptismal Tradition*, Syrian Churches Series 9 (Kottayam, 1979), pp. 6–7. It is quite possible that *gnn* rather than *škn* is the Semitic word ultimately underlying the Greek of Luke i.35.

29 *Commentary on Exodus* xii.3, CSCO, Scriptores Syri 71, p. 141. See further my 'Passover, Annunciation and Epiclesis', forthcoming in *Novum Testamentum* (1982).

Heinrich Graetz as Biblical Historian and Religious Apologist

R.E. CLEMENTS

It can only be a rather venturesome undertaking from the Christian point of view to offer some evaluation of the significance as a religious historian of the distinguished Jewish scholar Heinrich Graetz (1817–91).[1] From the Jewish side his reputation stands on the highest plane, and we need only to quote the comment of the eminent scholar S.W. Baron to substantiate this estimate: 'Through his *History* and, to a far lesser extent, through his biblical studies, he made lasting contributions to the knowledge of Judaism . . . Hardly any work of the science of Judaism achieved the success of Graetz's *History*.'[2] Yet among Christian scholars his work has largely been either ignored or considered as no more than a piece of religious apologetic. It might be in order, therefore, to attempt a fresh appraisal of the importance of Heinrich Graetz's contribution to a critical understanding of Jewish history in the biblical period as a mark of appreciation for the work of a scholar who has himself drawn attention to the creative significance of Graetz's work.[3] All the more is this so, since it was in lectures by Erwin Rosenthal that I first learnt of the many studies contributed by Graetz towards the

1 An appreciation of Graetz is given by I. Abrahams, 'H. Graetz, The Jewish Historian', *JQR* 4 (1892), 165–94, where a bibliography of his writings is also to be found (pp. 194–203). Further information is to be found in *JE*, vol. VI (New York–London, 1904), pp. 64–7; *EJ*, vol. VII (Jerusalem, 1972), cols. 845–50. Cp. also M.A. Meyer (ed.), *Ideas of Jewish History* (New York, 1974), pp. 217–44; I. Schorsch (ed.), *Heinrich Graetz: The Structure of Jewish History and Other Essays* (New York, 1975).

2 A. Hertzberg and L.A. Feldman (eds.), *History and Jewish Historians* (Philadelphia, 1964), p. 275.

3 Cp. especially E.I.J. Rosenthal, 'Hermann Cohen and Heinrich Graetz', *Salo Wittmayer Baron Jubilee Volume*, vol. II (Jerusalem, 1974), pp. 725–43, and his remarks in his essay 'Ismar Elbogen and the New Jewish Learning', *Year Book* 8 (of the Leo Baeck Institute, London, 1963), pp. 6–7 = *Stud. Sem.*, vol. I, pp. 330–1.

better understanding of the Hebrew Bible. In his extensive history of the modern critical study of the Old Testament since the Reformation, H.J. Kraus fails to mention him or his work,[4] which must be regarded as a surprising omission in view of the wide range of Graetz's contribution in the biblical field. Perhaps even more surprising is the failure to mention him in the monumental work by G.P. Gooch on *History and Historians in the Nineteenth Century* (London, 1913; 2nd edn, 1952), which includes a very interesting and informative chapter on 'The Jews and the Christian Church' (2nd edn, pp. 478–501). More recently still, John H. Hayes, in a chapter on the history of Israelite and Judean historiography in the modern period, gives so brief and unsympathetic an appraisal of that part of Graetz's work which touches on the biblical period as to discourage closer attention to it from the Christian side. We may quote his assessment: 'His work is not of major significance *per se* but because it represents the first modern history of ancient Israel and Judah by a Jew . . . Very few of the problems are given any detailed treatment.'[5]

This estimate by Hayes can scarcely be said to be entirely fair, and certainly tends to suggest that Graetz's work on the study of the biblical period of Israelite–Jewish history was neither particularly critical nor original. In fact it is quite decidedly both, and well deserves closer investigation, even now, so many years after Graetz's death, when so much more effort has been expended upon the study of Israelite–Jewish history. Two factors prompt a fresh look at Graetz and a new concern to evaluate the significance of his contribution to biblical historiography. The first is the simple apologetic one that the impartial and scientific character of biblical scholarship is called into question if there are major disagreements between Jews and Christians about what constitutes the right way of setting about the task of writing biblical history. The second factor is that there does appear today to be a new questioning about the very nature and aims of writing a history of Israel in Old Testament times. The very wealth of information that is now available outside the Bible, as well as the reconsidered results of more than a century of biblical criticism, suggest that it is right to look afresh at the historiographic

4 *Geschichte der historisch-kritischen Erforschung des Alten Testaments von der Reformation bis zur Gegenwart* (Neukirchen, 1956).

5 J.H. Hayes and J. Maxwell Miller (eds.), *Israelite and Judaean History* (London, 1977), p. 61.

aims of the great modern pioneers in this field. In a way the essay by J.H. Hayes is symptomatic of this extended interest. What is 'biblical' history? From a critical historian's perspective it breaks down into the political, cultic and sociological aspects of the historical process, as well as more generally containing a large measure of the history of ideas and of spiritual life. In fact a 'religious' history is a peculiarly difficult and many-sided phenomenon to attempt to present. It is important, therefore, to clarify what its aims are and to ask what the aims have been of those who have established the main paths that scholarship has followed in the past hundred years.

It is valuable in this light to look again at the work of Heinrich Graetz, not least because, although he undertook his task from a Jewish standpoint, he endeavoured to write a critical and impartial work of scholarship, not a philosophical or moralistic defence of Judaism. We can recognize the value of this all the more in noting that, among the many scholars who contributed to establishing the foundations of Old Testament history-writing in the nineteenth century, four names stand out: those of H.H. Milman (1791–1868),[6] Heinrich Ewald (1803–75),[7] Heinrich Graetz and Julius Wellhausen (1844–1918).[8] The work of Wellhausen has understandably acquired the greatest eminence and fame, and justifiably so in view of the importance of his contribution to the complex question of the literary history of the Pentateuch and its probable sources, and to that of the closely related history of Israel's religious institutions. It is certainly not out of place to suggest that Graetz does deserve examination and consideration alongside these other three, even though his contribution understandably lay in a very different direction from that pursued by Wellhausen. In recent years concern has been voiced at the apparent 'anti-Jewishness' of some of Wellhausen's conclusions, with the imputation that they arose out of a certain

6 *The History of the Jews* (London, 1829; 3rd edn, 1863). For Milman and his work cp. *DNB*, vol. XXXVIII (London, 1894), pp. 1–4; W.E.H. Lecky, *Historical and Political Essays*, rev. edn (London, 1910), pp. 227–50. For the historiographic background to the work of Milman an informative treatment is to be found in D. Forbes, *The Liberal Anglican Idea of History* (Cambridge, 1952), pp. 34ff.

7 *Geschichte des Volkes Israel*, 3rd edn (7 vols., Göttingen, 1864–7); Eng. trans. R. Martineau, J. Estlin Carpenter and J.F. Smith, *The History of Israel*, 4th edn (8 vols., London, 1883–6).

8 *Prolegomena zur Geschichte Israels*. Originally published as *Geschichte Israels* I (Berlin, 1878); Eng. trans. J. Sutherland Black and A. Menzies, *Prolegomena to the History of Israel* (Edinburgh, 1885); cp. also *Israelitische und Jüdische Geschichte* (Berlin, 1894; 5th edn, 1904).

Protestant theological prejudice,[9] and undoubtedly similar sentiments were felt much earlier by more than one Jewish scholar over Wellhausen's conclusions.[10] It is important therefore that we should be concerned to separate religious–theological evaluations from more narrowly historical ones. The hasty dismissal of Graetz's work by Hayes then becomes all the more striking in view of the relatively extended attention that he devotes to the work of Milman, whose *History of the Jews* was first published in 1829 and ran into three editions. Of the two scholars Graetz was incomparably the greater Hebraist, as his extensive contributions in this field show. More than this, however, he was also vastly more critical than Milman ever was in his evaluation of sources, concern over the dates and 'tendency' of particular sources, and overall appreciation of the way in which historical institutions develop. So too in regard to the 'miraculous' element in biblical history, a point over which Milman was heavily criticized by his contemporaries, Graetz was much more theologically discerning and critical. However, there are admittedly two factors that have greatly contributed to the impression of an insufficiency of critical rigour and have certainly encouraged the estimate of Graetz along these lines. The first concerns the manner and style of Graetz's writing, which is that of a free-flowing narrative, with no separate treatment either of critical issues concerning sources, or of those innumerable instances where the present biblical narrative requires to be probed if we are to arrive at what actually happened. Graetz has quite clearly made his own independent judgement on these questions, and puts down his personal estimate of the reality of what took place. It is therefore necessary for the reader to accept, or reject, this conclusion, since there is no footnote or appendix where the point can be followed through. In this measure Graetz undertakes a rather personal and eclectic type of history-writing, making no attempt to keep his conclusions in a separate compartment from the evidence on which he has reached them. So far as these are to be found at all they are present only in the many reviews and shorter articles that Graetz published.[11] From

9 Cp. C. Klein, *Theologie und Anti-Judaismus* (Munich, 1975), p. 66; Eng. edn *Anti-Judaism in Christian Theology* (London, 1978), pp. 62ff.

10 Cp. S. Schechter, 'Higher Criticism – Higher Anti-Semitism', in *Seminary Addresses and Other Papers* (Cincinnati, 1915), pp. 35–9. 'Wellhausen's Prolegomena and History are *teeming with aperçes* [author's italics] full of venom against Judaism, and you cannot wonder that he was rewarded by one of the highest orders which the Prussian Government had to bestow' (p. 36).

a modern critical point of view, such a method of writing history may not be particularly recommended, but it is certain that Graetz's work would never have attained the popularity that it did had he followed a more detailed and analytical approach. Like Milman, Graetz was undertaking a largely novel way of presenting biblical material to readers who could, for the most part, be assumed to be familiar with it. At this stage, in view of the pioneering nature of what was being attempted, it is hardly just to evaluate it as though a ready-to-hand readership existed, which could be assumed to be interested in, and appreciative of, such a fresh way of approaching a sacred subject matter.

The second feature in Graetz's work that has contributed to the impression of a rather romanticized and personal approach to the problem of presenting a biblical history is the marked tendency to reconstruct psychological reactions and attitudes on the part of the biblical personalities with whom he is dealing. We may cite his imaginative reconstruction of the reaction to the first sight of the land of Judah by the returning exiles as an example: 'The first sight of the long-cherished land, after a journey of four or five months, filled the returned exiles with unbounded joy. The prophecies, the hopes, the dreams had become a reality!'[12]

No doubt this injection of a psychological and spiritualizing attitude into situations where no hard historical evidence has come down to us marks a very bold and unwarranted filling-out of the material. From the writer's point of view it provides a way of introducing an element of evaluation, especially the evaluation of ideas, in which Graetz was himself obviously so deeply interested. It is undoubtedly an aspect of the 'popular' character of the approach undertaken by Graetz, who felt himself to be writing for a wide lay readership, not for a more narrowly academic one. If it is to be judged a fault in the method adopted for the work, it is a fault that nonetheless served to further the particular aspect of the history that Graetz regarded as of paramount importance. This aspect was to be found in the history of ideas, particularly in the way in which moral and spiritual issues were deeply embedded in religious and cultural

11 Graetz's rejection of the Documentary Hypothesis is set out in *Geschichte der Juden*, vol. II, part 1 (Leipzig, 1875), pp. 452–75. S.W. Baron, *History and Jewish Historians*, p. 448, n. 16, refers also to an essay by Graetz, 'Die allerneueste Bibelkritik Wellhausen–Renan', *MGWJ* 35 (1886), 193–204, 233–51.

12 *The Popular History of the Jews*, vol. I, p. 1 (5 vols., New York, 1930); Eng. trans. A.B. Rhine = *Volkstümliche Geschichte der Juden*, 1st edn (Leipzig, 1888–9).

features of ancient Israel's life and its background. It can hardly be said to be a mark of an uncritical attitude on Graetz's part, nor of any very special pleading as a Jewish apologist.

The comparison with the work of H.H. Milman immediately draws attention to a feature that stands out with extraordinary prominence when we consider the basic assumptions behind the nineteenth-century attempt to write a history of biblical Israel. Like Graetz, Milman regarded it as axiomatic that, in writing the history of Israel in Old Testament times, he was writing a history of 'the Jews'. Hence he regarded it as quite natural and proper to see the continuation of the nation of Israel, which effectively lost its full nationhood with the destruction of Jerusalem in 587 B.C. by the Babylonians, in the Jewish community of the post-exilic period and in the continuing history of the Jewish people after the second great political crisis with the Roman–Jewish war of A.D. 66–70. There was, as both Milman and Graetz viewed the history, a natural element of continuity of the Jewish people, which survived the loss of nationhood and which extended down into modern times. It is true that Milman saw a measure of 'completeness' – a national growth from childhood to maturity – manifesting itself in the biblical period, so that this period did in some measure stand by itself in a special way. Yet so also Graetz, who discerned an interesting structure of Jewish history in three main periods – national, post-exilic and post-biblical – could view the post-biblical period of Jewish existence as in a measure incomplete and distorted precisely on account of the lack of a truly 'national' dimension.[13] This is a point to which we shall have occasion to return in considering the structure of Graetz's work and its overall conception of the nature of Jewish existence.

The perspective of Graetz and Milman, however, stands in marked contrast to that adopted by H.G.A. Ewald, whose massive seven-volume work, *Geschichte des Volkes Israel* (Eng. edn, *The History of Israel*), viewed the rise of Christianity as the natural product and development of the history recounted in the Old Testa-

13 The comment by Forbes (p. 52) on the work of Thomas Arnold is illuminating: 'The nation remained for Arnold the instrument of moral growth, the means by which the individual and mankind are brought to perfection.' The same could certainly be said of Graetz's view of Jewish history, with the modification that the loss of this national dimension led to a wholly new emphasis upon the religious aspect that had remained hidden within the nationally-orientated social aspect. Certainly Graetz argued for a very close connection between Israel's moral life and its roots in the period of its existence as a nation.

ment. For him, the history of Israel found 'its own Consummation in ever-growing Christianity' (Eng. edn, vol. VI, p. 9). A similar perspective, although much more cautiously expressed, is to be found in J. Wellhausen's *Israelitische und Jüdische Geschichte.*[14] Milman, in fact, says virtually nothing regarding the separation of the early Christian community from Judaism, whereas Graetz regards the former quite explicitly as a heretical community for which there could be no natural home within Judaism.[15] It becomes all the more interesting, therefore, to note that Wellhausen took the view that Jesus 'never thought of leaving the Jewish community'.[16] Undoubtedly the immense development of research into the character and differing forms of Judaism in the immediate pre-Christian period since the time when both Graetz and Wellhausen were writing has served only to highlight still more the complexity of the question of the relationships of both Christianity and post-biblical Judaism to the Old Testament.

The work by Graetz was a massive eleven-volume undertaking, which began to appear with volume IV in 1853, and was not completed until 1874 with the publication of volume I. The first two volumes cover the biblical period with which we are concerned, dealing with the history down to the close of the Maccabean Revolt in approximately 160 B.C. Subsequently an abbreviated edition of the work, undertaken by Graetz himself, was published in Leipzig in 1888. Translations of this into a number of other languages appeared, as well as translations, and revised translations, of the original work. The international influence and reputation of Graetz was therefore understandably quite immense, although apparently not, as has been noted, among Christian biblical historians. This is in itself not at all difficult to appreciate in view of the fact that, when J. Wellhausen published in 1878 his *Geschichte Israels*, vol. I (called *Prolegomena zur Geschichte Israels* in later editions), he established an entirely new platform of scholarship upon which Christian scholars, more or less universally, have built.[17] In this the perspectives and interests that were paramount in the approach of Graetz had very little place.

14 Significantly, the book concludes with a chapter entitled 'Das Evangelium' (pp. 381ff).

15 *Geschichte der Juden*, vol. IV (Leipzig, 1853), pp. 88–128.

16 *Sketch of the History of Israel and Judah*, 3rd edn (Edinburgh–London, 1891), p. 227.

17 Cp. now M. Haran, *Temples and Temple-Service in Ancient Israel* (Oxford, 1978).

In Wellhausen's work the main foundation of the presentation of the history of Israel is achieved through setting out a history of the great religious institutions of the people: the Temple, its priests and ministrants, and its various rituals. In the course of this the history of the great political institutions of kingship and legal administration are also given extensive coverage. With Graetz the particular course of history through which these institutions passed is of much less importance. In setting out to achieve what he did, Wellhausen was following closely in the path of the great pioneer historian Barthold Niebuhr, who had used a study of the growth of the major political institutions of ancient Rome as a basis for presenting a new critical approach to the history of that great culture.[18] Niebuhr had been very influential in England, particularly with Thomas Arnold and J. Connop Thirlwall, and in some measure with Milman also. His influence upon the whole course of ancient historiography in the nineteenth century was therefore immense. Graetz was undoubtedly conscious in large measure of the whole historicist movement in Germany at the beginning of the nineteenth century and of the current philosophical and religious trends that made history-writing such a prominent scholarly occupation.[19] As a Jewish writer he had a particular forerunner in the work of I.M. Jost,[20] although this in itself cannot be regarded as the major stimulus for his own embarking upon so mammoth a task. For Graetz the particular characteristic that controls his methodology is a profound concern with ideas and their history, so that the way in which ideas governed and controlled experience becomes a significant feature of the presentation of history.

18 For Niebuhr cp. Gooch, *History and Historians in the Nineteenth Century*, pp. 14ff.

19 Cp. especially F. Meinecke, *Die Entstehung des Historismus* (Munich, 1936), Eng. edn *Historism. The Rise of a New Historical Outlook* (London, 1972); N.B. also E. Cassirer, *The Philosophy of the Enlightenment*, Eng. trans. F.C.A. Koelln and J.P. Pettegrove (Princeton, 1951), p. 199: 'History bears the torch for the Enlightenment; it frees the "neologists" from the bonds of Scripture dogmatically interpreted and of the orthodoxy of the preceding centuries' (= *Die Philosophie der Aufklärung* (Tübingen, 1932), pp. 266–7).

20 Jost (1793–1860) published his *Geschichte der Israeliten* in 1820–8 (9 vols., Berlin), and this represents the very beginning of modern Jewish historiography. A tenth volume, narrating the events of the author's own time, appeared in 1846–7. He subsequently published *Geschichte des Judentums und Seiner Secten* (3 vols., Leipzig, 1857–9). For Jost's work see S.W. Baron, *History and Jewish Historians*, pp. 240–62; M.A. Meyer (ed.), *Ideas of Jewish History*, pp. 175–86 (see n. 1 above).

In some ways as important for the religious historiographer as the *History* itself is the extended sketch that Graetz published in 1846, in which he explains the nature of his task as he saw it and the particular characteristics of Jewish history as he wished to demonstrate them.[21] The recent republication of this sketch, together with several of the prefaces to the individual volumes of the *History*, in an English translation (*Structure*, pp. 63–124), creates afresh an interest in Graetz as a historian, and in what may be termed the particular problems of dealing with Old Testament history in the pre-Wellhausen era. We may suggest two further reasons why an interest in the work of Graetz should be revived in the present and why in particular an interest should be taken in it from a Christian standpoint. The first of these is the new questioning that has arisen in respect of the famed four-document hypothesis in the source analysis of the Pentateuch with which Wellhausen's name has become inseparably associated.[22] This is not the place to consider these specific questions, and certainly not to concede that the Wellhausenian hypothesis can be said to have been overthrown. Rather what has taken place has been the setting of this hypothesis in a more critical perspective and the recognition that it is, itself, subject to several significant limitations. With sources that are all in some measure anthologies, it is obviously impossible to append precise dates to each item within each source, so that the value of being able to identify a specific source becomes of rather less significance and assistance in tracing a precise chronological development of institutions. Furthermore, the history of those institutions themselves, which forms a major part of the evidence for the four-document hypothesis, has forced certain modifications in the original thesis. This particularly applies to the so-called Priestly Source (Wellhausen's Q).[23]

The second reason for a new interest in the rise of nineteenth-century biblical historiography is that now, after more than a century of work, it is becoming all the more necessary to ask what kind of history it is that is being researched and presented. Is it a religious, political or social history? Or is it a history of ideas and, in some sense, a history that itself forms a part of a divine revelation?

21 Graetz, 'Die Konstruktion der jüdischen Geschichte', *Zeitschrift für religiösen Interessen des Judentums* 3 (1846), 270–3, 307–13, 349–52.

22 So especially R. Rendtorff, *Das überlieferungsgeschichtliche Problem des Pentateuch*, BZAW 147 (Berlin–New York, 1977).

23 Cp. especially M. Haran (see n. 17 above), pp. vi–vii.

It is evident in retrospect that only slowly have the separate facets of the history begun to appear as separately identifiable. It may be argued that in practice a biblical 'history' has provided a very broad introduction to questions of a literary, ethical, social and ideological nature, as well as to matters dealing more directly with religious and political institutions. It has become necessary to question what precisely is the 'Israel', the history of which is being pursued so painstakingly. In this respect it is salutary to reflect that, at the beginning of the nineteenth century, as important a scholar as W.M.L. de Wette argued that a critical history of Israel was neither possible nor desirable.[24] So powerfully, in fact, did the impulses and convictions of the historicist movement come to affect the study of religion, especially in regard to the questions concerning the origin of particular religions, that by the second half of the nineteenth century a critical historical study seemed to be essential to virtually everything in the way of religious practice and ideas.

Graetz was evidently not unmoved by all these things and we may note three factors that may be identified as having extensively affected his work. The first of these was the Enlightenment itself with its concern with history, and especially with a new critical approach to the task of historical writing.[25] Through his roots in the *Wissenschaft* movement in German Jewry Graetz was evidently freely at home in critical assumptions and methodology, so that he could not have expected or desired to write a history of the sort that he planned without the fullest immersion in critical questions. Most directly for Graetz this related to the Old Testament text and its interpretation, and to the problems of establishing a truly original and correct meaning.[26] In this he had learnt extensively from the newer classical workers in the field, even when this set him in opposition to the more traditional and Orthodox approach to the problem. That he extended this into a far-reaching literary criticism has already been noted, even though Graetz himself had neither the taste nor the rigour to carry it through with the determination that

24 Cp. R. Smend, *Wilhelm Martin Leberecht de Wettes Arbeit am Alten und am Neuen Testament* (Basel, 1957), p. 24; see also L. Perlitt, *Vatke und Wellhausen*, BZAW 94 (Berlin, 1965), pp. 91ff.

25 P.H. Reill, *The German Enlightenment and the Rise of Historicism* (Berkeley–Los Angeles–London, 1975), pp. 31ff.

26 As far as his work in the biblical field is concerned, Graetz's other major contributions were in the field of text criticism, especially in his commentary on the Psalms, *Kritischer Commentar zu den Psalmen* (2 vols., Breslau, 1882–3), for which he received severe criticism from his more conservative colleagues for the boldness of his emendations.

characterized Wellhausen. For the kind of history that he proposed to undertake the precise course of the rise and fall of such institutions as the Temple and its priesthood were not especially important. Graetz concerned himself more with the interpretation of the role of such archaic and obsolete institutions in forming the life, ideas and character of a people.

Certainly it is here, in the realm of ideas, that Graetz shows so much of the weaving together of nineteenth-century idealism and older, more traditional, interpretations of the ethical and doctrinal aspects of religion. So much has, in fact, been written and claimed with respect to the impact of Hegel and Hegelianism upon nineteenth-century biblical criticism that it is only with hesitation that such epithets and names can be mentioned. Yet there is undoubtedly a real measure of Hegelianism to be identified in Graetz's work, profoundly concerned as it is with the idea of Judaism and Jewishness.[27] In fact, for his *History* Graetz clearly had an ambition to bring out this particular ideological aspect of Jewish life and religion. In his own words (in translation): 'Thus, history is not only the reflection of the idea, but also the test of its power' (*Structure*, p. 65). From this he could go on to claim that, in its essence, all Jewish history exhibits but a single idea. Yet this idea was not monotheism as such, nor even the 'ethical monotheism' that formed so prominent a feature in the Wellhausenian reconstruction of Israel's theological and religious achievement. This fundamental ideological basis of Judaism emerges initially as the negation of paganism, but in the course of its historical development takes on a more and more positive form. 'For history merely ripens the seeds of an idea, and the variety of forms which history yields are only concrete manifestations of the idea' (p. 65). I could go on to cite further instances of this indirect influence of a philosophical idealism, with its loosely Hegelian character. What is important from a historiographic perspective is that, in itself, this concern with religious and ethical ideas, and with the broad spirituality of a people, constitutes the main centre of interest for Graetz. This is a point to which we shall need to return in considering the way in which the history bore a revelatory significance. It matters here, however, since it enabled Graetz

27 For the influence of Hegel on the Jewish *Wissenschaft* movement and its importance to Graetz's *History* see the introductory essay entitled 'Ideology and History' contributed by I. Schorsch to *Structure* (pp. 1–62), pp. 8ff. In a note on p. 308 Schorsch points to the influence on Graetz of the Hegelian philosopher Christian Julius Braniss at the University of Breslau.

to make a distinction between the 'external' history, which at times took the form of a history of suffering and endurance, and the 'inward' history, which constituted 'a comprehensive history of the mind'.[28] Thus he could treat the talmudic period as a manifestation of the channelling of Jewish life into a distinctive intellectual realm.[29] This realm was understandable, and even necessary in its time, but did not reveal the wholeness of Judaism or Jewish experience. In fact it was only through the totality of its history that the true nature of Judaism could be seen.[30] More than this, however, his conviction that an essential Jewish spirit manifests itself throughout the history of Judaism enabled Graetz to draw very positive and optimistic conclusions about the future of Judaism.[31] The fact that the first period of Jewish life held a kind of normative place within the whole story did not mean that this was the period in which the full fruits of the Jewish idea and experience were disclosed. This first period was that of national existence and began with the conquest of the land by Joshua and ended with the fall of Jerusalem to the Babylonians in 587 B.C.[32] Only in the future could the full flowering of the Jewish idea be attained.

This points us to the third important influence that we may discern within the structure and approach adopted by Graetz for his history. This lies within the greatly changed political and intellectual situation existing for Jews in Germany at the time when Graetz wrote. Loosely described, this has been termed 'emancipation', and represents in large measure the legacy of the Napoleonic upheavals upon the life and thought of central European Jewry. It is, in fact, almost impossible to separate the changed social and political context of life from the intellectual movements that accompanied it in Judaism. This witnessed the rise of *Wissenschaft* as a new way of approaching inherited religious riches, and the desire for reform and even full assimilation into European, especially German European, life. That Graetz held back from the idea of almost unrestricted

28 Cp. Graetz in 'Introduction to Volume Four of *The History of the Jews*' (reprinted in *Structure*, pp. 125–39), p. 125.

29 'Introduction to Volume Four', pp. 127ff.

30 Cp. Graetz, 'But the totality of Judaism is discernible only in its history', *Structure*, p. 65.

31 *Structure*, p. 72: 'Judaism is not a religion of the present but of the future.'

32 *Structure*, p. 74: 'The first page of Jewish history begins with the Book of Joshua, with the crossing of the Jordan, with the encampment at Gilgal. The Pentateuch, the slavery in Egypt, and the miraculous survival in the wilderness up to the death of the man of God with the radiant face constitute the interesting introduction and preparation thereto.'

'Reform', and from total assimilation into German life and citizenship, arose precisely out of his interpretation of Jewish history and of the peculiarly 'national' dimension that is identified in that history at its beginning.[33] It is here that we encounter some of the most interesting facets of Graetz's thought, and of the importance that he himself attached to his subject matter. Not only the age in which he wrote but also the impulses and tendencies of that age required the clarification of those features that were universally binding and eternally enduring within Judaism – what he himself could term 'the fundamental principle of Judaism'. Not surprisingly Graetz found this to lie in certain ideas and ethical principles, realities that could be applied and developed in an unlimited number of situations. They constituted in the Kantian sense 'universal truths'.[34] Yet these ideas, which were in Graetz's understanding the intellectual treasures of Judaism, had been received and expressed through a particular people and in particular times. In this measure therefore their universality had been limited and particularized through the exigencies and experiences of a concrete people and its life. There is, therefore, in the way in which the *History* is presented a strong, and not unexpected, apologetic element. Graetz is concerned to defend the right and propriety of the acceptance of change in Jewish life by demonstrating that throughout its history Judaism had been in a continuing process of change. This was not in a steady upward movement, but rather in a somewhat jerky series of phases.[35] More than this, however, he was able to present the history in such a way as to show that the period of emancipation made possible the recovery of something from the past, which life in the ghettoes had precluded. Judaism could therefore enter more fully into its inheritance by a recovery of the knowledge of its own past in the biblical

33 This point is brought out in the illuminating essay by E.I.J. Rosenthal, 'Hermann Cohen and Heinrich Graetz' (see n. 3 above). An appreciation by Cohen of the work of Graetz is to be found in 'Zur Jahrhundertfeier unseres Graetz' in H. Cohen, *Jüdische Schriften*, vol. II, 'Zur jüdischen Zeitgeschichte' (Berlin, 1924), pp. 446–53.

34 For the importance of the tensions and contrasts between universalism and particularism in relation to the study of the Old Testament cp. Smend (see n. 24 above), pp. 85–7n, and his essay 'Universalismus und Partikularismus in der Alttestamentliche Theologie des 19. Jahrhunderts', *EvTh* 22 (1962), 169–79.

35 Cp. Graetz, 'Introduction to Volume One of *The History of the Jews*' (Schorsch, pp. 173–89), p. 187: 'The history of the Israelite nation manifests, therefore, at the beginning a thoroughly irregular pattern.' We may contrast the summary by Forbes (p. 49) of the view of A.P. Stanley: 'In no people does the history move forward in so regular a course, through beginning, middle and end, as in the people of Israel' (taken from *The Eastern Church*, p. xxvi).

period. At the same time this knowledge of the past could bring to the fore those dimensions of Jewish life that had remained dormant for more than two millennia: in particular, the recognition that the ethical bases of biblical teaching pointed inevitably to the whole realm of man's political and social life for their full expression. 'The concept of God must immediately become a concept of the state' (*Structure*, p. 69). In this way Graetz believed that he was able to show from the character of the biblical material in the foundation period of Jewish existence the wholeness of revealed truth, which was of a profoundly ethical and spiritual nature.

This apologetic element in the structure of Graetz's work has, therefore, a special interest for the study of the development of Jewish thought in the nineteenth century. Interestingly enough also, it compares very strikingly with Wellhausen's parallel emphasis upon the national (pre-exilic) period of the Old Testament as necessarily the most spiritually creative and informative period of Israelite–Jewish life.[36] With Wellhausen, however, this led to a much sharper contrast between the pre- and post-exilic periods than Graetz was willing to endorse. Nevertheless, it is salutary to note that these similarities of emphasis upon the primary significance of the 'national' character of the revelation in the Old Testament exist between Graetz and Wellhausen. In this respect both scholars display their indebtedness to the larger nineteenth-century emphasis upon the nation as the appropriate unit for the study of history. In a wider apologetic context this led Graetz to make an interesting case for the universal significance of Judaism among the nations of the world. For him the study of this particular history did not lack a more universally relevant importance.[37]

However, it is perhaps most of all the way in which Graetz saw the eternal and enduring 'idea' of Judaism being tempered and modified in relation to the realities of history that gives his work a unique interest. In a sense he appears fully conscious that there exists a tension between the universality of ethical truths and the particularity of a special election and a special revelation to one individual people. This tension, however, is not to be overcome by accepting only the universality and all the consequences that might be drawn from it. On the contrary, the very concreteness of history and the historical past constitute a reason for retaining respect for,

36 Cp. Wellhausen, *Prolegomena* (see n. 8 above), pp. 368ff, 'Israel and Judaism'; Perlitt (see n. 24 above), pp. 218ff.

37 'Introduction to Volume One of *The History of the Jews*', pp. 177ff.

and attachment to, this element of particularity. In other words, Graetz appears to be arguing that the 'idea' of Judaism is not to be divorced from its history, but rather the two are to be seen in relation to each other. Thus Judaism is seen to consist not simply of a Torah that can be interpreted and applied to any number of given situations but to a Torah embodied in a people and related very directly to a land. As is well known, Graetz attached the greatest importance to 'Eretz Yisrael' – the Holy Land – as a given part of the history of Israel. Through the combination of religious and political factors in its history Judaism represents a combination of religious truths and political theory. 'The concrete expression for these abstractions is the revealed Law – the Torah – and the Holy Land. The attention of the people is directed to these two possessions. The Law is the soul, the Holy Land the body, of this unique political organism' (*Structure*, p. 71). From this foundation Graetz was able to proceed to a very striking and, in view of the time of its writing, very meaningful estimate of the essential character of Judaism. 'Judaism without the firm soil of national life resembles an inwardly hollowed-out and half-uprooted tree, which still produces foliage at the top but is no longer capable of sprouting twigs and branches' (*Structure*, p. 71).

In a way more striking still is the extraordinarily powerful influence that Graetz claimed that the land had exercised upon the people and their subsequent history. It exerted a kind of psychic force – a mystical sense of identity – over the people who had drawn their religious and cultural inheritance from it. Undoubtedly, Graetz had himself felt much of the attraction of this since he himself was unwilling to see the publication of his volume dealing with the biblical period until he had visited the Holy Land for himself, which he did in 1872. This interweaving of ideological, cultural and religious values with the concrete historical realities of place, time and event marks Graetz's work through and through so far as the biblical past is concerned. In the *Popular History*, vol. I, p. 1, it sets the scene and establishes the foundation from which the entire subsequent history is to be viewed: 'A country situated on the shore of a surging sea . . . will stimulate its inhabitants to higher impulses, and awaken within them the development of a psychic life all their own.'

It is not difficult to detect behind this the marked legacy of Romanticism upon Graetz's presentation of history. After all, Graetz was in so many respects a Central European, and his scholarship shows so much of the vigour and confidence that permeates the most creative years of the Historicist movement.[38] Nevertheless, the fact that all the great pioneers of biblical historiography reveal varying aspects of the contemporary influences that affected their understanding of their task should in no way surprise us. What has often proved unhelpful in the past has been the unexamined assumption that this influence could be described as Hegelianism and cast in one mould. This is evidently not so, and a glance at Graetz's work shows how many-sided these influences were. Certainly, the importance of the 'national' aspect of Israel's existence imposes its own structure upon the way in which the biblical period of Israel's history is viewed. Not only does it lead to the imposition of a three-stage structure on that history, with the Babylonian Exile marking the end of the first stage and the Roman–Jewish conflict the end of the second, but it also shows up in the way in which the historian must deal with the biblical source-material in relation to his subject. Thus the history of Israel does not truly begin until the age of Joshua and the conquest of the land. All that precedes this – the historical traditions now preserved in the Torah – comes by way of preparation. Furthermore, Graetz shows himself to be fully conscious of the problem that stood at the very fountainhead of Wellhausen's researches.[39] This concerns the evident lack of any serious attempt to live according to the Mosaic cultic and ethical legislation in the period of the Judges and the early monarchy.[40] In this regard Graetz's separation of the political–social factor from the more directly idealistic and religious allowed him to argue, not very convincingly, that this latter element was simply forced into the background.[41] Only slowly does it re-emerge into the forefront. Only, in fact, with the loss of nationhood does the religious dimension come more fully into its own. It is also interesting to note from the perspective of comparative historiography that the tendencies in

38 Cp. K. Löwith, *Meaning in History* (Chicago–London, 1949), p. 5: 'History, too, is meaningful only by indicating some transcendent purpose beyond the actual facts.'

39 Cp. Wellhausen, *Prolegomena* (see n. 8 above), pp. 3–4: 'I learned through Ritschl that Karl Heinrich Graf placed the Law later than the Prophets, and, almost without knowing his reasons for the hypothesis, I was prepared to accept it; I readily acknowledged to myself the possibility of understanding Hebrew antiquity without the book of the Torah.'

40 Cp. 'Introduction to Volume One of *The History of the Jews*', p. 184: 'Most of the kings, their sons, and courts behaved without restraint, as if there were no laws which set limits for their despotic will, as if they had never heard of the Ten Commandments of Sinai.'

41 *Ibid.* p. 184.

pharisaic and talmudic Judaism with which Wellhausen dealt so harshly were far from being held up as either typical or necessary expressions of the true Jewish ideal (*Structure*, pp. 90ff). They are, Graetz argues apologetically, an understandable and almost inevitable response of Judaism to a particular phase within its historical experience.

This brings us back to the way in which Graetz saw the importance of the totality of Jewish history:

> you may build a church and accept a creed for this refined and idealized Judaism 'in a nutshell'; nevertheless, you still will have embraced only a shadow and taken the dry shell for the succulent fruit. You possess neither the Judaism taught by the Bible in unambiguous terms, nor the Judaism molded by three thousand years of history, nor, finally, Judaism as it still lives in the consciousness of the majority of its adherents (*Structure*, p. 71).

This linking together, in tracing the structure and course of Jewish history, of the ethical and universal truths of divine revelation with the concrete realities of religious and political life as epitomized in the time of Israel's nationhood points to a kind of creative tension. The particularism of Israel's history is given a wider universal significance by the knowledge of God that has been granted to it and must ultimately be shared with all mankind. 'Judaism looks back to the burning bush of Sinai and forward to the time envisioned by the prophets, when the knowledge of God, justice, and happiness will unite all men in brotherhood' (*Structure*, p. 72).

One of the features that Graetz shared in common with Milman in dealing with the Old Testament period of Jewish history was a willingness to use the titles 'Jews' and 'Judaism' in dealing with the entire Old Testament period from the very beginnings of Israelite history. This was in marked contrast to the practice, beginning with W.M.L. de Wette and exemplified in H. Ewald and J. Wellhausen, of distinguishing sharply between the pre-exilic 'Israelite' period and the post-exilic 'Jewish' period.[42] Clearly there is a difference, occasioned by the loss of full national life with the fall of Jerusalem in 587 B.C. Graetz, as we have seen, is fully conscious of this and is willing to stress its importance; yet not to the point of seeing the post-exilic period as one of unfruitful decline and of a relapse into

42 Cp. Smend (see n. 24 above), p. 105. I.M. Jost had, before de Wette, made a distinction between 'Israelites' and 'Jews', a point over which Graetz took issue with him; cp. *Structure*, p. 72.

legalism. There is an essential unity that holds the two periods together:

> The bearers of the first historical era are political citizens, war heroes, and kings with only a touch of religious sentiment; those of the second era are pious men, sages, teachers, students, and sectarians who manifest only a passing social interest . . . However, is there no connecting link between these two divisions? Does not the influence of the pre-exilic period extend into that following the exile? Did not the prophets lay the groundwork for the piety of the second period? Judaism knows itself to be one and the same in both eras; it bears within it the self-consciousness that, despite all the differences resulting from external experiences and internal metamorphoses, it represents for itself an indivisible unity (*Structure*, p. 73).

It is evident on this particular question, that of the connection and continuity between the pre- and post-exilic periods of Israel's life, that the issues are complex and cannot be resolved simply by the application of particular labels. There is built into the Old Testament itself, as we can now see much more clearly than was possible towards the end of the nineteenth century, a deep literary connection between the pre- and post-exilic periods of Israel's life. The great literary collections, in the Pentateuch and the Former and Latter Prophets, as well as in Wisdom and Psalmody, all contain material and traditions from both phases of Israelite–Jewish life. No longer can 'Law' or 'Wisdom' or 'Psalmody' be ascribed to one particular phase of Israelite–Jewish life, whether that be regarded as very early and beginning with Moses, or very late and related to the Maccabean uprising. The different types of religious, prophetic and ethical sayings and collections belong to all periods of the Old Testament and in substantial measure straddle the dramatic upheaval occasioned by the Babylonian Exile. To this extent the discovery and delineation of the major literary 'sources' of the Old Testament can only be a task treated with reserve and caution so far as their relationship to particular events and personalities is concerned. This should certainly warn us against allowing the Babylonian Exile to control too strictly the particular way in which the biblical history is viewed. At this point also we must certainly raise fresh questions, in respect of both Graetz and Wellhausen, concerning the importance of the national dimension of Israelite life for biblical historiography.

It has already been pointed out that in more recent years the need has increasingly presented itself for breaking down this very unified conception of a national history into its component parts and for paying greater attention to social, territorial and more distinctively religious factors. In fact, with the work of both Graetz and Wellhausen, it is very hard to be clear whether we are dealing with a political history, set out according to recognized secular historiographic principles, or a more overtly religious history. Both scholars present a close interweaving of both aspects and defend their reasons for doing so. Yet in retrospect the two sides are distinct and the need remains for isolating historical judgements from more overtly theological ones. Perhaps at the end of the day the two can never be wholly separated, but it nevertheless remains essential to see the two in their separate spheres of reference.

In looking at the work of Heinrich Graetz as a religious historian, there is certainly no specific intention here to argue that he was somehow more right, or more far-seeing, than those other great pioneers of the nineteenth century who worked in the field of Israelite–Jewish history. In many respects we can still see how powerfully the work of Julius Wellhausen has towered above that of others. Nevertheless, it is also clear in retrospect that all the great figures who laid the foundations of biblical historiography in the nineteenth century were men of their time. Their particular aims and methods and the inevitable limitations that go with these must all now be seen in the particular context of culture and scholarship that found its major focus in the Historicist movement in Germany. It is no accident, therefore, that the major pioneers in this field were Germans, and even Milman owed not a little to the impulses of the German Enlightenment. What is clear, however, is that the work of Heinrich Graetz appears to have been quite peculiarly and unfairly ignored by Christian scholars, and not taken into account in the effort to attain some balanced assessment of the gains and losses of the historical movement in the study of the biblical history. He must surely be rescued from the unjust accusation of being 'uncritical'. From a Christian perspective he appears rather in the nature of a Jewish apologist, but against this must certainly be set the fact that the school of historical interpretation that took its lead from Wellhausen has appeared to be decidedly anti-Jewish. On this score alone it is obviously of the greatest importance to scholarship to avoid any confusion between historiographic method and theological evaluation. It is noteworthy that neither Milman nor Ewald achieved anything like a calm objectivity in such questions, and Ewald seems to have been only marginally interested in doing so, as is shown by the fact that almost the whole of three, out of eight, volumes of his *History of Israel* deal with Jesus and the origins of the Christian Church. In retrospect it is not misplaced to argue that all the great undertakings in the nineteenth century to write a clear and objective account of Israelite–Jewish history were over-ambitious. At that time much too little information existed regarding the political, cultural and religious life of the ancient Near East in which the Bible had arisen. The very aim of writing of biblical personalities as flesh and blood characters who had participated in a real history was fraught by the great lack of knowledge about the world in which they lived and its achievements. The very immensity of the range of discovery in the field of biblical archaeology in the present century shows how seriously handicapped all such writers were before this time. Inevitably, the tendency was to use the biblical material that was available and to create a background that was in no small part a construction of a sympathetic imagination. The materials simply were not available to do otherwise. All the great pioneer figures therefore, including Graetz, had largely to work from the Bible itself as their only substantial source. In doing so it was inevitable that they should portray that background as more primitive, more pagan and more crudely unethical than in reality it appears to have been. Their historical judgements and evaluations, therefore, could serve only partially as a critique and reappraisal of the biblical evidence. More often than not they simply served to reflect the attitude of the Bible itself. Yet by pioneering the task as they did, all these historians have left us an important legacy of scholarship.

More than this, however, it is the task of the historian to research into the causes and consequences of the great movements and events of history. Yet, when the sources of information with which to probe into such questions are so restricted, it is often far from easy to offer a satisfactory answer. The strong intellectual incentive in the early part of the nineteenth century to view history as 'the march of mind', and to see it as the reflection of certain distinctive ideas, has clearly left its mark. In this respect Graetz offers us a distinctively idealistic view of Jewish history with his contention that, at a fundamental level, it exhibits a single idea – the idea of Judaism. The reality was undoubtedly less homogeneous and more confusingly variegated than this. All too often it was possible to explain changes and developments as the consequence of the impact of this 'idea', without examining how consciously such an idea was present, or how men responded to, or reacted against, the ideas that they had inherited. The 'idea' itself becomes too vague and ill-defined an entity to account for the many political, religious and social forces that operated in the history itself.

It is of interest also, and largely in line with this view of the biblical history, that all the great pioneers, Milman, Graetz, Ewald and Wellhausen, should have been so deeply attracted to the heroic conception of Israel's history. T. Carlyle's *On Heroes and Hero-Worship* appears to have struck a profoundly resonant chord among biblical scholars of the time.[43] Yet it has proved very difficult for the serious historian to construct any very concrete portrait of the great Old Testament figures, Abraham, Moses, David and so on, because they lie so deeply embedded in the biblical narratives, and their real personalities are so completely hidden from us.

It is not difficult to see that, to a pattern of historical investigation that regarded source-criticism to be a first and paramount duty, Graetz's history-writing should have appeared to be uncritical. Yet it was certainly not so, and the more deeply the reader probes into its historiographic assumptions and aims, the more evident it becomes that he possessed a most interesting and stimulating conception of the critical historian's role. That it too must now appear dated and limited by the age and circumstances in which it was first written is inevitable. For the history of biblical scholarship, however, it is certainly far from being unimportant, and it well repays study by the serious student of biblical history.

43 T. Carlyle's work is mentioned by Graetz in 'The Correspondence of an English Lady on Judaism and Semitism', translated in *Structure*, p. 201 (with note, p. 311). His very words are interesting and worth citation: 'The gifted Thomas Carlyle has struck a powerful chord of the human keyboard: man's need for hero-worship.' For Carlyle and Wellhausen cp. Perlitt (see n. 24 above), p. 215.

The Extension of a Simile

DAVID DAUBE

Among Rab's dicta transmitted by his disciple R. Judah is the following:[1] 'He who marries his daughter to an old man or he who takes a wife for his infant son or he who returns a lost article to a Gentile, about him Scripture says [Deut. xxix.18f], "To join satiety to thirst – the Lord will not pardon him (for this act)."'

The Hebrew here translated 'to join satiety with thirst' is complicated. The biblical author may, for example, have used *sĕpōt* in the sense, not of 'to join', but of 'to sweep away'. Fortunately, for the purpose in hand, it is sufficient that 'to join satiety with thirst' approximately conveys the meaning that Rab assigns to the clause. However, even if we adopt his starting-point, we shall not find in the original deuteronomic context any reference to the cases he lists; and though it is easy to see how an imaginative exegesis might, unhistorically, connect the verse cited with an unequal coupling of lusty and dry, L. Goldschmidt understandably feels that the lost article is out of place.[2]

The explanation seems to lie in a phenomenon that is by no means uncommon: the repeated stretching of an attractive simile so that, in the end, it is applied to a situation it does not really fit. For the first of the three misdeeds, the handing over of your daughter to a pensioner, 'to join satiety to thirst' is a perfect metaphor: the concepts 'satiety' and 'thirst' are readily transferred to the sexual field. No wonder parallels exist in many literatures. In the Old Testament itself, the seductress says: 'Let us sate ourselves with love until

1 BT Sanh. 76*b*. According to traditional chronology Rab died in A.D. 247, R. Judah fifty years later.

2 See *Der Babylonische Talmud*, vol. VII (Berlin, 1903), p. 325, n. 34: 'Unverständlich ist jedoch, wieso dies aus dem angezogenen Schriftvers herausgedeutet wird.'

morning' (Prov. vii.18). Of course, the exhaustion contemplated in this setting is merely temporary. Jeremiah speaks of 'the thirst' of the nation whoring after strange gods, like a female animal in heat (ii.25). To the rabbis, then, Deuteronomy offered an obvious peg on which to hang their reproof of the union in question.

The phrase is slightly less suited to the second sin, that of taking an adult wife for your son below the age of puberty. 'Thirst' on her side is all right, but 'satiety' on his not quite. He does share the old man's lack of interest. But whereas the latter is 'sated', tired after a full life, he is not yet ready. Still, the discrepancy is not enormous. Once the simile was established for the first case, it was a small step to extend it to the second – or rather, to bring the second under the same scriptural warning that was believed to be directed against the first. The public would have no difficulty in going along with it.

The third wrong, the restoration of a lost object to a Gentile, represents a much more artificial enlargement of scope, involving a thorough reorientation of the metaphor. For one thing, the biblical verse is now taken to allude not, as in the previous two applications, to sexual relations but to property. So far so good. As for the specific treatment of 'satiety' and 'thirst', the former stands for the Gentile who has wealth more than enough – comparable to the old man no longer needing pleasure. This, too, is relatively ordinary: such an interpretation, however fanciful from the modern, scholarly point of view, would be universally intelligible in the talmudic period. It is when we come to 'thirst' that the going gets rough. The lost article 'joined', given back, to a Gentile is not capable of this sensation at all. It is the Jewish finder who, if he parts with it, is left suffering, incurs deprivation. (In a socialist tract, a thing might perhaps be depicted as 'thirsting' for service to a poor person rather than a rich one. We may confidently exclude this line from the present analysis.) Though a simile need not be absolutely precise,[3] the inclusion of this transaction under 'to join satiety to thirst' is over-ingenious, laboured. An audience would have to think hard to comprehend the analogy with the two preceding cases. This may indeed have been an effect far from unwelcome to the proponent of the dictum: from his angle, what we experience as a weakness was quite possibly a plus.

At a guess, the two cruel marriages had already been read into Deuteronomy before Rab and the startling reference to the lost

3 See D. Daube, *Ancient Hebrew Fables* (Oxford, 1973), p. 19.

article is his addition. The events accounting for his harsh attitude – persecutions by an anti-Jewish regime and, in particular, confiscations of Jewish property – have long been pointed out.[4]

4 See W. Bacher, *Die Agada der Babylonischen Amoräer* (Strassburg, 1878), p. 23; S. Funk, *Die Juden in Babylonien* (Berlin, 1902), pp. 66ff; *The Babylonian Talmud*, 'Sanhedrin', ed. I. Epstein (trans. H. Freedman, London, 1935), p. 517.

Two Genizah Fragments in Hebrew and Greek[1]

N.R.M. DE LANGE

Among the Cairo Genizah manuscripts in the Cambridge University Library there are several that are in Greek. They fall naturally into three groups:

(1) A number of palimpsests containing biblical texts (both OT and NT) in Greek uncials attracted attention almost as soon as the Taylor–Schechter Collection arrived in Cambridge. They are among the earliest manuscripts in the Genizah and are also among the first to have been published.[2] The Aquila fragments containing the tetragrammaton in Old Hebrew characters are likely to be of Jewish origin; the others were probably all copied by Christians.

(2) Two later fragments in Greek characters, which are not palimpsests, have so far escaped attention. One (T-S K24.27) is in a minuscule hand, with some headings in red uncials, and appears to contain some Christian hymns. The other (T-S 16.321), in a later and more cursive script, is also a Christian text.

(3) The third group consists of manuscripts containing Greek words and passages in Hebrew characters. The text of two of these is given below. There are others: a marriage contract from Mastaura

1 I am grateful to the Syndics of the Cambridge University Library for permission to publish these fragments, to the members of the Taylor–Schechter Genizah Research Unit for helpful advice and for access to their bibliographical index, and to Professor Simon Hopkins for drawing my attention to T-S Misc. 28.74. I should also like to express my thanks to Dr Sebastian Brock, to Professor Evelyne Patlagean and to Professor Robert Browning for wise counsel and encouragement.

2 F.C. Burkitt, *Fragments of the Books of Kings according to the Translation of Aquila*... (Cambridge, 1897)[T-S 12.184; 20.50]. C. Taylor, *Hebrew–Greek Cairo Genizah Palimpsests*... (Cambridge, 1900)[T-S 12.182, 186, 187, 188, 189, 208; 16.93]. J.H.A. Hart, 'The New Septuagint Fragment', *JTS* 4 (1903), 215–17; cp. Taylor, *ibid.* p. 130 [T-S 16.320]. Another palimpsest of this type [T-S 12.185] is still unpublished.

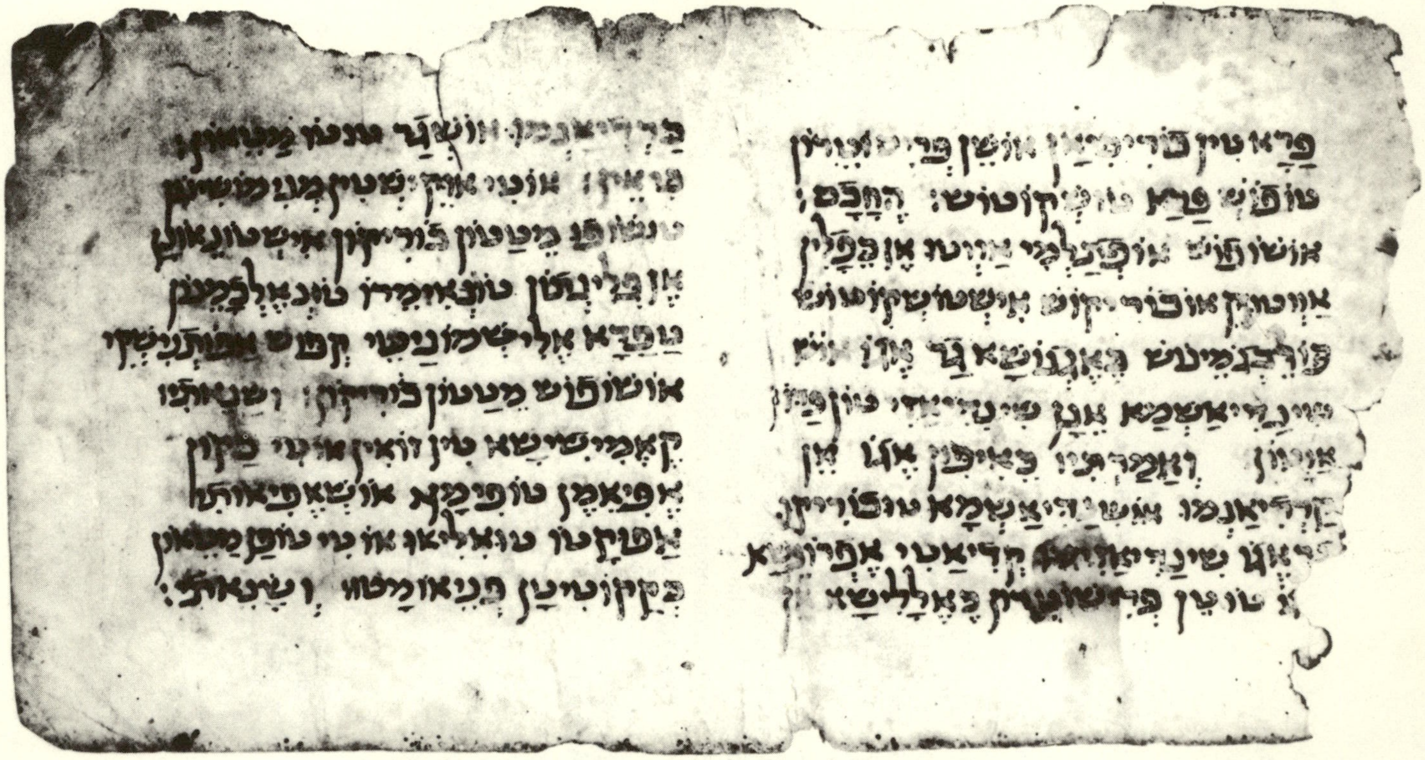

Plate 1 Recto of part of a Greek translation of the Book of Ecclesiastes (C.U.L. T–S Misc. 28.74)

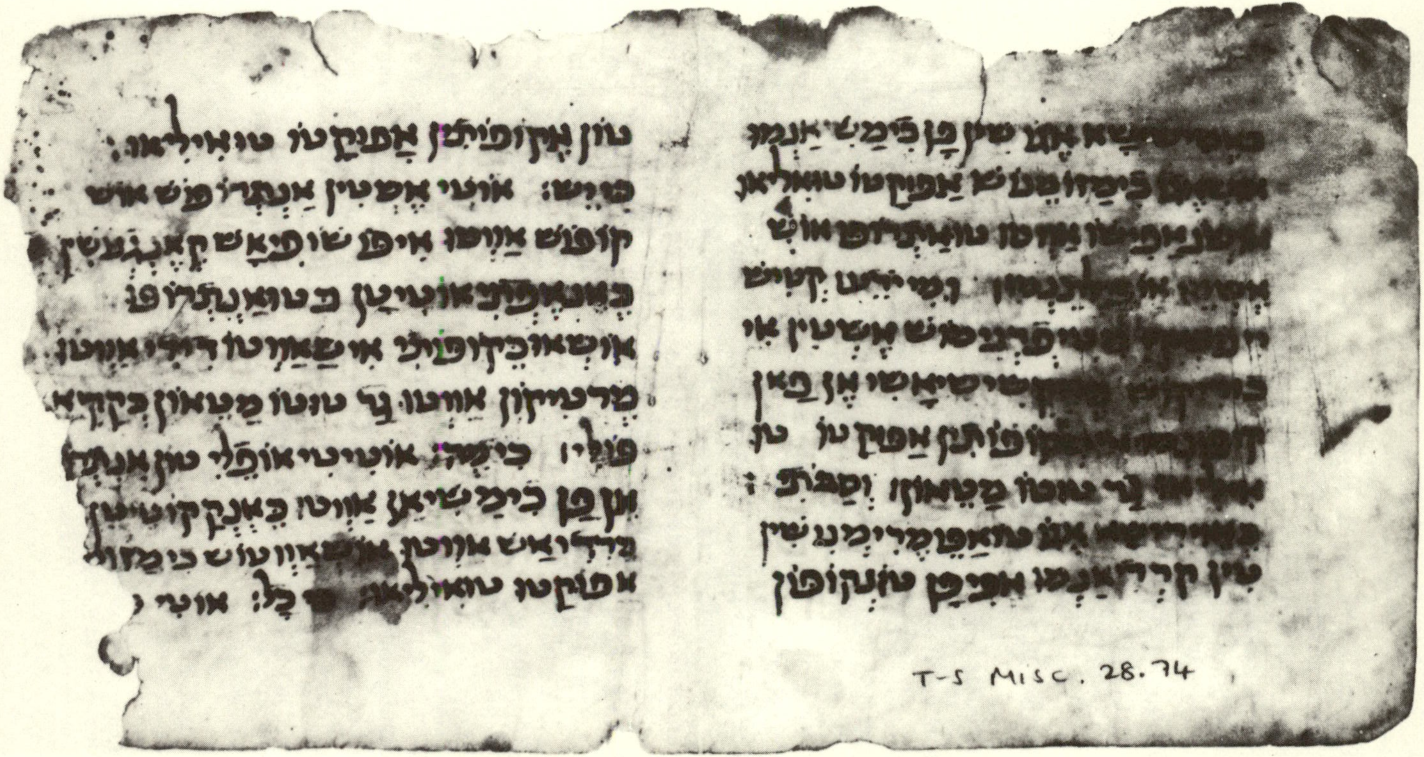

Plate 2   Verso of part of a Greek translation of the Book of Ecclesiastes (C.U.L. T–S Misc. 28.74)

containing a few Greek words (T-S 16.374),[3] a commentary on the Minor Prophets with some Greek glosses (T-S K25.288), and a glossary of difficult words in Malachi and Job (T-S NS 309.9).[4] It is likely that more may yet come to light. These texts add to our knowledge of the medieval Greek language, as well as throwing some light on the life and thought of the Greek-speaking Jewish communities of the Middle Ages.

I

T-S Misc. 28.74 (see plates 1 and 2)

Description

A single leaf of parchment. It is slightly damaged at the top and more seriously at one side, so that a few letters have been lost. The height is $4\frac{1}{2}$ in (115 mm), the maximum width $8\frac{5}{8}$ in (222 mm). The writing is in square Hebrew characters, pointed throughout. It is well preserved, although some of the vowel points may have disappeared.

The columns are of ten lines, 3 in (76 mm) high by 3–$3\frac{5}{8}$ in (76–92 mm) wide. There are two columns on each side, and the text continues from one side to the other, so that the codex apparently contained two columns per page.

I should hesitate to assign a date to the manuscript. A Greek transcription of the fragment was published by D.-S. Blondheim,[5] who dated both manuscript and translation approximately to the twelfth century.[6]

The text

The text is part of a Greek translation of the book of Ecclesiastes, beginning towards the end of ii.13 and breaking off after the first word of ii.23.[7] Each verse in Greek is preceded by the first word of the verse in Hebrew.

3 Text in J. Mann, *The Jews in Egypt and in Palestine under the Fāṭimid Caliphs*, vol. II (Oxford, 1922), pp. 94–6, translation in J. Starr, *The Jews in the Byzantine Empire 641–1204* (Athens, 1939), pp. 187–90.

4 I am obliged to Mr A. Spitzer of the Genizah Research Unit for bringing these two fragments to my attention. I have published the second in 'Some new fragments of Aquila on Malachi and Job?', *VT* 30 (1980), 291–4.

5 *REJ* 78 (1924), 14, reprinted in his *Les Parlers judéo-romans et la Vetus Latina* (Paris, 1925), p. 170.

6 *Ibid.* p. 3 and p. 159.

7 This identification was first made by J. Mann.

The system of transliteration is similar to that used in other such Greek texts in Hebrew characters. Words are often run together: in particular the article, καὶ and some prepositions are generally attached to the following word, and enclitic μου to the preceding word. Striking examples of this tendency are אישטונאונן (εἰς τὸν αἰῶναν) and כאנקקוטיטן (καὶ ἐν κακότηταν).

The orthography shows no attempt at consistency. Thus *pataḥ* and *qameṣ* are used indifferently for α, and ε/αι is rendered in four different ways. καὶ is written in six different ways: כְּ כֶּ כֵּ קְ קֶ קֵ. σ is generally שׁ, but once ס is used instead. On the other hand, תּ is never used for τ, as it is in our other text. No attempt is made to indicate breathings or accents.

The equivalents may be listed as follows:

α	◌ַ ◌ָ	ν	נ
αι	◌ְ ◌ֶ ◌ֵ ◌ֵי	ντ	דּ
αυ	◌ַוְו ◌ַוְ	ξ	קשׂ
γ	גֿ י	ο	◌וֹ
δ	דֿ	οι	◌ִי
ε	◌ְ ◌ֶ ◌ֵ	ου	◌וּ
ει	◌ִי	π	פּ
ευ	◌ֵבְ ◌ֶפְֿ ◌ֵו(?)	ρ	ר
ζ	ז	σ	ס שׁ
η	◌ִ ◌ִי	τ	ט
θ	תֿ	υ	◌ִ ◌ִי
ι	◌ִי	φ	פֿ
κ	כּ ק	χ	כֿ
λ	ל	ω	◌וֹ
μ	מ		

β and ψ do not occur.

The Greek

The language of the version is medieval Greek. Many of its peculiarities are due to the method of the translator (see below). The Hebrew scribe may also be responsible for some oddities. For example כֵּאִיפּוֹן (line 7) was read by Blondheim as καὶ εἶπιν, but it is more likely to be a mistake for כַּאִיפּוֹן, καὶ εἶπον. It is possible that the forms ἐξησιάσει (line 26) for ἐξουσιάσει and ἀπευμεριμνεῖ for ἀπομ- are due to a similar cause. It is difficult to know how to deal with the form אוֹשׂ, which renders the Hebrew relative -שׁ. Sometimes it seems best to take it as ὡς (e.g. lines 5, 11); more often, however, it appears to stand for the undeclined relative pronoun ὅς. This is borne out by the fact that the same Hebrew word, שעמלתי, is rendered once by ὅς ἐκοπώθην (line 27) and another time by τὸν ἐκοπώθην (line 31). The same use of ὅς is found in other Jewish Greek versions, such as those of the Pentateuch and Jonah.[8]

The dative case is not used. Instead, verbs are constructed with the genitive (e.g. συναντιάζει μου, line 9). Prepositions usually govern the accusative, but occasionally the genitive (ἀπουκάτω τοῦ ἡλίου, lines 19, 22, 27f, 31; ὑπὸ σοφίας, line 33). εἰς is used for 'in' (lines 4, 35), although ἐν + accusative is more usual. 'On' is ἐπὶ + accusative (lines 18, 30).

Participles are declined (lines 5, 14, 22). The temporal augment is used, even when not accented (e.g. lines 9, 10, 15). The aorist passive has -θ- (lines 18, 31, 35). 'That I may leave' is rendered by ὡς νὰ ἀφίσω (line 23).

οὐκ is correctly used (lines 12, 35). The genitive of πνεῦμα is πνεομάτου (line 20).

Great freedom is exercised in the use of *final ν*. It is frequently added where it does not belong, and once it is incorrectly omitted (line 14, τῶν ἡμερῶ). At line 18 the scribe shows some uncertainty: it is not clear whether he wrote ן and changed it to א or vice-versa.

The translation

The translation is a very faithful, word-for-word rendering of the Hebrew. Nothing is omitted, except for one word in the Hebrew (ושחכמתי, verse 19), which has probably been accidentally overlooked. Nor is anything added, not even the verb 'to be', which would often help the sense.

The *article* is rendered extremely carefully. It is consistently avoided in rendering such forms as עיניו (ὀφθαλμοὶ αὐτοῦ), where

8 The Pentateuch was printed at Constantinople in 1547 and reprinted by D.C. Hesseling, *Les cinq livres de la Loi* (Leiden, 1897). Hesseling also published the version of Jonah, in *ByZ* 10 (1901), 208–17. For examples of ὅς see Gen. i.7, 11, 12; Jonah i.5, 8, 10. See also the remarks of L. Belléli, *REG* 3 (1890), 290f; *REJ* 22 (1891), 262, 263.

the Hebrew has no article even though the noun is understood as definite. Only twice is the article introduced in the Greek where it is lacking in the Hebrew: εἰς τὸν αἰῶναν (verse 16) may be a conventional formula, and καὶ τοῦ ἀνθρώπου (verse 21) may be influenced by τοῦ ἀνθρώπου in verse 18.

A special case is presented by the particle -את, which indicates the direct object. This occurs four times in the passage and is treated differently each time. In verse 14 (את-כלם, τῶν πάντων αὐτῶν) it is rendered by the article; in verse 17 (את-החיים, τὴν ζωὴν) the noun already has the article, and the presence of -את is not indicated in the Greek; in verse 18 (את-כל-עמלי, σὺν πᾶν χειμασίαν μου) it is rendered by σὺν; and in verse 20 (את-לבי, σὺν τὴν καρδίαν μου) we find both σὺν and the article. σὺν never stands for עם ('with'), which is translated by μετὰ (verse 16).

There is no particular consistency in the treatment of *prepositions*. -ב ('in') is usually ἐν, but twice we find it rendered by εἰς (verses 14, 21) and once, surprisingly, by ὑπὸ (verse 21). -ל ('to') is only once translated by εἰς, in the formula εἰς τὸν αἰῶναν (verse 16). Otherwise it is rendered by the genitive of the indirect object (verses 16, 18, 21) or the accusative of the direct object (verse 22).

-ו ('and') is always represented by καί. כי is always ὅτι. -ש is ὡς or ὅς, except in verse 20, where it is rendered by τὸν (see above).

גם ('also') is always γὰρ (verses 14, 15, 19, 21), even though this rendering does not make sense in Greek.

The treatment of כל ('all') is curious. When it is followed by a noun (verses 18, 19, 20, 22) it is rendered by πᾶν, invariable. When it stands on its own, however, it is declined (verse 14, τῶν πάντων αὐτῶν; verse 16, τὰ πάντα; cf. verse 17, τὸ πᾶν).

The handling of *nouns* is straightforward. The translator seems to be at pains to respect the connection between nouns and verbs derived from the same root (verses 14f, συναντίασμα–συναντιάζειν; verse 17, ποί(η)μα–ποιεῖν; verse 18, χειμασία–χειμάζεσθαι; verses 19ff, κόπος–κοπωθῆναι). On the other hand he translates one Hebrew word by two different Greek ones (עמל = χειμασία or κόπος; חכם = σοφὸς or φρένιμος). He uses the same Greek word for the two words רעות (verse 17) and רעיון (verse 22). (It may be remarked that the LXX and the Targum both use one word to render these two Hebrew words, although each version interprets the meaning differently: LXX, προαίρεσις; Targum, תבירות.)

I am unable to explain the translation of בשכבר (verse 16) by ἐν πλίνθον.

Finally, there seems to be a partial attempt to deal systematically with the tenses of *verbs*. The Hebrew perfect is always rendered by a Greek aorist. The imperfect is rendered by the present tense in Greek, with two exceptions (verse 18, שאניחנו, ὡς νὰ ἀφίσω αὐτό; שיהיה, ὅς ἔσται). The Hebrew participle is usually rendered by a participle in Greek, but twice we find a present tense used instead (verse 19, יודע, γινώσκει; verse 22, הוה, ὠφελεῖ). In verse 20 the infinitive ליאש is translated τὸ ἀπευμεριμνεῖ(ν).

Comparison with other versions

The Septuagint. The oldest surviving Greek version of Ecclesiastes is that found in the LXX. It is of the καίγε type, and may have been produced in the circle of Aquila. Like our fragment, it follows the Hebrew very closely, and there are many similarities between the two versions, which may be illustrated by a comparison of a couple of verses[9]:

(verse 14)

LXX: τοῦ σοφοῦ οἱ ὀφθαλμοὶ αὐτοῦ ἐν κεφαλῇ αὐτοῦ
T-S Misc. 28.74: ὁ σοφὸς ὀφθαλμοὶ αὐτοῦ ἐν κεφαλὴν αὐτοῦ

καὶ ὁ ἄφρων ἐν σκότει πορεύεται καὶ ἔγνων καίγε ἐγὼ
καὶ ὁ χωρικὸς εἰς τὸ σκότος πορευγόμενος καὶ ἔγνωσα γὰρ ἐγὼ

ὅτι συνάντημα ἓν συναντήσεται τοῖς πᾶσιν αὐτοῖς.
ὡς συναντίασμα ἕναν συναντιάζει τῶν πάντων αὐτῶν.

(verse 15)

καὶ εἶπα ἐγὼ ἐν καρδίᾳ μου ὡς συνάντημα τοῦ ἄφρονος καίγε
καὶ εἶπον ἐγὼ ἐν καρδίαν μου ὡς συναντίασμα τοῦ χωρικοῦ γὰρ

ἐμοὶ συναντήσεταί μοι καὶ ἵνα τί ἐσοφισάμην ἐγὼ τότε
ἐγὼ συναντιάζει μου καὶ διατί ἐφρόνεσα ἐγὼ τότεν

περισσὸν ἐλάλησα ἐν καρδίᾳ μου ὅτι καίγε τοῦτο
περισσότερον καὶ ἐλάλησα ἐν καρδίαν μου ὡς γὰρ τοῦτο

ματαιότης.
μάταιον.

9 The LXX text is that of Rahlfs.

The similarities are so striking as to make a detailed analysis superfluous. They must raise a strong suspicion that our text is a revision of the LXX aimed at modernizing the language and following slightly different canons of translation. Such a hypothesis would help to explain the inconsistencies already noticed in our version. It is as if we have caught the reviser before his task has been completed. γὰρ has replaced καίγε, for example, but σὺν has not yet been completely eradicated. It could be argued that this process is already at work in our LXX, since σὺν for את is lacking in some places (verses 14 and 20).

Graecus Venetus (= *Ven.*)[10] This version is preserved in a unique manuscript in Venice, written in Greek characters and dated to the late fourteenth or early fifteenth century. It appears to represent a different revision of the LXX. It often agrees with the LXX against the Cambridge fragment, but sometimes displays uncertainty and occasionally agrees with our text against the LXX.

Thus הבל is ματαιότης, as in the LXX, whereas our text has μάταιον. In verse 21 it reads δώσει αὐτὸν μερίδα οἱ where the LXX has δώσει αὐτῷ μερίδα αὐτοῦ and our text has δίδει αὐτοῦ μερτικὸν αὐτοῦ. In verse 16 it has μνήμη for זכרון, like the LXX, where our text has μνημόσυνον.[11] In verse 15 it has ἐσοφίσθην for חכמתי where the LXX has ἐσοφισάμην and our text has ἐφρόνεσα, but in verse 19 the same verb is translated ἐφρόνησα. *Ven.* usually agrees with the LXX in translating כסיל by ἄφρων, although sometimes it prefers μωρός; our text uses χωρικός.

Ven. agrees strikingly with our fragment only in verse 21, κακία πολλή (LXX, πονηρία μεγάλη). There are also some less significant similarities, e.g. κάκωσις[12] in verse 17 for רעות, where our text has κακότηταν (LXX, προαίρεσις), and earlier in the same verse *Ven.* has τὸ πᾶν, like our text (LXX, τὰ πάντα).

More often *Ven.* disagrees both with our text and with the LXX; sometimes all three have different renderings. For example:

Verse	T-S Misc. 28.74	LXX	*Ven.*
13	ὡς ἐν περισσότερον	ὡς περισσεία	κατὰ τὴν ὑπεροχὴν
14	ὡς συναντίασμα	ὅτι συνάντημα	ὅτι συμβεβηκὸς
	συναντιάζει	συναντήσεται	συμβήσεται

10 Ed. O. Gebhardt (Leipzig, 1875).
11 Which is also, however, the rendering of Symmachus.
12 So too in ii.26. But in i.14 it has ἔφεσις. רעיון is ἀναπόλησις in i.17, μελέτη in ii.22.

Verse	T-S Misc. 28.74	LXX	*Ven.*
15	εἶπον	εἶπα	ἔφην
	περισσότερον	περισσὸν	μᾶλλον
	ἐλάλησα	ἐλάλησα	ἔφην
17	τὴν ζωὴν	σὺν τὴν ζωὴν	τὴν βιοτὴν
	τὸ ποί(η)μα	τὸ ποίημα	τοὖργον[13]
18	ὡς νὰ ἀφίσω	ὅτι ἀφίω	ἐπεὶ καταλείψω
19	καὶ ἐξησιάσει	καὶ ἐξουσιάζεται	δεσπόσει μέντοι
20	τὸ ἀπευμεριμνεῖ	τοῦ ἀποτάξασθαι	περιϊδεῖν
21	ἐν εὐθυότητα	ἐν ἀνδρείᾳ	ἐν καθαρότητι
22	ὅτι τί ὠφελεῖ	ὅτι τί γίνεται	τί γὰρ τυγχάνει
	ἐν κακότηταν	ἐν προαιρέσει	ἐν τῇ μελέτῃ

Moreover, *Ven.* constantly inserts the article where the other two are careful to leave it out.

The treatment of both גם and את is inconsistent in *Ven.* Whereas for גם our fragment always has γὰρ and the LXX always has καίγε, *Ven.* has ἔτι three times and καί twice. את is ignored in verses 17 and 20, but in verses 14 and 18, where it is joined to כל, *Ven.* has ξύμπασιν and ξύμπαντα, although elsewhere כל is rendered simply by forms of πᾶς. The ξυμ- seems to be a relic of the LXX σύν.

Like the LXX and our fragment, the translator of *Ven.* aims at a high degree of faithfulness to the Hebrew, although he sometimes permits himself small liberties, adding or omitting words or altering the word-order slightly. His language, unlike that of our fragment and the other medieval Jewish versions, is consciously and strictly classical, and he avoids neologisms and colloquial expressions.

Without entering into the vexed question of the origin of this version, it may confidently be stated that it is neither an ancestor nor a descendant of our text. Most likely, both stand in a similar tradition of translation, going back to antiquity, but incorporating changing attitudes to both the Hebrew and the Greek languages.

The Oxford Jonah. The version of Jonah published by D.C. Hesseling[14] is the only Greek translation of a biblical book in Hebrew characters surviving in its entirety in medieval manuscript. A comparison of it with our fragment is therefore of some interest. It is preserved in a manuscript now in the Bodleian Library,[15]

13 Symmachus τὸ ἔργον.

14 See n. 8 above.

15 Opp. Add. 8⁰ 19, no. 1144 in Neubauer's catalogue. There is also a fifteenth-century manuscript in Bologna, which contains some interesting modernizations, e.g. ψάρι for ἐχτύο ('fish').

which bears a note stating that it was sold in 1263. Like our fragment, it is written on parchment, in small format and in pointed square characters. Like our fragment, too, it is an extremely literal version in colloquial rather than literary Greek. Each verse of the Hebrew is followed by its Greek translation, whereas our text gives only the first word or two of each Hebrew verse.

The language of the Jonah version is similar to that of our fragment: there is no dative case; prepositions govern the accusative, rarely the genitive (ii.5, ἀπὸ ἐναντίου); 'in' is ἐν + accusative (never εἰς, which is used for 'to', side by side with πρὸς), and 'on' is ἐπὶ + accusative; the temporal augment is used; so is νὰ + aorist subjunctive (i.6, νὰ μεταμελεθῇ). Final ν is added with the same abandon that characterizes our fragment, and occasionally omitted (ii.5, ἐφταλμῶ for ὀφθαλμῶν).

The principles of translation are also similar, although there are signs of greater freedom or laxity. Thus the verb 'to be' may be inserted (iv.2, ἐσὺ εἶς for אתה). The article is sometimes omitted, or inserted where it is not explicitly present in the Hebrew, but we do often find renderings such as εἰς κεφάλι μου for לראשי (ii. 6). This inconsistency makes it hard to judge whether or not the translator has deliberately inserted the article to take the place of את־ (e.g. i.9, τὸγ γύριο for את־ה'). σὺν is not used. There is the same use of indeclinable ὃς (e.g. i.5) and πᾶν (ii.4) as in our fragment. גם does not appear in Jonah. Cognates are respected (i.16, ἐτάχτησαν τάγματα; iv.1, ἐκακώθην ... κακωσύνη).

The tenses of verbs are not handled as systematically as in our text, but we do find a curious use of the participle (i.3, καράβι ἐρχαμένη for אניה באה; i.13, ἡ θάλασσα πορευγόμενον καὶ λαιλαπίζον for הים הולך וסער). ל־ + infinitive is commonly rendered by such forms as τὸ ἐλθεῖ (i.3).

In other words, although the versions of Jonah and Ecclesiastes are not the work of the same translator, they display great similarities both in the Greek language and in the aims and methods of the translation. Many of the tendencies we have mentioned also appear in the 1547 Pentateuch,[16] and it would appear that we are dealing with a common tradition of Greek Jewish biblical translation.

16 See n. 8 above. There are, however, important differences. Most notably, גם is rendered by the curious word απατα, which is also used (for אף) in the translation of the Aramaic portions of the Bible by Elijah Afeda Beghi (1627), published by A. Danon in *JA* 11th series 4 (1914), 1–65.

The Jerusalem glosses. A manuscript in the Jewish National and University Library in Jerusalem[17] contains Hebrew notes and Greek glosses on Psalms xxi–xxvii and xlix–cl, Lamentations and Ecclesiastes. It is roughly written, eclectic in the words singled out for comment, some of which present no particular difficulty, and somewhat repetitious. It may represent a student's notes, or a teacher's. It is ascribed by D. Goldschmidt to the sixteenth century, and the language shows signs of Turkish influence (e.g. εἰς παζάρι for בשוק, Eccles. xii.5).

Unfortunately there are no Greek words in the section of Ecclesiastes contained in our fragment, apart from a supralinear gloss on ליאש (ii.20), which is so small as to be almost illegible.[18] The Hebrew comments on these verses in the Jerusalem text provide no helpful parallels to our text, except that ובכשרון (ii.21) is explained as 'straightness, correctness' (יושר ונכונה), which corresponds to the ἐν εὐθυότηταν of our fragment rather than to ἐν ἀνδρείᾳ of the LXX or ἐν καθαρότητι of *Ven.*

A few more points of comparison may be culled from other parts of Ecclesiastes:

i.2, הבל הבלים: 'nothing', οὐδὲν καὶ οὐδετίποτε
i.3, יתרון: 'benefit', ὀφειλοσύνη (?)
עמלו: 'his toil', κόπην (*leg.* κόπον?) αὐ(τοῦ)
i.14, ורעות: 'device' (מחשבה)

There is no evidence that the author was acquainted with our version; if anything, the indications are to the contrary.

Conclusions

Our text is a fragment of a Greek Jewish version of Ecclesiastes, which is in a tradition deriving ultimately from the ancient translation that is found in the Christian Greek Bible. The translator's object is to adhere as faithfully as possible to the letter of the Hebrew text, while making it intelligible to an uncultivated Greek-speaking audience by the occasional use of modern vocabulary and turns of phrase, without, however, inserting explanatory words into the text.

17 Ms. Heb. 8⁰ 2332. See the remarks of D. Goldschmidt in *Kirjath Sepher* 33 (1957–8), 133–4.

18 It looks like αποviασει. The Hebrew explanation is רפיון|בדבר והעברה ממנו.

In language and approach it is very similar to the medieval translation of Jonah, which dates from the early thirteenth or late twelfth century.[19] It is worth pointing out that, just as the book of Jonah was read publicly in synagogues on the Day of Atonement, Ecclesiastes was read on the Sabbath of Sukkot. Both the manuscripts containing the version of Jonah are prayer-books, and it is possible that our text, too, once formed part of a liturgical codex.

The lack of conclusive parallels in the later Jerusalem manuscript may indicate that our text is a local version, the use of which was not universal among Greek-speaking Jews, or that its use had died out before the sixteenth century.

The text

Recto Col. i

פָּרָא טִין כוֹרִיכִּיאַן אוֹשֵׁן פְּרִיסוֹטֵרוֹן
טוֹפוֹשׁ פַּרַא טוֹשְׁקוֹטוֹשׁ: הֶחָכָם:
אוֹשׁוֹפוֹשׁ אוֹפְתַלְמִי אַוְוטוּ אֶן כֵּפָלִין
אַוְוטוּ קֵאוֹכוֹרִיקוֹשׁ אִישְׁטוֹשְׁקוֹטוֹשׁ
פוֹרֵבְגֹמֵינוֹשׁ כֶּאֶגְנוֹשָׁא גַר אֶגוֹ אוֹשׁ
שִׁינַדִיאַשְׁמַא אֵנָן שִׁינַדִיאַזִי טוֹן פַּדוֹן
אַוְטוֹן: וְאָמַרְתִּי: כֵּאִיפּוֹן אֶגוֹ אֵן
קַרְדִיאַנְמוּ אוֹשְׁנַדִיאַשְׁמָא טוּכוֹרִיקוּ
גַ]ר אֶגוֹ שִׁינַדִיאַזִימוּ קְדִ̄יאַטִי אֶפְּרוֹנֵשַׁא
אֶ]גוֹ טוֹטֵן פְּרִישׁוֹטֵרוֹן כֶּאֶלָלִישָׁא אֵן

Col. ii

כַּרְדִיאָנְמוּ אוֹשְׁגַר טוּטוֹ מַטֵאוֹן:
כִּי אֵין: אוֹטִי אוּקֵישְׁטִין מְנִימוֹשִׁינוֹן
טוּשׁוֹפוּ מֵטַטוֹן כוֹרִיקוֹן אִישְׁטוֹנֵאוֹנָן
אֶן פְּלִינְתוֹן טוֹנְאִימֵרוֹ טוֹנְאֶלְכָמֵנוֹן
טַפָּדָא אֶלִישְׁמוֹנַיטֵי קְפּוֹשׁ אַפּוֹתְנִישְׁקִי
אוֹשׁוֹפוֹשׁ מֵטַטוֹן כוֹרִיקוֹן: וְשָׂנֵאתִי:
קֶאֶמִישִׁישָׁא טִין זוֹאִין אוֹטִי כַּקוֹן

19 There is no agreement on the place where Jonah was translated. Neubauer thought it was Corfu, Modena mentioned the Greek archipelago, and Belléli suggested that the Bologna manuscript originated in Crete (see Hesseling, *ByZ* 10 (1901), 208, 210).

אֶפִּיאָמֶן טוֹפִימָןﭏ אוֹשָׁאֶפִּיאוֹתִי
אַפּוּקְטוֹ טוּאָלְיָאוּ אוֹטִי טוֹפַן מַטַאוֹן
20   כְּקְקוֹטִיטָן פְּנֵיאוֹמָטוּ: וְשָׁנֵאתִי:

Verso Col. i

כָּאמִישִׁשָׁא אֶגוּ שִׁין פַן כִּימַשִׁיאָנְמוּ
אוֹשָׁאֶגוּ כִּימַזוֹזְמֶנוֹשׁ אַפּוּקְטוֹ טוּאָלְיָאוּ
אוֹשְׁנָאֶפִּישׁוֹ אַוְוטוֹ טוּאַתְרוֹפוּ אוֹשׁ
אֶשְׁטֵי אוֹפִּילְתְּנֶמוּ: וּמִי יָדַע: קְטִישׁ
25   יִינוֹשְׁקִי מְטִיפְּרָנִימוֹשׁ אֶשְׁטִין אִי
כּוֹרִיקוֹשׁ כְּאֶקְשִׁישִׁיאָשָׁשִׁי אֶן פַּאן
קוֹפוֹנְמוּ אוֹשְׁקוֹפוֹתִין אַפּוּקְטוֹ טוּ
אִילְיָאוּ גַר טוּטוֹ מַטַאוֹן: וְסַבּּתִי:
כָּאֶיְירְשָׁא אֶגוּ טוֹאַפוּמֶרִימְנִי שִׁין
30   טִין קָרְדִיאָנְמוּ אֶפִּיפָן טוֹנְקוֹפוֹן

Col. ii

טוֹן אֶקוֹפוֹתִין אַפּוּקְטוֹ טוּאָילְיָאוּ:
כִּי יֶשׁ: אוֹטִי אֶשְׁטִין אַנְתְּרוֹפוֹשׁ אוֹשׁ
קוֹפוֹשׁ אַוְוטוֹ אִיפוֹ שׁוֹפִּיאָשׁ קֶאָנְגְנוֹשִׁין
כְּאָנְאֶפְּתִיאוֹטִיטָן כְּטוּאַנְתְּרוֹפוּ
35   אוֹשָׁאוּכְּקוֹפוֹתִי אִישַׁאַוְוטוֹ דִידִי אַוְוטוּ
מֶרְטִיקוֹן אַוְוטוּ גַר טוּטוֹ מַטַאוֹן כְּקַקְיָא
פּוֹלִי: כִּי מֶה: אוֹטִיטִיאוֹפֶּלְי טוֹן אַנְתְּרוֹ‭[‬פוֹן
אֶן פַן כִּימַשִׁיאַן אַוְוטוּ כְּאָנְקְקוֹטִיטַן
כַּרְדִיאָשׁ אַוְוטוּ אוֹשָׁאַוְוטוֹשׁ כִּימַזוֹ‭[‬מֶנוֹשׁ
40   אַפּוּקְטוֹ טוּאָילְיָאוּ: כִּי כָל: אוֹטִי

Transliteration

(ii.13)   ... παρα την χωρικειαν ωσεν περισσοτερον
τοφως παρα τοσκοτος.
(14) οσοφος οφθαλμοι αυτου εν κεφαλην
αυτου καιοχωρικος εισтоσκοτος
5   πορευγομενος καιεγνωσα γαρ εγω ως
συναντιασμα εναν συναντιαζει των παντων
αυτων. (15) και ειπον εγω εν
καρδιανμου ωσσυναντιασμα τουχωρικου

γα]ρ εγω συναντιαζειμου καιδιατι εφρονεσα
ε]γω τοτεν περισσοτερον καιελαλησα εν
καρδιανμου ωσγαρ τουτο ματαιον.
(16) οτι ουκεστιν μνημοσυνον
τουσοφου μετατον χωρικονειστοναιωναν
εν πλινθον τωνημερω τωνελχαμενων
ταπαντα ελησμοναϊται καιπως αποθνησκει
οσοφος μετατον χωρικον.
(17) καιεμισησα την ζωην οτι κακον
επιεμεν το ποιμα(ν) οσεποιωθη
απουκατω τουηλιου οτι τοπαν ματαιον
καικατοτηταν πνεοματου.
(18) καιεμισησα εγω συν παν χειμασιανμου
οσεγω χειμαζομενος απουκατω τουηλιου
ωσναaφισω αυτο τουαθρωπου οσ-
εσται οπιλθενμου. (19) καιτις
γινωσκει μητιφρενιμος εστιν η
χωρικος καιεξησιασει εν παν
κοπονμου οσεκοπωθην απουκατω του
ηλιου γαρ τουτο ματαιον.
(20) καιεγυρισα εγω τοαπευμεριμνει συν
την καρδιανμου επιπαν τονκοπον
τον εκοπωθην απουκατω τουηλιου.
(21) οτι εστιν ανθρωπος ος
κοπος αυτου υπο σοφιας καιενγνωσιν
καιενευθυοτηταν καιτουανθρωπου
οσουκεκοπωθη εισααυτο διδει αυτου
μερτικον αυτου γαρ τουτο ματαιον καικακια
πολλη. (22) οτιτιωφελει τον ανθρω[πον
εν παν χειμασιαν αυτου καιενκακοτηταν
καρδιας αυτου οσαυτος χειμαζο[μενος
απουκατου τουηλιου. (23) οτι . . .

II

T-S K24.14 (see plates 3 and 4)

Description

This is also a single leaf of parchment, measuring $5\frac{3}{8}$ in (137 mm) by $9\frac{5}{8}$ in (250 mm) (maximum). There are traces of pricking at both ends.

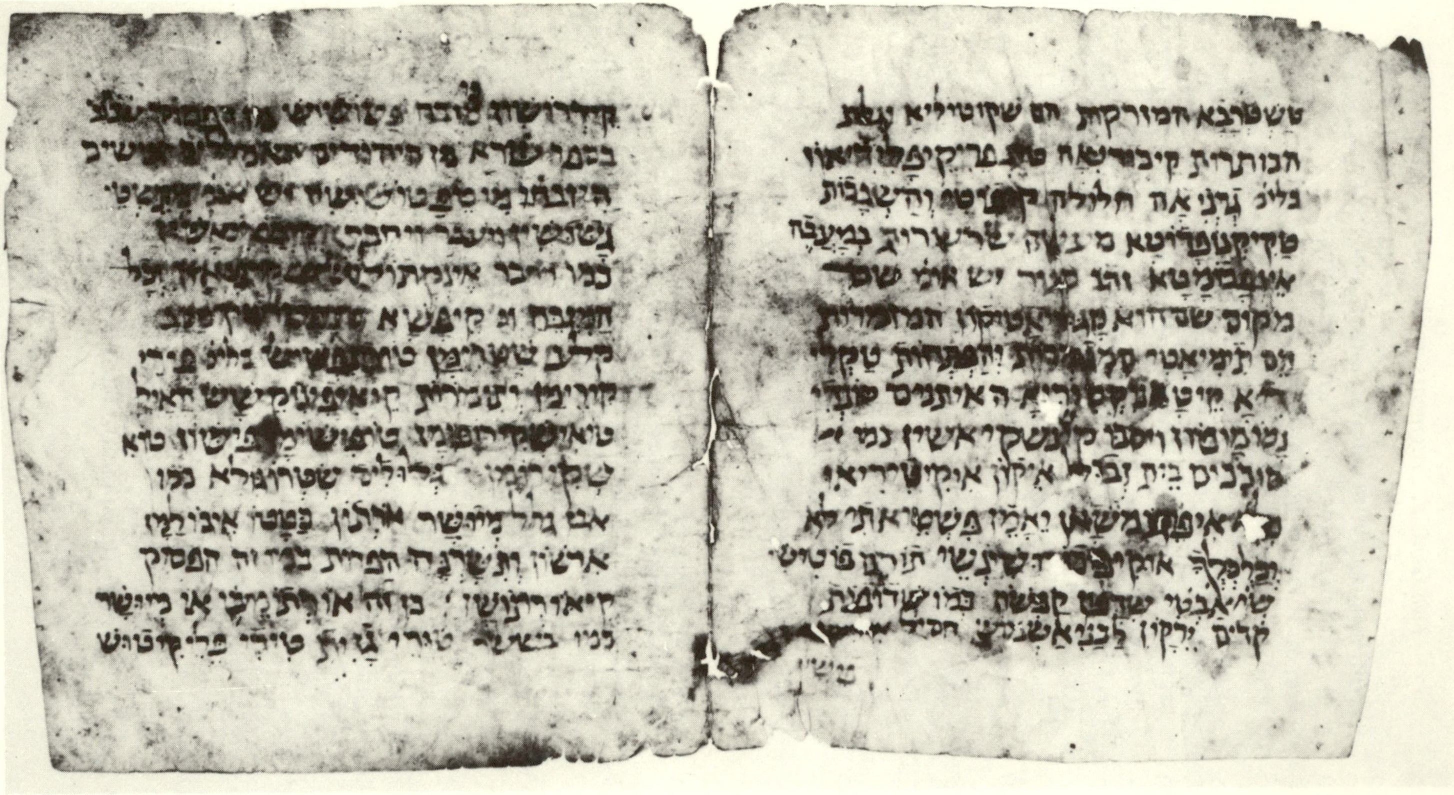

Plate 3 Recto of part of a glossary on the First Book of Kings (C.U.L. T–S K24.14)

Plate 4 Verso of part of a glossary on the First Book of Kings (C.U.L. T–SK24.14)

The writing is in square Hebrew characters, partly pointed. The columns measure $3\frac{7}{8}$ in (98 mm) in height by $3\frac{1}{8}$–$3\frac{1}{2}$ in (80–90 mm) in width, and contain fourteen lines each.

There is a central fold. The text begins on the left-hand side, continues overleaf in two consecutive columns and resumes on the right-hand side of the recto. This leaf was therefore the central leaf of its quire.

The text

The text is part of a glossary on the First Book of Kings. Our fragment begins at 1 Kgs vi.20, and breaks off at 1 Kgs viii.37. It consists of Hebrew comments and Greek glosses on selected words, in a similar manner to the Jerusalem manuscript mentioned above. The commentator confines himself for the most part to rare words and *hapax legomena*, of which this particular passage contains a high proportion. He rarely repeats himself (lines 6, 40f, 45f). He appears to have had a Greek translation before him, which he occasionally explains with a further Greek gloss (lines 7f, 13, 21, 24f, 45; cp. 31). Sometimes he provides two alternative Greek versions (lines 24, 27, 34, 40f; cp. 3).

The Hebrew lemmata do not always agree exactly with the Massoretic Text, particularly in the matter of full and defective spelling. This may be due to carelessness. There are many other signs of negligence, such as inconsistency of spelling and transliteration, and a rather haphazard approach to pointing. These factors, coupled with the untidiness of the writing, the poor state of preservation of the manuscript and the elliptic style, make it very hard in places to read the Greek words and to establish the sense of the text.

In view of all these difficulties I have not attempted to do more than to transcribe the text and to offer a slightly expanded translation. It should be stressed that some of the readings and interpretations are open to question. I have marked the most uncertain places with a question mark. In transcribing the text I have ignored the horizontal line that appears frequently over letters other than *b g d k p t*. The Greek specialist should be warned that it is not always easy to distinguish between certain letters, such as δ-ρ, ν-χ, π-φ.

In the translation I have added biblical references and the AV translation of the Hebrew words. These renderings have been inserted primarily to facilitate the identification of the biblical

Hebrew words by the non-Hebraist, and are not intended to imply any judgement about the meaning of the Greek glosses. I have not tried to translate the Greek words; in many cases even the transliteration has been offered with the greatest diffidence. I have deliberately kept the notes as brief as possible; much more work will be needed before this text is fully understood and explained.

The text

Recto Col. ii

כו
קֵידְרוֹשׁוֹן מזבח פַּטוֹשִׁישׁ מן הפסוק שנאׁ
בספר עזרא מן היהודים האמללים עושים
היזבחו מִיטֵפַּטוֹשׁוֹשִׁין יש אוםׂ מִתֵּשְׁטֵי
גָשׁוּשִׁין ויעבר ויחבר קֵיכֵמִינָאָשִׁין
כמו ויחבר אֶינְקָתוֹלוֹשַׁשׁ קרְפִיאָה וְכָל
הַמִּזְבֵּחַ וגׂ קֵיפָּשָׁא טנפטושין מסב
קלע שְׁטרימָן טוֹרְנֵפְּשִׁישׁ כלוםׂ פִּירֵי
קִירֵימַן וְתִימֹרוֹת קֵיאִיפִינִיקָשׁשׁ הָאַיִל
טוֹאִישְׁקִירוֹפִימָן טוֹפִישׁוֹמָן פִּישׁוֹן טוֹאִ
שְׁקֵירוֹמָן גְּלוּלִים שְׁטְרוֹגִילָא כמו
אבן גלל מְיוּשָּׁר אֹרְתוֹן כַּטָטוֹ אֵיגּוֹלַמָּן
אִישׁוֹן וְתִשָּׁרְנָה הַפרות כמו זה הפסוק
קֵיאוֹרְתוֹשָׁן: כן זה אוֹרְתוֹמֵינוּ או מְיוּשָּׁר
כמו בששר טוּרֵי גָזִית טורי פֵּלֵיקִיטוּשׁ

Verso Col. i

כלוםׂ דומוֹשׁ כְּרוּתוֹת אִיטַן כוֹמֵינָא קוֹפְּטוֹנְטָא
אִיפּוֹטִישְׁ אוֹדְדִינִיאָשׁ בוּל הוא····
מרחשון ולמה נקרא שְׁמוֹ בוּל על שֵׁם
מַבּוּל כי בְּמַרְחֶשְׁוָן ירד המבול ועל זה
נקרא שמו בול על אודות שנבלו האדם:
וּמַחֲזֶה אֶל־מַחֲזֶה קֵיאַפּוֹתֵיאַוְמָן פּרוֹשׁ
תֵיאַוְמָן כלוםׂ אַפּוֹפָונוֹן פְּרוֹשְׁפָנוֹן שלוש
פֵּרְפַּטִימָטָא בִימָטָא מֵחַלּוֹן אל חלון מְגוֹרָרֹת
בַּמְגֵרָה פְּרִיאוֹנִיזְמֵינֵישׁ אֵיפְּרִיאוֹנִין···
ודאׁ: אֵינְרוּכָנוֹן וּדְרִישָׁתוֹ שִׁירְמֵינֵשׁ
קֵאֵינְרוּקָנוֹן אַבְטוּ: וּמִמָּסָד עַד־הַטְּפָחוֹת במגרה

קֵיאַפּוטוֹתֵימֵילִיאוֹמָן אֵיאוֹשׁ טַפַּלֵשְׁטָא
וד א: קֵיאַפֵּוטוֹגְלַקְטִזְמָן: אֵנְכְרִיזְמָן כְּרוּתוֹת
פֵּרִיקֵפָּלִידִיאָ מוּצָק כִיטוֹן שְׂבָכִים מַעֲשֵׂה

Verso Col. ii

שְׂבָכָה קִיקְנוֹפָּדוֹטוֹן אֵרְגוֹן קִיקְנוֹפַּדוֹשִׁשׁ
וְהוּא כְמוֹ שְׂבָכָה יִתְהַלֵּךְ והוא פוֹדוֹבְרוֹכָא כלוֹמׂ
פֵּיזוֹבוֹלוֹן עַגוֹל שְׁטְרוֹגִילוֹן ביצוקתו אֵינְאִי
פִּכִישִׁין אָבְטוּ אלפים בת יכיל דִישְׁכִילִיאָ
בוּטִיאָ אֵיכוֹרִין: ויעש את המכונות טָאִיפּוֹתֵי
מָטָא ואת כנו פוֹלוּרוֹן לוּיוֹת כוּרְנִיאַ פֵּטוֹנִיאָ
פֵּיטוֹנִיאָה אֶרְגוֹן קַטֵפּוֹרוּ: וְאַרְבָּעָה
אוֹפַּנֵּי טְרוֹכֵיאָ וְסַרְנֵי נְחֹשֶׁת קֵיאַקְשׁוֹנָקָה
כַּלְקָה וְחִישּׁוּרֵיהֶם קֵיבְרֵגְמַטָא אַבְטוֹן כמו
חֶשְׁרַת חֶרְשַׁת־מים עבי שחקים וּמְלִיצָתוֹ
וְחוּרֵיהֶם כמו דודי שלח ידו מן החור
כְּמָעֵר אוֹשְׁ אַנַיִרְמָן [א]נדרוש לוּיוֹת...
פֵּיטוֹנִיאָה כְּמָעֵר אוֹשְׁ אַשְׁקִימוֹשִׁינִין
[כמו ל]מען הבית [ע]ל מְעוֹרֵיהֶם הַיָּעִים

Recto Col. i

טַשְׁטְרָבָא המזרקות הם שְׁקוֹטִילִיאָ וּגְלת
הכותרות קֵיכוּדְנִיאָה טוֹנְפֵּרִיקִיפָּלִידִיאוֹן
כלוֹמׂ גְרֵנִיאָה חלוּלה קוּפוֹטִי וְהַשְׂבָכוֹת
טַקִיקְנוֹפָּדוֹטָא מעשה שרשרות בְּמַעֲבֵה
אֵינְפַכוֹמָטָא זהב סגור יש אוֹמׂ שם
מקום שם הוא מָגוּרִיאָטִיקוֹן המזמרות
הם תִימִיאָטִי הַמְזַמְּרוֹת וְהַפְּתָחוֹת טַקְלִי
דִיאָ קֵיטָאַנִיקְטִירִיאָ האיתנים טוֹנְדִי
ש
נָמוֹמָוטוֹן ויסכו קינשקיאשין כמו..
סוככים בֵית זְבוּל אִיקוֹן אִיקִיטִירִיאוּ
מִ[לא] אִיפִּיגֵימַשַׁאן יֵאָמֵן פִּשְׁטֵוּאתִי לא
יְכַלְכְּלֶךָּ אוּקִיפִּיכוֹרוּשִׁינְשֵׁי תוֹרֵם פוֹטִישִׁי
שְׁ אַבְטִי שְׁדָפוֹן קַפּשׁוֹן כְּמוֹ שדופות
קדים יֵרָקוֹן לַכַנִיאַשְׁמוֹשׁ חסיל א[ ]יש
טִשִׁין

The translation

[? ארז (1 Kgs vi.18, 'cedar'):] κεδρωσιν. מזבח (vi.20, 'altar'): πατωσις, from the passage in the book of Ezra (Neh. iii.34), 'What do these feeble Jews? ... היזבחו (will they sacrifice?)': μητεπατωσουσιν, some say μητεστεγασουσιν. ויעבר (vi.21, 'and he made a partition'): 'and he joined', κεχεμινασιν (?), like ויחבר (?Exod. xxxvi.10 etc., 'and he coupled'): ενκαθολωσας καρφια. וכל־המזבח (vi.22, 'also the whole altar'): etc.: καιπασα τηνπατωσιν. מסב קלע (vi.29, 'he carved ... round about'): σταριμαν τορνεψις (?), i.e. πηρε κιρεμαν (?). ותמרת (*ibid.* 'and palm trees'): και οι φοινικεσας. האיל (vi.31, 'the lintel'): τοϊσκιροπιμαν τοπισομαν πισον τοϊσκιρομαν (?). גלילים (vi.34, 'folding'): στρογγυλα, like (?) 'to roll (גלל) a stone'. מישר (vi.35, 'fitted'): ορθον κατατο ἐγκόλαμμαν (?) ισον. We may compare to this passage 'and the kine took the straight way' (1 Sam. vi.12), καιορθωσαν: so too here (it means) ορθωμενο. Or else מישר is like בששר (Jer. xxii.14; Ezek. xxiii.14, 'with vermilion'). טורי גזית (vi.36, 'rows of hewed stone'): rows of πελεκητους i.e. δομους. (Verso i) כרתת (*ibid.* 'beams'): ηταν κομμενα κοπτοντα υποτης ωδεδινιας (?). בול (vi.38, 'Bul'): that is (the month) Marḥeshvan. And why is it called Bul? Because of the flood (*mabbūl*): because the flood came down in Marḥeshvan, and that is why it is called Bul, because mankind perished (*nābĕlū*). ומחזה|אל־מחזה (vii.4, 'and light was against light'): καιαποθεαυμαν προς θεαυμαν, i.e. αποφανον προσφανον, three περπατηματα (פעמים; *ibid.* 'ranks'), βηματα, from window to window. מגוררות במגרה (vii.9, 'sawed with saws'): πριονισμενες ε(ν)πριονιν. Another version: ενρουκανον, and it is interpreted συρμενες καιενρουκανον αυτου. וממסד עד־הטפחות (*ibid.* 'even from the foundation unto the coping'): καιαποτοθεμελιωμαν εως τα παλαιστα. And another version: καιαποτογλακτισμαν ενχερισμαν. כתרת (vii.16, 'chapiters'): περικεφαλιδια. מצק (*ibid.* 'molten'): χυτον. (Verso ii) שבכים מעשה שבכה (vii.17, 'nets of checker work'): κυκνοπαδωτον εργον κυκνοπα ωσι (?). It is like 'he walketh upon a snare (שבכה)' (Job xviii.8), which is ποδοβροχα, i.e. πεζοβολον. :עגל (vii.23, 'round'): στρογγυλον. ביצקתו (vii.24, 'when it was cast'): ενειπιχυσιν αυτου. אלפים בת יכיל (vii.26, 'it contained two thousand baths'): δισχιλια βουτια εχωρειν. ויעש את־המכנות (vii.27, 'and he made (ten) bases'): ταϋποθεματα. (cp.) ואת־כנו (Exod. xxx.28 etc., 'and his foot') φωλουρον (?). ליות (vii.29, 'certain additions'): χουρνια (?) πετονια πετονια εργον κατηφορου. וארבעה אופני (vii.30, 'and ... four ... wheels'): τροχαια. וסרני נחשת (*ibid.* 'and plates of brass'): καιαξωνακα χαλκα. וחשריהם (vii.33, 'and their spokes'): καιβρεγματα αυτων, like חשרת (in) 'dark waters, and thick clouds of the skies' (2 Sam. xxii.12), and its interpretation is 'and their holes', as in 'my beloved put in his hand by the hole' (Song of Songs v.4). כמער(־איש) (vii.36, 'according to the proportion of every one'): ως αναγυρμαν [α]νδρος. ליות (*ibid.* 'additions'): πετονια. כמער (*ibid.*): ως ασκημοσυνην, [as (in)] 'that thou mayest look [o]n their nakedness (מעוריהם)' (Hab. ii.15). (Recto i) היעים (vii.40, 'the shovels'): ταστραβα. המזרקות (*ibid.* 'the basons'): they are σκοτιλια. וגלת הכתרת (vii.41, 'and the (two) bowls of the chapiters'): καιχουδνια τωνπερικεφαλιδιων, i.e. γρενια (?), hollow, κουφοτη. והשבכות (*ibid.* 'and the (two) networks'): τακυκνοπαδοτα, 'chain work' (vii.17). במעבה (vii.46, 'in the (clay) ground'): ενπαχωματα. זהב סגור (vii.49, 'of pure gold'): Some say it is a place-name, μαγουριατικον (?). המזמרות (vii.50, 'the snuffers'): they are θυμιατοι. (?) המזמרות | והפתחות (cp. *ibid.* והפתות 'and the hinges'): τακλειδια καιταανοικτηρια. האתנים (viii.2, 'Ethanim'): τωνδυναμωματων. ויסכו (viii.7, 'and (the cherubims) covered'): και(συ)νσκιασειν (?), like סככים (Exod. xxv.20, xxxvii.9, 'covering'). בית|זבל (viii.13, 'an house to dwell in'): οικον οικητηριου. מלא (viii.15, 'hath ... fulfilled'): ειπιγεμισαν. יאמן (viii.26, 'let ... be verified'): πιστευωθη. לא יכלכלוך (viii.27, 'cannot contain thee'): ουκειπιχωρουσινσε. תורם (viii.36, '(that) thou teach them'): φωτισεις αυτη(?). שדפון (viii.37, 'blasting'): καψον, like 'blasted (שדפות) with the east wind' (Gen. xli.23). ירקון (*ibid.* 'mildew'): λαχανιασμος. חסיל (*ibid.* 'caterpillar'): ε[ ]ιστισιν (?) ...

Notes on the text

4 **κεχεμινασιν:** the text is not clear.

5 The meaning of this line is far from obvious.

7–9 I am uncertain about the transcription and meaning of the Greek words.

12 MT has וישרנה.

14 The word after גזית looks like טִידִי (τιδε?), but I cannot make sense of this, and prefer to take it as a repetition of .

15f I am not certain of the meaning of the Greek words, which go beyond a simple gloss. כרתות, which only occurs in this passage, is apparently derived from כרת, 'to cut'.

16ff The gist of this midrashic comment is found in several rabbinic sources (e.g. *Pĕsīqtā Rabbātī*, 6.5, fo. 24*b*), although not in the same words.

23 **ε(ν)πριονιν:** I have supplied the ν, which yields a fair translation of במגרה, literally 'in the saw'.

27 **ενχερισμαν:** the transcription is tentative. I have assumed a supposed etymology of טפחות from טפח, 'a handbreadth'. **כתרות:** the manuscript reads כרותות, as in line 15, but the Greek makes it clear that כתרות is intended (cp. line 44).

34 The quotation of ואת־כנו is curious, since the word כן occurs here at vii.29 and 31.

35 **πετονια εργον κατηφορου** is clearly intended as a translation of ליות מעשה מורד : literally 'garlands, work of descent'.

41 **πετονια:** cp. line 35.

42 Nahum iii.5 would have been a more appropriate parallel, since it uses the same word (מערך).

46 **τακυκνοπαδοτα:** cp. line 29.

47 זהב סגור also occurs earlier, in verses 20 and 21.

49 **המזמרות והפתחות:** this lemma does not appear in the text of 1 Kings, and indeed the word פתחות does not occur in the Hebrew Bible.

55 **αυτη:** from the Hebrew we should have expected αὐτούς.

The Translation and Interpretation of Isaiah vi.13

J.A. EMERTON

The first volume of Erwin Rosenthal's *Studia Semitica* brings together some of his publications on Jewish themes and reflects his scholarly interests over a period of many years. Eight articles are grouped under the general heading 'The Hebrew Bible and its exegesis', and they include several about medieval Jewish biblical scholars and their influence on Christian exegetes and translators of the Bible in the sixteenth and seventeenth centuries. Such studies are of interest for the light they shed on the history of biblical and Hebrew scholarship and of relations between Jews and Christians, and they can also be helpful to the twentieth-century exegete, whether he be Jew or Christian.

The present article will outline the principal ways in which Isa. vi.13 has been interpreted by Jewish and Christian scholars: how it was understood in the ancient versions, by several of the principal Jewish scholars in the Middle Ages, by some Christian commentators and translators in the sixteenth and seventeenth centuries, and by Jewish and Christian scholars since then, including those who have advanced theories on the basis of the A Scroll of Isaiah discovered in Cave 1 at Qumran in 1947. Any attempt to summarize in one article the work of two thousand years must leave out the contribution of innumerable writers and be open to the charge of superficiality. Nevertheless, there may also be an advantage in trying to see the picture as a whole.

The article has a further object. It will be asked whether any conclusions may be reached about the text and meaning of the verse. After all, the commentators of the past sought to clarify the meaning of the text, not to provide source material for the writing of the history of scholarship.

The text and its problems

ועוד בה עשיריה ושבה והיתה לבער כאלה וכאלון אשר בשלכת מצבת
בם זרע קדש מצבתה

A number of different translations will be examined later in the article, but we shall begin with the AV, the rendering that is best known in the English language:

> But yet in it shall be a tenth, and it shall return, and shall be eaten: as a teil tree, and as an oak, whose substance is in them, when they cast their leaves: so the holy seed shall be the substance thereof.

The context in which this difficult verse is found is the end of the account of Isaiah's call to be a prophet. He is commanded in verses 9 and 10 to proclaim a message that the people will not understand or accept. He therefore asks in verse 11: 'How long?', and the answer is given in verses 11–13: until the land is utterly desolate and without inhabitants; and the first part of verse 13 states that, even if a tenth part survives for a time, it too will be destroyed. The first three words of the verse (*wĕʿōd bāh ʿăśīriyyā*) are probably a circumstantial clause, which may legitimately be rendered 'And if there is still a tenth part in it'. Some commentators have supposed that this clause and the next words (*wĕšābā wĕhāyĕtā lĕbāʿēr*), taken with verses 11 and 12, imply that disaster will come in two stages, the first being perhaps the fall of the Kingdom of Israel and the second that of the smaller Kingdom of Judah. The AV's 'and it shall return' probably fails to represent correctly the sense of *wĕšābā* in this context (though we shall see that it has been understood to refer to repentance even by some translators in the twentieth century): here it is most likely used as an auxiliary verb meaning 'again', or rather 'in turn'. The tenth part, which has survived so far, will be subject to *lĕbāʿēr* in its turn. It is thus possible that disaster in two stages is implied, but it is by no means certain that the intention is so precise. The meaning may be no more than that, even if part of the population at first survives, their survival will be merely temporary, without there being two clear-cut and distinct major disasters separated from each other by many years. In contrast to the unrelieved gloom of the first part of verse 13, the last clause mentions 'holy seed', and it is usually thought to be an assurance that, in spite of everything, a holy remnant will survive. There thus seems to be a contrast, or even a contradiction, between the total disaster of which the beginning of the verse speaks and the hope that is implied at the end. Between the prediction of disaster and the last part of the verse stands a comparison with two trees, and it is disputed whether this comparison expresses disaster, like the earlier part of the verse, or hope, like the last clause. The latter interpretation is supported by the fact that the last clause identifies the *maṣṣebet* in the comparison and thus sees it as a sign of hope. On the other hand, the former interpretation is favoured by the fact that the comparison comes immediately after the prediction of disaster, and no conjunction, let alone an adversative particle, intervenes between the two; it is, therefore, natural to suppose that the comparison belongs with the prediction of disaster.

There are also problems of translation, vocabulary and text. First, it is uncertain precisely what kind of disaster is indicated by *lĕbāʿēr*, an infinitive construct *piʿel*. The verb is used in the *piʿel* in Isa. iii.14 of consuming, eating, and it may have the same meaning in Isa. v.14 – hence the AV's 'eaten' in vi.13. The *piʿel* can also mean 'to kindle' or 'to burn', and so in Isa. iv.4 perhaps 'to purify'. Further, it sometimes has the wider meaning 'to remove' or 'to destroy'. Any of these types of meaning would fit Isa. vi.13. Secondly, the trees mentioned are *'ēlā* and *'allōn*, which are usually thought to mean 'terebinth' and 'oak', respectively. Thirdly, the suffix of *bām*, 'in them', later in the verse, presumably has the two trees as its antecedent. There is a variant reading *bāh* with a third-person feminine singular suffix, and the antecedent is either the same trees understood in a collective sense (GK §145*k*) or *ʿăśīriyyā*. Fourthly, *bĕšalleket* ('when they cast their leaves' in the AV) is obscure. Its mention so soon after the words 'like a terebinth and like an oak' suggests that it is something to do with trees, and that probability remains even if the variant reading *bāh* is adopted and the relative clause in which it appears is thought to refer to the tenth. *bĕšalleket* consists of the preposition *b* attached to what is more probably a noun than a unique form of the infinitive construct *piʿel* of the root *šlk*. Nouns of this formation are often abstract in sense. The verb *šlk* is not attested in the *piʿel*, but the *hiphʿil* is used (with the *hophʿal* as its passive) to mean 'to throw, cast down' and (of a tree) 'to shed' leaves (cp. the AV). 1 Chron. xxvi.16 mentions a gate of the Temple called *šaʿar šalleket*, but it is not known why it was given that name. Fifthly, *maṣṣebet* also seems to be something to do with a tree, and most likely denotes part of a tree. It is probably a noun with a preformative *mem* from the root *nṣb* or perhaps *yṣb*, either of which would suggest a meaning connected with standing. We find a noun *maṣṣebet* in 2 Sam. xviii.18, where it is used of a pillar set up by Absalom as a memorial, and where it is thought to be a form of the more common *maṣṣēbā*, a word denoting a stone pillar, often a pillar used in Canaanite religion. In Isa. vi.13, however, it can scarcely refer to a stone pillar, for we have seen that the context suggests that it is part of a tree. It is not difficult to see why some exegetes have thought that it means a 'trunk' or 'stump', a part of a tree that might be thought to resemble a pillar – but we shall see that various suggestions about its meaning have been made.

The ancient versions

The earliest evidence (other than the text from Qumran) for Jewish interpretation of the verse is found in the ancient versions. Even the Vulgate can serve as evidence, for it is well known that, although Jerome was a Christian, his understanding of the Hebrew Bible owed much to Jewish scholars.

1. The Greek versions

It is convenient to begin with the A text of the LXX and the rendering given by Ottley:

> καὶ ἔτι ἐπ' αὐτῆς ἐστιν τὸ ἐπιδέκατον, καὶ πάλιν ἔσται εἰς προνομήν, ὡς τερέβινθος καὶ ὡς βάλανος ὅταν ἐκσπασθῇ ἀπὸ τῆς θήκης αὐτῆς.
>
> And still upon it is the tenth part, and again it shall be for plunder; as a terebinth, and as an oak, when it is torn from its place.

Apart from a longer reading at the end (which will be discussed below), the principal variants in other manuscripts are of comparatively little significance: ἐκπέσῃ, 'it falls', instead of ἐκσπασθῇ, 'it is torn'; and ἐκ, 'out of', instead of ἀπὸ, 'from'. There are several matters that need comment. First, εἰς προνομήν, which Ottley renders 'for plunder', corresponds to *lĕbāʿēr*. It appears at first sight to be a free rendering of the Hebrew, but it is possible that Ottley has not correctly represented the meaning intended by the translator. Liddell and Scott also give for the noun the meanings 'foraging' and 'provision of fodder', and such a meaning would fit *lĕbāʿēr* if it were understood to refer to eating by animals (cp. Worschech, p. 126). Second, 'when it is torn' or 'when it falls' may be a free translation of *bĕšalleket*, but Michaelis suggested as long ago as the eighteenth century that it was based on a reading *mušleket*, and it is interesting that 1QIsa[a] has *mšlkt*. Third, the LXX does not translate several words found in the MT, and they have often been thought to be *zrʿ qdš mṣbth* at the end of the verse. That opinion appears to go back as far as Origen and those scribes who followed him by adding at this point σπέρμα ἅγιον τὸ στήλωμα αὐτῆς from Theodotion. Budde, however, has argued convincingly (p. 167) that the word αὐτῆς, 'its', at the end of the verse in the LXX shows that *mṣbth*, with a suffix, was read, rather than *mṣbt* earlier in the verse. The words not translated are thus *mṣbt bm zrʿ qdš*. The omission is explained by him as due to homoioteleuton, but it would more accurately be ascribed to homoioarkton. Budde's suggestion is more likely than the alternative theory of Brownlee (1964, p. 237) that the LXX is based on a Hebrew text that ended with *mmṣbt bh*, where the MT has *mṣbt bm* or *bh* (though Kennicott records that one Hebrew manuscript has *mmṣbt* in place of *mṣbt*), for Brownlee does not account for the failure to translate the preposition *b*. Fourth, if εκ (or ἀπὸ) τῆς θήκης thus corresponds to the MT's *maṣṣabtāh*, the Greek preposition may have been added as part of a free translation. Alternatively, it may have been based on a Hebrew text that was thought to contain the preposition *min*, 'from': either the Hebrew text had *mmṣbth* (so Budde), or *mṣbth* was understood as *m*(*n*) + *ṣbth* (so Michaelis, except that he thought it was from *m*(*n*) + *ṣbt*). Fifth, it is possible to translate the last clause of the LXX differently: βάλανος can mean 'acorn' as well as 'oak', and θήκη can be understood in this context to denote 'acorn-cup'. The last clause can thus be translated 'and like an acorn when it falls from its cup' – and we shall see that the Peshitta and Jerome's commentary have a similar translation. Seeligmann (p. 49), who thinks that it is the final clause of the Hebrew that has not been translated in the LXX, suggests that the clause at the end of the Greek 'is rooted in the coagulated equation of' *mṣbt* 'with θήκη = gravestone, monument – with which the translator was, of course, perfectly familiar'. It is not clear exactly what he means. The meaning 'gravestone, monument' does not make sense in the LXX context, which demands 'place' or 'acorn-cup', and it may be that the words 'coagulated equation' mean that, although the translator did not intend to write of a gravestone or monument here, the correspondence between the Hebrew and Greek words was at the back of his mind. It is doubtful whether such an hypothesis is necessary.

The later Greek versions modify the LXX (see Field). Symmachus has εἰς καταβόσκησιν, 'for grazing', which is a possible meaning of *lĕbāʿēr*; *bšlkt* is then understood to refer to a tree's shedding of its leaves, which is one of the meanings of the verb *šlk* in Hebrew. *mṣbt* is rendered ἵσταται μόνη, 'stands alone', in accordance with the Hebrew word's derivation from *nṣb* or *yṣb*, 'to stand', and *mṣbth* is translated ἡ στάσις αὐτῆς; Symmachus reproduces the verse in full and does not have a shorter text like the LXX. As we have seen, Theodotion has 'holy seed is its pillar' at the end of the verse, and Aquila's version has the same meaning, although it has στήλωσις instead of τὸ στήλωμα αὐτῆς.

2. *Latin*

> et adhuc in ea decimatio et convertetur et erit in ostensionem sicut terebinthus et sicuti quercus quae expandit ramos suos semen sanctum erit id quod steterit in ea.

The Vulgate's translation of *lbʿr* by 'in ostensionem' is strange, and it may be asked whether it has arisen from a confusion between *bʿr* and *bʾr*, of which the *piʿel* means 'to make plain'. In contrast, Jerome's commentary has 'in depraedationem', which betrays the influence of the LXX's εἰς προνομήν, though not perhaps the meaning intended by it. The translation of *bšlkt* (or, according to Michaelis, *mašleket*) is free, and there is no obvious counterpart to *mṣbt bm* (or *bh*). The commentary here has 'quae proiecit fructus suos', and it explains the figure of speech in a way that recalls a possible understanding of the LXX: 'In tantum, ut terebintho et quercui, comparetur.' It is not clear what has become of *mṣbt bm* (or *bh*). It is difficult to see how 'ramos suos' can have been derived from the Hebrew except by an attempt to convey the meaning of the figure of speech as a whole. Sawyer compares the Aramaic word *maṣṣēbā*, or *maṣṣabtā*ʾ (in fact, he quotes a slightly different form), 'planting', but it may be doubted whether it accounts for the Vulgate's somewhat different rendering. Finally, *mṣbth* is understood by Jerome, as it had been earlier by some Greek translators, from the meaning 'to stand'.

3. *Aramaic*

The Targum of Jonathan, which occupied a position of particular importance for later Jewish commentators, has the following translation of Isa. vi.13:

> וישתארון בה חד מן עסרא ויתובון ויהון לצרבא כבוטמא וכבלוטא
> דבמיתר טרפיהון דמן ליבישין ועד כען רטיבין לקיימא מינהון זרעא

כין גלוותא דישראל יתכנשון ויתובון לארעהון ארי זרעא דקודשא נצבתהון

And a tenth will be left in it, and they will again be burnt, like a terebinth and like an oak which, when their leaves fall, are as if they are withered, but they are still moist to preserve seed from them; so the exiles of Israel will be gathered and will return to their land, for the holy seed is their plant.

bšlkt is taken to refer to the trees' shedding of their leaves. *mṣbt* and *mṣbth* are understood in different ways: the former is thought to mean that the trees retain their moisture, and the latter is translated *niṣbātĕhōn*, 'their plant', and the second rendering is an Aramaic word with the same radical consonants as the Hebrew.

4. Syriac

wdpyšyn bh ḥd mn ʿsrʾ wttwb wthwʾ lyqdnʾ ʾyk bṭmtʾ wʾyk blwṭʾ dnpl mn qʿrth zrʿʾ hw qdyšʾ nṣbth

And those that remain in it (will be) a tenth, and it will return and be burnt like a terebinth and like an acorn that has fallen from its cup; the holy seed is its plant (*or* power of reproduction).

The rendering of *bšlkt* probably betrays the influence of the LXX reading ἐκπέσῃ. Here again, *mṣbt* and *mṣbth* are understood in different ways, and the translation of the first recalls the LXX's rendering of the second. The Peshitta, however, understands the second in the same way as the Targum, and the Syriac word *neṣbteh* is from the root *nṣab*, 'to plant'. Despite the Peshitta's agreement in places with the LXX, it also has a point of contact with the Targum, and it is based on a longer Hebrew text than that underlying the LXX.

The above study of the versions shows that there was no uniform tradition about the meaning of Isa. vi.13. *lbʿr* and *bšlkt* (or perhaps *mšlkt*) were understood in different ways. So too were *mṣbt* and *mṣbth*, and none of the extant versions understands both words in the same way.

Some medieval Jewish scholars

First, an interpretation of the verse is offered by Saadya, 'whose Arabic Bible translation', as Erwin Rosenthal has written, 'became authoritative and whose linguistic attainment and commentaries made possible the flowering of Bible Study in East and West during the later Middle Ages' (*Stud. Sem.*, vol. I, p. vii). J. and H. Derenbourg offer the following French translation:

> et il y restera un dixième (des habitants), au point qu'elle redevienne un pâturage. Comme le térébinthe et le chêne sont à (la porte de) Schaleketh où ils se dressent, ainsi se dressera la génération sacrée.

Several parts of the translation deserve comment. First, *lĕbā'ēr* is understood to refer to grazing (*r'y'*), as in Symmachus. Second, *bĕšalleket* is taken to be the name of the gate in Jerusalem mentioned in 1 Chr. xxvi.16. Third, both occurrences of the word *maṣṣebet* are thought to refer to standing (*mntṣbyn* and *nṣbthm*), and we are reminded of Symmachus and the Vulgate (for the second).

Secondly, Rashi's comments on the verse are brief enough to be quoted in full in translation:

> *w'wd bh 'śyryh*: even against that remnant will I turn my hand with testing after testing. *whyth lb'r* until only the perfectly righteous are left, who will return to me with all their heart. *k'lh wk'lwn* which in the time of their *šlkt* shed (*mšlykyn*) their leaves in the days of autumn until nothing is left but the *mṣbh*. So too the holy seed, who remain in it steadfast [literally 'standing' – *'wmdyn*] in their holiness, will be a *mṣbt* to it. Another interpretation of *mṣbth* is its 'planting'. Therefore I am not making an end of them, (for) I planted them as holy seed. And some offer the interpretation that there was a gate Shallecheth in Jerusalem, as Ezra mentioned [in 1 Chr. xxvi.16], and there were planted there a terebinth and an oak.

Rashi thus notes two interpretations of *bĕšalleket*: shedding leaves and the name of a gate in the Temple. The former recalls Symmachus and the Targum, and the latter Saadya. There are also two interpretations of *maṣṣebet* and *maṣṣabtāh*. One is that the word denotes what is left when a tree has shed its leaves. Behind that interpretation may lie the view of the Targum that there is something in trees that enables them to grow fresh leaves after they have shed the old ones. It would also be possible to understand the explanation to refer to the trunk (and perhaps the branches) of a tree, which remains when the leaves have fallen. The other interpretation is that *maṣṣabtāh* means 'its planting' (cp. the Targum, and the Peshitta).

Thirdly, Ibn Ezra discusses the verse at greater length, but it will suffice to summarize his interpretation. He understands *lĕbā'ēr* to mean 'to make an end of' (cp. Deut. xxi.21) and so to refer to the Exile, though he also notes the opinion that it means 'to burn, kindle' (Exod. xxxv.3). *ʿăśīriyyā* is regarded by him as the ordinal numeral and distinguished from the fraction meaning 'a tenth part', which would be *ʿăśīrīt*, and he thinks that there is a reference to the ten reigns between the time of the vision and the Exile of Judah. *šalleket* is taken by him, as by Saadya, to be the name of the gate, and he thinks that the point of the comparison is that there were two trees there that were sturdy. He rejects the view of those who suppose that metathesis has occurred and identify *šalleket* with *liškat* ('the hall of') or derive it from the verb *šlk*, which is used in the *hiphʿil*, not the *piʿel*. Finally, he follows those who connect *maṣṣebet* with the root meaning 'to stand': the people are compared to a tree (cp. Isa. lxv.22), and to say that there is *maṣṣebet bām* means that there will be those who will endure – the holy seed are thus those who will return from exile in Babylon. Once again, the Targum's understanding of the passage appears to lie in the background, despite the fact that *bĕšalleket* is understood differently.

Fourthly, David Qimḥi understands *ʿăśīriyyā* to be a noun referring to the ten kings who will reign before the Exile, and thinks that *lĕbāʿēr* means 'to make an end of'. Although he is aware of the theory that *šalleket* is the name of a gate, he appears to prefer the view that it denotes the shedding of leaves. When a tree sheds its leaves it appears to be dried up, but *maṣṣebet bām* signifies that there is moisture remaining in it, and new leaves will grow again in the spring. Thus, although the people will go into exile, a holy seed will again sprout and flourish and will return to their land. He also notes that the Targum understands *maṣṣabtāh* to be a noun meaning 'a plant' with a suffix referring to the land.

Some English versions of the Bible

Erwin Rosenthal's articles on 'Rashi and the English Bible' (1940) and 'Sebastian Muenster's knowledge and use of Jewish exegesis' (1943) (reprinted in *Stud. Sem.*, vol. I, pp. 56–85 and 127–45, respectively) discuss Jewish influence on Christian translations of the Old Testament in the sixteenth and seventeenth centuries. The following section of the present article will consider several English versions of Isa. vi.13, but will not discuss the exact channels by which the Jewish traditions were transmitted to the translators.

The similarity between the Great Bible (London, 1539 – here quoted from a reprint of 1540) and Jewish exegesis of the verse is at once obvious:

> . . . yet in yt shall succeade .x. kinges, and the lande shall retorne and be layde waste. And as The terebint tre and oke in winter cast ther leaves, and yet haue ther sappe in them so shall the holy sead contynue in theyr substance.

The Jewish opinion that *ʿăśīriyyā* refers to ten kings, which had been known to Nicolaus of Lyra, was familiar to Calvin too, but he preferred the other view, also held by Jewish commentators, that it means a tenth part. Further, his exposition of the meaning of the comparison with the trees follows the familiar pattern: *maṣṣebet* means 'subsistentia', and it would be impossible for the trees that had shed their leaves to grow new ones 'nisi in media etiam hyeme vigorem intus aliquem retinerent'. The Geneva Bible of 1560 follows Calvin's interpretation of the verse:

> But yet in it *shalbe* a tenth, and shal returne, and shalbe eaten vp as an elme or as an oke, which have a substance in them, when they cast *their leaves*: *so* the holie sede shalbe the substance thereof.

A note on 'a tenth' records as an alternative interpretation that 'it was reuiled to Isaiáh for the confirmation of his prophecie, that ten Kings shulde come before their captivitie, as were from Vzziáh to Zedekiáh'. Another note speaks of the comparison to a tree that loses its leaves in winter and seems to be dead, 'yet in sommer is fresh, and grene'.

The Bishops' Bible of 1568 follows the Great Bible's understanding of the verse, and does not adopt Calvin's explanation of *ʿăśīriyyā*. In 1611, however, the AV, which was quoted above on p. 86, agrees with the Geneva Bible in understanding the word to mean 'a tenth'. *wĕšābā wĕhāyĕtā lĕbāʿēr* is thought to mean 'and it shall return, and shall be eaten' or, according to the margin, 'when it is returned, and hath been broused'; and *bĕšalleket* is understood to refer to trees casting their leaves. The text follows a familiar tradition in translating both occurrences of *maṣṣebet* by 'substance', but the margin notes an alternative rendering: 'stock' or 'stem'; and behind the marginal rendering lies Luther's 'Stam' in his German translation of 1522–46. Similarly, the Italian scholar F. Foreiro (Forerus) comments in 1563: 'Ego *stipitem* dixi: nam Hebraeum מצבת est à verbo quod sign. *stare*, nempe יצב . . . unde pro *statuis* frequentissimè accipitur: hîc autem pro *statua arboris*, i. trunco seu stipite.' He thus translates this part of the verse: 'sicut ilex, & sicut quercus, quibus in defluxu (foliorum) stipes [est]: semen sanctum, stipes eius'. The same interpretation of *maṣṣebet* is given in J. Buxtorf's *Lexicon Hebraicum*, 2nd edn (London, 1646) and, as we shall see, has established itself widely in modern translations of the verse. Such an understanding of *maṣṣebet* recalls one way of understanding Rashi's comment that it is what is left when a tree's leaves have fallen.

Study of Isaiah vi.13 since the sixteenth century

We have seen that the influence of Jewish exegesis on the understanding of Isa. vi.13 by Christians was strong in the century or so before the AV of 1611. In the following period, however, the study of Hebrew by Christian scholars moved forward on its own, although Jewish comments on the verse were not ignored.

Several developments in the exegesis of Isa. vi.13 by Christian scholars may be noted. One of them displayed continuity with Jewish tradition: the understanding of *ʿăśīriyyā* as 'a tenth' became dominant at the expense of the alternative Jewish tradition that it meant 'ten' and referred to ten kings. The other developments moved a greater distance from Jewish exegesis of the verse. First, de Dieu suggested an active sense for *lĕbāʿēr*: 'erit ad urendum aut ad depascendum, nempe hostes'. His suggestion did not win general support, but we shall see later that the recent interpretation of the verse by Cazelles bears some resemblance to it. Second, the belief that *maṣṣebet* means 'stock, stem, trunk, stump, or rootstock' became general. The meanings 'trunk' and 'stump' are not identical, but a stump is what remains when most of a trunk is cut down, and it is not difficult to see how the Hebrew word could be understood in either sense; and the English word 'stock' can have either meaning. The view that the Hebrew word means 'stem', 'trunk', or the like was held in the eighteenth century by such notable scholars as Vitringa, Le Clerc, and Lowth, though caution was expressed by Michaelis, who noted that none of the ancient versions had understood the Hebrew word thus. It received the weighty support of Gesenius in the nineteenth century and was accepted by, for example, Roorda and Cheyne. The rendering 'stump' was given in the influential lexicon of Brown, Driver and Briggs near the beginning of the twentieth century, and was adopted in the standard commentaries of Skinner, Gray and Wade. Despite its thoroughness on many matters, Gray's commentary does not even mention the fact that many have understood the word in other ways, and it is ironical that Sawyer refers in 1964 to 'the traditional translation "stump"' (p. 113). The similar rendering 'rootstock' or 'Wurzelstamm' was favoured by some leading scholars in the last century such as Ewald, Franz Delitzsch, Dillmann, Duhm and Marti, and in the present century by the lexicon of Gesenius–Buhl. A different interpretation, which understands the word to mean 'shoot' or the like, was favoured by Hitzig, Knobel and Orelli, and we shall see below that the idea has been revived in the twentieth century. Third, *běšalleket* was understood by many scholars to refer to the falling or felling of a tree – an idea that is obviously related to the view that *maṣṣebet* is a stump. We find such an understanding of *běšalleket* in a variety of forms in the writings of, for example, Vitringa, Le Clerc, Lowth, Gesenius, Hitzig, Knobel, Ewald, Delitzsch, Orelli, Dillmann, Duhm, Marti and Gesenius–Buhl, and in the twentieth-century British writers mentioned above.

So it was that the Revised Version of 1884 could refer to 'a terebinth, and . . . an oak, whose stock remaineth, when they are felled', and could relegate 'substance' and 'cast *their* leaves' to the margin. In more recent years, the Revised Standard Version has abandoned the marginal translations altogether. The Good News Bible goes even farther:

> Even if one person out of ten remains in the land, he too will be destroyed; he will be like the stump of an oak tree that has been cut down.

Those responsible for this translation, who thus understand the tenth in an individualistic way and ignore the terebinth, go on to commit the version to the view that the last clause of the verse is a gloss by adding it in brackets after the closing of the quotation marks at 'cut down'. At the same time, they refrain from using the word 'holy' (even though it seems to have been unavoidable in verse 3): '(The stump represents a new beginning for God's people.)'. The New American Bible is more conservative: it renders *maṣṣebet* by 'trunk', but reverts to an older understanding of *běšalleket* as 'when the leaves have fallen'. Although the Jerusalem Bible has 'stock' for *maṣṣebet*, and appears to understand *běšalleket* to denote felling, a trace of another rendering of the latter word appears to have survived: the country 'will be stripped like a terebinth of which, once felled, only the stock remains'. The New International Version understands the verse in another way:

And though a tenth remains in the land,
  it will again be laid waste.
But as the terebinth and oak
  leave stumps when they are cut down,
  so the holy seed will be the stump in the land.

A contrast is thus seen between the beginning and end of the verse. The first part, as far as *lĕbāʿēr*, describes disaster and is translated as a complete sentence. The second, from *kāʾēlā*, is understood to be a prophecy of hope: the comparison with what happens to the trees is concerned with hope for the seed and not with disaster. The contrast is emphasized by introducing a new sentence with 'But'. There is, however, no adversative particle, or any conjunction, in the Hebrew text corresponding to the English word 'But'. Further, the comparison with trees that are cut down comes immediately after a reference to the destruction of even the tenth that has survived so far, and it is arguable that the simile is concerned with disaster rather than with hope for the future. The presence of 'But' in the translation is difficult to justify.

A different kind of development in exegesis, which had an influence on the interpretation of Isa. vi.13, was the acceptance in the nineteenth century of a critical view of the Bible involving a more favourable attitude towards emendation of the Hebrew text and a willingness to recognize the work of redactors and glossators. The contrast between the disaster described in the first part of Isa. vi.13 and the hope implied in the last clause of the verse has been regarded by many scholars since Duhm and Marti as so sharp that both cannot be attributed to the same hand. The first part, it is argued, does not allow for the permanent survival of any portion of the people, and the comparison with what happens to a terebinth and an oak, which follows immediately, must be intended to express disaster, not hope. The last clause of the verse, which implies that the 'holy seed' will survive, has, therefore, been regarded as a gloss intended to introduce a happy ending to the prophecy of doom. The argument has sometimes been reinforced by the claim that the last clause was not in the Hebrew text used by the LXX translator – though we have seen that the LXX cannot be legitimately used to support such an argument.

We turn now to the ways in which Jewish scholars of more recent times have understood Isa. vi.13. Many of them have taken into account exegesis of the verse by Christian scholars as well as Jewish tradition, and there has sometimes been a willingness to emend the text. The varied work of Jewish biblical scholars in the past century or so will be illustrated by a few examples.

Three Jewish scholars of the nineteenth century will be considered. First, Luzzatto's commentary on Isaiah, which appeared between 1855 and 1867, makes no explicit reference to the work of contemporary exegetes on Isa. vi.13. He understands *lĕbāʿēr* to mean that the land will be near to destruction (*qĕrōbā liklāyā*). According to him, *bĕšalleket* denotes what the trees cast to earth, namely their fruit, which when planted in the earth will grow into a new plant (*nĕṭīʿā ḥădāšā*). He then follows the Targum, which he quotes, in interpreting *maṣṣebet* to mean *nĕṭīʿā*. Second, Barth (1885) accepts without question the view that *bĕšalleket* and *maṣṣebet* mean, respectively, 'beim Fällen' and 'Wurzelstamm'. He does not, however, accept the opinion that the first part of the verse predicts complete destruction, and here he expresses disagreement with Luzzatto. How could there be complete destruction when Isaiah elsewhere expresses hope for the future, and the last clause of vi.13 itself teaches that 'ein heiliges Stamm' will remain? Moreover, there is no adversative particle, which would have been expected if the first part of the verse had predicted disaster in contrast to the second part's hope. He suggests, therefore that *lĕbāʿēr* here denotes, not destruction, but grazing: the land will again be grazed (cp. xxx.23), and the beginning of the verse is an oracle of hope. Barth fails, however, to do justice to the destructive connotation of *bʿr* when it is used of grazing, and his interpretation of the verse is improbable. If it is rejected, then his own argument for interpreting both parts of the verse in the same way raises a difficulty for accepting the view that the second part was originally a prophecy of hope. If there had been a contrast between the two parts, we might have expected an adversative particle. Third, Graetz, whose textual notes on Isaiah were published posthumously in 1892, suggests two emendations. One of them, the addition of *ʾak* before *kāʾēlā*, supplies an adversative particle. The other is an attempt to solve the problem of the obscure *bĕšalleket* by emending it to *bĕšalhebet*.

Early in the twentieth century (1909), Halévy (pp. 381, 397) follows Giesebrecht (p. 89) in reading *wĕʿad* for *wĕʿōd* to continue the sense begun by *ʿad* in verse 11. He removes the apparent contradiction between the two parts of verse 13 by emending *lĕbāʿēr* to *lišĕʾār* (cp. *tiššāʾēr* in verse 11). *bĕšalleket*, he thinks, does not denote the falling of leaves or branches, or the felling of trees. Instead, he follows Saadya and Ibn Ezra (whom, however, he does not mention) in seeing here a reference to the Temple gate of that name, which was 'connue pour posséder de beaux chênes verts'. He adopts the variant reading *bāh* for *bām*, and changes *maṣṣebet* and *maṣṣabtāh*, respectively, to *maṣṣabtām* and *maṣṣabtōh*:

> De même que le térébinthe et le chêne qui ont leur emplacement fixe à Šaleket.
> De même la semence saint (Israël épuré) aura un emplacement dans elle (à Jérusalem).

Three years later, Ehrlich maintains that *lĕbāʿēr* means 'nicht brennen, sondern wegräumen, säubern' (cp. 1 Kgs xiv.10). The second half of the verse is given up by him as hopelessly corrupt.

We shall now consider four examples of Jewish scholarship of the period since the Second World War. Kaufmann (p. 208) understands the first part of the verse to speak of complete destruction (*klywn gmwr*) and yet maintains that the prophet believed in a remnant. He recognizes that the verse is difficult, but does his best to solve the problem. *bĕšalleket* is understood by him to denote, not the cutting down of a tree, but its being stripped of its leaves, and he refers to the Targum, Rashi and Qimḥi. His interpretation of *maṣṣebet* is presumably derived from the context: it is the skeleton (*šld*) of the tree after its leaves have fallen—and we have seen that Rashi's comment is capable of being understood in such a way. *maṣṣebet bām* is emended by Kaufmann to *maṣṣabtām*. Tur-Sinai (pp. 168–9), like Ibn Ezra (whose name he does not mention), denies that *ʿăśīriyyā* means 'a tenth part' and thinks that the word would have to mean 'a (group of) ten men', and (unlike Ibn Ezra) that such a meaning does not fit the context. Moreover, he asks why the land should be threatened with further punishment when no reason is given. He therefore emends the text to read *rišʿā*: 'And yet there is still *her wickedness* in her; so it shall again be expurged.' His other suggestion is that *maṣṣebet* denotes 'new planting', and he compares the verb *nĕṣab*, 'to plant', in Aramaic and Syriac. The verse, he thinks, refers to 'the new growth to come forth after the trees have been entirely denuded of foliage and fruit'. His words imply that he understands *bĕšalleket* to refer to the shedding of leaves. Although he does not mention the Targum or Peshitta, the resemblance between his understanding of *maṣṣabtāh* and theirs is obvious. Unlike Kaufmann and Tur-Sinai, Hartom does not emend the text. He understands the verse to mean that, although part of the tenth who have survived so far will be destroyed, the destruction will not be complete. The survivors will be like the stump that continues to exist when the rest of the tree has been cut down. The last example is the treatment of the verse in the Jewish Publication Society's recent version, *The Prophets – Nevi'im* (Philadelphia, 1978):

> But while a tenth part yet remains in it, it shall repent. It shall be ravaged like the terebinth and the oak, of which stumps are left even when they are felled: its stump shall be a holy seed.

The resemblance between the renderings of *bĕšalleket* and *maṣṣebet* and those in other modern English versions is worthy of note. On the other hand, the translation of *wĕšābā* and the fact that a full stop is put immediately after it differentiate this version from the others. According to this translation, the tenth part is not completely destroyed, but repentance occurs and there are survivors, just as stumps remain after trees have been felled. It is thus possible to see in the verse a prophecy of a brighter future after judgement.

The text of 1QIsa[a]

A new stage in the discussion of Isa. vi. 13 began for both Jewish and Christian scholars when fresh textual evidence was unexpectedly discovered at Qumran in 1947. Among the scrolls in Cave 1 was a manuscript of Isaiah, which came to be known as Scroll A (in distinction from Scroll B, of which the part containing Isa. vi.13 has not survived) or 1QIsa[a]. Apart from purely orthographical details, its text differs from that of the Massoretes in three ways. First, 1QIsa[a] has *mšlkt* in place of *bšlkt* – and it will be remembered that Michaelis suggested in the eighteenth century that the Hebrew text underlying the LXX had the *hophʿal* participle *mušleket* (a reading later favoured as an emendation by Condamin), and that the Vulgate presupposed the *hiphʿil* participle *mašleket*. The difference between the Qumran manuscript and the MT involves a confusion between the letters *beth* and *mem*, and Friedrich Delitzsch has drawn attention to a number of such examples (pp. 113–14). The Qumran reading is usually pointed *mušleket* and thought to agree either with the feminine singular noun *'ēlā* (though *'allōn* is masculine) or, more probably, if the participle is regarded as a feminine singular with a collective sense (so Driver), with both *'allōn* and *'ēlā* (cp. GK §145*k*). Albright, however, points it *mošlākōt*, a feminine plural participle with the two trees as its subject (and presumably attracted to the gender of the first noun). While it is possible that the obscure *bšlkt* was changed by a scribe to the easier *mšlkt*, it is an attractive hypothesis that the latter reading is original, and that the MT's reading has arisen through confusion between *mem* and *beth*. Worschech (p. 133) prefers the MT because it has the *lectio difficilior*, but an incautious use of that principle could lead to the favouring of any variant in the Hebrew Bible (and Kennicott has listed a large number) that fails to yield sense. Secondly, 1QIsa[a] has *zrʿ hqwdš* instead of *zeraʿ qōdeš*. The Qumran reading differs from the MT only by having the definite article with the noun *qwdš* (apart, of course, from the *plene* spelling) after *zrʿ*, which is in the construct state, and it is difficult to decide whether either reading is inherently more probable than the other. Worschech (pp. 136–7) strangely writes of *hqwdš* as 'the adjective' and wonders why 'the noun it qualifies (*zrʿ*) stands without the article', but the difficulty disappears once the words are correctly defined. Thirdly, where the MT has *bām* or the variant reading *bāh*, 1QIsa[a] has *bmh*, and the word is separated by a space from what follows and so, it may be supposed, is intended to be construed with what follows – and it would be difficult to construe 'in them', which has a masculine plural suffix, with what precedes in a text with the feminine participle *mšlkt*. Sawyer suggests that the first word in the clause *bmh zrʿ hqwdš mṣbth* is the interrogative *bammeh*: 'Wherein is the holy seed? Its stump!' or 'How can the Holy Seed be its stump?' It is also possible, as several scholars have observed, that *bmh* is, like *bām* in the MT, the preposition *b* with the third-person masculine plural suffix. A final *h* is often added after certain suffixes in 1QIsa[a], and we find *bmh* in place of *bm* in xi.6. If so, the scribe intended the clause to mean 'in them [presumably, in the trees] the holy seed is *mṣbth*'. The space before *bmh*, which thus implies a particular understanding of the syntax, may be regarded as evidence for one aspect of an early Jewish interpretation of the verse.

A different explanation of *bmh* has been advanced by some scholars, who identify it with *bāmā*, 'high place', and either ignore the space before it or suggest (so Brownlee, 1964, p. 239) that it did not exist in the original text. Some scholars emend the text, but Hvidberg thinks that good sense can be obtained from the Qumran reading without alteration:

> Like the terebinth and the oak, that lie flung down . . . upon the masseba in the bama. The holy seed is its [the bama's] masseba!

Hvidberg explains the last clause by suggesting that there is a reference to the gardens of Adonis (Isa. xvii.10–11) and that the seed sown in them was thought to be identical with the Canaanite god, who was also identified with the *maṣṣēbā*. In his opinion, 'the prophet contemptuously calls' the holy tree and the *maṣṣēbā* '" the holy seed" of the bama'. His theory is unconvincing. First, he has not justified the use of 'upon' in his translation (cp. Burrows, p. 148). Secondly, his explanation of 'holy seed' is questionable, and it may be doubted whether the prophet who spoke of 'the Holy One of Israel' would have been likely to use the word 'holy' in a contemptuous sense, particularly after hearing the cry of the seraphim in verse 3. Thirdly, Hvidberg does not explain the force of the comparison 'Like', which is not identical in meaning with 'and also'. If the pagan high places were to be destroyed, a prediction of their destruction might have been expected before anything else was compared to the destruction.

Another attempt to make sense of the Qumran text without emendation is made by G.R. Driver. He reads *mušleket miṣṣebet bāmā*, and explains the second word as the preposition *min* with a noun *ṣebet* meaning 'standing, position, site', which is comparable in form to *šebet* from *yšb*. The comparison thus means 'like an oak or a terebinth which is cast away from the site of a high place', and he explains: 'that is, the remnant shall be burnt like the poles from a dismantled high place'. His article does not explain what he thinks about the last clause of the verse, but he once expressed the opinion to me that it means 'sacred seed (thrown out) from its position', and that it is a gloss explaining *ʿăšīriyyā* as well as *ʾēlā* and *ʾallōn*. His explanation of *mṣbt* is conjectural, but it is at least as likely as some other suggestions that have been made. It is interesting to note that Michaelis had earlier suggested that the Hebrew text underlying the LXX may have had either *miṣṣabbātām*, 'Tanquam ex *testudine sua*' (cp. *ṣab* in Num. vii.3), or *miṣṣabtām* from *ṣebet*, 'fasciculus' (cp. Ruth ii.16), and he also compared the Syriac. To return to Driver, he has failed, like Hvidberg before him, to explain how the comparison came to be made.

The other suggestions, which have been made by Brownlee (who was the first, in 1951, to offer a suggestion about the verse on the basis of 1QIsa^{a}'s reading), Iwry, Albright and the New English Bible, all involve conjectural emendation of the consonantal text. Brownlee moves *wkʾlwn* to a position after *mšlkt*: 'As an oak when it is thrown down, //And as the terebinth by the sacred column of a high place'. The others all change the relative particle *ʾšr* to *ʾšrh*, that is, *ʾăšērā*, the goddess Asherah or her symbol. Iwry also puts *w* before it, and then reads *hmšlkt mmṣbt bmh*, 'when flung down from the sacred column of a high place'. Burrows pertinently comments that 'it is hard to see why and how the trees would be flung down from the sacred column or stone pillar' (pp. 142f). Albright's restoration is similar, but he points *k'lh* as *kĕ'ēlā*, 'Like the terebinth goddess', and he reads *mošlākōt bĕmaṣṣĕbōt bāmā*, 'Cast out with the stelae of the high place'. Both Iwry and Albright find the prosaic relative particle *'ăšer* strange in poetry – though it is found in verse 11 and, as Brownlee points out (1964, p. 238), in a number of other places in Isaiah. Albright further sees in *mṣbt* a reference to 'the commemorative stelae of important deceased persons (or of "heroes" who may never have lived on earth at all)' (p. 255), but his theory about the commemorative function of high places has been questioned (see Vaughan, and Barrick). Finally, the New English Bible reads *'ăšērā mušleket miṣṣebet bāmā* (Brockington gives the form *maṣṣebet*, but that is surely a mistake): 'a sacred pole thrown out from its place in a hill-shrine'.

The difficulty with such theories is both their resort to conjectural emendation of the consonantal text (cp. Hasel, p. 236) and, as we have seen, the assumption that the destruction of a high place was something sufficiently common to be a suitable disaster with which the devastation of the people could be compared. Brownlee seeks to meet the second difficulty by suggesting that this part of the chapter reflects what happened, not at Isaiah's call in the year of Uzziah's death, but during Hezekiah's reformation many years later, and Iwry thinks of 'a familiar iconoclastic scene of ancient Palestine' (p. 228; cp. p. 238). It is doubtful whether such iconoclasm was so 'familiar' before Hezekiah's reformation, and the fact that Brownlee needs to resort to the supplementary hypothesis that verse 13 comes from a later time than Isaiah's call does not help his main argument. In any case, it may still be doubted whether the comparison is a natural one.

The reading *mšlkt* in 1QIsa[a] may be correct, but it is questionable whether *bmh* should be understood as a high place and whether the text should be emended conjecturally. Nor does the manuscript shed any direct light on the meaning of *mṣbt*.

The text and meaning of Isaiah vi.13

So far, the present article has sought primarily to describe, and only secondarily to evaluate. Now, however, we must ask whether it is possible to reach any conclusions about the text and meaning of Isa.

vi.13. The variety of opinions expressed over a period of more than two thousand years bears witness to the obscurity of the verse, and no interpretation has established itself as self-evidently right. There is no single, standard tradition about the meaning to serve as a starting-point for exegesis. Further, the discovery of 1QIsa[a] has raised more problems than it has solved. An outline of the history of exegesis has been sketched in the preceding part of the present article, but it will be necessary to mention some further scholars and theories in the detailed discussion of the meaning of the verse that follows.

(1) *The first part of the verse*

We begin with the first part of the verse (as far as *lĕbāʿēr*), which is widely thought to speak of the destruction of the tenth that remains in the land, whether *lĕbāʿēr* is understood to refer to consuming, burning, removing or destroying. The case for such an interpretation is strong, but it is necessary to consider now some attempts to explain the text differently.

We have seen that Barth believed this part of the verse to be a prophecy of hope, a prediction that the land would again be grazed by flocks. A similar interpretation was advanced, apparently independently, by Seierstad in 1946 (pp. 107–9). When the *piʿel* is used of consuming, it normally connotes the destruction of what is consumed, but Seierstad claims that the *hiphʿil* and the *piʿel* do not have such a connotation in Exod. xxii.4; and he may be right, although even there the idea of damaging someone's property is present. Yet the analogy of Isa. v.5 strongly suggests that vi.13 is speaking of damage to the tenth, and the statement that it will be consumed is most naturally understood as a prediction of doom. Further, Seierstad advances three arguments against Duhm's view that the verse speaks of the burning of the tenth. First, *lĕbāʿēr* is not used of burning in Isaiah, and Seierstad believes that the verb in the *piʿel* means 'weiden' in iii.14 and 'abweiden' in v.5. Yet the context implies damage in the latter verse, which is the closest parallel to vi.13, and it is strange that Seierstad does not accept the same meaning here. Moreover, the evidence is insufficient to prove that the *piʿel* cannot mean anything other than 'to graze, pasture' in Isaiah, and that only the *qal* is used for the meaning 'to burn' (quite apart from the possibility of vocalizing the text differently). Seierstad recognizes that the verb does not have precisely the same meanings in iii.14 and v.5, and it may be added that the *piʿel* may denote purification by burning in iv.4. Second, he claims that the meaning 'to burn' does not fit *wĕšābā wĕhāyĕtā lĕbāʿēr*, for the tenth had not been burned before. The meaning may, however, be that there will again be devastation, and so there will be a repetition of disaster, even though a different figure of speech is used to describe the disaster. Third, he claims, it was not the custom to burn the stumps of trees. Even if he is right (and Ahlström, p. 171, thinks differently), he fails to consider the possibility that it was the felled or fallen trunks of the trees, not their stumps, that were burned. Whether or not Duhm is right in believing that *lĕbāʿēr* means 'to burn' in this verse, Seierstad's arguments against him are weak.

A different way of seeing in the beginning of verse 13 a prophecy of hope is to understand *lĕbāʿēr* in an active sense. We have seen that de Dieu's theory that it means that Israel would burn or consume its enemies did not win support in the past. In 1975, Cazelles advanced the comparable theory that the beginning of the verse means 'mais dans (le pays) il y a encore un dixième et il recommencera à brûler' (pp. 104–5). He compared Isa. x.17, xxxi.9, and the light in ix.1, and also the passages that speak of the Davidic dynasty having a lamp in Jerusalem (2 Sam. xxi.17; 1 Kgs xi.36, xv.4; 2 Kgs viii.9). Isa. vi.13 thus speaks of a light that will be beneficial to those who are faithful to the Davidic dynasty, but dangerous for the rebels. Cazelles argues his case well, but it is difficult to accept his interpretation of the verse. First, *bʿr* suggests burning, rather than giving light, and that does not favour the attempt to connect the verse with the lamp of the house of David. Second, it is more natural to interpret vi.13 on the analogy of v.5, and to see in it a prediction of disaster. Third, if Cazelles were right, we should expect the imagery of burning to be developed more fully, as it is in i.31, ix.17, x.17, xxx.27–33, to which he refers. It would be strange if it were introduced suddenly and not developed, and if the verse then turned abruptly to a quite different matter.

We may, therefore, conclude that the first part of verse 13 is a prediction of doom, not of hope. If so, the translation of *wĕšābā* as 'and will repent' must be rejected. The next words are *wĕhāyĕtā lĕbāʿēr* and it is improbable that the verse would say that repentance would be followed immediately by destruction. The understanding of *wĕšābā* as an auxiliary verb is thus confirmed.

A further corollary of the understanding of the first part of the verse as a prediction of disaster is that the comparison with a terebinth and an oak is probably a figure of doom. There is nothing to indicate a contrast between the figure of speech of the trees and the disaster that has just been mentioned, and it is natural to expect a continuation of the same thought.

(2) *The comparison with the trees in the Massoretic Text*

We shall next examine the comparison with the trees in the MT, and it will simplify the discussion if the text of 1QIsa[a] is considered separately later. The comparison begins with the words 'like a terebinth and like an oak', and continues with the relative particle *'ăšer* and two clauses. The first clause may end with *bām* (or the variant reading *bāh*), but we must also consider the possibility that it ends with *maṣṣebet* (as in 1QIsa[a]). If the antecedent of the two readings *bām* and *bāh* is the same, namely the two trees (viewed as a plurality and as a collective, respectively), it makes no difference to the sense which reading is adopted. We note, however, that *maṣṣabtāh* has a third-person feminine singular suffix, and that there is an inconsistency between it and the reading *bām*, with the third-person masculine plural suffix, if both have the same antecedent. The inconsistency would appear less surprising if it were held that a glossator had expanded the verse, for he might not have followed the grammar of the original writer. On the other hand, it is also possible that the antecedent of the feminine singular suffix is *'ăśīriyyā*.

How is *bĕšalleket* to be explained? Although the *hiph'il* of *šlk* can be used of a tree shedding its leaves, such a meaning seems too weak as a figure of speech for the disaster that has just been described. It is more likely that the reference is to the trees being cast down or felled, and such a meaning may be derived without difficulty from the meaning 'to throw, cast'. If *bĕšalleket* consists of a noun denoting the state of being cast down preceded by the preposition *b*, the meaning may be rendered idiomatically in English 'when they have been felled'. The meaning would not be very different if it were thought that *šalleket* is an unusual form of the infinitive construct *pi'el* and that no subject is expressed: 'when (someone) fells (them)'. The meanings of the two ways of understanding the form are thus similar, and it will be convenient to use only one of them, namely, the former, in the following discussion.

If the clause beginning with *'ăšer* ends with *bām* (or *bāh*), it means 'in which is *maṣṣebet* when they have been felled', or the like. If, on the other hand, *bām* does not belong with the words that precede it, the clause is a nominal clause introduced by *'ăšer* without a retrospective pronoun (GK §138*b*) and means 'which are *maṣṣebet* when they have been felled'.

We turn next to *maṣṣebet.* The meaning 'pillar', which the word has in 2 Sam. xviii.18 (where it seems to be a by-form of *maṣṣēbā*), has usually been regarded as inappropriate to the context of Isa. vi.13. Cazelles has, however, recently claimed to find in the verse an allusion to a pillar. He believes that *maṣṣebet* is 'la pierre dynastique qui symbolise la perpétuité de la dynastie' of David (p. 96), and he refers to the *'ammūd* of 2 Kgs xi.14, xxiii.3, and also compares the stone in Isa. xxviii.18 and Zech. iv.7. He translates the MT as follows: 'Comme le chêne et le térébinthe où il y a maṣṣebet lors de l'abattement son maṣṣebet est une ligne sainte.' His rendering of *'ăšer . . . bām* as 'où' presumably gives to *b* the meaning 'at, by'. It is a disadvantage to the theory that that sense of the preposition is rare, and that, of the four examples given in BDB, one (Deut. ii.4) has the meaning 'in', one (1 Sam. xxix.1) is textually uncertain, and the better attested examples are only Ezek. x.15, 20 (and the corresponding expressions in Ezek. i.1, 3, x.22 use *'al*). While Cazelles's translation of Isa. vi.13 is possible, it would be more natural to translate *'ăšer . . . bām* 'in which'. Further, the translation postulates a strange mixture of imagery: a comparison to a pair of trees combined with a statement that the two figurative trees are by a literal, though symbolic, pillar. It is difficult to see how the trees and the pillar are related to each other in the comparison.

If *maṣṣebet* does not mean 'pillar' in Isa. vi.13, does any other meaning that has been suggested fit the context? The theory that it denotes 'substance', 'moisture' or the like is ancient, but it is probably derived chiefly from an understanding of the context as a prophecy of hope. It does not fit the context if it is concerned with disaster, and we have seen that the latter interpretation of the comparison with the trees is more probable.

The theory that *maṣṣebet* is derived from a root cognate with Aramaic *nĕṣab*, 'to plant', goes as far back as the Peshitta and, for *maṣṣabtāh*, the Targum, and we have seen that Tur-Sinai gives to the noun the meaning 'new growth' (cp. the earlier suggestions of Hitzig, Knobel, and Orelli). His theory is regarded as possible by Baumgartner and is favoured in the recent commentary of Wildberger. Although translations of this kind usually involve an understanding of the verse as a prophecy of hope, it is also possible to explain the figure of speech in a context of disaster. If the relative clause means 'on which is new growth when they have been felled', the point of the comparison may be the eating by animals of the new growth on the stump of a tree that has been felled (cp. Job xiv.7–9). On this understanding of *maṣṣebet*, the verb *lĕbā'ēr* denotes eating or grazing. The last clause of the verse is then probably an addition by a later scribe who misunderstood the prophecy as one of hope: 'the holy seed is its new growth'.

The next theory to be considered is that *maṣṣebet* means 'trunk' or 'stump'. It is not difficult to speculate about the way in which the meaning may have developed: what looks like a pillar, what stands up, a place where something stands, etc. Yet it is better to base the argument primarily on the context, rather than on any possible semantic development. Sawyer has argued that the translation 'stump' derives some support from a comparison with the Accadian words *nanṣābu*, *namṣābu*, *nāṣābu*, *nenṣābu*, 'support, post or stand' of wood or other material, but his argument is based on what C. Bezold says in *Babylonisch–Assyrisches Glossar* (Heidelberg, 1926), p. 203, whereas a different understanding of the Accadian words has appeared since Sawyer wrote. W. von Soden, *Akkadisches Handwörterbuch*, vol. II (Wiesbaden, 1972), p. 757, gives the meaning 'Abflussrohr', and the comparison with the Hebrew word must be abandoned.

The theory that *maṣṣebet* means 'trunk' or 'stump' encounters the difficulty of finding a suitable translation for the preposition *b* in *bām* (or *bāh*). If the relative clause ends with *bām*, it may be translated 'in which is a trunk (or stump) when they are felled'. But what is meant by 'in'? A trunk or stump is scarcely 'in' a tree, and it is questionable whether the meaning of the preposition may legitimately be extended to 'of (which . . . remains)' (Hasel, p. 236), 'part of (which)', 'to (which belongs)', or the like. While some such meaning cannot perhaps be excluded, it is not free from difficulty. If the relative clause does not include *bām* and if *maṣṣebet* is understood collectively, it is possible to obtain good sense: 'which are trunks (or stumps) when they have been felled'. It is not, however, so easy to dispose of the difficulty of the preposition, for it is still necessary to explain its meaning in the last clause of the verse: 'in them the holy seed is its [or 'their'] trunk [or 'stump']'. If the last clause is a gloss, it is perhaps easier to understand the preposition. A glossator may have used it in the margin to introduce a reference to the trees, with which his gloss is concerned, and 'in them' may have seemed all right in the circumstances. There is also another possibility. Perhaps the reading *bāh* is original, and the antecedent is *ʿăśîriyyā*: 'in it [i.e. 'the tenth'] its trunk [or 'stump'] is the holy seed'.

The renderings 'trunk' and 'stump' have so far been treated as alternative forms of the same type of theory. Now we must ask whether it is possible to choose between them. The word 'trunk' would be suitable in the clause beginning with *'ăšer* in a prediction of disaster: the trees would be cut down and their trunks removed or destroyed. It would, however, be unsuitable in the last clause of the verse. That clause is probably the work of a glossator, but it is reasonable to suppose that he understood the meaning of *maṣṣebet*, although it is obscure to us. Even if he was desperate to find a message of hope in the verse, it would have been difficult for him to identify the holy seed, on whom the future of the nation depended, with the severed trunk of a tree. It is more likely that a stump would have been seen as a sign of survival and hope for the future. The author of the last clause of the verse is more likely to have understood *maṣṣebet* to mean 'stump' than 'trunk', and it is best to accept the former rendering.

Three types of translation of the MT from *'ăšer* to the end of the verse thus seem possible (apart from sub-divisions depending on the differences between the readings *bām* and *bāh* and between possible antecedents of the third-person feminine singular suffixes):

(1) 'in which is new growth when they have been felled: the holy seed is their [or 'its'] new growth';

(2) 'in which are stumps when they have been felled; the holy seed is their [or 'its'] stump';

(3) 'which are stumps when they have been felled; in them [or 'it'] the holy seed is their [or 'its'] stump'.

Translation 1 probably implies that *lĕbāʿēr* earlier in the verse denotes grazing: the new growth will be eaten by animals. The meanings 'burn', 'remove', and 'destroy' all fit translations 2 and 3. It is not necessary to suppose that the stump was burned, removed, or otherwise destroyed, for the verb may refer to what happened to the rest of the tree, which was cut down leaving only a stump.

While all three translations are possible, the last clause of the verse can again help us to choose among them, for it gives us a reason to prefer either 2 or 3 to 1. If 1 is the meaning, then the person responsible for the last clause misunderstood the earlier part of the verse completely. He thought that the new growth was a sign of hope for the future, whereas it was intended as part of the picture of destruction. The last clause in translations 2 and 3 also implies a departure from the intention of the earlier part of the verse, but not quite a contradiction. If the first part of the comparison with the trees is speaking, not of clearing the ground by rooting out stumps, but of felling wood for fuel or some other purpose, then the point is that the trees were cut down and their trunks and branches removed and, in due course, destroyed. The stump is not the point of comparison and nothing is said about its destruction. The glossator may have correctly understood what was said in the comparison and seen that the existence of a stump was compatible with the hope of survival. That was not the intention of the original text (despite the opinion of Hasel (p. 245) that we have here 'both a symbol of destruction... and a symbol of resurgent life'), but the figure of speech left open the possibility of a future for the stump, and the glossator could believe in such a future without contradicting what was said in the comparison. If it is reasonable to ascribe to the glossator some understanding of what lay before him, even though he changed the purpose of the comparison, then it is more likely that he understood *maṣṣebet* to mean 'stump' than 'new growth'.

(3) *A different vocalization of the consonants of the Massoretic Text*

The discussion of the comparison with the trees has so far followed the standard vocalization of the MT. There is, however, a different tradition of vocalization that is implied by two of the versions, and we shall now consider it with the consonants of the MT. Unless the LXX is merely rendering the Hebrew freely or presupposes a reading *mmṣbth*, it appears to understand *mṣbth* as the preposition *m*(*n*) with a noun *ṣbt* and a third-person feminine singular suffix. The Peshitta understands *mṣbt* in a similar way (apart from the absence of a suffix), though it should be noted that a variant reading *mmṣbt* is recorded by Kennicott. If the *m* of *mṣbt* and *mṣbth* is so understood, and if the existence of a noun *ṣbt* is postulated, it must be asked whether sense can be made of the verse. We recall that Michaelis thought that the LXX and the Peshitta presupposed a noun *ṣebet*, and that Driver postulated its existence in 1QIsa[a]. The latter scholar derived it from the root *yṣb*, but it could also be derived from *nṣb* (cp. *śĕ'ēt* and *nāśā'*). The meaning is unlikely to be the same as that of *ṣĕbātīm*, 'bundles' of grain, in Ruth ii.16, or of the Post-biblical Hebrew *ṣebet*, 'pair, set', or *ṣĕbāt*, 'tongs', which are from the root *ṣbt*, but the meaning 'stump' (which is not the one suggested by Driver) would fit the context. If the existence of such a noun were postulated and if the relative clause were thought to end with *mṣbt*, the sense would be good: 'which have been felled from the stumps'. The trees have been felled, and so the trunk of each tree has been separated from its stump. The next clause would mean 'in them [or 'it'] the holy seed is from their [or 'its'] stumps', that is, the holy seed comes or grows from the stumps.

The translation of *mṣbt* offered above contains the definite article ('the stumps'), although the word is indefinite in Hebrew (it has neither the definite article nor a pronominal suffix). The construction may be similar to the way in which *miššōreš* is used in Job xxviii.9: 'he overturns mountains from (their) roots'. A comparable, though somewhat different, idiom is sometimes found when there is a reference to what has happened since the time when a person was in his mother's womb. While it is possible to say *mēreḥem 'immō* (Num. xii.12), *mibbeṭen 'immō* (Judg. xvi.17; Psalm xxii.11; Job i.21, xxxi.18), *mibbeṭen 'immī* (Eccles. v.14), or *min-habbeṭen* (Judg. xiii.5, 7), it is also possible for the word to be indefinite: *mēreḥem* (Jer. i.15, xx.17; Psalms xxxii.11, lviii.4 and perhaps cx.3; Job iii.11, x.18, xxviii.8), and *mibbeṭen* (Isa. xliv.2, 24, xlviii.8, xlix.1, 5; Hos. ix.11; Psalms xxii.10, lviii.4, lxxi.6; Job iii.11, x.19).

If the existence of a noun *ṣbt*, 'stump' is postulated, and if the consonantal text of the Massoretes is vocalized so as to include it, good sense can be obtained. On the other hand, it has no advantage over the traditional vocalization, and it is unnecessary to postulate the existence of the noun in order to escape the difficulties of the MT.

(4) *The comparison with the trees in 1QIsa[a]*

Whether or not its reading is original, the text of 1QIsa[a] needs to be discussed. It will be assumed in what follows that the reading *mšlkt* is a feminine singular participle with the trees, viewed as a collective, as the subject.

The relative clause consists of the words *'šr mšlkt mṣbt* and is clearly separated from the next clause by a space. The participle has been understood as either a *hiph'il* or a *hoph'al*. Sawyer believes it to be a *hiph'il*, and he offers the translation 'which throws out a stump'; he adds in n. 6: 'The meaning "to throw away or out, cast off (leaving behind as useless)", etc., depends on the meaning of' *mṣbt*. It is not clear precisely what his translation is intended to mean, or how a tree can be said to cast off a stump. The *hiph'il* is also obviously unsuitable if *mṣbt* means 'a pillar', and the sense is not much better if it is said to cast down its own trunk or fresh growth. The participle is probably to be regarded as a *hoph'al*, and three translations deserve consideration. First, the clause may mean 'which are cast down as trunks'; that is, the destruction of the tenth is compared to trees when they are felled (and 'stumps' would be inappropriate in this translation). For the syntax of *mṣbt* see GK § 118*q*, and P. Joüon, *Grammaire de l'hébreu biblique*, 2nd edn (Rome, 1947), §126*c*. Against such a translation stands the argument, which was advanced above, that it creates a difficulty for the last clause, if that clause is understood as a prophecy of hope. Second, Cazelles translates the relative clause 'qui (ont) une massebet quand (ils sont) abattus' (p. 105), but it is difficult to justify 'ont', even in brackets, without adding *lāhem* to the text or at least reading *la'ăšer*. Third, there is Driver's suggestion that *mṣbt* should be parsed as the preposition *mn* with a noun *ṣbt*. The meaning suggested by him for the noun is related to his understanding of *bmh* as a high place, which was seen above to be improbable, but the translation of *ṣbt* 'stump' was proposed as an alternative. Although the postulating of a noun *ṣbt* offers no help in explaining the MT – and it was not Driver's intention that it should – it can make sense of the relative clause in 1QIsa[a]: 'which are cast down from their stumps'. Indeed, it has the advantage of avoiding the difficulties of the other proposed translations.

The interpretation of the last clause in the verse depends partly on the way in which *bmh* is translated. The theory that it means 'high place' has been rejected, for none of the proposed translations yields a satisfactory meaning – and the scholars who adopt the meaning but emend the text have abandoned the task of translating what is actually found in 1QIsa[a]. Sawyer's suggestion that *bmh* is the interrogative particle *bammeh* is possible. One of the two translations he mentions, 'How can the Holy Seed be its stump?', is suggested by him only as an interpretation of the text by the Qumran sect as an ironical and polemical question concerning the claim of the Jerusalem hierarchy to be the remnant – and the suggestion may be right. It is not suggested by him as the original meaning of the text, which he believes to be 'Wherein is the holy seed? Its stump!' Such a translation is possible, but an objection arises from the difficulty in finding a satisfactory translation of *mṣbt* in the previous clause unless it means 'from the stumps'. If the *mem* is the preposition meaning 'from', it is surprising to find it in an answer to a question introduced by *bmh*, 'Wherein ...?' We should expect an answer with the preposition *b*, that is, *bṣbth*, 'In its stump!' The other way of understanding *bmh*, namely, that it is, like the MT's *bām*, the preposition *b* with a third-person masculine plural suffix, results in the translation 'in them the holy seed is its stump' or, if the probable view that the *m* of *mṣbth* is a preposition is accepted, 'in them the holy seed comes from its stump'.

The most satisfactory way of understanding the text of 1QIsa[a] (apart from a possible reinterpretation in a polemical sense by the Qumran sect) is to postulate the existence of a noun *ṣbt* (as Driver has suggested). The last two clauses of the verse may then be translated: 'which are cast down from their stumps; in them the holy seed comes from its stump'.

(5) *Which text is more original?*

Of the four differences between the MT and 1QIsa[a], two probably have little significance for an attempt to determine the original text. If *bmh* in 1QIsa[a] is understood as *b* with the third-person masculine plural suffix, it merely illustrates the tendency of the manuscript to add *h* at the end of certain pronominal suffixes and is identical in meaning with the MT's *bām*. It does, however, attest the antiquity of the reading *bm*(*h*) in contrast to the variant reading *bāh*. It may be suspected that the space before *bmh* in the manuscript reflects an interpretation of the text at the time of the scribe, rather than being a faithful continuation of a tradition going back to the author of the verse. The division of clauses may, nevertheless, correspond to the intention of the original writer, and the MT is capable of being understood in the same way. The *plene* spelling of *hqwdš* is another instance of the orthographic character of 1QIsa[a]. Its use of the definite article is a more substantial difference from the MT's *qōdeš*, but it makes little difference to the meaning whether or not the definite article is used, and it is difficult to tell which is inherently more probable in this context, though 1QIsa[a]'s reading may be an assimilation to Ezra ix.2. The most important variant in the verse is the spelling *mšlkt* in contrast to the MT's *bšlkt*. The former reading is easier in that the *hiph'il* is found elsewhere, whereas the latter is a *hapax legomenon* and its use here is awkward. Whether the conclusion to be drawn is that the more usual form is more likely to be original, or that the unusual form is more likely to have been changed to the usual form in 1QIsa[a], is impossible to determine. If *mšlkt* is more original, it is best to follow Driver and understand the *m* at the beginning of *mṣbt* as a preposition (cp. the LXX and the Peshitta).

In the last resort, it is impossible to be sure whether *bšlkt* or *mšlkt* is more original. A scholar must be content to do his best to find satisfactory translations and explanations of both readings.

(6) *The last clause of the verse*

The opinion of many modern commentators that the last clause of the verse is secondary was accepted above because of the contrast between its implied hope and the unrelieved gloom of the beginning of the verse. To hold that the clause is an addition is not necessarily to be committed to the opinion that Isaiah never hoped for a better future, for it is possible to see in Isa. vi.11–13 a prophecy of complete disaster and yet not to press the logic of the passage so far as to exclude any trace of hope elsewhere. The phrase *zera' qōdeš*, 'holy seed', recalls *zera' haqqōdeš* in Ezra ix.2, where it is used of the Jewish community after the Exile, and it would be compatible with, although it does not demand, a post-exilic date for the end of Isa. vi.13 – and it is strange that Seeligmann (pp. 63–4) appears to regard the verse in Ezra as evidence for the pre-exilic date of the end of the verse in Isaiah. The view that the clause is an addition is not based on its alleged omission from the Hebrew text implied by the LXX, for the reason given above. On the other hand, it would be absurd to go to the other extreme and follow Engnell in regarding the LXX as 'wholly conclusive proof that the whole expression in question was there from the beginning' (p. 15); he gives no reason for supposing that no addition could have been made to the Hebrew text before the time of the LXX.

Conclusions

The principal conclusions of this discussion of the text and meaning of Isa. vi.13 may now be summarized, and it need scarcely be said that they are no more than tentative. No choice is offered between the readings *bām* and *bāh*, and the question of the antecedents of the suffixes on *bāh* and *maṣṣabtāh* is left open. Nor is a choice made between the readings of the MT and 1QIsa[a], but interpretations of both texts are suggested. Since it is possible to translate both texts, it has been unnecessary to discuss all the emendations that have been proposed, though some have been mentioned in passing.

The conclusions are as follows:

(1) The first part of the verse describes the destruction of the tenth part of the people, who have survived so far. *wĕšābā* is used as an auxiliary verb and does not speak of repentance; *lĕbāʿēr* denotes burning or some other kind of destruction.

(2) The comparison with the trees probably goes with what precedes and was originally intended to illustrate destruction, not survival.

(3) The MT from *kāʾēlā* to the end of the verse is best translated either

> like a terebinth and like an oak in which are stumps when they have been felled; the holy seed is their [or 'its'] stump
>
> or
>
> like a terebinth and like an oak which are stumps when they have been felled; in them [or 'it'] the holy seed is their [or 'its'] stump.

(4) The theory that the words *maṣṣebet* and *maṣṣabtāh* have been wrongly vocalized and that the *m* represents the preposition *min*, 'from', (cp. the LXX and the Peshitta) followed by a noun *ṣbt* offers no help in understanding the traditional consonantal text, but may well be right for the text of 1QIsa[a].

(5) The text of 1QIsa[a] from *kʾlh* to the end of the verse is best translated 'like a terebinth and like an oak which are cast down from their stumps; in them the holy seed comes from its stump'.

(6) The last clause of the verse is probably a later addition intended to modify the preceding prophecy of destruction by allowing for the survival of the holy seed. The addition is not, however, as blatant a contradiction of the earlier part of the verse as is often believed. The comparison with the trees was originally concerned with the destruction of the branches and trunks, and not with what happened to the stumps. The later writer saw that the mention of the stumps left open the possibility of survival and hope for the future.

LIST OF WORKS CITED

G.W. Ahlström, 'Isaiah vi. 13', *JSS* 19 (1974), 169–72.

W.F. Albright, 'The high place in ancient Palestine', *Volume du Congrès: Strasbourg 1956*, SVT 4 (Leiden, 1957), pp. 242–58.

W. Boyd Barrick, 'The funerary character of "high-places" in ancient Palestine: a reassessment', *VT* 25 (1975), 565–95.
J. Barth, *Beiträge zur Erklärung des Jesaia* (Karlsruhe–Leipzig, 1885).
W. Baumgartner (and L. Koehler), *Hebräisches und aramäisches Lexicon zum Alten Testament*, 3rd edn, fasc. 2 (Leiden, 1974).
L.H. Brockington, *The Hebrew Text of the Old Testament. The Readings Adopted by the Translators of the New English Bible* (Oxford–Cambridge, 1973).
W.H. Brownlee, 'The text of Isaiah vi 13 in the light of DSIa', *VT* 1 (1951), 296–8.
The Meaning of the Qumrân Scrolls for the Bible with Special Attention to the Book of Isaiah (New York, 1964), pp. 236–40.
K. Budde, 'Über die Schranken, die Jesajas prophetischer Botschaft zu setzen sind', *ZAW* 41 (1923), 154–203.
M. Burrows, *More Light on the Dead Sea Scrolls* (New York–London, 1958).
J. Calvin, *Commentarii in Isaiam Prophetam*, Corpus Reformatorum 64 (Brunswick, 1888).
H. Cazelles, 'La vocation d'Isaïe (ch. 6) et les rites royaux', in A. Alvarez Verdes and E.J. Alonso Hernandez (eds.), *Homenaje a Juan Prado* (Madrid, 1975), pp. 89–108.
T.K. Cheyne, *The Book of the Prophet Isaiah. A New English Translation* (London–New York–Stuttgart, 1898).
A. Condamin, *Le livre d'Isaïe* (Paris, 1905).
Franz Delitzsch, *Commentar über das Buch Jesaia*, 4th edn (Leipzig, 1889).
Friedrich Delitzsch, *Die Lese- und Schreibfehler im Alten Testament* (Berlin–Leipzig, 1920).
J. and H. Derenbourg, *Version arabe d'Isaïe de R. Saadia Ben Josef Al-Fayyoûmî, Oeuvres Complètes*, vol. III (Paris, 1896).
L. de Dieu, *Animadversiones in Veteris Testamenti Libros omnes* (Leiden, 1648).
A. Dillmann, *Der Prophet Jesaia* (Leipzig, 1890).
G.R. Driver, 'Isaiah i–xxxix: textual and linguistic problems', *JSS* 13 (1968), 36–57.
B. Duhm, *Das Buch Jesaia* (Göttingen, 1892).
A.B. Ehrlich, *Randglossen zur hebräischen Bibel*, vol. IV (Leipzig, 1912).
I. Engnell, *The Call of Isaiah* (Uppsala–Leipzig, 1949).
H. Ewald, *Die Propheten des Alten Bundes*, 2nd edn, vol. I (Göttingen, 1867).
F. Field, *Origenis Hexaplorum quae supersunt* (Oxford, 1875).
F. Foreiro (Forerius), *Jesaiae Prophetae vetus et nova ex Hebraico versio* (Venice, 1563).
W. Gesenius, *Der Prophet Jesaia* (Leipzig, 1820–1).
W. Gesenius and F. Buhl, *Hebräisches und aramäisches Handwörterbuch*

über das Alte Testament, 17th edn (Leipzig, 1915).
F. Giesebrecht, *Beiträge zur Jesaiakritik* (Göttingen, 1890).
H. Graetz (ed. W. Bacher), *Emendationes in plerosque Sacrae Scripturae Veteris Testamenti Libros*, fasc. 1 (Breslau, 1892).
G.B. Gray, *Isaiah I–XXVII* (Edinburgh, 1912).
J. Halévy, ' Recherches bibliques. Le livre d'Isaïe (*Suite.*) ', *Revue sémitique* 17 (1909), 363–401.
E.S. Hartom, *spr yšʿyhw* (Tel-Aviv, 1969).
G.F. Hasel, *The Remnant. The History and Theology of the Remnant Idea from Genesis to Isaiah*, 2nd edn (Berrien Springs, 1974).
F. Hitzig, *Der Prophet Jesaja* (Heidelberg, 1833).
F. Hvidberg, 'The Masseba and the Holy Seed', *Interpretationes ad Vetus Testamentum pertinentes Sigmundo Mowinckel septuagenario Missae* (Oslo, 1955), pp. 97–9.
S. Iwry, ' *Maṣṣēbāh* and *bāmāh* in 1Q Isaiah^A 6 13', *JBL* 76 (1957), 225–32.
Jerome, *Commentariorum in Esaiam Libri I–XI*, Corpus Christianorum Series Latina 73 (Turnhout, 1963).
Y. Kaufmann, *twldwt h'mwnh hyśr'lyt*, vol. III, bk 1 (Tel-Aviv, 1947).
B. Kennicott, *Vetus Testamentum Hebraicum cum variis lectionibus* (Oxford, 1776–80).
A. Knobel, *Der Prophet Jesaia* (Leipzig, 1843).
J. Le Clerc (Clericus), *Veteris testamenti Prophetae, ab Esaia ad Malachiam usque* (Antwerp, 1622).
H.G. Liddell and R. Scott (ed. H.S. Jones and R. McKenzie), *A Greek–English Lexicon*, 9th edn (Oxford, 1940).
R. Lowth, *Isaiah* (London, 1778).
S.D. Luzzatto, *Il Profeta Isaia* (Padua, 1855–67).
K. Marti, *Das Buch Jesaja* (Tübingen–Freiburg i. B.–Leipzig, 1900).
J.D. Michaelis, *Deutsche Uebersetzung des Alten Testaments*, vol. VIII (Göttingen, 1779).
Supplementa ad lexica hebraica (Göttingen, 1792).
Nicolaus of Lyra, *Textus Biblie* (Basel, 1506–8), vol. IV.
C. von Orelli, *Die Propheten Jesaja und Jeremia* (Nördlingen, 1887).
R.R. Ottley, *The Book of Isaiah According to the Septuagint (Codex Alexandrinus)*, vols. I and II (Cambridge, 1904 and 1906).
PESHITTA: the Urmia edition of 1852 and G. Diettrich, *Ein Apparatus criticus zur Pešitto zum Propheten Jesaia* (Giessen, 1905).
D. Qimḥi: L. Finkelstein, *The Commentary of David Kimhi on Isaiah* (New York, 1926).
T. Roorda, 'Annotatio ad Vaticiniorum Iesaiae Cap. I–IX:6', in T.G.J. Juynboll, T. Roorda and H.E. Weijers (eds.), *Orientalia*, vol. I (Amsterdam, 1840), pp. 65–174.
J. Sawyer, 'The Qumran reading of Isaiah 6, 13', *Annual of the Swedish Theological Institute* 3 (1964), 111–13.

I.L. Seeligmann, *The Septuagint Version of Isaiah* (Leiden, 1948).
P. Seierstad, *Die Offenbarungserlebnisse der Propheten Amos, Jesaja und Jeremia* (Oslo, 1946).
SEPTUAGINT: J. Ziegler, *Isaias* (Göttingen, 1939) – *see also* Ottley.
J. Skinner, *The Book of the Prophet Isaiah Chapters I–XXXIX*, 2nd edn (Cambridge, 1915).
TARGUM: A. Sperber, *The Bible in Aramaic*, vol. III (Leiden, 1962).
N.H. Tur-Sinai, 'A contribution to the understanding of Isaiah i–xii', in C. Rabin (ed.), *Studies in the Bible*, Scripta Hierosolymitana 8 (Jerusalem, 1961), pp. 154–88.
P.H. Vaughan, *The Meaning of 'bāmâ' in the Old Testament* (Cambridge, 1974).
C. Vitringa, *Commentarius in librum prophetiarum Jesaiae* (Leeuwarden, 1714).
G.W. Wade, *The Book of the Prophet Isaiah*, 2nd edn (London, 1929).
H. Wildberger, *Jesaja*, vol. I (Neukirchen–Vluyn, 1972).
VULGATE: R. Weber *et al.* (eds.), *Biblia Sacra iuxta Vulgatam versionem*, 2nd edn (Stuttgart, 1975).
U.F.C. Worschech, 'The problem of Isaiah 6: 13', *Andrews University Seminary Studies* 12 (1974), 126–38.

Terra Sancta and the Territorial Doctrine of the Targum to the Prophets[1]

ROBERT P. GORDON

It is not difficult to understand why the concept of 'the land' is one of the dominant notes in the Hebrew Bible. The tradition of a promise of territory for Abraham's descendants was already old by the time the patriarchal stories began to be written down;[2] when in the fullness of time those descendants created a kingdom and then an empire for themselves, the tradition assumed still greater significance as 'a formative, dynamic, seminal force in the history of Israel'.[3] Possession of 'the land' became a visible sign of the unique relationship between God and Israel. Israel was the land of the divine presence, and even when this land proved as vulnerable to Assyrian depredations as any other in the Near East, the idea of 'the land of the presence' was perpetuated, albeit now in the myth of the inviolability of Zion. In 587 B.C. both Zion and the myth were destroyed by the Babylonian forces of Nebuchadrezzar II, but the concept of 'the land' lived on, and in the rabbinic period we find it being developed and applied in new and sometimes surprising ways.

As I have noted elsewhere, some rabbinical authorities saw fit to introduce the territorial factor into their discussions of the subject of resurrection.[4] So close was the link between resurrection and 'the

1 The following abbreviations have been used in addition to those listed at the beginning of this volume: DSS (Dead Sea Scrolls); PTg (Palestinian Targum); Tg (Targum); TJ (Targum Jonathan to the Prophets, ed. A. Sperber); TO (Targum Onqelos to the Pentateuch, ed. Sperber); PsJ (Targum Pseudo-Jonathan, ed. M. Ginsburger).

2 Cp. R.E. Clements, *Abraham and David* (London, 1967). For a recent discussion of the pentateuchal promises in relation to 'the land' see D.J.A. Clines, *The Theme of the Pentateuch* (Sheffield, 1978).

3 W.D. Davies, *The Gospel and the Land: Early Christianity and Jewish Territorial Doctrine* (Berkeley–Los Angeles–London, 1974), p. 18.

4 'The Targumists as Eschatologists', *SVT* 29 (1978), 117–21.

land' in some minds that R. Eleazar ben Pedat could deny the privilege of resurrection to Israelites buried beyond the borders of Israel (BT Ket. 111*a*). The lengths to which exegesis could go in order to accommodate this view can be seen in Tg Song of Songs viii.5, where it is suggested that deceased expatriate Israelites would, on the day of resurrection, be conducted to the Mount of Olives by means of underground channels. The problem of the expatriate is also addressed in the fragment of Palestinian Targum to Ezek. xxxvii published by A. Díez Macho in 1958.[5] Here too it is asserted that Israelites buried abroad will participate in the resurrection.[6] But territorial considerations affected other equally important areas of Jewish belief and practice, and it is the purpose of this essay to examine three of these with particular reference to the Targum to the Prophets.

(1) Land and cult

TJ is a keen advocate of the law of the central sanctuary (cp. Deut. xii.5ff), even to the extent of compensating for the apparent lapses of the MT in this connection. Only in 'the land', and specifically in Jerusalem, were sacrifices to be offered to the God of Israel. The targumic commitment to this view probably accounts for its modification of the MT at Jonah i.16 where, instead of saying that the sailors on board the ship of Tarshish 'offered a sacrifice to the LORD', TJ avers only that they 'promised to offer a sacrifice before the LORD'. We can be sure that TJ is not concerned merely with the question of the availability of a sacrifice there and then aboard ship, so much as with the unwelcome suggestion that Gentile idolaters offered sacrifice to Israel's God, and on a profane altar.[7] Considerations of this sort will have given rise to the tradition that the mariners' sacrifice consisted of the blood of their circumcision:

> They returned to Joppa and went up to Jerusalem and circumcised the flesh of their foreskins, as it is said, 'And the men feared the LORD exceedingly; and they offered a sacrifice unto the LORD.' Did they

5 'Un segundo fragmento del Targum Palestinense a los Profetas', *Biblica* 39 (1958), 198–205.

6 Cp. especially verse 11.

7 Cp. É. Levine, *The Aramaic Version of Jonah* (Jerusalem, 1975), p. 70. P. Churgin, *Targum Jonathan to the Prophets* (New Haven, 1927), p. 113, notes how TJ differentiates in its terminology between Israelite and pagan altars.

offer sacrifice? But this (sacrifice) refers to the blood of the covenant of circumcision, which is like the blood of a sacrifice.[8]

On the other hand, Naaman's professed intention of offering burnt offerings and sacrifices to the LORD when he returned to his native Syria appears with minimal alteration in TJ (2 Kgs v.17). The Targum, introducing its own brand of 'Name Theology', simply substitutes 'to the name of the LORD' for the MT's 'to the LORD'. Whether this is a substantive difference is difficult to tell; normally TJ speaks of offering sacrifice 'before the LORD' (cp. 1 Sam. vii.9; 2 Sam. vi.17). However, targumic scruples could not be denied amid such uncertainties, and the record is put straight in an alternative version of 2 Kgs v.19, which has survived in the margin of Codex Reuchlinianus.[9] Elisha, according to this version, informed Naaman that altars in non-Israelite territory were ritually unclean but that he could, if he wished, send his offerings each year to 'the place which [the LORD] has chosen to place his name there' and they would be accepted. The reference to the name of the LORD is interesting in view of our observation about the standard Targum's treatment of verse 17, but there are insufficient grounds for thinking of an 'abridgement theory' of the type advanced by Grelot in connection with the tosephtic Targum to Zech. ii.14f.[10]

The question of the proper location of cultic activity is also raised by Mal. i.11: 'For from the rising of the sun to its setting my name is great among the nations, and in every place incense is offered to my name, and a pure offering; for my name is great among the nations, says the LORD of hosts.' If, as our translation suggests, the prophet is speaking of a present reality, is he referring to Gentiles worshipping God in ignorance, or is he thinking of the worship of the Jewish Diaspora?[11] In either case the territorial factor is involved. For all that modern commentators have tended to credit Malachi with a universalist outlook, TJ plies in the opposite direction: 'and on every occasion when you fulfil my will I hear your

8 *Pirkê de Rabbi Eliezer*, ch. 10 (Eng. trans., G. Friedlander (London, 1916), p. 72)

9 W. Bacher, 'Kritische Untersuchungen zum Prophetentargum', *ZDMG* 28 (1874), 17ff, lists this reading among several that cannot be traced to a known midrashic source.

10 P. Grelot, 'Une Tosephta targoumique sur Zacharie, II, 14–15', *RB* 73 (1966), 197–211. Fundamental criticisms of Grelot's argumentation are presented by R. Kasher in 'The Targumic Additions to the *Haphtara* for the Sabbath of Ḥannuka' (Hebrew), *Tarbiẓ* 45 (1975–6), 27–45.

11 See J.G. Baldwin, 'Malachi 1 : 11 and the Worship of the Nations in the Old Testament', *Tyndale Bulletin* 23 (1972), 117–24.

prayer and my great name is hallowed on your account, and your prayer is like a pure offering before me'. TJ has thus dismissed the question of location by substituting 'occasion' for 'place', and the effect is reinforced by the equation of 'incense' with 'prayer'. For the targumist there is no question of Gentile worship being acceptable to God, nor can he allow the unique cultic status of Jerusalem to be compromised. It is a matter of theological orthodoxy, and the fact that *Didache* XIV.3 has 'in every place and time' in its paraphrase of Mal. i.11 scarcely requires the conclusion that there was a variant reading, which is otherwise attested only in TJ.[12] Theological considerations of a different kind account for the wording of *Didache*, for Mal. i.11 was a pliant text for Christians as well as for Jews in the early centuries of the common era.

Cultic and territorial issues inevitably confronted the targumists when they came to deal with Isa. xix.18. The MT speaks of five cities in the land of Egypt whose inhabitants would in a future day speak 'the language of Canaan'. One of these cities is named, though the ancient texts disagree over the form of the name. The MT has 'city of destruction (*heres*)'; 1QIsa[a], some Hebrew manuscripts and Symmachus have 'city of the sun (*ḥeres*)', while TJ appears to combine both readings in 'the city, Beth-shemesh [literally 'house of the sun'], which is to be destroyed'. The LXX ploughs a lonely furrow with πόλις ασεδεκ ('city of righteousness'), almost certainly influenced by Isa. i.26. It would seem that, to some degree, these variants reflect differing attitudes to the Jewish temple erected *c*. 160 B.C. by Onias IV, at Leontopolis in Egypt.[13] Josephus' account of the circumstances in which the temple was built makes it plain that Isa. xix.18 was popularly regarded as having a bearing on Onias' venture; indeed he represents Onias as quoting from Isa. xix to back up his request to the Ptolemy for permission to build (*Ant*. XIII.3.1 (68)).

Obviously the LXX – and its *Vorlage*, for πόλις ασεδεκ points to a Hebrew original – looked upon this development favourably, as would be expected of a work originating in Alexandria. Enthusiasm for the Onias temple is also expressed in the *Sibylline Oracles* (bk 5, lines 492–511), and in M. Menaḥ. 13.10 it is even suggested that

12 Cp. my note, 'Targumic Parallels to Acts XIII 18 and Didache XIV 3', *Novum Testamentum* 16 (1974), 287ff.

13 Cp. M. Delcor, 'Le temple d'Onias en Égypte: Réexamen d'un vieux problème', *RB* 75 (1968), 201. On the problems raised by Josephus' accounts of the Onias temple see V. Tcherikover, *Hellenistic Civilization and the Jews* (New York, 1974), pp. 275–81.

sacrifices offered at Leontopolis were, in certain circumstances, valid. But there are also indications of hostility towards this rival to the Jerusalem Temple. The circumstances in which the project was launched were short of ideal, for, as Josephus notes, Onias cherished a grudge against the Jerusalem authorities who had banished him from the city, and thought that he could create a following for himself by establishing a rival centre of worship (*War* VII.10.3 (431)). Disapproval of the Onias temple appears to be expressed by the MT at Isa. xix.18, where the original reading almost certainly was 'city of the sun'. The alteration in the consonantal Hebrew text is slight and of a kind sometimes made in pursuit of an exegetical point.[14] Strictly, 'city of the sun' would correspond to Heliopolis, the ancient centre of Egyptian sun-worship, but Leontopolis was 'in the nome of Heliopolis', according to Josephus, and would therefore come within the terms of Isa. xix.18 in the reckoning of ancient translators and exegetes.[15]

As has already been noted, TJ possibly shows awareness of the two readings, 'city of the sun' and 'city of destruction', though the fact that the Targums sometimes insert a clause such as 'which is to be destroyed' must also be taken into account. At all events it is scarcely to be doubted that TJ is predicting the destruction of Leontopolis, and if we are guided by other passages in which the devastation of cities or countries is predicted with the use of the formula *ʿĕtīd lĕ* we shall conclude that here too it is used with hostile intent (cp. PTg Gen. xv.12; Tg Isa. xxi.9; Tg Zech. iv.7 (Sperber's manuscript *c*)). Even in Tg Jer. ii.12, where the prediction concerns Israel and the Temple in Jerusalem, the idea of judgement predominates. So we have another instance of the territorial doctrine of TJ at work: 'Jerusalem is the place where men ought to worship' (John iv.20).

It is known from Josephus' account of the First Jewish War that the Onias temple was destroyed by the Romans *c.* A.D. 73, as a measure to prevent further outbreaks of rebellion among the Jewish population in Egypt (*War* VII.10.4 (433–6)). Is it therefore to be concluded that Tg Isa. xix.18, for which the destruction appears to lie in the future, assumed its present form before A.D. 73? Tg Isa. xxi.9 was used in this kind of way by Pinkhos Churgin when he attempted to settle the question of the dating of the final redaction

14 For an example involving the same consonants see BT Yoma 76*b*.

15 On, the Hebrew equivalent of Egyptian *'Iwnw* (Greek Heliopolis), is transliterated in the 'official' Targums (cp. Gen. xli.45, 50; xlvi.20; Ezek. xxx.17).

of TJ.[16] Or is it possible that, as at Jer. ii.12, TJ is speaking from the standpoint of the prophet whose message it is interpreting? There can be no certain answer to this question; the most that can be said is that a date before A.D. 73 for the composition of Tg Isa. xix.18 is a possibility.

(2) The land and prophecy

The territorial doctrine of the rabbis also figured in their discussions of prophecy and the canonical prophets. Some rabbis upheld the view that prophecy was a medium of revelation intended for use within Israel and nowhere else. Jonah i.3 was quoted to show that the divine presence was restricted to Israel, but others enlisted Psalm cxxxix.7–12 and Amos ix.2ff in support of the opposite view.[17] However, the strongest objection to this territorial circumscription of prophecy lay in the fact that Jeremiah, Ezekiel and Jonah prophesied outside ' the land '. One of the answers offered in solution of this problem was that extra-territorial prophecies were special concessions granted because certain conditions had been fulfilled, such as that the vision was experienced in a ' pure ' place, for example beside water (cp. Dan. viii.2, x.4; Ezek. i.3).

Some rabbis reconciled the territorial view with the undoubted fact that prophets occasionally did prophesy abroad by declaring that once a prophet had prophesied on the *terra sancta* of Israel it was permissible for him to fulfil his vocation in foreign parts. Jeremiah certainly satisfied this condition, since his Egyptian pronouncements (Jer. xliii–xliv) came after a long period of prophetic activity in Judah.

Ezekiel presented more of a problem. In its present form the book that bears his name seems to allow only a Babylonian ministry; viii.3–xi.24 are no exception, for the prophet's trip to Jerusalem was of a visionary nature. So it was propounded that Ezekiel had already functioned as a prophet in Judah before he received his visions in Babylonia. Exegetical support for this idea was furnished from Ezek. i.3 where the words *hāyō hāyā* were interpreted to mean, '[the word of the LORD] had come [i.e. in Palestine] and came [i.e. now

16 Pp. 28f. Churgin's views on the final redaction of TJ are rejected by S.H. Levey in his article 'The Date of Targum Jonathan to the Prophets', *VT* 21 (1971), 186–96.

17 Cp. *Mekilta*, Pisḥa 1 (ed. J. Z. Lauterbach (Philadelphia, 1933–5), vol. I, pp. 4–7); see also BT Mo'ed Qaṭan 25*a*. See P. Schäfer, *Die Vorstellung vom heiligen Geist in der rabbinischen Literatur* (Munich, 1972).

in Babylonia]', the infinitive absolute being given the force of a pluperfect.[18] This is quite illuminating when we turn to Tg Ezek. i.3. For the MT's 'The word of the LORD came to Ezekiel the priest, the son of Buzi, in the land of the Chaldeans' the Targum has: 'A word of prophecy from before the LORD was with Ezekiel the priest, the son of Buzi, in the land of Israel; it returned a second time and spoke with him in the province of the land of the Chaldeans.'[19] It is clear that the earliest Targum texts had no direct equivalent of *hāyō*, but it is equally evident that the targumic assurance that Ezekiel first prophesied in Israel has a great deal to do with the explanation of the infinitive absolute given in the *Mekilta*. And it is the Targum's commitment to territorial doctrine that accounts for its divergence from the MT.

The prophetic ministry of Jonah, as described in the canonical book, was also exercised beyond the borders of Israel. In this case, however, TJ leaves territorial considerations alone. The probable explanation is that Jonah's mission to Nineveh was held to have been undertaken after the prophesying attributed to him in 2 Kgs xiv.25.[20] Jonah's utterances concerning the expansion of Israel under Jeroboam II were not unreasonably regarded as having been made within 'the land'. It is interesting in this connection to note Levine's suggestion that, in translating the MT's 'ship of Tarshish' by 'a ship that was going on the sea' (Jonah i.3; cp. iv.2) TJ 'may also be reflecting the midrash tradition that Jonah fled to the sea due to his primitive conception of divine revelation not taking place there' (p. 56; see n. 7 above). The difficulty with this is that, as Levine himself notes, the Targums commonly translate 'Tarshish' by 'sea' (cp. Isa. ii.16, xxiii.14), and Jerome is aware of the same exegetical tradition: 'naues Tharsis: id est maris' (Commentary on Jonah i.3). There is the further consideration that the targumic rendering has recently been commended as preserving something of the original sense of 'Tarshish'.[21] C.H. Gordon explains the word as originally meaning 'red', cognate with the Coptic *trošreš*. He also connects it with the Hebrew *tīrōš* ('wine') and compares the

18 *Mekilta*, *loc. cit.* (ed. Lauterbach, vol. I, p. 6). This separation of the infinitive absolute and the accompanying finite verb forms part of the hermeneutical stock-in-trade of the Targums (cp. TO Exod. xxxiv.7; Tg Nahum i.3).

19 For a similar type of explanatory expansion see Tg Nahum i.1.

20 So *Pirḳê de Rabbi Eliezer* (Eng. trans., Friedlander, p. 65); see also BT Yebam. 98*a*.

21 C.H. Gordon, 'The Wine-Dark Sea', *JNES* 37 (1978), 51ff.

common Homeric epithet for the sea, οἶνοψ ('wine-dark'): 'Both *taršîš* and *oinops* are reflexes of an ancient East Mediterranean tradition where the sea was called wine-dark.'

(3) The land and the future

In rabbinic thinking Israel would not only occupy a special position in the messianic age or World to Come but would also extend its boundaries as in its imperial heyday. This expectation is summed up in Tg Mal. i.5: 'And your eyes shall behold, and you shall say, "Great is the glory of the LORD *who has extended* [MT 'beyond'] the border of Israel."'

But first let us observe the unique status accorded to Israel in the new age by Tg Mic. vii.14. To appreciate the manner in which TJ has adapted the MT to suit its own purpose it will be useful to set out the respective Hebrew and Aramaic versions in translation. The MT reads:

> Shepherd thy people with thy rod, the flock of thy inheritance, who dwell alone in a forest in the midst of a garden land; let them pasture in Bashan and Gilead as in the days of old.

In TJ this becomes:

> Sustain thy people by thy Word, the tribe of thy inheritance; in the world which is to be renewed they shall dwell by themselves; those who were [or, 'for they were'] desolate in the forest shall be settled in Carmel, they shall be sustained in the land of Bashan and Gilead as in the days of old.

Exactly the same idea is propounded in TO at Deut. xxxii.12, with perhaps even less support from the MT: 'The LORD will settle them by themselves in the world which is to be renewed, and the worship of idols shall not be established before him.'[22] And TO returns to the same theme at Deut. xxxiii.28 (manuscripts). The expectation that the world will be renewed is voiced elsewhere in the Targums (cp. Tg Jer. xxiii.23; Tg Hab. iii.2); in the case of Mic. vii.14 its introduction has the effect of converting the prophet's depiction of the plight of Israel, surrounded by predacious enemies, into a picture of future prosperity when the nation will have taken possession of all the territory to which it laid claim (cp. Jer. 1.19). B. Stade's interpretation of the MT as a prayer for the separation of Israel

22 See also TO Num. xxiii.9; in both cases cp. PsJ.

from the pagan world around has a certain amount in common with TJ, but both depart from the plain sense of the Hebrew.[23] In reaffirming Israel's claim to the regions of Bashan and Gilead in Transjordan TJ exceeds the anticipation of Ezekiel, for whom the river Jordan was the eastern boundary of his ideal kingdom.[24]

A more striking statement about the extent of the kingdom of Israel in the new order occurs in Tg Zech. ix.1. Whereas the MT declares that the word of God will alight in judgement on Hadrach and Damascus, TJ sees a reference to the future enlarging of Israel's coasts: 'The oracle of the word of the LORD is in the land of the south, and Damascus shall again belong to the land of his presence.' The claim of Israel's God to sovereignty over Hadrach and Damascus[25] is thus made concrete in a prediction of their physical inclusion in a new and enlarged state of Israel.[26] TJ can speak of the return of Damascus to the Israelite fold because of David's subjugation of this city-state (cp. 2 Sam. viii.5f). Israelite suzerainty over Damascus had, however, been short-lived, and the Aramean state, once independent, proved a troublesome neighbour to Israel and Judah.

The location of Hadrach puzzled some of the rabbis, though others affirmed with no lack of confidence that it was situated in the same general area as Damascus. Nowadays it is usually identified with the Ḫatarikka mentioned in Assyrian inscriptions and situated about 16 miles (25·7 km) south of Aleppo. TJ's substitution of 'the south' for Hadrach obviously knows nothing of such an identification, and it is in any case doubtful whether it is to be regarded as offering a serious geographical datum.[27] There is a slight tendency in the Targums to assign places of uncertain location to 'the south' (cp. Tg 1 Sam. ix.4, xiii.17; Isa. xlix.12); perhaps the same applies to Tg Zech. ix.1.[28] The reference to the south is probably intended to balance the mention of Damascus, which, even for targumists, lay to

23 'Streiflichter auf die Entstehung der jetzigen Gestalt der alttestamentlichen Prophetenschriften', *ZAW* 23 (1903), 169.

24 Ezek. xlvii.18. Cp. also Num. xxxiv.10ff, though there the allocation of Transjordanian territory to the two-and-a-half tribes is assumed (cp. verses 13ff).

25 Cp. the widely accepted emendation of MT 'the eyes of man' to 'the cities of Aram' in verse 1.

26 In verse 2, TJ also predicts the inclusion of Hamath in 'the land'.

27 Cp. B. Otzen, *Studien über Deuterosacharja* (Copenhagen, 1964), p. 235.

28 This possibility renders unlikely the suggestion of G. Vermes (*Scripture and Tradition in Judaism* (Leiden, 1961; 2nd edn, 1973), p. 47n) that *'ĕra' dārōmā* should be translated 'the land of the height (*rûmā*)'.

the north of Israel.[29] TJ would then be making the point that Israel's boundaries were to be extended to the north and to the south, in keeping with Tg Isa. liv.3 ('you [*sc*. Jerusalem] will be strengthened to the south and to the north').

Basically the same interpretation of Zech. ix.1 is given in *Song of Songs Rabba* 7.5 and in *Sifre* on Deuteronomy.[30] Commenting on its occurrence in *Song of Songs Rabba*, W.D. Davies makes a suggestion about the historical circumstances in which it may have originated:

> In the age of the Rabbis concerned, Jerusalem was out of bounds to Jews, who were scattered from that city as far away as Damascus. Such Jews lacked the comfort of living in the land, as its boundaries were understood in the first century, and lacked the consolation of living with easy access to Jerusalem, the centre of their world. But, it was natural that they should want to claim that they, although scattered to Damascus, were still to be considered as belonging to the land where the Messiah was to appear. At the same time, they had no desire to question the age-long centrality of Jerusalem. Aware of this twofold aspect of the yearnings of Jews, did the Rabbis in their Messianic hopes, for their comfort, expand Jerusalem to include Damascus? (pp. 232–3 (see n. 3 above)).

Unfortunately Davies does not include TJ in his discussion; much less does he take account of Vermes's submission (p. 49; see n.28 above) that the targumic exegesis of Tg Zech. ix.1 and the symbolical interpretation of Damascus in the DSS reflect a common exegetical tradition. The origins of the interpretation presented in TJ and the midrash would then have to be traced to a time considerably in advance of the Hadrianic decree that expelled all Jews from Jerusalem and its environs. It is also a moot point whether the phrase *'ĕraʿ bēt šĕkīnĕtēh* in Tg Zech. ix.1 should be translated 'the land of the house of his presence', or simply, 'the land of his presence'.[31] If the latter is preferable – would Damascus belong *again* to 'the land of *the house of* his presence'? – then the Targum must be understood to

29 Cp. 'the land of the north' for Damascus in CD VII.14. See C. Rabin, *The Zadokite Documents* (Oxford, 1958), p. 29.

30 Ed. L. Finkelstein and H.S. Horovitz (Berlin, 1939; reprinted in New York, 1969), Pisqā 1, pp. 7–8.

31 Vermes (n. 28 above), p. 47 opts for the former alternative. For *bēt* in its various combinations see J. Levy, *Chaldäisches Wörterbuch über die Targumim*, vol. I (Leipzig, 1867), pp. 96ff.

refer to 'the land' in the broad sense, and not specifically to Jerusalem. This could be a significant point in view of the possibility that TJ represents an earlier stage in the interpretation of the verse than is given in *Song of Songs Rabba*.[32]

The annexation of Philistine territory by Israel in the latter days is also envisaged in Tg Zech. ix. Verses 5–8 in the MT announce the impending destruction of Philistia and give intimation of its incorporation in the revived Israelite empire:

> it too shall become a remnant for our God;
> it shall be like a clan in Judah,
> and Ekron shall be like the Jebusites.
> (verse 7)

TJ develops this idea of annexation. Even the statement that 'a mongrel people shall dwell in Ashdod' (verse 6), intended merely as a threat of judgement on that city, is pressed into higher service: 'and the house of Israel shall dwell in Ashdod where they were as foreigners'. Otzen suggests that TJ has been influenced by Zeph. ii.7, which actually refers to Ashkelon, and possibly also by the account of the visit of the ark of the covenant to Ashdod (1 Sam. v.1–8) (p. 238 (see n. 27 above)). But it is more to the point to note that, according to Josh. xv.47, Ashdod was allocated to Judah at the time of the settlement. The Israelites did not capture Ashdod at that time (cp. Josh. xi.22, xiii.1ff), but 2 Chr. xxvi.6 reports that Uzziah broke down its walls and founded cities in its territory.

The precise manner of the incorporation of Philistia in the Israelite kingdom is outlined by TJ in its rendering of verse 7: 'and the strangers who are left among them, they also shall be added to the people of our God and shall be as princes of the house of Judah, and Ekron shall be filled with the house of Israel like Jerusalem'. It is not just, as the MT would have it, that Philistia would become 'a remnant for our God'; rather, the 'strangers' who are left in it after divine judgement has been executed are to be included in the reconstituted Israel. Since it is unlikely that 'strangers' here denotes expatriate Israelites, for it would hardly be said of them that they would be 'added to the people of our God', *giyyōr* must be used in

32 This is not the place to enter into discussion of the dating of the Targums and midrashim; on *Song of Songs Rabba* see J.W. Bowker (*The Targums and Rabbinic Literature* (Cambridge, 1969), p. 83) who follows S.T. Lachs in suggesting a date between 600 and 750.

the technical sense of 'proselyte'.[33] TJ lies somewhere in between the polarities of universalism and particularism.

Boundary extension specifically in connection with Jerusalem seems to be indicated by Tg Zech. xiv.10. The idea of territorial expansion is already present in the MT, though strictly with reference to 'the whole land', which is to be converted into a plain 'from Geba to Rimmon south of Jerusalem'. The boundaries of the new Jerusalem are also delineated, but in fairly conventional terms. One of the reference points mentioned is 'the king's wine presses', which must denote some royal holding in the vicinity of Jerusalem. TJ, which, as a matter of interest, has a contemporizing reference in this verse to the Hippicus Tower built by Herod the Great, does not at first sight appear to deviate from the MT in the matter of the royal wine presses: for the MT's *yiqĕbē hammelek* it has *šīḥē malkā*. But the translation of *yiqĕbē* by *šīḥē* is worthy of comment. In the first place this is the only instance of BH *yeqeb* being rendered by *šīḥā* in the Targums; *šīḥā* is used for a pit or cavity rather than a wine press.[34] In fact, the key to TJ's translation is provided by *Song of Songs Rabba* 7.5 where, in relation to the latter-day expansion of Jerusalem, the words 'as far as the king's wine presses' are explained as meaning 'up to the pits of Ripa [var. Yapho], up to the wine presses that the supreme king of kings, the holy One blessed be he, hollowed out'. The pits in question are the depths of the Mediterranean Sea; Jerusalem is to extend to the Mediterranean coast. Ripa does not offer as good sense as Yapho (= Jaffa) in this connection, and it is likely that an original reading דיפו was corrupted into ריפע.[35] Since *Song of Songs Rabba* uses the root *šyḥ* for 'pit' we may reasonably infer that its singular occurrence in Tg Zech. xiv.10 betrays the Targum's awareness of the interpretation spelled out in the midrash. This is a good example of the way in which a single word in the 'official' Targums may connect with an aggadic tradition developed at greater length in a talmudic or midrashic source.[36]

That this survey of the territorial doctrine of TJ should conclude with reflections on the place of Jerusalem in the new earth is entirely

33 For a discussion of *giyyōr* and related terms in the Targums to the Pentateuch see M. Ohana, 'Prosélytisme et Targum palestinien: Données nouvelles pour la datation de Néofiti 1', *Biblica* 55 (1974), 317–32.

34 *Pace* Levy (n. 31 above), vol. II, p. 475.

35 So M. Jastrow, *A Dictionary of the Targumim, the Talmud Babli and Yerushalmi, and the Midrashic Literature* (London–New York, 1903), p. 586.

36 Cp. J.W. Bowker, 'Haggadah in the Targum Onqelos', *JSS* 12 (1967), 51–65.

appropriate, for there is a sense in which, as Tg Zech. xiv.10 implies, Jerusalem and ' the land ' are, eschatologically, coterminous.

> At the end of days it was Jerusalem that was to be the scene of the eschatological drama when Gentiles would come to Mount Zion to worship at God's Holy Mountain. Any area that might be desirous of inclusion in that drama (and after the Fall of Jerusalem and the scattering of Jewry there were many such), was simply taken over geographically into the orbit of the city. Any rivalry that might have arisen between such areas and Jerusalem was thereby cut at the root (Davies, p. 234f (see n. 3 above)).

What came to full flower in the midrashim of which Davies speaks can be seen *in nuce* in Tg Zech. xiv.10.[37]

I welcome this precious opportunity to record my appreciation of Dr E.I.J. Rosenthal, distinguished scholar and exemplary teacher.

Postscript

Since this essay was written there has appeared yet another explanation of Tarshish, relating it to the Greek θαλάσσης (gen.), 'sea', and again invoking targumic support. See S. B. Hoenig, 'Tarshish', *JQR* N.S. 69 (1979), 181f. Two recent studies focusing on 'land theology' are mentioned here at the suggestion of Dr S. C. Reif: E. M. Meyers and J. F. Strange, *Archaeology, the Rabbis and Early Christianity* (London, 1981), pp. 155–65 ('Jewish and Christian Attachment to Palestine'); B. H. Amaru, 'Land Theology in Josephus' *Jewish Antiquities*', *JQR* N.S. 71 (1981), 201–29.

37 For information on studies with a bearing on targumic topography, principally in connection with the pentateuchal Targums, see A. Díez Macho, *Neophyti 1*, vol. v, 'Deuteronomio' (Madrid, 1978), pp. 13*ff.

The Bible in Medieval Hebrew Poetry [1]

R.J. LOEWE

Where Jewish history is concerned the term 'medieval' can be unhelpful, especially if one is dealing with Jewry and Judaism in the sixteenth century or later, but its function in the foregoing title is as an indicator of what may be excluded on grounds of its higher antiquity, and in this sense 'medieval' is perhaps less confusing. But let us be specific. I am not concerned here with what may be termed the prolongation of biblical Psalmody, whether in the latest biblical texts themselves (e.g. Chronicles) or in apocryphal literature such as Ecclesiasticus xliv, or the Hodayoth scroll from Qumran, or similar pieces, the original language of which may or may not have been Hebrew, e.g. the Song of the Three Holy Children or the Magnificat (Luke i.46f). These compositions simply maintain the style of the biblical exemplars and sources, sometimes indeed so slavishly as to betray, perhaps, a feeling in their very authors of belonging to the *fin de siècle* – that is, of standing within a literary tradition not yet closed, feeling themselves to be continuators rather than creators of admittedly reproduction furniture. Some of these pieces may have been composed with liturgical use in view, and we may deal no less brusquely with the earliest surviving pieces in the Jewish liturgy proper. Early liturgical Hebrew is basically prose writing, albeit an exalted prose of a type that may have been slightly archaic already at the time of its formulation – a situation that has a parallel in sixteenth-century Anglican liturgical history. Biblical quotations and allusions figure here, but they are introduced more rarely, self-consciously and, one might say, more portentously than is the case in later Jewish liturgical compositions, the authors of which were quite aware of themselves as hymnologists rather than liturgical

1 Based on a paper read to the Society for Old Testament Study in London on 4 January 1974.

formulators. A fair example is the second benediction of the ʻAmidah or Eighteen Benedictions, being itself a test formula designed to exclude from leadership in public prayer one who could not avow assent to notions of resurrection. It is a short collect,[2] clear allusion to which occurs in Mark xii.26f, where it is represented as familiar to Jesus (as it probably was).[3] Short reminiscences of the Psalms occur therein, God being praised as *sōmēk nōpĕlīm* (Psalm cxlv.14) and *mattīr ʼăsūrīm* (cxlvi.7); but the highlight, so to speak, is the assertion that God keeps faith with 'those that sleep in the dust' (*līšēnē ʻāpār*), thus linking the prayer overtly with the last chapter of Daniel (xii.2) and so with one of the only two unequivocal references in the Hebrew Bible to a future life.

The same verdict may be pronounced on the early mystical compositions known as *hēkālōt*, i.e. 'angelic palaces', which, although still written in exalted and lyrical prose, do make use of the simpler forms of parallelism to be found in the Bible. The following example is particularly significant: in the plural form as here transcribed it is familiar as forming the opening of the prayer with which most Jewish services conclude,[4] but in its original form beginning with the singular *ʻālay* the prayer is to be found amongst the *hēkālōt*:[5]

ʻālēnū lĕšabbēaḥ laʼădōn hakkōl:
lātēt gĕdullā lĕyōṣēr bĕrēʼšīt

It is our bounden duty to praise the LORD of all:
To ascribe greatness to him who wrought the Creation.

Until recently these texts were assigned, conjecturally, to the latter part of the first millennium of the common era, although in the case of *ʻālēnū lĕšabbēaḥ* itself there are some grounds for crediting it to Rab in the third century within whose New-Year liturgical arrangement it is embedded.[6] However, comparison of them with gnostic

2 Found in all (traditional) prayer-books, e.g. *The Authorised Daily Prayer Book*, ed. S. Singer (London, 1890), pp. 44–5.

3 See H. Loewe in C.G. Montefiore and H. Loewe, *A Rabbinic Anthology* (London, 1938), p. 369. In an article that I cannot now trace T.W. Manson applauded the interpretation of 'the powers of God' as a reference to the *gĕbūrōt* benediction (*ʼattā gibbōr ... mĕḥayyē mētīm*), but it would seem that commentators on Mark's Gospel have not yet noticed it. See now R. Loewe, '"Salvation" is not of the Jews', *JTS* N.S. 32 (1981), 358f.

4 E.g. *Prayer Book* (see n. 2), p. 76.

5 See G.G. Scholem, *Jewish Gnosticism, Merkabah Mysticism, and Talmudic Tradition*, (New York, 1965), pp. 27f, 105f. See also briefly *EJ*, vol. II, p. 557.

6 *Pĕsīqtā dĕrab Kāhănā*, ed. S. Buber (Wilna, 1925), *Baḥōdeš haššĕbīʻī*, fo 150a etc.; I. Elbogen, *Der jüdische Gottesdienst*, 2nd edn (Frankfurt-am-Main, 1931), p. 264; *EJ*, *loc. cit.*, and vol. XV, p. 915.

texts and their heavy use of 'chariot'-mysticism has led Scholem to propose a significantly higher date, so that he can now write with confidence that there is 'no doubt' that parts of them ascend to talmudic times and that the central ideas, as well as many details, go back to the first and second Christian centuries – or, in other words, to the period of the definitive closure of the Jewish biblical canon.[7]

It is that event which is our true starting-point, as a feature in the foregoing quotation strikingly demonstrates. The first word of Gen. i.1 *bĕ* + *rē'šīt* has, thanks to that context, become fused into a noun, *bĕrē'šīt*, that can be preceded by a construct (e.g. *yĕmē bĕrē'šīt*) and itself be used alone, idiomatically, for [*ma'ăśē*] *bĕrē'šīt*, 'creation'. If the change is no more radical than the passage of *affidavit* from a verb in Latin to a noun in English, the point here is that whereas within Latin *affidavit* could not have undergone that sea-change, *bĕrē'šīt* has sustained it within its own home territory without entirely losing the availability of the biblical *rē'šīt* to mean 'beginning', alongside the commoner rabbinic *tĕḥillā*. The canonization of the Hebrew scriptures was a formal act that acknowledged the position of authority that they occupy and the affection that they inspire in Jewish sentiment, such that minor linguistic features – or apparently dispensable details – could be elevated to a new level of meaningfulness in virtue of their assumed deliberate and inspirational selection, and each tiny part may thus be taken and cherished as representative of the whole. The biblical text acquires a dynamism that makes it, in contemporary terms, a source of energy to be exploited, canalized, and variously applied. On the halakic side, which concerns personal and social ethics and, bound up with these, the institutional life of the Jewish people, textual *minutiae* could be mobilized to point a moral, to inculcate some practical lesson or even to yield formal authority for stultifying a biblical institution that was, or had become, socially unworkable.[8] In midrash, the availability of a textual approach of great rigour could become a vehicle of poetic insight expressed through the forcing of a suffix, the association of discrete texts from different parts of the Bible etc. The fact that during the talmudic period we encounter no formal Hebrew poetry does not, in my view, indicate a few centuries' hibernation of any Jewish capacity for poetic response

7 *EJ*, vol. x, p. 500.

8 E.g. the law regarding the child beyond parental control (*bēn sōrēr ūmōre*) in Deut. xxi.18f, as in effect construed out of applicability in the Mishnah (Sanh. 8.1–4).

but rather that we are looking for it in the wrong medium: it is there, expressed in midrashic anecdotage and parable-making, and in the themes – and sometimes in the economy of expression – of rabbinic exegesis.[9] And when Hebrew poetry does re-emerge as a self-conscious art form, the biblical element contributes to the subject-matter of its new settings a dimension of depth, to the analysis and illustration of which I shall return below (p. 138f).

Considerations of space may be allowed to excuse some chronological telescoping of a millennium into a single paragraph, and the summary statement that the factors that produced a poetic revival concern both content and form. The themes for long remain exclusively religious, i.e. either linked to a specific liturgical setting or else concerned with *rites de passage* – birth, circumcision, marriage, death. It is not until the eleventh century that so-called secular poetry appears, and friendship, women, love, nature, wine and even battle figure, but even in the case of battle the term 'secular' is scarcely apposite to compositions written by poets who were themselves believers – however cynical their passing mood – and who wrote in an idiom thoroughly impregnated with biblical flavouring. Before these genres appear, the novelty in respect of content consists in the plaiting together of the several strands of the heritage of the Bible regarded as a self-contained, an inspired and a classical document. That is to say, there are introduced into Hebrew poetry elements of aggadic exegesis as elaborated in the midrashim, and sometimes elements of institutional Judaism, that have been text-linked through the hermeneutical processes of halaka. These are the distinguishing features of the early *piyyūṭ*, or liturgical poem, the very name of which – deriving, through *payyĕṭān*, from the Greek ποιητής – points to an external stimulus.

This brings us to the question of form. *Piyyūṭ*, which at first uses the assonance of suffixes and terminations and then develops to adopt the use of rhyme proper, appears in Palestine, apparently before the Arab conquest of 636, and it has several features of a markedly formal similarity to Byzantine hymnology.[10] The

9 E.g. BT Soṭa 36*b* on Gen. xxxix.11, where Joseph's intention of 'getting on with his business' (*la'ăśōt mĕla'ktō*) is interpreted by (?) Mar Samuel as indirectly indicating that Joseph had been virtually won over by the importunities of Potiphar's wife, until a vision of his father's likeness shocked him into reasserting himself. We here have an insight into the subject of the Phaedra theme that invites comparison with its treatment by Euripides and Racine.

10 On the Byzantine background to the *piyyūṭ* see P.E. Kahle, *The Cairo Geniza*, 2nd edn (Oxford, 1959), pp. 43ff.

piyyūṭ-form reached Jewish Europe through southern Italy and spread northward, reaching its zenith in the Rhineland communities of the period of the first crusade. Another branch ran westwards through Fatimid Egypt, leaving its traces in the Cairo Genizah, along the series of settlements of Jews on the North African seaboard, but it was followed, and ultimately eclipsed, by another environmental influence regarding form. I refer here to Arabic poetry and long syllables is very different from that in Classical Arabic, and rhyme. In the tenth century this was adapted to the strait-jacket of massoretically formalized Hebrew in which the distribution of short and long syllables is very different from that in classical Arabic, and this gave rise to a rigorously self-disciplined Hebrew classicism that invites comparison with Roman treatment of Greek models, e.g. what Vergil made of the Greek hexameter as compared to its earlier Latin handling, or Horace's treatment of the Sapphic and Alcaic metres. I must hereafter leave consideration of *piyyūṭ* on one side, since its degree of dependence on halakic reminiscence would require greater space for adequate demonstration than is here available.

I revert now to the dimension of depth that the biblical factor infuses into medieval Jewish poetry. It is easy to caricature the Hebrew poetry of the Middle Ages as but a pastiche of quotations and reminiscences of the Bible that can recall to those of us who are old enough to have received a traditional English grammar-school education the Latin elegiacs and the Greek iambics of our youthful lucubrations, or the Latin plays that used to be produced at Westminster School each December with topical curtain-raisers, likewise in Latin, the quotations and puns in which *The Times* would helpfully italicize. But to approach Hebrew poetry from such an angle is to misconceive it. For the medieval Jewish poets, for their contemporary readership and for those in subsequent generations whose Jewish education has been adequate for full appreciation, the Hebrew Bible was, and has remained, a heritage too familiar and too intimate for their attitude to it to be reckoned purely 'literary', in the way that the Greek and Latin classics were loved by (say) Macaulay, Gladstone or those of our own age who left school with a significant acquaintance with Aeschylus and Vergil. To get on to the right wave-length, so to speak, one ought rather to try to get inside the mind of the audience – be it peasant or proletarian – of a medieval miracle-play performed on a stage of bare boards laid athwart a waggon. If the dramatic effect is to come across there must of course be a convincing evocation of a familiar literary heritage, but this in itself is not enough; it has to be combined with successful appeal to a common stock of experience, folk-lore and oral tradition. When all these elements meet and are expressed in a form that is both memorable and impressive, true poetry is present.

The medieval Jewish parallels are easily recognized. First, the circumstance that Jewish education made it possible to presuppose, from an early age, close familiarity with, at any rate, the Pentateuch, those parts of the prophetic canon that occur as haphṭarot and the Psalms. Secondly, Jewish historical experience, in both biblical and post-biblical times, senses synchronically rather than viewing diachronically: for the Jew, his people's history is like a rolling snowball, regarding which it is arbitrary – and sometimes futile – to pronounce how much is core and where the outer skin begins. And, thirdly, that experience is crystallized in biblical exegesis and scriptural association. This last associative aspect is of particular importance, as it may sometimes contribute a level of meaning that has accrued to a text independently of, or even in defiance of, its original context or meaning, in virtue of the use that has been made of it, *obiter dictum*, in the Talmud. A Christian parallel to the latter factor is afforded by the use made of the Old Testament in the New. In short, when the medieval or the traditionally-minded modern Hebrew poet uses a biblical quotation, he is not indulging in a piece of mere literary virtuosity. Rather, he is setting out to achieve the effect that the composer aims at when, instead of using a simple note, he draws on the full depth and subtlety of a chord.

The following is a good illustration of the way in which the obscurity of a biblical phrase can find itself transcended by the intensity of the emotional setting into which it has been taken up in the Talmud, to be used in turn by a medieval poet in order to evoke its talmudic association, the function of the biblical original being, as seen retrospectively by the poet, comparable not to a seed, but rather to the irritant grain deliberately inserted into an oyster to stimulate it to produce a pearl. Psalm xvii.15 is a very difficult text. The rendering offered by the New English Bible begins the verse with *ḥarbĕkā*, which in the MT is the last word of verse 14, and it involves emending the curious *mimmĕtīm* (= 'from men'(?)) to

11 L.H. Brockington, *The Hebrew Text of the Old Testament ... Adopted by ... the New English Bible* (Oxford–Cambridge, 1973), p. 124. One wonders whether the rendering of *hămītēm* by 'make an end of them' is intended to nod towards an alternative emendation *hătimmēm*.

hămītēm,[11] rendered 'make an end of them' with the marginal note 'probable reading; Hebrew unintelligible'. The translation therefore reads:

> Make an end of them with thy sword. With thy hand, O LORD, make an end of them; *thrust them out* of this world *in the prime of their life*, gorged as they are with thy good things, blest with many sons and leaving their children wealth in plenty. (verse 16) But my plea is just: I shall see thy face, and be blest with a vision of thee when I wake.

The italicized words correspond to the operative phrase vocalized in the MT *ḥelqām baḥayyīm*, *ḥelqām* being revocalized by the translators, following the LXX, as *ḥallĕqēm*. Verse 16 has here been added because in the talmudic passage to be cited immediately it is probably to be considered in the background by association even though it is not quoted.[12] The text is a celebrated one, dealing as it does with the martyrdom of R. 'Aqiba, whose death under Hadrian became, in virtue of its circumstances, archetypal for the Jewish martyr. Somewhat abbreviated, it may be rendered as follows:

> When the hour for R. 'Aqiba's execution arrived, it happened to be the time for prayer and therefore for the recitation of the Shema'. His torturers were combing his flesh off him whilst he was acknowledging the authority of the kingdom of heaven over himself by reciting the Shema' ... and he protracted his articulation of the closing *'eḥād* until with it upon his lips he expired. A divine voice proceeded from heaven, saying: 'Happy indeed art thou, Rabbi 'Aqiba, that thy soul goeth forth with the proclamation of the divine unity upon thy lips.' The ministering angels said to God; 'Is this then what Torah means, and is this the sort of reward that it merits? *Mimmĕtīm yādĕkā 'ădōnāy* – rather than by men['s cruelty, death should have come to him by] thine [own] hand, O LORD!' [so Rashi *in loc.*]. God answered with the words that follow almost immediately in the psalm: '*ḥelqām baḥayyīm* – their portion [i.e. that of 'Aqiba and his fellow martyrs] is in life [eternal].' Then a divine voice proceeded from heaven, saying: 'Happy indeed art thou, Rabbi 'Aqiba, in that thou art destined for the World to Come.'

The emotional significance of this incident for the Jewish sense of identity is so powerful that the passage quoted takes in its stride the virtual unintelligibility of the MT, the meaning that it has imposed upon the words being integral to its own dramatic unity. And on it Solomon ibn Gabirol could draw, writing in the eleventh century, in

12 BT Ber. 61*b*.

his great metaphysical poem *Keter Malkūt*, in the confidence that those for whom he was writing would pick up his allusion:[13]

וְאַחַר כָּבוֹד תִּקָּחֵנִי, וּבְעֵת מִן הָעוֹלָם הַזֶּה תּוֹצִיאֵנִי, לְחַיֵּי הָעוֹלָם
הַבָּא בְּשָׁלוֹם תְּבִיאֵנִי, וְאֶל עָל תִּקְרָאֵנִי, וּבֵין חֲסִידֶיךָ תּוֹשִׁיבֵנִי,
וְעִם הַמְּנוּיִם מֵחֶלֶד חֶלְקָם בַּחַיִּים תִּמְנֵנִי, וְלֵאוֹר בְּאוֹר פָּנֶיךָ תְּזַכֵּנִי.

. . . when doth sound
The hour for Thee to lead me hence, and send
Me peaceful to the life of that world without end:
And when thy summons cometh, raised on high
Let me with saints for company recline,
Mustered midst martyrs, *they that qualify*
For everlasting life; may thy face shine
On me, as worthy in that wondrous light
To find all my delight.

By contrast, the following example – likewise from Ibn Gabirol – shows us the poet fusing his biblical heritage not merely with his own experience but, if I am not mistaken, with his feeling for the history of his own, non-Jewish environment. His patron Yequthiel ben Ḥasan 'al-Mutawakkil,[14] who was apparently regarded as a father-figure throughout Spanish Jewry, was judicially murdered in a *coup d'ėtat* in Saragossa in 1039. In his great lament on his death Ibn Gabirol compares Yequthiel to the rock captured by King Amaziah from which he flung down his 10,000 Edomite captives and which he named Yoqte'el (2 Kgs xiv.7).[15] Ibn Gabirol died in Spain and it is not known that he ever left its shores. He was born in Malaga, not so far from Gibraltar, which even if he never saw he cannot have failed to know by repute. When, therefore, he writes that 'Yequthiel was even as the crag Yoqte'el, whence hostile strangers were flung headlong, aye, smashed to pulp', it is difficult to think that Gibraltar, stout bastion against wave and foe, was far from his mind, seeing that its name, albeit somewhat corrupted in its

13 The translation is from my own forthcoming poetic version of the complete *keter malkūt*. All verse renderings in this article except that by H. Loewe on p. 148 are by myself; other than that by me on p. 155, none of mine have hitherto appeared in print.

14 See *JE*, vol. VII, p. 91.

15 *Bīmē yĕqūtī'ēl 'ăšer nīgmārū*, Gabirol's poems, ed. H.N. Bialik and J.H. Rawnitzki (Tel-Aviv, 1927–32), vol. I, p. 52. I have translated the poem into English verse in *Judaism* 18 (1969), 343ff. For the line here discussed (*hāyā yĕqūtī'ēl kĕselaʿ yoqtĕ'ēl*) see pp. 347, 351.

modern form, preserves in the Arabic Jebel 'al-Tariq the name of the commander who captured it in 711.

When we turn to metaphysics – within which both personal experience and awareness of tradition and identity must be subsumed – again we find Ibn Gabirol constructing a short liturgical poem on the basis of a talmudic legend that holds up mirrors, both biographical and psychological, in order to scrutinize the aesthetics of the fivefold repetition of the phrase *bārĕkī napšī 'et-'ădōnāy* in Psalms ciii.1, 2, 22 and civ.1, 35. Simi bar ʿUqba (or possibly ʿUqba himself)[16] asserted that the five exhortations by David to his soul to bless the LORD correspond to the five points of similarity between the soul and God: God fills the world, the soul the body; both have power to see but are themselves invisible; God sustains the whole world, the soul the whole body; both God and the soul are pure; and both of them dwell in the innermost chambers. 'How appropriate, therefore', he said, 'that something possessed of these five qualities should praise him in whom those same five are found.' The motif obviously lends itself to linkage with the Magnificat, so to say, of the morning service for Sabbath and festivals, *nišmat kol-ḥay tĕbārēk 'et-šimĕkā 'ădōnāy*,[17] 'the breath of all that lives shall praise thy name, O LORD', and it was made the theme of an exordium (*rĕšūt*) to *nišmat* by Ibn Gabirol that incorporates in its first line (*šĕḥī lā'ēl yĕḥīdā hahăkāmā*)[18] allusion to the rational soul (διανοητικός, *maśkelet*), possession of which is the prerogative of man:

שְׂחִי לָאֵל יְחִידָה הַחֲכָמָה   וְרוּצִי לַעֲבֹד אֹתוֹ בְּאֵימָה
לְעוֹלָמֵךְ פְּנִי לֵילֵךְ וְיוֹמֵךְ   וְלָמֶה תִרְדְּפִי הֶבֶל וְלָמָּה
מְשׁוּלָה אַתְּ בְּחַיּוּתֵךְ לְאֵל חַי   אֲשֶׁר נֶעְלַם כְּמוֹ אַתְּ נֶעֱלָמָה
הֲלֹא אִם יוֹצְרֵךְ טָהוֹר וְנָקִי   דְּעִי כִּי כֵן טְהוֹרָה אַתְּ וְתַמָּה
חֲסִין יִשָּׂא שְׁחָקִים עַל־זְרֹעוֹ   כְּמוֹ תִשְּׂאִי גְוִיָּה נֶאֱלָמָה
זְמִרוֹת קַדְּמִי נַפְשִׁי לְצוּרֵךְ   אֲשֶׁר לֹא שָׁם דְּמוּתֵךְ בַּאֲדָמָה
קְרָבַי בָּרְכוּ תָמִיד לְצוּרְכֶם   אֲשֶׁר לִשְׁמוֹ תְּהַלֵּל כָּל־נְשָׁמָה:

Line 7 cp. Psalms ciii.1, cl.6

16 BT Ber. 10*a*. The identity of the speaker referred to (*'ămar lēh hākī qā'āmēnā lāk*) is not certain, other named rabbis being also involved in the discussion. Alternative applications and biographical reconstructions of the repeated refrain come first.

17 E.g. *Prayer Book* (see n. 2), p. 125.

18 I. Davidson, *Thesaurus of Mediaeval Hebrew Poetry* (New York, 1924–33), vol. III, p. 442, no. 802.

My one true self, to God in worship bend,
  Thou soul endow'd with reason, haste thy flight
In reverence to serve Him every night,
  Each day, think on that world that waits thy end:
Nor chase vain bubbles – thou that canst pretend
  To liveliness like God's own life: from sight
Like Him conceal'd; be He that form'd thee hight
  Purest, thou canst thy pure perfection tend;
His arm sustains the welkin – even so
  Dost thou thy frame, that but for thee were dumb.
To thy Rock, then, my soul, thy singing raise
  Who made nought like to thee on earth below,
That Rock to whom shall all within me come
  Blessing the One whom all that breathe do praise.

Although it is tempting to stay with the Sephardi poets, to whose classicism the Arabic influence adds a dimension, it is important to illustrate the richness achieved by others, not heirs of the Spanish tradition, who were prepared to subject themselves to the co-ordinated disciplines of biblicism and purism in rhyme. In order so to do, I turn to one of the early *payyĕṭānīm*, Eleazar Qallir, of whose personal history virtually nothing is known; his Palestinian origin is assumed, and his possibly sixth-century date rests on sheer surmise.[19] His style is often much more rugged than appears in the acrostically arranged example here chosen,[20] which is an elegy for the fast commemorating the destruction of Jerusalem on 9 Ab. Like many pieces on this theme it makes significant play with the word *'ēkā*, 'how could it be?', which, standing at the beginning of Lamentations, gives the book its regular Hebrew title. It is here reserved as a climax, the poem ending with the first words of Lam. ii, *'ēkā yāʿīb bĕ'appō*, 'how comes it that [God] hath clouded with his anger [the daughter of Zion]?' It is led up to by the recurrent *lāmmā*, 'why, why?', tolling like a passing-bell at the beginning of the second line of each stanza: and the concluding word *'appō*, which determines that the key rhyme to the whole poem must be *-pō*, has prompted the choice for the punch-lines of each stanza of verse-fragments ending with the word *pō*(*h*), 'here'. The effect is to communicate something of an existential quality to the poem, which proves to be less elegy than expostulatory questioning of God's apparently sub-

19 See, most recently, *EJ*, vol. x, pp. 713ff, with bibliography.
20 Davidson (see n. 18), vol. I, p. 67, no. 1452. A. Rosenfeld, *The Authorised Kinot for the Ninth of Av* (London, 1965), pp. 104ff. See below, p. 143.

lime disregard of justice, and in my view it can stand comparison with Job and with the protest-poems that have grown out of the anguish of Hitler's concentration-camps. Every stanza except for the last is constructed on the same pattern, the speaker being the Jewish people stunned by the enormity of its own tragedy as typified in the loss of the Temple: referred to, be it noted, as *'ohŏlī* – '*my* tent', not 'God's house'. This is followed in every stanza by a reminder to God of his own one-time loving concern for the Temple. Thus the first stanza begins by glancing at the rabbinic exegesis of Jer. xvii.12,[21] according to which the Temple, like the divine throne, existed before creation. The expostulatory 'why?' invariably introduces a verb in the passive, adverting to some aspect of the tragedy that contrasts starkly with the feature of divine favour to which reference has just been made; this in turn being always followed by *wĕnihyētā*, addressed to God – 'and thou hast turned into' either a declared enemy, or else so craven and benighted a friend as to be helpless in the face of the hatred for Israel that God is himself responsible for having permitted to spring up. The immediacy and the continued relevance down the tortured generations of Jewish history are reinforced by the climactic *pō*(*h*) quotations – 'here and now'. But the poet has not lost his faith, and therefore inevitably in the penultimate stanza a re-evaluation concedes that the cause of the tragedy lies not in the Godhead but in Israel's own sin, and specifically the sinful desire for gain – *'ăwōn biṣ'ī*, or Aristotle's τὸ ἐπιθυμητικόν – and allusion to Psalm xxx.6 brings assurance that God's anger is but for a moment whilst in his goodwill there is life. But the question that the poem asks is too powerful to admit of simplistic or sentimentalizing answers, so that this reassurance is no sooner mentioned than it is postponed into the mists of messianic distance by the words of the conclusion – *wĕ'ad 'attā 'ēkā yā'īb 'appō* – that may well be so, but for the time being blackness is unrelieved.

	אָהֳלִי אֲשֶׁר תְּאַבְתָּ עַד־לֹא בְּרֵאשִׁית, עִם־כִּסֵּא כָבוֹד לְצָרְפוֹ.
Song of Songs i.7	לָמָּה לָנֶצַח שֻׁדַּד בְּיַד שֹׁדְדִים, וְנִהְיֵיתָ כְּרֹעֶה בְּעֹטְיָה,
Isa. lii.5	וְרַעַשְׁתָּ וְרָגַזְתָּ, וְעַתָּה מַה־לִּי־פֹה:
Gen. xxvii.33	אָהֳלִי אֲשֶׁר קוֹמַמְתָּ לְאֵיתָנֵי עוֹלָם בְּחֶרְדַּת מִי־אֵפוֹא.
Psalm cii.8	לָמָּה לָנֶצַח צֻמַּת בְּיַד צָרִים, וְנִהְיֵיתָ כְּצִפּוֹר בּוֹדֵד עַל־גָּג,
(Jer. xi.15)	מַר צוֹרֵחַ, מֶה לִידִידִי פֹה:
Deut. v.28	אָהֳלִי אֲשֶׁר פִּצַּתְּ לְמַעֲנוֹ לְצִיר, וְאַתָּה עֲמֹד עִמָּדִי פֹּה.

21 BT Pesaḥ. 54*a*.

לָמָּה לָנֶצַח עָרְעַר בְּיַד עֲרֵלִים, וְנִהְיֵיתָ כְּשֹׂנֵא וְצָר,	
וְאַיֵּה אִוּוּי מוֹשָׁב פֹּה:	Psalm cxxxii.13
אָהֳלִי אֲשֶׁר נָחִיתָ בְּעַנְנֵי הוֹד, לְאֶת־אֲשֶׁר יֶשְׁנוֹ פֹּה וְאֵינֶנּוּ פֹּה.	Deut. xxix.14
לָמָּה לָנֶצַח מֹאַס בְּיַד מֹרְדִים, וְנִהְיֵיתָ כְּלֹא יוּכַל לְהוֹשִׁיעַ,	
מַה־לְּךָ פֹּה וּמִי־לְךָ פֹּה:	Isa. xxii.16
אָהֳלִי אֲשֶׁר כּוֹנַנְתָּ מָכוֹן לְשִׁבְתְּךָ, לְחֹפֵף בְּחֶפּוֹ.	Deut. xxxiii.12
לָמָּה לָנֶצַח יֹעָה בְּיַד יְהִירִים, וְנִהְיֵיתָ כְּטָס בֶּחָלָל,	
וְאֵין־עוֹד נָבִיא, וְנָמְתָּ, הַאֵין פֹּה:	1 Kgs xxii.7
אָהֳלִי אֲשֶׁר חָנִיתָ מֵאָז בְּתָאָיו, מִפֹּה וּמִפֹּה.	Ezek. xl.21
לָמָּה לָנֶצַח זֻנַּח בְּיַד זָרִים, וְנִהְיֵיתָ כְּוָתִיק יֹצֵא חוּצָה,	
וְלֹא־עָבַר פֹּה:	(Jer. ii.6)
אָהֳלִי אֲשֶׁר הֲכִנוֹתָ לְהַשְׁלִיךְ בּוֹ לְפָנֶיךָ, גּוֹרָל פֹּה.	
לָמָּה לָנֶצַח דֹּחָה בְּיַד דּוּמִים, וְנִהְיֵיתָ כְּגֵר בָּאָרֶץ,	
וְנָמְתָּ, כִּי־לֹא נָסֹב עַד־בֹּאוֹ פֹּה:	1 Sam. xvi.11
אָהֳלִי אֲשֶׁר בַּעֲוֹן בִּצְעִי, חָשְׁכוּ כּוֹכְבֵי נִשְׁפּוֹ.	Job iii.9
לָמָּה לָנֶצַח אֻפַּל בְּיַד אֲחֵרִים. וְנִהְיֵיתָ כְּאוֹרֵחַ בְּמָלוֹן,	
וְעוֹד מִי־לְךָ פֹּה:	Gen. xix.12
אָחוֹר וָקֶדֶם מִפֹּה וּמִפֹּה. לְכָל־דּוֹר וָדוֹר נוֹדַע קִצְפּוֹ וְחֶפּוֹ. עַל	Psalm cxxxix.5
מֶה מִכָּל־אֹם, שָׁת עָלַי כַּפּוֹ. זֹאת לְבַעֲלִיל, כִּי־פִיד חָקוּק בְּכַפּוֹ.	
רִפְאוּתִי בְטוּחָה, כִּי רֶגַע בְּאַפּוֹ. וְעַד־עַתָּה, אֵיכָה יָעִיב בְּאַפּוֹ:	Psalm xxx.6; Lam. ii.1

My tent it was, whereon thy yearning played
  Or e'er the world began, linked to thy throne,
The twain primeval: wherefore, then, betrayed
  For aye to foes and fell destruction?
And Thou – the Shepherd – strayest, to appear
Resentful; musing: 'What should keep Me here?'

My tent – for my forebears 'twas pitched by Thee
  In ancient times where fear struck Isaac cold,
His sire's near-holocaust: must it then be
  Cut off for aye, fast cramped in foemen's hold?
While from the roofs a love-bird's plaint sounds clear,
Thy moan – 'No longer place for my mate here'.

My tent – Thou didst display to mine envoy
  Its pattern, bidding him: 'Here, by Me stand
On Sinai': just for Gentiles to destroy,
  A ruin, wrecked by sacrilegious hand?
And Thou, against what Thou didst once hold dear
Turned foe – what of thy sighs: 'Here stay I, here'?

My tent – that thine own glory's cloud did lead
  Through deserts, as a sign that should imply
'Both to those here this day, and to their seed
  Not yet here, keep I tryst': spurned must it lie
In rebel hands, thy saving power turned sheer
Unmanliness? Whose grave wouldst Thou dig here?

My tent – Thou stablished it, to be a bower
  Wherein thy hovering Presence e'er should stay:
Why, then, did those, high-handed in their power,
  Self-vaunting come, and sweep that shrine away,
Whilst Thou, a swooping vulture, canst but jeer
  And prey – 'No prophet of the Lord left here?'

My tent – the camp wherein Thou didst erect
  Long since thine own pavilion, well placed
'Twixt flanking ranges: why, down years unchecked
  Hath it lain derelict, the strangers' waste?
And Thou, thine elder years enfeebled, sere,
Must take the road, nor evermore come here.

My tent – where Thou didst sacred lots ordain
  To find the scapegoat of my sins, and grant
Each tribe inheritance it should retain:
  Thrust down! Why, why shall foreigners supplant,
And Thou, part alien-guest dost muse, part seer,
'We sit not down till Jesse's son be here'?

My tent: nay, 'twas through mine own sin of greed
  That darkness swathed its twilight stars in gloom;
Yet wherefore to each gloom must gloom succeed
  While cursed hands make endless night its doom,
And Thou, a wayfarer forlorn, must hear
Man's wry reproach – 'What, hast Thou folk still here?'

. . .

On this side and on that, age after age
  His anger is made known – to front, to rear;
Why must He lay his hand on me in rage
  Greater than any people else must bear?
When on his palms my name He graved, no page
  More grimly showed Catastrophe *writ clear:*
True, one brief moment all his ire can gauge
  But his goodwill spells life to give me cheer,
Though yet his healing shall my pain assuage
  Still Zion feels his fury's storm-cloud near.

But let us turn to a happier theme, the good cheer and the spiritual peace of the Sabbath table. In the poem that I wish to consider next an acrostic gives the author's name as Israel, after which the initials of *haššāmayim*, *gam*, and *rĕʾū* spell out *haggēr*.[22] L. Zunz noted this, but circumspectly inserted a qualifying *vielleicht*[23] – a caution that I must commend, having myself once composed a short Hebrew metrical poem without realizing until it was finished that the first three lines gave the acrostic 'Levi'.[24] Nevertheless, there is strong internal evidence that the poet was indeed avowing with pride his adoption of Judaism, the arguments being both textual and exegetical. First, rather than *gam hāʾāreṣ* we might have expected the author to write *wĕgam hāʾāreṣ*. Secondly, Isa. lxvi.2, which is alluded to, reads *wĕʾet-kol-ʾēlleh yādī ʿāśātā*, and although *wĕʾet* is admissible both grammatically and metrically it has been replaced by *rĕʾū*. (It might be argued that this was with the object of alluding also, by a sort of shorthand *enjambement*, to Isa. xl.26, [*śĕʾū-mārōm ʿēnēkem*] *ūrĕʾū mī bārāʾ ʾēlleh*, but this would not weaken the apparent insistence on making the *rēš* acrostically significant.) Clearly, one could not put too much weight on evidence of this nature, but there is more. The third stanza may be translated: 'eat rich fare, drink sweet wines, for to them that cleave unto him (*bō dĕbēqīm*) God gives raiment to wear and victuals unfailing, flesh, fish, and every delicacy'. The phrase *bō dĕbēqīm* picks up Deut. iv.4, a verse that may be expected to carry a particularly intimate meaning for a proselyte. But what settles the matter, in my opinion, is the hint at the assertion in Deut. x.18 that God loves the *gēr* to give him food and raiment. The poet has slightly changed the deuteronomic formulation in order to echo Jacob's vow (Gen. xxviii.20) contingent upon God's providing him with *leḥem leʾĕkōl ūbeged lilbōš*, this making it virtually certain – as exegetical matter to be cited immediately will show – that the author chose to understand Deut. x.18 as meaning that God loves the 'proselyte' (*gēr*). An anecdote connects that verse with Onqelos or Aquila (the recensions differ)[25] – both of

22 Davidson (see n. 18), vol. III, p. 338, no. 1733.

23 *Literaturgeschichte der synagogalen Poesie* (Berlin, 1865), p. 511.

24 The piece, written in honour of Ibn Gabirol on the occasion of the alleged 950th anniversary of Ibn Gabirol celebrated in Malaga in 1972, will be found in the printed record (*Seis conferencias en torno a ibn Gabirol* (Malaga, 1973), p. 56; also *The American Sephardi* 6 (1973), 69.

25 *Bĕrēšīt Rabbā*, 70.5, on Gen. xxviii.20 (Wilna, 1878), fo 137*a*; ed. J. Theodor and Ch. Albeck, 2nd edn (Jerusalem, 1965), pp. 802f; *Tanḥuma* ed. S. Buber (Wilna, 1885), Genesis, *Lek lĕkā*, fo 32*a*, n. 53.

them proselytes, if indeed they be not one and the same. Aquila said to R. Eliezer: 'Why should the mere assurance of food and clothing prove, as Deuteronomy asserts, that God loves the *gēr*? I myself possess peacocks and pheasants in such profusion that my very slaves think nothing of them.' R. Eliezer rebuked him for taking for granted, as if automatic, a providence that is in fact divinely dispensed and also for depreciating an item that Jacob, in formulating his vow, had regarded as of primary importance. So Aquila turned to R. Joshua, who calmed him down by pointing out that *leḥem* in Deut. x.18 is a metaphor for Torah, the bread of wisdom in Prov. ix.5, whilst *śimlā* alludes to the *ṭālīt* and thus perhaps to the (rabbinical) gown.[26] In other words, the Bible is assuring the proselyte that the Torah and its expertise are available in their fullest measure to him no less than to one born a Jew. Nay, more, the terms 'bread' and 'raiment' point also to the sacrificial dues and the raiment worn by priests, inasmuch as there is no impediment to the descent of a high priest of Israel from one who was a proselyte to Judaism. It needs little imagination to appreciate how meaningful this piece of exegetical history would be to a medieval convert to Judaism who had mastered both the Hebrew Bible, and the conventions of medieval Hebrew poetry, with the degree of competence that this Sabbath hymn evinces.[27]

יוֹם זֶה מְכֻבָּד מִכָּל־יָמִים, כִּי בוֹ שָׁבַת צוּר עוֹלָמִים: שֵׁשֶׁת	Isa. lviii.13
יָמִים תַּעֲשֶׂה מְלַאכְתֶּךָ, וְיוֹם הַשְּׁבִיעִי לֵאלֹהֶיךָ, שַׁבָּת לֹא	Exod. xx.9–11
תַעֲשֶׂה בוֹ מְלָאכָה, כִּי כֹל עָשָׂה שֵׁשֶׁת יָמִים: יום זה	Lev. xxiii.2–3
רִאשׁוֹן הוּא לְמִקְרָאֵי קוֹדֶשׁ, יוֹם שַׁבָּתוֹן יוֹם שַׁבַּת קוֹדֶשׁ, עַל כֵּן	
כָּל־אִישׁ בְּיֵינוֹ יְקַדֵּשׁ, עַל שְׁתֵּי לֶחֶם יִבְצְעוּ תְמִימִים: יום זה	
אֱכוֹל מַשְׁמַנִּים שְׁתֵה מַמְתַקִּים, כִּי אֵל יִתֵּן לְכָל־בּוֹ	Neh. viii.10
דְבֵקִים, בֶּגֶד לִלְבּוֹשׁ לֶחֶם חֻקִּים, בָּשָׂר וְדָגִים וְכָל־מַטְעַמִּים: יום ז	Deut. x.18 + Gen. xxviii.20
לֹא תֶחְסַר כֹּל בּוֹ וְאָכַלְתָּ וְשָׂבָעְתָּ, וּבֵרַכְתָּ	Deut. viii.9f
אֶת יְיָ אֱלֹהֶיךָ אֲשֶׁר אָהַבְתָּ, כִּי בֵרַכְךָ מִכָּל־הָעַמִּים: יום זה	
הַשָּׁמַיִם מְסַפְּרִים כְּבוֹדוֹ, גַּם הָאָרֶץ מָלְאָה חַסְדּוֹ, רְאוּ	Psalms xix.2, xxxiii.5;
כִּי כָל־אֵלֶּה עָשְׂתָה יָדוֹ, כִּי הוּא הַצּוּר פָּעֳלוֹ תָמִים: יום זה	Isa. lxvi.2; Deut. xxxii.4

26 The context requires reference to a garment worn as a mark of privilege, and therefore presumably the rabbinical garb mentioned in *Šĕmōt Rabbā*, 27.9 (Wilna, 1878), fo 49*a*, on which see my note in *HTR* 58 (1965), 158, n. 28.

27 The translation is by Herbert Loewe; see his *Mediaeval Hebrew Minstrelsy* (London, 1926), p. 91.

Crown of days, above all blest,
The Rock of Ages chose thee for his rest.

Six days are for toil created
But the seventh God has consecrated.
'Do no labour!' Thus He bade us;
In six days a world He made us.

First of all his feasts renownèd,
Holy Sabbath day, with glory crownèd.
With our cup we speak thy blessing,
With twin loaves his grace confessing.

Eat thy fill, then drink thy pleasure,
For He granteth of his richest treasure:
Gifts to all his word believing,
To his faithful promise cleaving.

Lacking naught, give thanks abounding,
Satisfied, then let thy praise be sounding.
Love the Lord thy God who loved thee.
From all nations He approved thee.

Hark, the heavens his praise are singing;
With his mercy, hark, the spheres are ringing!
Look, He wrought these works enduring,
True his word our weal assuring.

Crown of days, above all blest,
The Rock of Ages chose thee for his rest.

If a proselyte's spiritual joy in his adoption of Judaism is the counterpoint in the piece just considered, a diametrically opposite situation forms the major theme handled in the next, by Abraham ibn Ezra. His son Isaac[28] was the friend and assistant of the distinguished scholar and physician Nethane'el b. ʿAli Ibn Malka of Baghdad, known in Arabic as Hibat Allah abū'l Barakāt, *'awḥad 'al-zaman* ('unique in his generation').[29] The latter in his old age apostatized to Islam, and Isaac ibn Ezra followed his patron, although in a poem he protested that despite his conversion he remained a loyal and observant Jew. True, about the same time Maimonides was maintaining that profession under duress of the formula recitation of which makes one a Muslim does not compromise

28 On Isaac ibn Ezra see *EJ*, vol. VIII, p. 1170, with bibliography.
29 See *Encyclopaedia of Islam*, 2nd edn (1960), vol. I, pp. 111ff, and *EJ*, vol. VIII, pp. 461 ff. Both include bibliographies.

Jewish monotheism;[30] but little imagination is required to picture the reaction of Abraham ibn Ezra to the news of what had befallen his son. In this poem[31] the intensity of feeling, and the structure, are integrally linked with the climactic series of quotations, all of them verses (or rather verse-fragments) culminating in the name 'Isaac' at the end of each stanza. In the exordium Abraham ibn Ezra endeavours to come to terms with a loss viewed as a sacrifice like to that which was all but required of his forefather and namesake (Gen. xxii.2). There follow a first movement in which Isaac's apparent apostasy is felt to spell his spiritual death (Gen. xxxv.29); a second, in which the elder Ibn Ezra laments the tribulations that a father must sustain in looking helplessly on at his son's vicissitudes and in some sense living them out vicariously, even as the biblical Isaac's history was troubled with domestic problems (Gen. xxv.29); a third movement, of dark despair, with allusion to the first Isaac's agony of realization that it is the wrong son to whom he has given the blessing (Gen. xxvii.30); and then in the fourth the triumph of faith. In this last symphonic movement Ibn Ezra prays that his son – still in his eyes a mere lad – may find his spiritual way home, and that the tradition that his father has held in reverence may prove in the end to be the destiny of the son, just as the old servant beside the well prayed that a girl's good manners might lead him to identify the wife providentially designated 'for thy servant, even for Isaac' (Gen. xxiv.14). Isaac ibn Ezra used the Arabic name Abu Saʿd, but one is tempted to suggest that on conversion to Islam he may have

30 *'Iggeret haššĕmad*, chs. 1 and 4, ed. M.D. Rabinovitz, *'Iggĕrōt hārambam*, pp. 31–2, and 61. This letter, written in 1162–3, is now generally regarded as authentic, despite the arguments advanced by M. Friedländer (*The Guide of the Perplexed of Maimonides* (London, 1881), vol. I, pp. xviif, xxxiiif) that it is at least in its present form a pseudograph. The passages indicated are pertinent, though perhaps not crucial, to the question of whether Maimonides himself temporarily professed Islam under duress. *EJ*, vol. XI, pp. 780–1, lists bibliographically the scholars who assert that he did profess Islam and those who deny it, adding but few items to those listed by D. Yellin and I. Abrahams (*Maimonides* (London, 1903), pp. 25, 162, n. 9), who conclude that the evidence warrants no more than a presumption that Maimonides was content to keep a low profile and that he succeeded in avoiding any constructive avowal of Islam. The author of the article in *EJ*, vol. XI, pp. 754–5 (L.I. Rabinowitz) implies that the essential evidence comes from Muslim sources and is to be discounted. On Isaac ibn Ezra's protestation of his Jewish loyalty see Brody-Albrecht (n. 31 below), p. 159.

31 Davidson (see n. 18), vol. I, p. 10, no. 172. H. Brody and K. Albrecht, *The New-Hebrew School of Poets of the Spanish–Arabian Epoch* (London, 1906), pp. 137ff; see below, p. 150.

also taken the name ʻAbdullah, analogously to the adoption of the name Obadiah by those who, formerly Christians, embraced Judaism. Be that as it may, the great closing chord of the poem, *lĕʻabdĕkā lĕyiṣḥāq*, constitutes the victory of faith over despondency, achieved through the recognition that no theology of Jewish peoplehood is feasible without ecumenical corollaries. And this conclusion surely merits comparison with that of Beethoven's Ninth Symphony. The allusiveness of the original makes it impossible to translate without rendering the biblical parallels a degree more explicit, with the consequent loss of subtlety, but a verse rendering, however inadequate, does at least impose the obligation of attempting to match the terseness of the Hebrew.

	אֲבִי הַבֵּן קָרֵב לִסְפֹּד	כִּי אֵל מִמְּךָ רָחָק
Gen. xxii.2	אֶת־בִּנְךָ אֶת־יְחִידְךָ	אֲשֶׁר־אָהַבְתָּ אֶת־יִצְחָק:
Lam. iii.1	אֲנִי הַגֶּבֶר רָאָה	שֶׁבֶר וּמְשׂוֹשׂוֹ גָּלָה
Mic. vi.7	הָהּ פָּקַדְתִּי פְּרִי בִטְנִי	וְעַל־לִבִּי לֹא עָלָה
	כִּי חָשַׁבְתִּי לְעֵת זִקְנָה	הֱיוֹתוֹ לְרֶוַח וְהַצָּלָה
Isa. lxv.23	אַךְ לָרִיק יָגַעְתִּי	וְיָלַדְתִּי לַבֶּהָלָה
Gen. xxxv.29	כִּי אֵיךְ יִשְׂמַח לִבִּי	וַיִּגְוַע וַיָּמָת יִצְחָק:
Lam. i.2; Mic. ii.4	בָּכֹה אֶבְכֶּה בְּכָל־רֶגַע	וְאֶשָּׂא נְהִי נִהְיָה
Exod. xviii.3	בְּזָכְרִי זֶה שָׁלֹשׁ שָׁנִים	מוֹתוֹ בְּאֶרֶץ נָכְרִיָּה
	וְצֵאתוֹ מִמָּקוֹם לְמָקוֹם	וְנַפְשִׁי עָלָיו הֹמִיָּה
	עַד־שֶׁהֲבֵאתִיו אֶל־בֵּיתִי	לַיְלָה וְיוֹמָם בּוֹכִיָּה
Gen. xxv.19	כַּמָּה תְלָאוֹת מְצָאוּנִי	וְאֵלֶּה תּוֹלְדֹת יִצְחָק:
	רֵעַי הַרְפֵּה מִמֶּנִּי	אִם תְּנַחֲמֵנִי תְנִיעֵנִי
	מַחֲלַת נַפְשִׁי אַל־תִּזְכֹּר	וּשְׁמוֹ אַל־תַּשְׁמִיעֵנִי
	גַּחַלְתִּי אֲשֶׁר נִשְׁאֲרָה לִי	כִּבָּה זְמָן וְאִם יְרוֹעֵנִי
Ezek. xxxv.9, xxiv	שִׁמְמוֹת עוֹלָם הֱשִׁמַּנִי	וַיִּקַּח מַחְמַד עֵינִי
Psalm lxxiii.26; Gen. xxvii.30	כָּלָה שְׁאֵרִי וּלְבָבִי	כַּאֲשֶׁר כִּלָּה יִצְחָק:
	מָעוֹן אֲשֶׁר הַכֹּל בְּיָדוֹ	וְחֶפְצוֹ עֹשֶׂה בְּכָל־יְצוּרָיו
	דַּבֵּר עֲלֵי־לֵב אָב נִכְאָב	יָרֵא שִׁמְךָ מִנְּעָרָיו
	רוּחַ תַּנְחוּמִים עוֹרֵר	עָלָיו וְיַעֲבֹר בֵּין בְּתָרָיו
	הוֹרֵה חֲמוּדוֹ יִרְאָתְךָ	לָלֶכֶת בְּדֶרֶךְ הוֹרָיו
Gen. xxiv.14	עוֹדֶנּוּ נַעַר אוֹתָהּ	הֹכַחְתָּ לְעַבְדְּךָ לְיִצְחָק:

I am a father: and myself must hear
Say: ' Mourn, for God from thee did alienate
Thy son – thine only son, that one most dear,
Isaac ', whose name hints at our forebears ' fate.

I am that man whom tragedy did find,
Through joy exiled; and I am brought to book
By forfeiture that I had ne'er divined
Of issue of my body – I did look
To him that should to mine old age prove kind,
Yet toiled in vain: for consternation took
Mine offspring hence. Shall joy my heart elate?
Isaac, his spirit fled, as dead must rate.

Weep, weep must I, nor let my tears relent
One moment, but with lamentation sigh
As I recall how three years are now spent
Since he – for all that he still lives – did die
In foreign fields. Forth from his Place he went
Elsewhere: from morn to night my soul must cry,
Till home I fetch him, troubles must frustrate
Cares that another Isaac's cares equate.

Friend, let me be. Thy words, that would console
Set me aflutter. Mention not his name
For whom compassion yearns within my soul;
Time's fateful march has quenched that single flame
My ember held – would I had been the coal
For him to crush. An endless ruin came
On me, with mine eye's joy made confiscate,
When Isaac's end left me exanimate.

God, our eternal home, by thy hand swayed
All creatures do thy will: comfort the ache
Within a father's heart, who ever paid
To thy name reverence. Consoling, wake
Relief to him by covenant conveyed:
He taught his loved one fear of Thee, to take
His forebears' way – still may his youth await
That way, the spouse for Isaac designate.

But let us return to Ibn Gabirol and conclude with specimens that illustrate the biblical element in two features that are characteristic of him in a pre-eminent degree. The first of these is his sheer virtuosity in the handling of the Hebrew language for poetic purposes (it is worth reminding ourselves here that his prose works were composed in Arabic) in a manner that recalls the mastery of Chopin over the keyboard of the piano; and the second is his *amor dei intellectualis*, the intensity of which served to sublimate and canalize Ibn Gabirol's marked streak of eroticism. Of the pieces here selected, the first may exemplify how the Jewish poet draws on his biblical tradition in treating an intellectual and quasi-scientific commonplace, itself older than the Bible, in order not merely to hebraize it but indeed to 'biblicize' it, i.e. to naturalize it within the context of specifically Jewish cultural tradition. The second illustrates his treatment of a specifically Jewish concept that, although itself post-biblical, derives from exegetical address to the Bible: a concept that the poet makes the more real by exploitation of his own awareness of the original level of meaning of the biblical text, which the exegetical approach has sought to transcend.

In Ibn Gabirol's masterpiece, the *Keter Malkūt*, the theme of human frailty and capacity for penitence is correlated with the creatorship of God and the position within the physical and metaphysical scheme of creation occupied by the human soul. The cosmology is ptolemaic albeit supplemented by a tenth sphere, which does not here concern us, and after dealing briefly with Earth and the four elements the description works outward through the planetary spheres and arrives at the zodiac.[32] The Hebrew names for the signs themselves were, of course, of long standing by Ibn Gabirol's time. One may be tempted to smile at the literary conceit by which Virgo is introduced with language borrowed from the biblical licence for a priest to attend his unmarried sister's funeral (Lev. xxi.3), Ishmael becomes the type of Sagittarius (Gen. xxi.20) and Jonah's whale that of Pisces (Jonah ii.1), but to yield to the temptation to smile is to miss the point. Judaism, no less than the author of the Fourth Gospel, knows of the Word, the same that was at the beginning, by which – rather than by whom – all things were made; for as the Palestinian Targum understands, *bĕrēʾšīt* can be taken as meaning 'by the instrumentality of *rēʾšīt*', that *rēʾšīt* with which Wisdom, and so Torah, identifies herself as 'the beginning of God's way' (Prov. viii.22; cp. iii.19). It was Torah, as if it were an architect's plan, into which God looked when he created the cosmos;[33] since, therefore, it existed before creation,[34] it is natural enough for (the primordial prototype of) Ishmael, *rōbe qaššāt* (which Ibn Gabi-

32 See below, p. 153.

33 *Bĕrēšīt Rabbā*, 1.1 on Gen. i.1 (Wilna) fo 6*a*, ed. Theodor and Albeck, p. 1 (n. 25 above).

34 *Bāraitā* in BT Pesaḥ. 54*a* etc.

rol possibly thought of as meaning 'great archer' rather than 'a shooter , a bowman') to have fulfilled a cosmic function and to have prefigured Sagittarius as well as predetermining the name of the son whom Hagar would bear to Abraham.[35]

מִי יֵדַע הֲלִיכוֹתֶיךָ בַּעֲשׂוֹתְךָ לְשִׁבְעָה כּוֹכְבֵי לֶכֶת הֵיכָלוֹת,
בִּשְׁתֵּים עֶשְׂרֵה מַזָּלוֹת. וְעַל טָלֶה וְשׁוֹר אָצַלְתָּ כֹּחֲךָ בְּהִתְיַחֲדָם,
וְהַשְּׁלִישִׁי תְּאוֹמִים כִּשְׁנֵי אַחִים בְּהִתְאַחֲדָם, וּדְמוּת פְּנֵיהֶם — Ezek. i.10
פְּנֵי אָדָם. וְלָרְבִיעִי וְהוּא סַרְטָן, גַּם לְאַרְיֵה נָתַתָּ מֵהוֹדְךָ עָלָיו, — Num. xxvii.20
וְלַאֲחוֹתוֹ הַבְּתוּלָה הַקְּרוֹבָה אֵלָיו. וְכֵן לְמֹאזְנַיִם וּלְעַקְרָב אֲשֶׁר — Lev. xx.3
בְּצִדּוֹ הוּשָׁת, וְהַתְּשִׁיעִי הַנִּבְרָא בְּצוּרַת גִּבּוֹר בְּקֶשֶׁת כֹּחוֹ לֹא
נָשָׁת. וַיְהִי רוֹבֶה קַשָּׁת. וְכֵן נִבְרָא גְּדִי וּדְלִי בְּכֹחֲךָ הַגָּדוֹל, — Gen. xxi.20
וּלְצִדּוֹ הַמַּזָּל הָאַחֲרוֹן וַיְמַן יְיָ דָּג גָּדוֹל, וְאֵלֶּה הַמַּזָּלוֹת גְּבוֹהִים — Jonah ii.1
וְנִשָּׂאִים בְּמַעֲלוֹתָם, שְׁנֵים עָשָׂר נְשִׂיאִים לְאֻמֹּתָם. — Gen. xxv.16

What man may thy eternal ways divine?
Thou, for the seven planets designate
Didst make the twelve signs mansions palatine,
Lending thine own strength to invigorate
The *Ram*, paired with the *Bull*, and that third sign
Of *Gemini*, the twain inseparate
Visaged like men, and then the fourth in line,
Cancer, and *Leo*, whom Thou didst instate
With some part of thy majesty to shine
Close by his sister *Virgo* radiate;
Libra, next whom is placed the serpentine
Scorpio; and that ninth, Thou didst create
A warrior bold, ne'er knowing his strength pine,
Who aims his bow an Ishmael constellate:
Thy might formed *Capricorn*, and did assign
Aquarius, pail in hand, to be their mate:
Last, lonely *Pisces* didst Thou place in trine
That Jonah's whale be seen predestinate.
These fill the zodiac's exalted list,
Twelve princes, each his nation's own protagonist.

My final specimen is a wedding-hymn by Ibn Gabirol,[36] and it illustrates the manner in which a piece of allegorical interpretation can establish itself so firmly in popular acclaim that the allegory, having become almost an article of faith, can find itself being ap-

35 From my forthcoming translation (see above, n. 13).
36 Davidson (see n. 18), vol. III, p. 432, no. 637. See below, p. 154.

plied to a situation not so very far from its own literal launching-pad in the text. As is well known, the Song of Songs was allegorized in rabbinic Judaism as the love-dialogue of God and Israel,[37] a scheme that was inherited and modified by the Church.[38] But independently of this motif the rabbis, in conformity with the positive attitude towards sex that is characteristic of nearly all traditions within Judaism, set about domesticating human sexuality by theologizing it. As R. ʿAqiba himself pointed out,[39] the *yod* and the *he* of *Yah* are to be found in *'īš* and *'iššā*, signifying the divine Presence (*šĕkīnā*) wherever the marriage is a successful one, but where the couple can find no room for it in their matrimonial life, both *'īš* and *'iššā* are reduced to mere *'ēš*, the fire of consuming passion. Thus it comes about that the notion of God's relationship to Israel as his bride can be reflected in Jewish marriage as an institution, and the Song of Songs, which begins as the love-idyll of the countryside or of the Court and is then made the subject of theological allegory, can form the sub-stratum of a wedding-hymn composed, like the Song of Songs itself, in dialogue form, and designed to inspire the bridal couple with the will to make their own union a reflection of that peculiarly Jewish ἱερὸς γάμος with which the Synagogue also endowed the Church. The wheel has come full circle: appropriately enough, in that Ibn Gabirol's first name was Solomon.[40]

שׁוֹכַנְתְּ בַּשָּׂדֶה	עִם אָהֳלֵי כוּשָׁן,	Hab. iii.7; Psalm cxx.5
עִמְדִי לְרֹאשׁ כַּרְמֶל	וּצְפִי לְהַר בָּשָׁן.	
לַגַּן אֲשֶׁר נֶחְמַס,	יָפָה, שְׂאִי עַיִן	
וּרְאִי עֲרוּגָתֵךְ	כִּי נִמְלְאָה שׁוֹשָׁן.	
מַה־לָּךְ, צְבִי נֶחְמָד,	כִּי תַעֲזֹב גַּנִּי	
לִרְעוֹת בְּגַן יָקְשָׁן	וּבְתוֹךְ עֲצֵי דִישָׁן.	Gen. xxv.2
הַב נֵרְדָה לַגָּן	נֹאכַל מְגָדִים שָׁם	Song of Songs vi.2, iv.13,
וּבְחֵיק יְפַת־עַיִן	תִּשְׁכַּב וְגַם תִּישָׁן.	iv.1

37 BT Šĕbu. 35*b*. The most elaborate development of the notion is the Targum to the Song of Songs; see R. Loewe, 'Apologetic Motifs in the Targum to the Song of Songs', in A. Altmann (ed.), *Biblical Motifs*, Studies and Texts 3 (Cambridge, Mass., 1966), pp. 159ff, especially pp. 169ff.

38 In particular, Origen's commentary on the Song of Songs was accepted as a classical exposition of the Christian interpretation; see R. Loewe, 'Apologetic Motifs', pp. 173f, 196; R. Kimelman, *HTR* 73 (1980), 567f.

39 BT Soṭa 17*a*.

40 The translation was privately printed in an *Order of Service for Hakaphot*, *Eve of Simḥat Torah*, by the Spanish and Portuguese Jews' Congregation (London, 1965), p. 10.

'Mid alien tents still must thou dwell, forlorn,
Out on the heath? Nay, up, to Carmel's top,
My fairest maid, on Bashan's heights to gaze,
Our garden bower to scan
Laid out ere time began:
See how, for thee, its beds with lilies blaze.'

'Why, then, my heart's desire, hast Thou forsworn
So long my garden close, elsewhere to crop,
A lonely hart, in foreign fields to graze?
Our garden screened shall keep
The joys we taste: aye, sleep,
Lull'd on thy true-love's breast, at peace, always.'

Some Notes on Šelomo Almoli's Contributions to the Linguistic Science of Hebrew

SHELOMO MORAG

Our biographical knowledge of Šelomo Almoli[1] is rather meagre. He was born between 1480 and 1490, probably in Spain.[2] His literary activities, at any rate, took place in Constantinople, where he lived from about 1515 until his death (after 1542), earning his livelihood by serving as a judge of the rabbinical court (*dayyān*) and a physician. In this article I shall concern myself with Almoli's grammatical treatise,[3] הליכות שבא, 'the ways of the *šĕwā*'.[4] The main purpose of this work is to present rules for making the distinction between *šĕwā* on the one hand and *ṣērī*/*sĕgōl* on the other.[5] In fact, it contains much more than these rules, in the domain of phonological theory as well as in that of the traditional pronunciations of Hebrew. The significance of the work therefore extends

1 The name, written אלמולי, may be transcribed as either Almoli or Almuli. Both forms, as well as Almeli and Almali, appear in documents relating to the history of the Jewish communities of Spain (see F. Baer, *Die Juden im Christlichen Spanien*, vol. I (Berlin, 1929), indices, p. 1100; mentioned by Ḥ. Yalon, *HŠ*, p. פב). The abbreviation *HŠ* will be used in this article to denote Yalon's admirable edition of הליכות שבא (Jerusalem, 1945).

2 There is no definitive evidence on this point.

3 For information regarding Almoli's other works see Yalon, *HŠ*, pp. עט–פא; *EJ*, vol. II, pp. 663–5, s.v. 'Almoli'.

4 The name is a pun, based on Job vi.19 where הליכות שבא possibly means 'the routes of Sheba' (namely, the travellers using these routes; NEB: 'travelling merchants of Sheba'). The spelling שבא for שְׁוָא is common in medieval grammatical works (see, e.g., Ben-Yehuda's *Thesaurus*, p. 6819). In the work under discussion, Almoli himself mostly uses the form with *w*, not the one with *b*, although he considers the latter to be etymologically correct (see *HŠ*, p. טו).

5 In the traditional pronunciation of the author, as in those of the Sephardi communities, the realizations of the *šĕwā* and the *ṣērī*/*sĕgōl* were identical. Hence the significance for Sephardi *naqdānīm* of rules for distinguishing *šĕwā* from *ṣērī*/*sĕgōl*.

far beyond the problem of *šĕwā*; it should, in fact, be regarded as a milestone in the study of the structure of Hebrew phonology.[6]

In size, *HŠ* is a small treatise consisting, in Yalon's edition, of seventy small pages.[7] The work is divided into three parts. In the first part, which has three chapters, the author presents some important elements of his phonological theory (to which I shall later return); locates the place of the *šĕwā* within the system of Hebrew vowels; discusses the 'seven typical features' (Hebrew *sĕgullōt*) of the *šĕwā*; and states rules for the distribution of mobile and quiescent *šĕwā'īm* and for the phonetic realizations of the mobile *šĕwā*.

Different in scope and nature is the second part, which consists of two chapters. Whereas the first part is, in the main, concerned with theory, the second is practically orientated: the author introduces, in the first chapter of this part, the nine 'fundamental rules',[8] which determine whether, in a certain position of the word, or in a certain nominal or verbal pattern, the vowel is a *šĕwā*, and not a *ṣērī*/*sĕgōl*. As mentioned above, the making of this distinction is the central theme of Almoli's treatise, around which revolve his far more valuable theoretical discussions.

The second chapter of this part deals with the composite *šĕwā'īm*, namely, the *ḥăṭāpīm*. The author first explains the nature of the *ḥăṭāpīm* and analytically presents the reasons for their use; there then follow five 'fundamental rules' (*haqdāmōt*), which describe the distribution of the *ḥăṭāpīm* in various syllabic positions and their occurrences in nominal patterns.

The third part is devoted to the morphology of the noun. In its first chapter Almoli lists the nominal patterns occurring in Biblical Hebrew; in the second these patterns appear again, this time accompanied with lists of nouns that actually belong to them.

The link attaching the third part to the first two is the *šĕwā*: the author's primary aim in presenting the nominal patterns is to show

6 The debt owed by students of the history of Hebrew grammar to Ḥ. Yalon should here be mentioned. In his edition of *HŠ*, the value of which cannot be overestimated, Yalon established Almoli's place in the history of Hebrew grammar. Cp. also his paper '*Mā bēn rabbī Šĕlōmō 'Almōlī lĕrabbī 'Eliyāhū Baḥūr*', *Lĕšonénu* 27–8 (1964), 225–9. Yalon also edited a treatise on poetics, *Šeqel Haqqōdeš*, which he attributed to Almoli (Jerusalem, 1965), and several chapters from Almoli's *Hammĕ'assēp lĕkol hammaḥănōt*, in his *Pirqē Lāšōn* (Jerusalem, 1971) pp. 218–32.

7 Substantial parts of these pages consist of Yalon's footnotes.

8 I use 'fundamental rule' to translate Hebrew *haqdāmā*.

when and where a *šĕwā* appears in them or, morphophonemically, in their declensions.[9] Almoli's treatment of the nominal patterns, however, goes far beyond the primary aim. This third part is, in fact, a succinct and clear description of the morphology of the noun.

Almoli's stature as a Hebrew grammarian cannot be appreciated through this brief synopsis of the structure and contents of *Hălīkōt Šĕbā*. His originality is reflected in the analytical and critical approach that led him to establish, as we shall see, a new structural theory of the vowel-system, and to take a stand of his own on such relevant points as standard and norm. Judged by these criteria, Yalon's evaluation of Almoli as one of the greatest Jewish students of the Hebrew language seems fully justified.[10]

I shall now present some features of Almoli's phonological theory, as well as some of his views on normativity and on traditional pronunciations.

The vowel-system of Hebrew

Almoli's system of Hebrew vowels consists of five 'kings' (*mĕlākīm*) and five 'servants' (*ʿăbādīm*). Each of the 'kings' has his specific 'servant', that is, a vowel that 'serves' only him. In the following table the respective 'servants' appear against their 'kings':

'kings'	'servants'
ā (qāmēṣ)	*a (pātaḥ)*
ē (ṣērī)	*e (sĕgōl)*
ī (ḥīreq followed by a silent *yōd)*	*i (ḥīreq* not followed by a silent *yōd)*
ō (ḥōlam)	*å (qāmēṣ qāṭān)*[11]
ū (šūraq)	*u (qibbūṣ)*

Almoli's 'kings' and 'servants' are the counterparts of the long (*tĕnūʿōt gĕdōlōt*) and short (*tĕnūʿōt qĕṭannōt*) vowels of the Qimḥis' school. The structure of the vowel-system of Hebrew, designed by the Qimḥis, is based on the notion of quantity (length) as a major feature. Joseph Qimḥi (*c.* 1105–1170), the father of

9 See Almoli's words (pp. נה, נט) explaining why he included this third part in *HŠ*, which is a work devoted to the *šĕwā*.

10 *HŠ*, p. ח.

11 Almoli uses the term *ḥăṭap-qāmēṣ* for the *qāmēṣ qāṭān* (*HŠ*, p. י). This use is common in medieval grammatical terminology. Cp. Yalon's n. 14 on the same page.

David, appears to have been the first[12] to identify this feature as a distinctive mark pervading the entire vowel-system (with the exception of the *šĕwā* and the *ḥăṭāpīm*) and creating a tenfold system divided into two parallel categories, namely, the long and the short vowels.[13] Joseph's sons, Moses (died *c.* 1190) and David (*c.* 1160–1235), adopted this concept of the vowel-system,[14] also incorporating in the theory underlying it the principles formulated by Ḥayyūğ.[15] The Qimḥis' theory of the structure of the vowel-system

12 As to the very principle of using the notion of quantity as a marker distinguishing vowels, he seems to be indebted to Ḥayyūğ. For the latter's theory see below n. 15.

13 See his *Sepher Sikkaron* (= *Zikkārōn*), ed. W. Bacher (Berlin, 1888), p. 17.

14 See Moses Qimḥi's *Mahălak Šĕbīlē Hadda'at* (Hamburg, 1785), p. 12*b*; David Qimḥi's *Miklōl* (Lyck, 1842), pp. 136*a*ff.

15 Cp. W. Chomsky, *David Kimhi's Hebrew Grammar* (*Mikhlōl*) (New York, 1952), p. 31, n. 11. For Ḥayyūğ's concept of quantity see his *kitāb al-tanqīt* (= *Sēfer hanniqqūd*), published in T.W. Nutt (ed.), *Two Treatises on Verbs containing Feeble and Double Letters by R. Jehuda Ḥayug of Fez* (London–Berlin, 1870), pp. Iff (the Arabic original), pp. 120–1 (Abraham Ibn Ezra's Hebrew translation). Ḥayyūğ deals with this question also in his *kitāb al-'af'āl ḏawāt ḥurūf al-līn* (published by M. Jastrow, as *The Weak and Geminative Verbs in Hebrew by Abû Zakariyyâ Ḥayyûĝ* (Leiden, 1897) p. 8. Moses Giḳatilla's Hebrew translation of this book was published by Nutt; for the passage referred to, see *ibid.* pp. 6–7).

Some notes on Ḥayyūğ's notion of quantity (vowel-length) are in order. For Ḥayyūğ, quantity is a feature resulting from the syllabic structure and depending, in part, on orthography, actual or reconstructed. Thus, e.g., the *ḥōlam* of שְׁכוֹר and the *ḥīreq* of פָּלִיט are to be considered long because of the vowel letters; the same holds good for the *qāmēṣ* of שָׁמַר, which is potentially to be regarded as being followed by a silent א (= שָׁאמַר) and is therefore long. (The occurrence of the *qāmēṣ* in an open, unstressed syllable, as well as in a closed, stressed syllable, results, according to Ḥayyūğ, from the hypothetical existence of a silent א, *nāḥ nistār*, after the *qāmēṣ*.) Similarly, the first *ṣērī* in יֵצֵא is followed by a hypothetical silent י, and is, therefore, long.

Ḥayyūğ's basic principles are evident in both Moses Qimḥi's and David Qimḥi's exposition of the structure of the vowel-system. Moses Qimḥi says in *Mahălak* (above, n. 14), p. 12*b*:

כי התנועה הקטנה אחריה נח נראה והתנועה הגדולה אחריה נח נסתר

'The short vowel occurs before a vowelless consonant while the long vowel occurs before a vowel letter.'

Similarly, David Qimhi, in *Miklōl*, p. 136*a*:

ודע כי חמש התנועות הגדולות אחריהן נח לעולם

'One should know that the five long vowels are always followed by a vowel letter.'

Both Qimḥis evidently use the term 'a vowel letter' to refer either to an actual one or to one existing potentially. (See שָׁאמַר mentioned earlier in this note.)

spread widely, through the writings of David Qimḥi and his followers, and was accepted, being a part of Qimḥi's grammatical text-book, by Jews as well as by Christian Hebraists.[16]

In spite of the external similarity, Almoli's concept of the relationship between the 'kings' and the 'servants' differs from that of the long and short vowels in the Qimḥis' school. Although he must have been well acquainted with the writings of David Qimḥi, whom he mentions several times,[17] Almoli did not adopt the Qimḥis' theory of the structure of the vowel-system. Almoli's own concept of the vowel-system is based on the notion of hierarchy. The hierarchy in the system consists of four levels that, starting from the top, are:

(1) 'kings' = the Qimḥis' long vowels
(2) 'servants'[18] = the Qimḥis' short vowels
(3) mobile *šĕwā*
(4) quiescent *šĕwā* = 'zero'

From Almoli's remarks regarding the position of the mobile *šĕwā* in the scale we can infer that the four levels are evenly graded: 'the mobile *šĕwā* is intermediate in position between the five servants and the quiescent *šĕwā* . . . so that the mobile *šĕwā* is to be regarded a "king" in relationship to the quiescent, and the quiescent is a "servant" in relationship to the mobile'.[19]

The introduction of this structure of the vowel-system, comprehensive (including, as we have seen, also the mobile *šĕwā* and 'zero'), symmetrical and rather simple, is to be considered an important stage in the history of the phonological theory of the Hebrew grammarians.

What are the logical foundations of the vowel-system that Almoli proposes? There appear to be three such foundations, namely, (*a*) discrepancy between phonology and orthography;[20] (*b*) syllabic structure and vowel-quantity; and (*c*) morphophonemic relations.

16 Cp. S.C. Reif, *HUCA* 44 (1973), 211ff.
17 See Yalon's index, *HŠ*, p. קטו.
18 I use 'servants' to translate Almoli's *ʿăbādīm*, preferring this translation to 'slaves'; because of the semantic associations, 'servants' appears to be more appropriate.
19 *HŠ*, p. יג. Although Almoli makes no explicit statement about the grading of the 'servants' in relation to the 'kings', it seems that all four levels are evenly graded.
20 In 'orthography' I also include the vowel-signs.

(*a*) *Discrepancy between phonology and orthography*

Almoli's pronunciation of Hebrew, like all the Sephardi pronunciations, had only five vowels: *i*, *e*, *a*, *u*, *o*.[21] These vowels were the realizations of the following vowel-signs:

i = *ḥīreq* (whether followed by a *yōd* or not)	*u* = *šūraq* and *qibbūṣ*
e = *ṣērī* and *sĕgōl* (mobile *šĕwā* and *ḥăṭap-sĕgōl*)	*o* = *ḥōlam*, *qāmēṣ qāṭān* (and *ḥăṭap-qāmēṣ*)
a = *qāmēṣ*, *pātaḥ* (and *ḥăṭap-pātaḥ*)	

The number of the vowel-signs extant in the vocalization is thus much larger than the number of the vowels used in the actual pronunciation.[22] This rather baffling situation requires an explanation, and the hierarchic system Almoli introduces is in fact an attempt to present a logical explanation of this discrepancy between phonology and orthography. Because of some fundamental features of Hebrew, which he discusses (see below, (*b*) and (*c*)), every vowel that actually exists phonetically has to be represented by two vowel-signs; for this purpose the parallel series of 'kings' and 'servants' had to be created.

I might add that the problem of discrepancy mentioned above also underlies the Qimḥis' theory of the structure of the vowel-system. Earlier grammarians of the Spanish school, whose pronunciation was Sephardi while the vocalization they used was the 'ten vowel-signs' (Tiberian), were also definitely aware of the existence of this problem.

(*b*) *Syllabic structure and vowel quantity*

Presenting the most explicit explanation for the existence, in the vocalization, of the five 'servants' (Qimḥi's short vowels) *versus* the five 'kings' (Qimḥi's long vowels), Almoli says:[23]

לפי שפעמים יתחייב בדבור להאריך בתנועה מעט ולהוליד נחות אחריה
ופעמים להמשיכה במרוצה מבלי נחות כלל

21 This is also the case in the present-day traditional Sephardi pronunciations. The vowel-system of modern Hebrew, which also has this system, is based upon the Sephardi pronunciation.

22 Almoli (following in this respect David Qimḥi) speaks of ten vowel-signs. He counts the *ḥīreq* with a *yōd* and the *ḥīreq* without a *yōd* as two signs, the *ḥōlam*, whether with a *wāw* or not, as one sign (independent of the *qāmēṣ qāṭān*, realized as *o*) and excludes the mobile *šĕwā*, realized as *e*.

23 *HŠ*, p. י.

> For speech may occasionally necessitate a little lengthening of the vowel, thus creating a closed syllable; on the other hand, it may be necessary to have the vowel articulated 'runningly', without creating a closed syllable.[24]

The 'creator of the language'[25] has established, according to Almoli, these two categories of vowel-signs in the vocalization, in order to denote the quantitative (length) differences in the realizations of a vowel, e.g.,[26] between the *pātaḥ* in זָכַר, 'he remembered', which has 'a little lengthening', and the *qāmēṣ*, which is 'articulated runningly'.[27] Although Almoli is rather brief here, his conception of vowel-quantity not as an inherent feature of the vowel-system (as it is in the Qimḥis' school), but rather as an element resulting from syllabic structure, can quite clearly be grasped. We might note in passing that Ḥayyūǧ's theory of vowel-quantity also relates this feature to syllabic structure.[28] Almoli's approach may have its roots in Ḥayyūǧ's theory; as things stand, however, in the text of *HŠ*, it cannot be considered an adaptation of the latter.

(*c*) *Morphophonemic relations*

Almoli's hierarchy of vowels is primarily based on the concept of 'serving'.[29] Any of the vowels of level (2), the 'servants', and the mobile *šĕwā*, serve the vowels of a higher level. That is, every 'servant' of level (2) serves its corresponding 'king'; the mobile *šĕwā*, the 'servant' *par excellence*,[30] has multiple serving functions.

24 By 'a little lengthening' Almoli means a relatively short realization of a vowel; in saying that a vowel may be extended 'runningly' he has in mind a relatively long realization. The expression להמשיך במרוצה apparently means here 'to articulate'. (Cp. *HŠ*, p. יב: להחטיף את האות ולהמשיכה במרוצה מבלי שום תנועה, 'to denote that the consonant has to be articulated without any vowel following it'.) For Almoli's other uses of הריץ (literally 'make to run') as a phonetic term, see *HŠ*, p. יז, line 9; p. יט, line 11; p. כ, line 4 from bottom; p. כח, last line. Cp. also below, n. 49.

25 בעל הלשון (*HŠ*, p. י), literally: 'the master of the Hebrew language'.

26 The example is mine. Almoli does not, however, deal with the problem of a *qāmēṣ* occurring in the same syllabic conditions as *pātaḥ* (e.g. זָכָר, 'a male' versus זָכַר, 'he remembered').

27 Our interpretation of Almoli's statement regarding vowel-quantity is in agreement with that of Yalon (*HŠ*, p. , n. 15).

28 See above, n. 15.

29 Hebrew: שרות; the term appears on p. יד, line 5 from bottom. Cp. also משמש, 'serves', on line 4 from the bottom.

30 The *šĕwā* is *ʿebed ʿăbādīm*, 'servant of servants' (*HŠ*, p. יד).

Almoli does not say explicitly what he means by 'serving'; from several passages in his treatise, however, it may perhaps be adduced that the meaning of the term would come quite close to that of 'appearing as a morphophonemic alternant' in modern linguistics. Thus, for example, when he says that 'it is the nature of the king that he does not serve ... but the servants always serve them [= the kings]',[31] he may be referring to such alternations as דְּבַר־ in relation to דָּבָר, or לֶב־ in relation to לֵב, where the 'servants', *pātaḥ* and *sĕgōl*, 'serve' the 'kings', *qāmēṣ* and *ṣērī*.[32]

So far Almoli's theory of the vowel-system. As observed above, medieval Hebrew grammarians had to tackle a great difficulty, namely, the discrepancy created by the relationship of their Sephardi pronunciation with the vowel-system reflected by the Tiberian vocalization. Almoli's theory probably constitutes the last attempt to offer an interpretation of this inconsistency.

The concluding section of my discussion of this pertinent problem in the history of Hebrew grammatical thought is perhaps a good place to present in a comparative way some of the main features of the Hebrew vowel-system (in particular, those pertaining to the quality-quantity relationship), as they appear in practice and theory in four schools concerned with medieval transmission of Hebrew and its study. These schools are: the Tiberian Massoretes; Ḥayyūğ; the Qimḥis; Almoli.[33]

31 *HŠ*, p. י: וזהו דרך המלך שאינו משמש... אבל העבדים לעולם בהם יעבודו..

32 Note also that Almoli speaks of 'change' and 'turn' when referring to morphophonemic alternations. *HŠ*, p. מ:

לפעמים ישתנו השואים אל בלתי־שוא והבלתי־שואיים אל שוא

'The *šĕwā'īm* sometimes change into "*non-šĕwā*" and the "*non-šĕwā'īm*" into a *šĕwā*.'

Ibid.:

ולזה המלכים והעבדים יחזרו לשוא והשוא לא ישוב אליהם

'And so the "kings" and the "servants" turn into a *šĕwā* but the *šĕwā* does not turn into them.'

33 Not in all medieval Hebrew schools can these features be traced in full. It is particularly unfortunate that Saadya's theory of vowel-length has not reached us. (The Leningrad manuscript from which S.L. Skoss published Saadya's 'Study of Hebrew vowels' breaks off where the author starts his discussion of the shortenting and lengthening of the *ḥōlam*: see *JQR*, N.S. 42 (1952), 316.)

Tiberian Hebrew		Ḥayyūǧ	The Qimḥi School	Almoli
Qualitative distinctions are made between all seven vowels (*qāmēṣ* – *pātaḥ* – *ṣērī* – *sĕgōl* – *ḥōlam* – *ḥīreq* – *šūraq*/*qibbūṣ*); *quantitative* (length) distinctions are consistently made between ordinary and ultra-short vowels,[34] but not among ordinary vowels.	In actual pronunciation:	No distinctions, either qualitative or quantitative,[35] are made between *qāmēṣ gādōl* and *pātaḥ*; *ṣērī* and *sĕgōl*; *ḥōlam*, *ḥăṭap-qāmēṣ* and *qāmēṣ qāṭān*		
	In theory:	The notion of quantity is present; it depends partly on orthography and partly on syllabic structure, making it possible, in certain cases, to distinguish *qāmēṣ* from *pātaḥ*, *ṣērī* from *sĕgōl*, and *ḥōlam* from *qāmēṣ qāṭān*.[36]	The notion of quantity is a fundamental feature of the entire vowel system, which consists of five long vowels and five short vowels; in addition, Ḥayyūǧ's syllabic principles are included.	There is a hierarchy in the vowel-system, the two highest levels being the 'kings' and the 'servants' (corresponding to the Qimḥis' long and short vowels); relationships between the 'kings' and the 'servants' depend on syllabic structure and vowel-quantity as well as on morphophonemic considerations.

(footnotes 34, 35, 36 are on page 166).

Some aspects of the pronunciation of Hebrew

As observed above, Almoli's phonological theory emerged out of the need to account for a distinction extant in Tiberian Hebrew but missing in the Sephardi pronunciation, namely, the distinction between *ṣērī/sĕgōl* and *šĕwā*. Related to this central theme are his discussions of several aspects of the traditional pronunciation of Hebrew, both his own and that of former generations. These discussions are occasionally intertwined with critical observations of statements and rules made by other grammarians, primarily David Qimḥi, the great medieval master. I shall here briefly present two of Almoli's observations that are of some interest for the history of Hebrew pronunciation.[37]

(1) *Medial* šĕwā, *preceded by a long vowel: mobile or quiescent?*

Almoli does not agree with David Qimḥi's opinion regarding the nature of a medial *šĕwā* preceded by a long vowel, that is, a *šĕwā*

34 Hebrew, as pronounced by the Tiberian Massoretes, had two systems of vowels, which were qualitatively identical, but differed quantitatively, namely:

(*a*) ordinary (that is 'normal', neither short nor long)

i (*ḥīreq*)	*u* (*šūraq/qibbūṣ*)
e (*ṣērī*)	*o* (*ḥōlam*)
ɛ (*sĕgōl*)	*å* (*qāmēṣ*)
a (*pātaḥ*)	

(*b*) ultra-short ('*ḥăṭūpōt*')

ĭ	*ŭ*
ĕ	*ŏ*
ɛ̆	*å̆*
ă	

Explanatory notes for (*b*): *ă* is the basic realization of *šĕwā* (and of *ḥăṭap-pātaḥ*);

ĭ is the realization of a *šĕwā* preceding a *yōd*, or ', *h*, *ḥ* or ʿ when these letters are vocalized with a *ḥīreq*;

ĕ, *ŭ*, *ŏ*, are the realizations of a *šĕwā* preceding ', *h*, *ḥ*, or ʿ when they are vocalized with *ṣērī*, *šūraq/qibbūṣ* or *ḥōlam*, respectively;

ɛ̆ is the realization of *ḥăṭap-sĕgōl* and of a *šĕwā* preceding ', *h*, *ḥ*, or ʿ, when they are vocalized with a *sĕgōl*;

å̆ is the realization of *ḥăṭap-qāmēṣ* and of a *šĕwā* preceding ', *h*, *ḥ*, or ʿ, when they are vocalized with a *qāmēṣ*.

For some medieval sources that expound the Tiberian rules for the realizations of the *šĕwā*, see my *The Hebrew Language Tradition of the Yemenite Jews* (Jerusalem, 1963) (Hebrew), pp. 160–6.

35 What I here have in mind are constant, regular, distinctions.

36 See above, n. 15.

37 Some of Almoli's observations also shed light upon some aspects of the present-day communal pronunciations of Hebrew.

in words like שׁוֹמְרִים, שָׁמְרוּ etc.[38] According to David Qimḥi this *šĕwā* is mobile.[39] Taking a stand against this opinion of David Qimḥi, Almoli says:[40]

> We do not, at the present time, pronounce [the *šĕwā* mentioned above] in this way [that is, as a mobile *šĕwā*], nor have we heard anywhere about such a pronunciation; everybody pronounces it as quiescent. We ought, therefore, to regard this custom of [the communities of] Israel, to which they all adhere, as a tradition from which we should not deviate.

The passage in question ends with a significant principle, namely, the precedence of tradition over prescribed grammatical rules. This principle is reformulated in another passage, where Almoli describes the various realizations of the mobile *šĕwā*:[41] 'it is in order to keep the customs [based on tradition] that are in agreement with what the books say; but we should in no way practise the customs that are prescribed in books but which nobody actually follows'.[42]

To return to the former passage treating the medial *šĕwā*: a significant item of information for the history of Hebrew pronunciation is provided here. Almoli unequivocally states (and he appears to be the first grammarian to do so) that in the pronunciation of his community (and of other communities, apparently Sephardi, known to him), this medial *šĕwā* is quiescent. This means that the Sephardi communities of Almoli's time did not follow Qimḥi's rule in their realization of the medial *šĕwā*.[43]

It is of some interest to note that the present-day reading traditions of the Sephardi communities reflect the difference between Qimḥi and Almoli:[44] in reading the Bible these communities realize the medial *šĕwā* as mobile (that is, they follow Qimḥi's rule), while in their reading of the post-biblical literature, primarily the Mishnah and the Hebrew parts of the Talmud, this *šĕwā* is quiescent (that

38 In this section I shall henceforth refer to this *šĕwā* as 'medial *šĕwā*'.

39 Almoli quotes Qimḥi's *'Ēṯ Sōfēr* (for the passage in question see the Lyck 1864 edition of the book, fo. 3*a*; cp. also *Miklōl*, p. 136*b*).

40 *HŠ*, p. כא.

41 *HŠ*, p. כח.

42 By 'customs' (*minhāgīm*) Almoli refers here to features of pronunciation.

43 To be more precise: those communities whose pronunciations were known to Almoli.

44 The term 'Sephardi communities' is employed here in a broad sense, including all oriental communities except the Yemenite.

is, in reading these texts the Sephardi communities are in agreement with Almoli's statement).[45]

One may surmise that in Almoli's time the medial *šěwā* was realized as quiescent in the Sephardi reading traditions of both biblical and post-biblical texts, and that its realization as mobile in the Sephardi reading traditions of biblical texts reflects a development that took place after Almoli's time. This development may be due to the influence of David Qimḥi, whose Hebrew grammar, the *Miklōl*, attained a great measure of popularity in Jewish communities.[46] Another explanation might also be feasible: the Sephardi communities differed among themselves, from times prior to David Qimḥi's, as to the realization of the medial *šěwā*. Some of them regarded it as mobile in reading the Bible and quiescent in reading post-biblical literature; others regarded it as quiescent in reading all texts, whether biblical or post-biblical. David Qimḥi's rule is based on the practice of the former communities,[47] while Almoli's observation reflects that of the latter.

(2) *A medial mobile* šěwā *following a quiescent: quantitative aspects*

In presenting the constraints that do not allow the occurrence of two consecutive mobile *šěwāīm*,[48] Almoli employs the phonetic notion of 'semi-deletion' (חצי־חטיפות). This notion is introduced to denote the realization of the second of two consecutive *šěwā'īm*.

In order to grasp the meaning of this expression, we should note that in Almoli's terminology *ḥăṭīpūt* is used in the sense of 'zero',

45 It should, however, be borne in mind that Almoli makes no distinction between biblical and post-biblical Hebrew.

For the nature of medial *šěwā* in the traditional pronunciations of the Sephardi communities see S. Morag (ed.), *The Hebrew Language Tradition of the Baghdadi Community: The Phonology* (Hebrew: *Edah Velashon*, vol. I (Publications of the Hebrew University Language Traditions Project) (Jerusalem, 1977)), pp. 79ff; K. Katz, *The Hebrew Language Tradition of the Community of Djerba* (Tunisia), (Hebrew: *Edah Velashon*, vol. II (Jerusalem, 1977)), pp. 116ff; S. Morag, 'A "Semi-Mobile" *Shěwā*', *Proceedings of the Fifth World Congress for Jewish Studies* (Jerusalem, 1973), pp. 173–81.

46 This explanation was offered by Yalon, *HŠ*, p. קא.

47 As one would expect, David Qimḥi refers in his rule only to the reading of the Bible.

48 *HŠ*, pp. ל–לא.

'absence of any vowel' (= quiescent *šĕwā*).[49] In other words, according to Almoli a mobile *šĕwā* following a quiescent *šĕwā* is, in its duration, in an intermediate position between a full vowel[50] and 'zero', while an initial *šĕwā* is a full vowel. Almoli thus makes an interesting distinction, based on duration, between a mobile *šĕwā* following a quiescent *šĕwā* and other kinds of mobile *šĕwā'īm*. As far as I know, we possess no evidence for an actual distinction between the former *šĕwā* and other kinds of mobile *šĕwā'īm* in any traditional pronunciation of Hebrew; it might be worthwhile noting, however, that the present-day traditional pronunciation of the Baghdadi community discloses a similar, although not identical, distinction between the phonetic realization of two kinds of mobile *šĕwā'īm*. In this pronunciation, a medial *šĕwā* preceded by a vowel (after which no gemination occurs) is differently realized, quantitatively and occasionally also qualitatively, from other categories of *šĕwā'īm*.[51]

49 See p. לא. Cp. the use of להחטיף האות (*HŠ*, pp. יב׳, יד׳) in the meaning of 'to indicate that a letter is not followed by any vowel (that is, is followed by "zero")'. The fuller form of the term is probably *ḥăṭīpūt šĕlēmā*, 'complete deletion' (for this term see pp. לא–לב); *ḥăṭīpūt* is used elliptically for *ḥăṭīpūt šĕlēmā*.

50 As stated above, in the Sephardi pronunciation, which was Almoli's, an initial *šĕwā* (as well as a medial *šĕwā* coming with a geminated letter) is in its duration a full vowel identical with *ṣērī/sĕgōl*. I follow here Yalon's interpretation of Almoli's discussion of this point. See *HŠ*, pp. צט–ק.

51 The above *šĕwā* is known in this tradition as נע מעט = 'semi-mobile'. For a detailed description see S. Morag (ed.), *The Hebrew Language Tradition of the Baghdadi Community*, pp. 79ff.

Discourse Analysis and the Dating of Deuteronomy

CHAIM RABIN

The date of composition of the book of Deuteronomy is one of the most widely discussed questions in the history of the Pentateuch. There is no point in recapitulating here the various views, which can be found in convenient summaries in introductions to Deuteronomy and to the Hebrew Bible. The various datings proposed are based on two types of argumentation. The one is drawn from known or assumed historical facts with which the book could be connected, mainly the discovery of a Torah in the time of Josiah, the increasing concentration of the cult in Jerusalem, or the development of prophetism and of *ḥokmā* and the influence of the one or the other school of thought upon teaching that had initially been the prerogative of the priests. The other collects words and phrases typical of Deuteronomy and measures the degree of occurrence of the same linguistic elements in other biblical books, either on the assumption that these expressions were used during a certain period only and their co-occurrence can be taken as evidence of approximate contemporaneity, or with the intention of showing either that Deuteronomy had influenced the other work or works or that the latter had influenced the writer(s) of Deuteronomy.

As a linguist, I do not pretend to any competence in weighing historical evidence, except perhaps in pointing out that historians have not reached any agreement in the case under discussion. With regard to the conclusions drawn from words and phrases, however, these appear to me to be founded on misconceptions about the nature of language and linguistic usage. It is of course legitimate to collect words and phrases from the work of a single author in order to determine what denotations and connotations they had for him – though even there experience shows that speakers and writers are apt to vary the meanings of the words they use. But when it comes to comparing the usage of different writers, especially in literary texts, we must always keep in mind that the linguistic elements they use are drawn from a large reservoir characterized by built-in redundancy, i.e. the availability of different ways to say the same thing, ranging from full synonyms to the semantic equivalence of single words and combinations of words, whether this equivalence is dependent on certain contexts or universal. The number of words listed in a Biblical Hebrew dictionary is between 7000 and 8000, depending on the way one counts. Obviously this is only a small sample of the words that at any time were actually in use. Statistical Linguistics assumes that the average person has a working vocabulary of 25 000 words, and languages of which the vocabulary is sufficiently well known seem to range from some 80 000 words upwards. Since Biblical Hebrew is so rich in synonyms, it is probable that it had a rather large vocabulary. Moreover, the Hebrew we encounter in the Bible was a literary language and, as such, marked both by a large store of equivalent ways of expression and by a tradition that retained such semantic material rather longer than a purely colloquial language might do. As the users of a literary language learn it from existing literary works, words and phrases can also reappear after having lain dormant for a time. Since it is also certain that the works included in the Hebrew Bible represent only a fraction of the literature available in writing at the time (not to mention the immense body of oral literary expression), we have no means of assessing the variety of equivalent ways to say the same thing which were at the disposal of a Hebrew writer at any given point in the biblical period. For the same reasons we can never be sure whether a certain phrase was created by the writer in whose text we find it. Even if the context strongly suggests that the phrase or word was used for a situation not previously encountered, we cannot know whether it was put together by the author for that purpose, or existed in the literary or spoken language of his time in another meaning and was merely adapted by him to the new need. The evidential value of any particular linguistic expression for dating the segment of text in which it occurs, leave alone a whole text, is thus rather small.

Apparent exceptions are so-called 'fashion words', i.e. words or phrases that, for various reasons, more or less suddenly spread widely in a society, and words of known date of introduction, which are either fashion words or denote new concepts, objects or institutions (this includes borrowing from another language). However, such cases can be ascertained only in our own contemporary language, where we (or the person who noticed the item) have actually witnessed the innovation, or at most, though with less certainty, when we have large bodies of written documents in almost continuous sequence. In a situation like that of biblical literature we cannot recognize fashion words or innovations, as is amply demonstrated by some discussions in which borrowings from other languages are with equal force used to prove early and late dating of the same text.

This does not mean that linguistic material is useless for dating. Even words and phrases can successfully be used in cases where we can show more or less systematic replacement of elements in reworking an earlier text (e.g. Chronicles, and the Qumran reworkings of Deuteronomy and Isaiah). The systematic character is inherent in spelling and in morphology, and these are of course widely employed for dating inscriptions. But they also happen to be the aspects of a text most often changed by copyists, and thus can be adduced only with the greatest caution in a literature, the oldest manuscripts of which represent the result of a large number of recopyings. Syntax, which is a good deal more difficult to alter, provides a better possibility for recognizing and utilizing gradual changes in usage, and there certainly might accrue considerable benefit to biblical studies if this neglected branch of Hebrew grammar were pursued more energetically and with the application of suitable modern techniques.

In recent years, linguists have begun to extend their systematic analysis of structures beyond the limits of the sentence, ranging from a paragraph to the integrated study of entire works (especially the German *Textologie*). The 'texts' investigated are not only written ones; in fact Conversation Analysis, in which the entire interchange between the different participants is treated like a continuous text, has produced some most interesting results. The new branch of linguistics, called Discourse Analysis, investigates such features as reference between different parts of the text (Cohesion), distribution of the information into sentences and paragraphs, density of information and quantity of non-informational features, such as emphasis, modality (expression of the speaker's feeling) and rhetoric, choice of words and grammatical constructions, as well as the ways in which the words are strung together (Collocation). One of its important results is the awareness that texts are of different kinds (*Textsorten*), largely corresponding to social conventions dictating different varieties of one and the same language to be employed in circumscribed social situations (Registers). The differences, which are culture-bound and thus transcend individual choice, include all the features enumerated, as well as prosodic features (rhythm, rhyme, parallelism, speed) and, in speech, pronunciation – in written texts, punctuation.

The concept of culturally and socially conditioned text-forms partly covers the same ground as the theory of literary genres on the one hand and that of biblical Forms or *Gattungen*, with their *Sitz im Leben*, on the other. It differs from them by integrating their domains within a theory that can deal with non-literary, and indeed with non-contrived, texts. It is also in most of its manifestations closely linked to Socio-linguistics and to a general study of human behaviour.

The important feature of the phenomena studied by Discourse Analysis for our problem of dating texts is that they are distributed over the text in such a way that they are practically secure against alteration by scribes. A scribe may alter a feature here and there, but the statistical differences between text-types are in most cases so large that this does not obliterate them. Moreover, being culture-bound, they persist for longer times, and changes consisting in renouncing one text-type for another as being appropriate to a given social purpose are clearly identifiable. And of course, in former periods, more governed by tradition and social convention than ours, we can be certain that the use of a text-type was socially meaningful and not a matter of individual whim.

The book of Deuteronomy is stylistically the most integrated of the Pentateuch and therefore, no doubt, a text in the Discourse Analysis sense. It also clearly defines its social purpose: a speech by a leader to his people. Most discussions of the book mention its rhetorical character and, where we can compare its paragraphs with corresponding ones found in other pentateuchal books, we can clearly see the rhetorical amplifications. Its choice of words and phrases, too, brings it somewhat closer to what is called in the study of the Bible poetical language. All this is well known, and has played a role in the arguments for a late, approximately Josianic dating.

This is of course by no means an isolated example of rhetoric in the Hebrew Bible. We find it in speeches, some long and some short, by Joshua, Jotham, David and Solomon. A great number of the short utterances of kings and heroes have rhetorical form, and it is of some interest that in his analysis of the syntax of pre-exilic poetry R. Sappan has found parallels to some specific poetical features in the direct speech of exalted personalities in the books of Samuel and Kings.[1] But the largest body of speeches is to be found in the books of the Latter Prophets. The most outstanding pre-exilic prophets were more or less contemporary with the Josianic Reform, the most widely accepted date for the composition of Deuteronomy. That these speeches had a distinctive text-type or register, we can ascertain by comparing them with narrative material interwoven with them in the same book: the speeches are marked by parallelism and poetic vocabulary, whereas the narrative has neither.

I have designedly called the words of the prophets 'speeches' and not 'rhetoric', for in introductions to the Bible and in works on Form Criticism this text-type is called poetry.[2] Since parallelism and poetical language are generally considered the only sure marks by which to recognize and describe biblical poetry (the question of metre still being a matter of debate), and these features are shared by undoubtedly poetical texts, such as the Psalms, the pentateuchal *šīrōt*, the Song of Deborah and the Prayer of Hannah on the one hand, and the main creations of Wisdom literature and the speeches of the Prophets on the other, all these are described as poetry. I think that it is possible to show significant discourse differences between the texts socially identifiable as poetry or songs (and sometimes called *šīr*, *mizmōr* etc.) and those identifiable socially as speeches, and suggest that we talk of parallelism and poetical language as features of literary texts, which can then be classified by other linguistic features into poetry, Wisdom and rhetoric. Proofs for this are not, however, necessary for my argument, which is that the speeches of prophets at work in the last stage of the Monarchy were characterized by extensive and systematic use of parallelism and poetical language, while these are absent from Moses' speech in Deuteronomy, as well as from the speeches of Joshua and Jotham, and the Prayer of Solomon in 1 Kings viii.

It seems to me most unlikely that, at a time when prophets delivered political speeches in parallelism before the people, high officials or the king, someone should have put in the mouth of the venerated ancient leader a speech lacking this essential feature of rhetoric and thus inferior to those of contemporary representatives of his teaching. There can be no doubt that the author of Deuteronomy was

1 *The Typical Features of the Syntax of Biblical Poetry* (Jerusalem, 1981).
2 Cp. K. Koch, *Was ist Formgeschichte?* (Neukirchen–Vluyn, 1964), p. 106 = Eng. edn *The Growth of the Biblical Tradition* (London, 1969), p. 97.

familiar with parallelism, since he incorporated into his book two long poems in this form. Even if he did not incorporate them himself, he could hardly have been ignorant of poems contained in Genesis, Exodus and Numbers, on which he drew for his legal materials and historical details. To say that the author of the book was unable to write in parallelism would be incongruous in view of his proven virtuosity in his own style of rhetoric. Nor is it believable that he should have avoided parallelism because he knew that in the time of Moses speeches were given in straight prose and, moreover, expected his audience to be conscious of this archaeological detail. And if we were prepared to attribute to an eighth-century writer such a feat of mystification and pastiche, we would only involve ourselves in a further problem: from where did the author of Deuteronomy take the model for his pastiche of rhetoric without parallelism? If we assume that he had access to the text of ancient speeches, how could he expect his readers to identify the style as rhetoric, unless they were likely to have read the same book or books, in which case they would know that this was a style used by people who lived a century or two earlier, and might not believe that it was used by Moses.

There is another apparent way to get out of the dilemma. We might assume that use of a style connected with poetry was thought in the eighth century B.C. to be suitable for prophets who were 'seized by the spirit', for one who was *'īš hārūaḥ* and *měšuggā'*,[3] but not for an *'īš hā'ělōhīm* (Deut. xxxiii.1) such as Moses, 'like whom no other prophet ever arose in Israel' (Deut. xxxiv.10). This would still fail to explain the source of the rhetorical style of the author of Deuteronomy. But it fails on another ground: Nathan, Elijah and Elisha were prophets of the spirit, and yet the things they say are not in parallelism. There was thus a change in the style in which prophets spoke in **ancient Israel.**

Thus there are a number of examples of speeches without the feature of parallelism, all of which belong to an older period, and may be called the Old Rhetoric, and a larger group of speeches, all belonging to a later period, beginning with Hosea and Amos, which exhibit parallelism, and may be called the New Rhetoric. The speeches in the book of Job (where again the narrative is in a different register), as well as Proverbs chs. i–ix, might also be included in

3 Cp. the Arabic *kāhin*, 'soothsayer', who spoke in *saj'* 'rhymed prose'. It is probable that *saj'* is cognate with Hebrew *měšuggā'*.

the latter class.[4] It is not known how it came about that discourse features that had formerly been reserved for poetry came to be extended to speeches, and whether this was a local development in Judah, or one in Israel (cf. Hosea and Amos) that spread to Judah, or perhaps an importation from outside. There is a parallel in Arabic, from a much later time, when the use of rhymed prose, at first restricted to soothsayers and prophetic utterances, became a feature of Wisdom literature and history.[5]

It may, however, be assumed that when the new fashion of speeches in parallelism came into Israelite society, there was a period of transition during which both types of rhetoric were employed according to personal preference. This period may be responsible for the prose accounts of the utterances of Elijah and Elisha and, on the other hand, for putting a prayer in strict parallelism into the mouth of Samuel's mother (1 Sam. ii.1–10).[6]

The book of Deuteronomy, except for its last chapters, would then belong either to the period of the Old Rhetoric or to the hypothetical transition period, but not to the period when the New Rhetoric had won general acceptance. This, in my view, would exclude a Josianic date, but would allow for the early Monarchy, until the time when the Elijah stories were written up, i.e. during or somewhat after the time of Jehu and Jehoash. At the time of the transition period, people would still identify speeches with parallelism as a novelty, and thus an author presenting Moses would choose the traditional manner rather than the new one. Be the actual date of Deuteronomy as it may, there can be no doubt that its style represents an elaboration and refinement of the Old Rhetoric to which we have no parallel in the samples of that genre preserved in the Hebrew Bible.

4 But not the rest of Proverbs, since in many languages proverbs are cast into poetic forms, such as rhyme in English.

5 I may mention as a parallel closer in time the use of poetic language (close to the 'Hymnic–Epic Dialect') in the inscriptions of the later kings of Assyria. On the other hand the use of metres in Sanskrit and Arabic for scientific text-books is not a matter of register, but a utilitarian device for assisting memorization.

6 Unless Hannah's prayer is a royal psalm, as argued by some modern scholars, or, as I believe, a piece from an ancient epic.

A Midrashic Anthology from the Genizah

STEFAN C. REIF

Introduction

It was in the course of the academical year 1973–4, not many months after I had been appointed to be responsible for the Taylor–Schechter (Genizah) Collection at Cambridge University Library, that a few fragments in one of the many boxes comprising that rich source of scholarly discoveries first caught my eye. The fact that notes on three of the folders[1] attributed the contents to Rashi almost discouraged me, as it had no doubt discouraged many more distinguished scholars before me, from embarking on a thorough investigation, but the study of a whole leaf provided a clear refutation of the attribution and excited a strong curiosity to replace it with more accurate information. I identified five separate leaves, at various numbers through the box, as belonging to the same original manuscript, ordered and transcribed the Hebrew text and reached a tentative conclusion that the material was part of an as yet unidentified medieval Bible commentary, or late midrashic anthology. Unfortunately, however, although I briefly discussed the fragments with some other scholars[2] I was unable at that time to devote to them the substantial degree of attention that they seemed to deserve and my intense involvement over the subsequent five years in build-

1 T-S C6.55, 56 and 95.

2 I am particularly grateful to my distinguished teacher, Professor N. Wieder and to Dr S.A. Birnbaum, that pioneer in Hebrew palaeography, for their responses to my written enquiries, and to Professors J. Sussmann, M. Benayahu and M. Beit-Arié, for their interesting comments on photocopies of the manuscript. I also benefited from a discussion of this article with Professors D. Weiss-Halivni and H. Soloveitchik and Drs M. Assis and J. Tabori at a seminar that I led while a visiting scholar at the Institute for Advanced Studies at the Hebrew University. Needless to say, responsibility for the conclusions here reached remains entirely my own.

ing a comprehensive Genizah project at Cambridge prevented me from offering any more than an occasional well-meaning nod in their general scholarly direction. In the last few months a happy combination of circumstances has provided me with the opportunity of returning to the topic. The desire to honour my dear friend and senior colleague Erwin Rosenthal with a suitable contribution not unworthy of his own important efforts in the field of medieval Jewish Bible exegesis was given the opportunity of fulfilment when the University of Cambridge generously enabled me to accept the kind invitations of the Hebrew University of Jerusalem and the Oxford Centre for Postgraduate Hebrew Studies to spend some time with them as a Visiting Scholar.[3] It seems to me singularly appropriate that Jerusalem, Oxford and Cambridge should each have played a part in enabling me to offer a token of my affection and esteem to a scholar of international standing.

The physical description of the five fragments at Cambridge University Library is as follows:[4]

T-S C6.55: Commentary on Gen. xxv.13–23; paper; one leaf; 27 × 18·2 cm; four outer margins indicated by ruling with a hard point and providing a writing area of 19·5 × 12·9 cm all used except for about 50–75 mm at foot of recto; 30 lines on each side; left-hand margin justified by anticipation, dilatation and diagonal writing upwards, with one line left short; wire lines barely visible; 'תולדות' in top left margin of recto indicates *sēder* to which folio belongs; torn and stained; text well preserved with the exception of the top inside margins where some adhesion has been removed with consequent damage to the legibility; oriental hand.

T-S C6.56: Commentary on Gen. xxv.23–32; paper; one leaf; 27 × 18·4 cm; written area 19·8 (verso 19·5) × 12·9 cm; 30 lines on each side; left-hand margin justified

3 Acknowledgement is gladly made to these institutions for their various kindnesses and to the Syndics of Cambridge University Library for permission to publish its Genizah material.

4 The decision about which characteristics to note in these descriptions owes much to Beit-Arié's excellent volume *Hebrew Codicology* (Paris, 1976) as well as being influenced by the format of the catalogues in Cambridge University Library's *Genizah Series*.

by dilatation and diagonal writing upwards, with one line left short; wire lines (and remnants of chain lines?) barely visible; תולדות in top left margin of recto indicates *sēder* to which folio belongs; torn and stained; text very well preserved except that some blotting from opposite pages has occurred on the top inside margins; oriental hand (see plates 5 and 6).

T-S C6.84(A): Commentary on Gen. xxiv.58–xxv.13; paper; one of two leaves; 27 × 18·2 cm; written area 19·5 × 12·9 cm; 29 lines on each side; left-hand margin justified by dilatation and diagonal writing upwards, with two lines left short; wire lines barely visible; חיי שרה may have been written in the top left margin of recto but no longer clearly visible; torn, holed, rubbed and stained; signs of having been folded; text reasonably well preserved except that the lower outside quarter is rubbed and there is some blotting from opposite pages on the top inside margins; oriental hand.

T-S C6.95: Commentary on Gen. xxxvii.29–xxxviii.1; paper; one leaf; 27 × 18.2 cm; written area 20 (verso 19·7) × 12·9 cm; 32 lines on recto, 30 on verso; left-hand margin justified by dilatation and diagonal writing upwards, with some lines left short; wire lines barely visible; וישב in top left hand margin indicates *sēder* to which folio belongs; torn, holed, rubbed and stained; signs of having been folded; text reasonably well preserved on recto except that the top right margin is rubbed and the bottom left is blotted from an opposite page; text on verso very well preserved; oriental hand.

T-S C6.163: Commentary on Gen. xxxvii.13–29; paper; one leaf; 27 × 18·1 cm; written area 19 (verso 20) × 13 cm; 29 lines on each side; left-hand margin justified by anticipation, dilatation and diagonal writing upwards; wire lines visible; וישב in top left margin of recto indicates *sēder* to which folio belongs; torn, holed, rubbed and badly stained; signs of having been folded; text reasonably well preserved except that the top inside margin is rubbed and blotted from an opposite page and the bottom outside margin is similarly blotted; oriental hand.

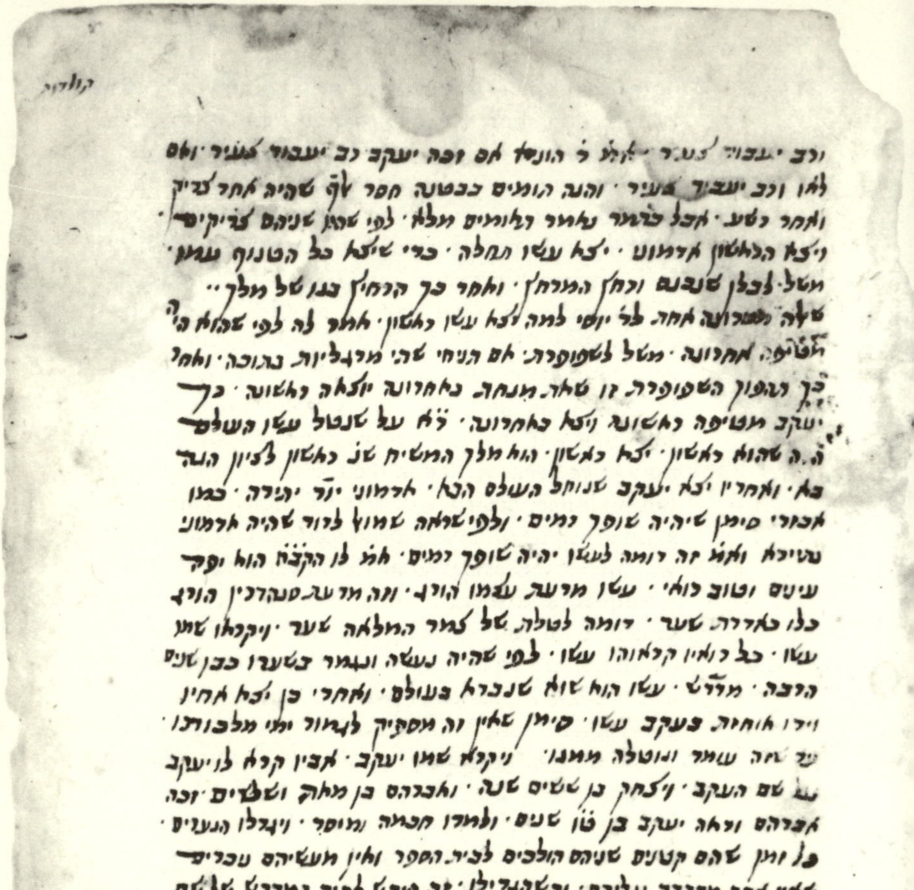

Plate 5 Recto of a commentary on Gen. xxv.23–xxv.32 (C.U.L. T–S C6.56)

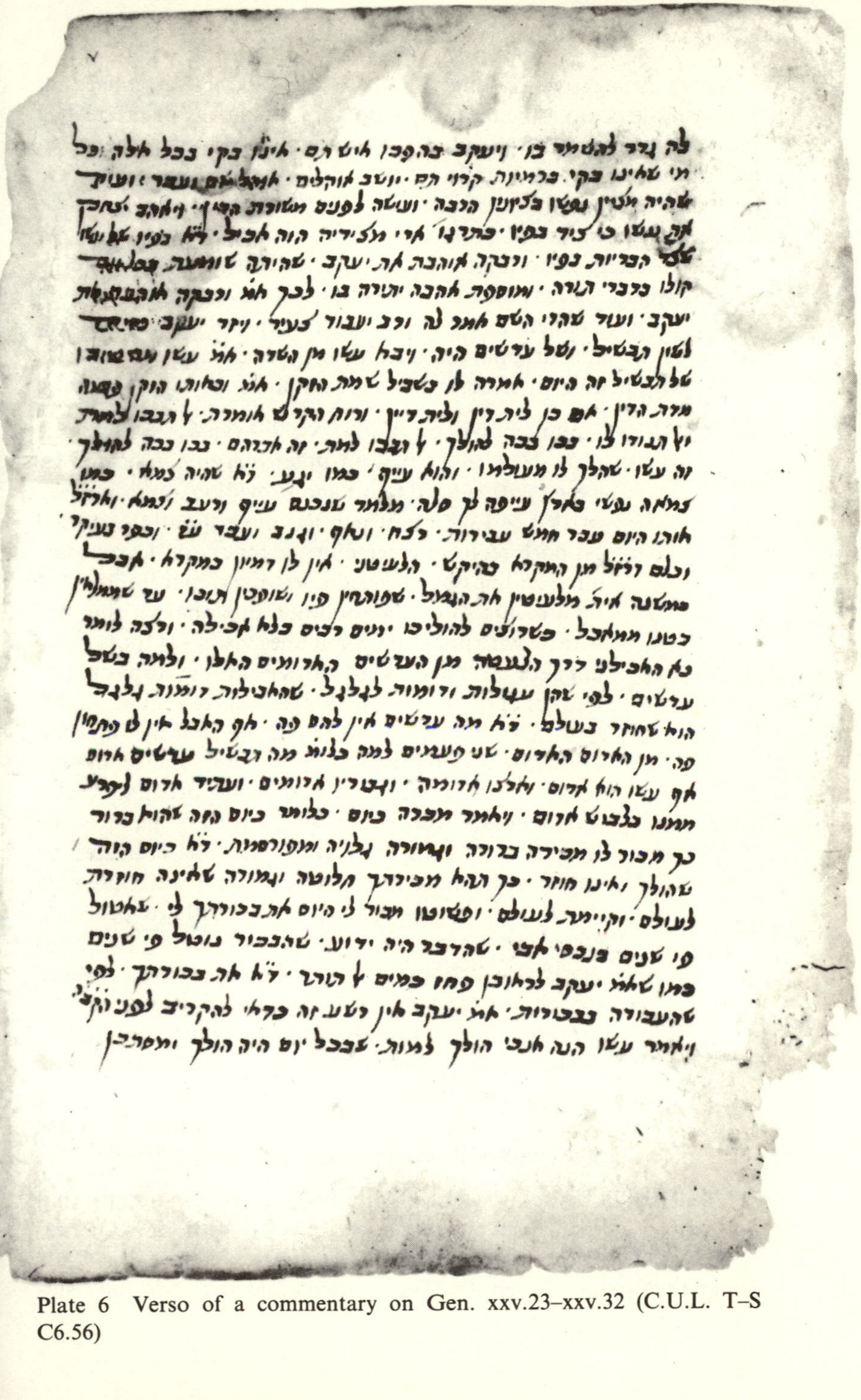

Plate 6 Verso of a commentary on Gen. xxv.23–xxv.32 (C.U.L. T–S C6.56)

As far as negative evidence is concerned it should be noted that there is little or no indication of chain lines, no means of preserving the order of quires or leaves and a very limited use of ruling techniques. Before further details are provided of those folios that have been chosen as the basis of the text offered in this article, it will be necessary to comment on another five fragments which, though similar to them, have finally been excluded from the text edition, and to explain the reasons for their exclusion.

The second fragment in T-S C6.84 and that in T-S C6.81 probably belong to the same original manuscript as the five fragments already described. Their physical description is as follows:

T-S C6.84(B): Commentary on Exod. xvi.24–xvii.5; paper; one leaf; 27 × 18·3 cm; four outer margins indicated by ruling with a hard point and providing a writing area of 19·1 × 13·4 cm, which has been slightly exceeded on both recto and verso at the inner and lower margins; 28 lines on each side; left-hand margin justified by anticipation, dilatation and diagonal writing upwards; wire lines and chain lines visible at foot; בשלח appears to have been written in the top outside margin of recto but is no longer clearly visible; slightly torn, holed and stained, with signs of having been folded; text well preserved except for some smudging on the lower outside quarter of recto; oriental hand.

T-S C6.81: Commentary on Exod. vii.22–viii.17; paper; one leaf; 27 × 18·5 cm; four outer margins indicated by ruling with a hard point and providing a writing area of 19 × 13·4 cm, which has been slightly exceeded on recto and verso at the ends of lines and on the lower margins; 30 lines on recto, 28 on verso; left-hand margin justified by dilatation and diagonal writing upwards; wire lines barely visible; torn, holed, rubbed and stained, with signs of having been folded; text reasonably well preserved except for some blotting and rubbing on recto and some smudging and rubbing on verso; oriental hand.

It will readily be acknowledged, on the basis of these details, that these two fragments have enough in common with those earlier described to constitute at least a *prima facie* case for the claim made about their original identity. The contents and the style tally sufficiently well to provide further support for the claim, although it must be admitted that T-S C6.84(B), in contrast to the fragments used in the text edition, stresses the halakic and aggadic sense rather than the plain meaning of Scripture. This is, however, no doubt due to the legal nature of the biblical passage, and the only remaining reason for excluding these fragments is that they deal with a different biblical book.

With regard to the fragment in T-S C6.72 the evidence is ambiguous. Although the nature of some of the content, the extent of the written area and the paper size (but not its quality?) are approximately the same, there are serious differences in the depth of coverage, the set-out and the handwriting. The number of lines, the length of right-hand margin and the spacing between lines are at odds, and there are some letters such as *'āleph* and *zayin* that obviously do not tally. In sum, there is enough doubt to justify its exclusion.

The elements that fragments T-S C6.53 and C6.90 have in common with our manuscript are limited to the immediate general appearance of the handwriting and the size of the page, and the fact that they clearly contain Bible commentary. The nature and methodology of their commentaries, and all other physical characteristics do, however, strongly militate against their being identified with our manuscript and they have consequently been excluded.

It should also be pointed out that other Genizah collections outside Cambridge remain to be searched for further fragments of our manuscript. My attention has already been drawn to the existence of four folios in the Jewish Theological Seminary of America in New York and the likelihood of more such discoveries being made appears strong.[5]

Although the text reproduced in the five fragments is generally satisfactory the copyist was not without his deficiencies. There is little consistency and some occasional originality in the use of *plene* and defective spelling[6] and of ligatures;[7] there are examples of

5 The folios are ENA 960.74–5 and 1069.25–6 and they cover Gen. xxxii.9–21 and xxxiii.10–15, and Exod. xii.47 – xiii.16 respectively. I owe this reference to my good friend, Professor Jacob Sussmann.

6 Cp. e.g. הדור (I, 8); העיבור (IV, 18); ארחת (VIII, 8); אורחת (VIII, 23); בתפילה (IV, 3); תפלת (IV, 10); יודע (VII, 2); יודיע (IX, 17); גהנם (X, 11); גיהנם (X, 12); פירות (I, 5); בירכו (II, 4); לטלת (V, 15); בשלם (VII, 3); הזמן (VIII, 11); and הדבר (for הדיבור? I, 26).

7 Cp. e.g. the words ישמעאל in II, 14 and III, 18; אלהי in III, 17 and גבריאל in VII, 9, as well as לשאל (VII, 3).

dittography,[8] homoioteleuton,[9] and simpler textual errors that have not been detected by the copyist;[10] not surprisingly, biblical and rabbinic sources are not indicated; verses are sometimes inaccurately cited.[11] When the copyist has himself noticed an error he has, depending on the circumstances, inserted a word above the normal text,[12] overlined a word or letter to be removed,[13] or overwritten the original text.[14] The 'three angels' of one well-known midrash have become 'three kings' due to the omission of an *'āleph*,[15] while in at least three out of a number of substantial variations from standard midrashic texts there is some reason to suspect that what are being dealt with are no more than scribal errors.[16]

Even if all these variations are regarded as authentic and valuable for the text-critical history of midrashim a linguistic analysis of the fragments hardly reveals anything exciting. There are no Hebrew transliterations of vocabulary from other languages and little Aramaic. In two cases, indeed, the Aramaic of the original sources has been translated into Hebrew.[17] It is clear that the author is totally committed to the use of simple, Rabbinic Hebrew, particularly as it is found in the later midrashic works.[18] He is in fact so fond of citing large sections from these and other sources, at times almost verbatim, with their own characteristic linguistic expressions and introductory formulae, that no uniform linguistic style here emerges. While the matter of vocabulary is under discussion, it may also be noted that the abbreviation most commonly used for introducing alternative interpretations is ד״א, although י״א and its fuller form also perform this function and there is one strange instance of the use of מלמד for the same purpose.[19]

Although there are some instances involving a degree of exegetical innovation, the commentary's importance lies in the way in which it deals with earlier sources rather than in any striking

8 See IX, 6–7.
9 See III, 4–5.
10 E.g. עשי for עשו (II, 4); נוצל for ניצל (III, 17) and כבוד ואם (IX, 31).
11 As in V, 11; VII, 5, 9.
12 As in I, 5, 23; III, 17.
13 As in I, 19; III, 24; VII, 17, 26, 28; IX, 22; X, 16, 30.
14 See III, 22; V, 20.
15 See VII, 10; but such defective spelling is known from other manuscripts.
16 In addition to the variants noted in nn. 1, 12, 97 and 133 on the Hebrew text there is also the variant *qāṭĕrā* for *qāšĕrā* in I, 28.
17 See nn. 63 and 132 on the Hebrew text.
18 Lines 13–16 contain numerous examples to justify this claim.
19 See n. 47 on the Hebrew text.

originality.[20] The tendency with midrashim is to alter their content, order and length in order to achieve an adjustment of stress. It is not always apparent why this adjustment is necessary, but there are instances in which it would seem to have been motivated by a desire to follow a more rational line of thought or, possibly, a more up-to-date philosophy.[21] In one case the compiler engages in a form of analysis by explaining by which hermeneutical principles the talmudic rabbis arrived at certain aggadic notions.[22] His text thus becomes important not only for his citations from earlier sources but also for the modifications he makes to them and for the possible reasons he may have had for doing so. These considerations also apply to those comments that are literal rather than midrashic. The compiler demonstrates a considerable interest in grammar, vocabulary and chronology.[23] He is also clearly aware of the distinction between *pĕšaṭ* and *dĕrāš* and introduces some of his comments with a specific characterization of this nature.[24] Constituting as it does a neatly integrated anthology of midrashic and literal comment on the biblical text, the work has significance for the history of the manner in which these two approaches vied with each other for dominance in this field of study.

When this attempt at integration is borne in mind, it clearly comes as no surprise to discover that the work is often similar to Rashi's commentary, and sometimes identical with it, and that for literalist comment it is heavily indebted to Ibn Ezra more than to any other commentator with such a bent. The thought had occurred to me at an early stage of research on the fragments that I might here be dealing with an early recension of Rashi's commentary, or indeed a source of his commentary, but once the broader picture emerged it became clear that the context in which the commentary is to be placed is that of the popular midrashic anthologies of the centuries immediately following Rashi's period. Although *Bĕrēšīt Rabbā* is the primary source of much of his midrashic material, the compiler's formulation has much in common with those of *Yalqūṭ Šim'ōnī* and *Leqaḥ Ṭōb* and, to a lesser extent, *Midraš haggādōl* and *Śēkel Ṭōb*. That *Leqaḥ Ṭōb* was a particularly popular anthology in the medieval oriental communities is apparent from the number of texts of

20 But see nn. 8, 16, 18, 26, 70, 121 and 136 on the Hebrew text.
21 See nn. 37, 70 and 133 on the Hebrew text.
22 See VI, 15.
23 See X, 25–30.
24 As in VI, 26; VII, 11; VIII, 23; X, 10 for the former, and V, 17; VII, 12 and X, 11 for the latter.

the work discovered in the Genizah. What is being edited here is probably another such popular anthology, possibly even an adaptation of the *Leqaḥ Ṭōb*. The original work almost certainly dealt with Genesis and Exodus and may well have covered the whole Pentateuch.

The lack of incontrovertible evidence makes it difficult to arrive at definitive conclusions about the date and provenance of the original commentary. Its similarity to the late midrashim of the anthological variety, its preference for the synthetical approach rather than a commitment to either the midrashic or literal and its dependence on Rashi and Ibn Ezra all point to a *terminus a quo* in the thirteenth century. In addition, Jacob Mann discovered a fragment in the Cambridge Genizah collection forty years ago with characteristics that have much in common with those of the manuscript that is the subject of the present article and placed it in the thirteenth-century orient.[25] Further support for such a date may be adduced from the similarity of the manuscript's content to that of the Genesis commentary of Samuel b. Nissim Masnut of thirteenth-century Syria.[26] With the greater availability and popularity of the standard Bible commentators and primary midrashim through the spread of printing the interest in such anthologies waned and it therefore seems reasonable to fix a *terminus ad quem* in the sixteenth century. It also appears to me that the fragments here being dealt with would warrant our antedating the commentary even further. Although the handwriting has characteristics in common with some eastern oriental hands of later centuries as much as with earlier Syro-Egyptian-Palestinian styles, the codicological practices reflected in the fragments and detailed above, as well as the paper itself, point to about the fourteenth or fifteenth century.[27] Unless, then, this Genizah manuscript is in holograph, it would appear to have been written between the thirteenth and fifteenth centuries.

The provenance is, if anything, even more difficult to ascertain

25 'A Commentary to the Pentateuch à la Rashi's' in *HUCA* 15 (1940), 497–527. That commentary is also heavily indebted to Rashi and borrows from Ibn Ezra and *Leqaḥ Ṭōb*. Its linguistic style, exegetical method and use of rabbinic sources are also reminiscent of what has just been described here.

26 *Midraš Běrēšît Zûṭā*, ed. M. Hakohen (Jerusalem, 1962). It should also be borne in mind that Jacob b. Ḥananel Sikili did similar work in Syria at this period.

27 This judgement is based on the criteria used by Beit-Arié to assist in the dating of Hebrew manuscripts; see his *Hebrew Codicology*, pp. 29–37, 50–9, 72–5 and 87–103. Somewhat paradoxically, Beit-Arié's instinct when I showed him photocopies of the manuscript was to date it much later (possibly in Persia) but without an examination of the original he was obviously hesitant about committing himself.

than the date. In their heyday the kind of midrashic anthology with which this manuscript has such obvious affinities was popular with Jewish communities spread over a wide area from Germany and the Balkans to Persia and Yemen,[28] and the oriental appearance of the manuscript may not be crucial. The fact that no vernacular has been utilized by the compiler would appear to make Franco-German, Persian or Arabic-speaking countries, where *lĕʿāzīm* were so popular, less likely candidates, although it has to be admitted that much of what has been written above would make the thirteenth century a strong possibility. If this earlier date is preferred, there is less reason to rule out Spain or Italy, while a dating a century or two later would make such a provenance unlikely in view of the way in which Bible commentaries developed there at that time. In the absence of more concrete evidence either the problem of provenance must be left unsolved or a conjecture must be offered in the hope that the guess may ultimately turn out to be an inspired one. Is it sufficient for the moment to say that the source of the commentary is to be sought in the eastern Mediterranean, or perhaps in the Balkans?

In the text edition printed below the *sēder* headings, lines, punctuation and abbreviations have been given as in the manuscript. To these have been added the Cambridge University Library class-marks, with indications of recto and verso, and each of the pages has been given a Roman numeral and the lines numbered, for ease of reference. Also supplied are references in Arabic numerals to the verses being commented upon, references in Hebrew type to other biblical texts and non-biblical sources, and references in smaller, raised Arabic numerals to my notes. An asterisk indicates a word inserted above the line by the copyist and for typographical reasons the use of brackets is in accordance with the following system:

( ) = restoration of *lacunae*
[ ] = words to be omitted
[ ] = words being supplied

28 See *Encyclopaedia Judaica*, vol. XI, pp. 1511–14 and the works already referred to above for confirmation of this wide range. Further evidence may be adduced from Louis Ginzberg's 'Midrash and Aggadah' in *Genizah Studies in Memory of Doctor Solomon Schechter*, vol. I (New York, 1928); Jacob Mann's *The Bible as read and preached in the Old Synagogue* (Cincinnati, 1940, 1966); E.E. Urbach's *Sefer Pitron Torah* (Jerusalem, 1978); Y. Sabar's *Pešaṭ Wayehî Bešallaḥ* (Wiesbaden, 1976); and M. Weiss's *Sēper Rūšaynā* (Jerusalem, 1976). Z.M. Rabinovitz' *Ginzé Midrash* (Tel Aviv, 1976), deals with other types of midrashim but demonstrates what a variety of midrashic material remains to be uncovered, especially in Genizah collections. Cp. also M. Katz's introduction to his edition of *Rabbenu Meyuhas ben Elijah: Commentary on Deuteronomy* (Jerusalem, 1968), esp. p. 12.

The purpose of the notes is to provide a brief explanation of the sense of the comments and to indicate how the latter relate to various midrashim and medieval Bible commentaries. Allusion is usually made to aggadic motifs; it has not, however, been my intention to expound the concepts and methodology of the original midrashic sources but simply to place the present commentary in correct context.[29] Where a rabbinic source has been cited without specific mention of chapter and sub-section the reference is to the comment made in that source on the verse being discussed in the text-edition.

Although these notes are primarily intended for the specialist in Rabbinics who is interested in how this commentary is related to similar but better-known works, the translation that follows them is provided rather for those students of the Hebrew Bible who are less at home with rabbinic literature but are nevertheless anxious to become acquainted with the kind of interpretations followed by the Jews in the Middle Ages. I have therefore tried, while remaining true to the original, to produce a readable English version that avoids the slavish commitment to the Hebrew characteristic of some renderings and the loose inaccuracies of others. I have used square brackets to indicate any part of the translation that is not explicitly or implicitly contained in the Hebrew text and have thereby avoided the use of explanatory notes, which interrupt the flow of the commentary and hamper the reader interested in understanding the general tenor of the exegesis. Word-plays and similar midrashic devices are notoriously difficult to represent in English translation, but I have, wherever possible, made efforts to overcome rather than evade this difficulty in the hope of producing one or two renderings that may encourage other translators to take up this important challenge. The page and line numbers in the margin of the English text refer to the Hebrew original.

The following abbreviations have been employed in addition to those already listed at the beginning of this volume (where titles are also given in Latin characters in the original these have been preferred to my own transliteration):

AB ʾ*Ăggādat Bĕrēšīt*, ed. S. Buber (Cracow, 1903).
B Baḥya b. Asher, *Bīʾūr ʿal hattōrā*, ed. H.D. Chavel, vol. I (Jerusalem, 1971).

29 For further explanation of the original midrashim see Ginzberg, 'Midrash and Aggadah', vol. I, pp. 296–321; vol. II, pp. 9–32; vol. V, pp. 262–78 and 327–33.

BR *Bereschit Rabba*, ed. J. Theodor and Ch. Albeck, 2nd edn (Jerusalem, 1965).

BRT *Midraš Berešit Rabbati*, ed. Ch. Albeck (Jerusalem, 1940).

Ginzberg L. Ginzberg, *The Legends of the Jews*, vols. I–VII (Philadelphia, 1909–38).

IE Abraham Ibn Ezra, *Pērūšē hattōrā*, ed. A. Weiser, vol. I (Jerusalem, 1977).

JQ Joseph b. Simeon Qara, *Pērūš hattōrā* in *Sēper Ḥămišā Mĕʾōrōt haggĕdōlīm*, ed. J. Gad (Johannesburg, 1952); but see the comments of M. Ahrend, *Le Commentaire sur Job de Rabbi Yoseph Qara'* (Hildesheim, 1978), pp. 33–4.

LT *Lekach-Tob*, ed. S. Buber (Wilna, 1880–4).

MA *Agadischer Commentar zum Pentateuch* (*Midraš ʾĂggādā*), ed. S. Buber (Vienna, 1894).

MG *Midraš haggādōl*, ed. M. Margulies, vol. I (Jerusalem, 1947).

N Moses b. Naḥman, *Pērūšē hattōrā*, ed. H.D. Chavel, vol. I (Jerusalem, 1959).

PRE *Pirqē Rabbī ʾĔlīʿezer* (Warsaw, 1852); *Pirḳê de Rabbi Eliezer*, Eng. ed. G. Friedlander (London, 1916).

PRK *Pĕsīqtā dĕrab Kāhănā*, ed. S. Buber (Wilna, 1925); or ed. B. Mandelbaum, vol. I (New York, 1962).

Q David Qimḥi, *Pērūšē R. D. Q. ʿal hattōrā*, ed. M. Kamelhar (Jerusalem, 1970).

R *Raši ʿal hattōrā*, ed. A. Berliner (Frankfurt-am-Main, 1905).

RS Samuel b. Meir, *Commentarium ... in Pentateuchum*, ed. D. Rosin (Breslau, 1881).

S Saadya Gaon, *Pērūšē R. S. G. ʿal hattōrā*, ed. J. Kafiḥ (Jerusalem, 1963).

ST *Sechel Tob*, ed. S. Buber (Berlin, 1900).

T-A Notes of Theodor and Albeck on BR *q.v.*

TJ *Pseudo-Jonathan* (*Targūm Yōnātān*), ed. M. Ginsburger (Berlin, 1903).

TN *Midraš Tanḥūmā* (Warsaw, 1875).

TNB *Midrasch Tanchuma*, ed. S. Buber (2 vols., Wilna, 1885).

TO *Targūm ʾOnqĕlōs* in *The Bible in Aramaic*, ed. A. Sperber, vol. I (Leiden, 1959).

WR *Wayyikra Rabba*, ed. M. Margulies (5 vols., Jerusalem, 1953–60).

YS *Yalqūṭ Šimʿōnī* (Warsaw, 1876); ed. I. Shiloni, vol. II (Jerusalem, 1973).

Hebrew text

I (C6.84r)

חיי שרה

מ(רמ)זים הילדה שלא תלך[1]·· ותאמר אֵ͡לֵך מעצמי איני מעכבת[2]·· [24 : 59] ואת מנקתה זו דבורה[3]· [24 : 60] את היי לאלפי רבבה· את וזרעך תקבלו הברכות שנאמרו לאברהם בהר המוריה· והרבה ארבה את זרעך [בראשית כב: יז]· יהי רצון שיהיה אותו הזרע ממך[4]· ואע״פ כן לא נפקדה רבקה· עד שהתפלל עליה יצחק שלא יאמרו* תפלתינו עשתה פירות[5]· [24 : 62] באר לחי רואי· הלך שם יצחק להביא הגר· כי (ישבה?) על הבאר ואמרה להקב״ה ראה בעלבוני[6]· [24 : 63] לשוח בשדה· להתפלל כמו ולפני יי׳ ישפוך שיחו [תהלים קב: א][7]· וי״א שהיה הולך ומתבודד בין השיחים[8]· [24 : 64] (ו)תרא את יצחק· ראתה אותו הדור ועומד וידין [צ״ל: וידיו] שטוחות בתפלה אמרה אדם גדול הוא זה[9]· ותפול מעל הגמל· השמיטה עצמה לארץ ברצונה· כתרגו׳ ואתרכינת[10]· [24 : 65] ותקח הצעיף ותתכס· שתים נתכסו בצעיף· רבקה ותמר· ושתיהן ילדו תאומים[11]· [24 : 66] ויספר העבד ליצחק· גילה לו הניסים שנעשו לו בדרך וגם שנזדווגה לו רבקה במענה פיו[12]· [24 : 67] האהלה שרה אמו· האהל של שרה אמו[13]· ד״א שנעשת דוגמה לשרה אמו· שכל זמן שהיתה שרה קיימת היה נר דלוק באהלה מערב שבת לערב שבת וברכה מצויה בעיסה· וענן קשור על האהל· ומשמתה אמו פסקו· וכשבאתה רבקה חזרו[14]· וינחם יצחק אחרי אמו· דרך ארץ שכל זמן שאמו של אדם קיימת כרוך הוא אחריה· ומשתמות מתנחם הוא באשתו[15]· ד״א וינחם יצחק שהיה מתייאש למצא אשת חיל (כשירה) כמו שרה· אמו עד *ש/ת̄/*מצא רבקה שדומה לה· לכך וינ(חם) יצחק וג׳[16] [25 : 1] ויוסף אברהם ויקח אשה· זש״ה בבקר זרע זרעך ולערב אֵ͡ל תנח וג׳ [קהלת יא: ו] ר׳ אליעזר אומ׳ אם זרעת בזמן הבכיר· תזרע באפי(ל שא)ין אתה יודע איזה מתקיים· ואם למדת תורה בבחרותך ל(מו)ד תורה בזקנותך· שאין אתה יודע* איזה מתקיים· ר׳ שמואֵ͡ל בר נחמני אומ׳ אם היו לך בנים בבחרותך ומתה אשתך קח אשה בזקנותך ותעמיד בנים· שאין אתה יודע מי מתקיים· ממי אתה למד· מאברהם· הה״ד ויוסף אברהם וג׳ ד״א ויוסף אברהם על פי הדבר· כד״א ויוסף יי׳ דבר אֵ͡לי [ישעיה ח: ה][17]· ד״א ויוסף שהוסיף לו הקב״ה תאוה על תאותו[18] ושמה קטורה· היא הגר· ולמה נקרא שמה קטורה· שנאים מעשיה כקטורת· ד״א שקטרה פתחה ולא נזדווג לה אדם· מיום שיצאה מעם אברהם· ואפי׳ שנ׳ בה ותלך ותתע במדבר באר

II (C6.84v)

שבע[19] [בראשית כא: יד]. [25 : 5] ויתן אברהם את כל אשר לו ליצחק מאי היא ברכה שאמר לו הקב״ה והיה ברכה [בראשית יב: ב]. כלומ׳ הברכות מסורות לך לברך מי שתרצה. ומסר אברהם זה הדבר ליצחק[20]. וי״א דייתקי וקבורה במערה[21] ר׳ חמא ב״ר חנינא אמ׳ לא בירכו שצפה עשי [צ״ל: עשו] יוצא ממנו שיוצא לתרבות רעה. אלא נתן לו מתנה ממש כל נכסיו. משל למלך שהיה לו פרדס ונתנו לאריס. והיו בו שתי אילנות כרוכות זו על גב זו. אחת של סם חיים ואחת של סם המות. אמר האריס אם אני משקה של סם חיים. זה של סם המות (שותה) וחי תמיד עמו. ואם אין אני משקה של סם חיים היאך יחיה. אמ׳ האריס איני משקה אותם. אלא יבא בעל הפרדס ויעשה מה שירצה. כך אמר אברהם. אם אני מברך את יצחק יכנס עשו בברכה. אלא יבוא בעל הברכות ויברך מי שירצה. כך כיוון שמת אברהם נגלה הקב״ה על יצחק ובירכו הה״ד ויהי אחרי מות אברהם ויברך אלהים את יצחק בנו [בראשית כה: יא][22]. [25 : 6] ולבני הפילגשים לא היה לו רק פילגש אחת[23]. והיא הגר. בימי אלכסנדרון מוקדון. באו בני ישמעאל לעורר על ישראל בדבר הבכורה אחז״ל מי ילך וידון עמהם אמ׳ גביהה בן פסיסא אני אליך. אם אנצח מוטב. ואם לאו אתם אומרים מה זה (הפחות) שידון עלינו. הלך ודן עמהם. אמרו מי תובע. אמרו הישמעאלים אנחנו תובעים (מידם). ומתורתם אנו באים עליהם דכתי׳ כי את הבכור בן השנואה יכיר (לתת לו) פי שנים וג׳ [דברים כא: יז] וישמעאל היה בכור. אמר להם גביהה יכול אדם לעשות מנכסיו בחייו כל מה שירצה. או לאו. אמרו לו יכול הוא (אמר להם הא?) כתי׳ ויתן אברהם את כל אשר לו ליצחק [בראשית כה: ה] מיד נסתלקו (כלם במבושה)[24].. [25 : 7] ואלה ימי שני חיי אברהם. מאת שנה ושבעים שנה וחמש שנים. בן מאה כבן שבעים. ובן שבעים [כבן] חמש לחט׳[25] [25 : 8] זקן ושבע. מלמד שהקב״ה מראה לצדיקים שכינתו בשעת מיתתם ונפשם שביעה[26]. ויאסף אל עמיו. שהנפש בהיותה מתעסקת בצרכי הגוף היא כחלק הנפרד ממקומו. וכשתפרד מן הגוף יאסף הכבוד אל עמיו[27]. [25 : 9] ויקברו אותו יצחק וישמעאל. מכאן שעשה ישמעאל תשובה שבא מן המדבר לגמול חסד לאברהם והקדים יצחק לפניו. ועשה עצמו טפל לו והיא שיבה טובה שנאמרה לאברהם[28].. [25 : 11] ויהי אחרי מות אברהם ויברך אלהים את יצחק. בירכו תנחומי אבלים[29]. [25 : 13] בשמותם לתולדו(תם)

III (C6.55r)

תולדות

סדר ליד(תן ז)ה אחר זה[30]· [25 : 17] ואלה שני חיי ישמעאל· אמ׳ ר׳ חייא בר אבא למה

נמנו שנ(ות)יו של (יש)מעאל· לפי שעשה תשובה בחיי אביו שנ׳ ויגוע ולא

נאמרה ג(וי)עה אלא בצדיקים[31]· [25 : 18] על פני כל אחיו נפל· דרך הנוסעים

ממקום למקום לומר עליהן לשון נפילה· כמו אל הכשדים אתה נופל [ירמיה לז: יג][32]

[ד״א שכן כמו ומדין ועמלק וכל בני קדם נופלים בעמק [שופטים ז: יב] כאן הוא אומר נופל][33]

ולהלן הוא אומ׳ על פני כל אחיו ישכון [בראשית טז: יב]· כל זמן שהיה אברהם קיים

(יש)כון כיוון שמת נפל·· [25 : 19] יצחק בן

ואלה תולדות

(אב)רהם וג׳ זש״ה עטרת זקנים בני

(בני)ם ותפארת בנים אבותם [משלי יז: ו]· האבות עטרה לבנים· והבנים עטרה

(לאבו)ת· האבות עטרה לבנים· שנ׳ ותפארת בנים אבותם· והבנים

(עט)רה לאבות שנ׳ עטרת זקנים בני בנים· אברהם נתעטר בזכות

יעקב שכשהשליכו נמרוד לכבשן האש ירד הקב״ה להצילו· אמרו

מלאכי השרת רבונו של עולם לזה אתה מציל· הלא כמה רשעים עתידין

לצאת ממנו· אמ׳ להם הקב״ה אני מצילו בשביל יעקב בן בנו· וזהו שנ׳

לכן כה אמר יי׳ אל בית יעקב אשר פדה את אברהם [ישעיה כט: כב] זכות יעקב·

פדה את אברהם· /זכות יעקב פדה את אברהם/ ומניין שנתעטרו /ו]

הבנים באבות· שבשעה שרדף לבן אחר יעקב ונתוכח עמו· אמר

יעקב לולי אלהי אבי אלהי* אברהם וג׳ [בראשית לא: מב] הרי בזכות אברהם נוצל [צ״ל: ניצל] יעקב מלבן[34]·

ד״א ואלה תולדות יצחק בן אברהם· אחר שהזכיר תולדות ישמעאל

בקצור· הזכיר תולדות יצחק והאריך בעניינו[35]· ועל ידי שאמ׳ יצחק

בן אברהם· נזקק לומר אברהם הוליד את יצחק· שהיה דומה לו··

שהמלאך הממונה על הצורה צר קלסתר פניו של יצחק דומים לשל

אברהם· וכל רואהו יעיד שאברהם הולידו· ועוד שכל מי שהיה /רואה/

רואה מעשיו הטובים· אומ׳ בודאי אברהם הוליד את יצחק[36]·· [25 : 20] ויהי

יצחק בן /אבנ/ ארבעים שנה וג׳ יש מרז״ל אמ׳ כשבא אברהם מהר

המוריה נתבשר שנולדה רבקה· ויצחק היה בן ל״ז שנה כשנעקד

שהרי שרה בת תשעים שנה היתה כשנולד· ובת מאה ועשרים ושבע

כשמתה ובו בפרק מתה· ובו נתבשר שנולדה בת זוגו הרי לא היתה

רבקה כי אם בת שלש שנים· ואל תתמה על שיצאה למעיין והשקתה

הגמלים והיא בת שלש שנים· שאין דורות ראשונים כדורות אחרונים[37]

בת בתואל הארמי להגיד שבחה שהיתה בת רשע ואחות רשע רמאי ומקומה

IV (C6.55v)

אנשי רשע רמאים ולא למדה ממעשיהם· אלא כשושנה בין החוחים [שיר ב: ב] היתה[38]· לו לאשה· ראוייה לו והוגנת צדקת כמותה לינשא לצדיק[39]· פדן ארם שדה ארם [הושע יב: יג][40]· [25 : 21] ויעתר יצחק· הרבה והפציר בתפילה· עד שנתרצה לו· כמו ה העתירו ﭏ יי׳ [שמות ט: כח] ויעתר לו נתרצה לו· ד״א ויעתר לשון הפוך· (שהכלי שמ(הפך?) בו התבואה נקרא עתר· וגדול כוחן של צדיקים שהופכים גזירות (רעות) לטובה[41]· לנוכח אשתו זה עומד בזוית זו ואומ׳ רבון העולמים (כל בנים) שאתה עתיד ליתן לי יהיו מן צדקת זו· והיא עומדת בזוית א(חרת) ואומרת רבון העולמי׳ כל בנים שאתה עתיד ליתן לי יהיו מן הצ(דיק) הזה[42]· כי עקרה היא· לא נתפלל עליה עד שידע שהיא עקרה· (שצפה?) עשר שנים ולא ילדה[43]· ויעתר לו· ולא לה· שאין דומה תפלת צדיק בן (צדיק) לתפלת צדיק בן רשע[44]· [25 : 22] ויתרוצצו הבנים כתרגו׳ ודחקין בניא במעיה· כמו טומאה רצוצה [משנה טהרות ח: ב][45]· ד״א לשון מרוצה· כמו כברקים ירוצצו [נחום ב: ה][46]· מלמד[47] כשהיתה עוברת על פתחי ע״ז היה עשו מפרכס לצאת· כמו שנ׳ זורו רשעים מרחם [תהלים נח: ד]· וכשהיתה עוברת על פתח בית מדרש של שם ועבר· היה רץ יעקב ומפרכס לצאת כעניין שנ׳ בטרם אצרך בבטן ידעתיך ובטרם תצא מרחם הקדשתיך [ירמיה א: ה]· ד״א ויתרוצצו זה רץ להרוג את זה וזה רץ להרוג את זה· ד״א זה מתיר ציוויו של זה· וזה מתיר ציוויו של זה[48]· הבנים נקראו בנים על שם סופן[49]· ותאמר אם כן הוא צער העיבור· למה זה אנכי מתפללת ומתאוה על ההירין[50]· והיתה מחזרת על פתחי הנשים ואומרת להם הגיע לכם כצער הזה[51]· ותלך לדרוש את יי׳· להקריב קרבן[52] ד״א לדרוש במדרש של שם ועבר· להגיד לה מה יהיה בסופה[53] ולבקש רחמים על עיבורה[54]· ולמדנו שכל המקבל פני זקן· כﭏו מקבל פני שכינה[55]· [25 : 23] ויאמר יי׳ לה על ידי נביא· שהרי שם ועבר ואברהם נביאים היו ובחיים היו· שני גוים שני גאים· זה מתגאה בעולמו זה מתגאה בעולמו· זה מתגאה במלכותו וזה מתגאה במלכותו· אדריינוס באומות· ושלמה בישראל· ד״א שני גוים שניהם שונאים [צ״ל: שנואים?] כל העולם שונאים את עשו· וכל העולם שונאים את ישראל[56]· ושני לאומים אין לאום ﭏא מלכות· וכן תרג׳ ומלכו ממלכו יתקף[57] ממעיך יפרדו· אמ׳ ר׳ ברכיה מכאן שנולד יעקב מהול[58]· ד״א ממעיך יפרדו זה לרשעתו וזה לצדקתו ולתומו[59]· ולאום מלאום יאמץ לא ישוו בגדולה· כשזה קם· זה נופל[60]

V (C6.56r)

תולדות

ורב יעבוד צעיר· אמ׳ ר׳ הונא אם זכה יעקב רב יעבוד צעיר· ואם לאו ורב יעביד צעיר[61]· [25 : 24] והנה תומים בבטנה חסר אל״ף שהיה אחד צדיק ואחר רשע· אבל בתמר נאמר תאומים מלא [בראשית לח: כז]· לפי שהיו שניהם צדיקים[62]· [25 : 25] ויצא הראשון אדמוני· יצא עשו תחלה· כדי שיצא כל הטנוף עמו· משל· לבלן שנכנס ורחץ המרחץ· ואחר כך הרחיץ בנו של מלך·· שאלה מטרונה אחת לר׳ יוסי למה יצא עשו ראשון· אמר לה לפי שהוא היה מטיפה אחרונה· משל לשפופרת· אם תניחי שתי מרגליות בתוכה· ואחר כך תהפוך השפופרת זו שאת מנחת באחרונה יוצאה ראשונה· כך יעקב מטיפה ראשונה ויצא באחרונה[63]· ד״א על שנטל עשו העולם הזה שהוא ראשון· יצא ראשון· [הוא מלך המשיח שנ׳ ראשון לציון הנה בא [צ״ל: הנם. ישעיה מא: כז]]· ואחריו יצא יעקב שנוחל העולם הבא[64]· אדמוני יו״ד יתירה· כמו אכזרי סימן שיהיה שופך דמים· ולפי שראה שמואל לדוד שהיה אדמוני נתיירא ואמ׳ זה דומה לעשו יהיה שופך דמים· אמ׳ לו הקב״ה הוא יפה עינים וטוב רואי [שמואל א טז: יב]· עשו מדעת עצמו הורג· וזה מדעת סנהדרין הורג[65] כלו כאדרת שער· דומה לטלת של צמר המלאה שער[66]· ויקראו שמו עשו· כל רואיו קראוהו עשו· לפי שהיה נעשה ונגמר בשערו כבן שנים הרבה[67]· מדרש· עשו הוא שוא שנברא בעולם[68]· [25 : 26] ואחרי כן יצא אחיו וידו אוחזת בעקב עשו· סימן שאין זה מספיק לגמור ימי מלכותו· עד שזה עומד ונוטלה ממנו· ויקרא שמו יעקב· אביו קרא לו יעקב על שם העקב[69]· ויצחק בן ששים שנה· ואברהם בן מאה וששים· זכה אברהם וראה יעקב בן ט״ו שנים· ולמדו חכמה ומוסר[70]· [25 : 27] ויגדלו הנערים· כל זמן שהם קטנים שניהם הולכים לבית הספר ואין מעשיהם ניכרים שאין אדם מדקדק עליהם· וכשהגדילו· זה פירש לבית המדרש של שם ועבר וזה פירש לע״ז· משל לעצבונות והדס· שגדילים זה על זה ולא היו נכרים· הפרידו· זה נותן ריחו· וזה נותן חוחו[71]· ויהי עשו איש יודע ציד מלא מרמות· שהצודה חיות· צריך להיות בעל חכמה ומרמות[72] ד״א שהיה צד אביו ומרמהו· שואלו אבא היאך מעשרין את המלח ואת התבן· וכסבור אביו שמדקדק במצות[73]· ד״א שהיה צד הבריות בפיהם ואומר להם לא גנבת· מי גנב עמך· לא הרגת מי הרג עמך[74]· איש שדה בטל· צד בקשתו חיות ועופות[75]· ד״א עשה עצמו כשדה (ש)אין

VI (C6.56v)

להּ גדר להשמר בו[76]· ויעקב בהפכו איש תם· אינו בקי בכל אלה וכל מי שאינו בקי ברמיות קרוי תם[77]· יושב אוהלים· אוהל שם ועבר ועוד שהיה מציין נפשו בציונין הרבה· ועושה לפנים משורת הדין[78]· [25 : 28] ויאהב יצחק את עשו כי ציד בפיו· כתרגו׳ ארי מצידיה הוה אכיל· ד״א בפיו של עשו שצד הבריות בפיו[79]· ורבקה אוהבת את יעקב· שהיתה שומעת בכל יום קולו בדברי תורה· ומוספת אהבה יתירה בו· לכך אמ׳ ורבקה אוהבת את יעקב[80]· ועוד שהרי השם אמר לה ורב יעבוד צעיר[81]· [25 : 29] ויזד יעקב נזיד לשון תבשיל· ושל עדשים היה[82]· ויבא עשו מן השדה· אמ׳ עשו מ(ה טיבו) של תבשיל זה היום· אמרה לו בשביל שמת הזקן· אמ׳ ובאותו הזקן פ(געה) מדת הדין· אם כן לית דין ולית דיין· ורוח הקדש אומרת· אַל תבכו למת ואַל תנודו לו· בכו בכה להולך [ירמיה כב: י]· אַל תבכו למת· זה אברהם· בכו בכה להולך· זה עשו· שהלך לו מעולמו[83]· והוא עייף· כמו יגע· ד״א שהיה צמא· כמו צמאה נפשי כארץ עייפה לך סלה [תהלים קמג: ו]· מלמד שנכנס עייף ורעב וצמא[84]· וארז״ל אותו היום עבר חמש עבירות· רצח· ונאף· וגנב ועבד ע״ז· וכפר בעיקר· וכלם דרז״ל מן המקרא בהיקש[85]· [25 : 30] הלעיטני· אין לו דמיון במקרא· אבל במשנה[86] אית׳ מלעיטין את הגמל [שבת כד: ג]· שפותחין פיו ושופכין תוכו· עד שממלאין בטנו ממאכל· כשרוצים להוליכו ימים רבים בלא אכילה· ורצה לומר נא האכילני דרך הלעטה מן העדשים האדומים האלו[87]· ולמה בשל עדשים· לפי שהן עגולות ודומות לגלגל· שהאבילות [דומות] גלגל הוא שחוזר בעולם· ד״א מה עדשים אין להם פה· אף האבל אין לו פתחון פה[88]· מן האדום האדום· שני פעמים למה כלומ׳ מה תבשיל עדשים אדום אף עשו הוא אדום· וארצו אדומה· וגבוריו אדומים· ועתיד אדום ליפרע ממנו בלבוש אדום [ישעיה סג: א–ב][89]· [25 : 31] ויאמר מכרה כיום· כלומר כיום הזה שהוא ברור כך מכור לו [צ״ל: לי] מכירה ברורה וגמורה גלויה ומפורסמת[90]· ד״א כיום הזה שהולך ואינו חוזר· כך תהא מכירתך חלוטה וגמורה שאינה חוזרת לעולם· וקיימת לעולם[91]· ופשוטו מכור לי היום[92] את בכורתך לי· שאטול פי שנים בנכסי אבי· שהדבר היה ידוע· שהבכור נוטל פי שנים כמו שאמ׳ יעקב לראובן פחז כמים אַל תותר [בראשית מט: ד][93]· ד״א את בכורתך· לפי שהעבודה בבכורות· אמ׳ יעקב אין רשע זה כדאי להקריב לפני הקב״ה[94] [25 : 32] ויאמר עשו הנה אנכי הולך למות· שבכל יום היה הולך ומסתכן[95]

VII (C6.163r)

וישב

[37 : 13] (מכל מת?) ולא חשדם[96]· ודברים אלו היה יעקב נזכר· והיו מעיו מתהפכים
ואמ׳ יודע הוא שאחיו שונאים אותו· והוא אומ׳ לי הנני[97]· [37 : 14] והשיבני
דבר· מכאן שצריך האדם לשאל בשלם דבר שיש לו הנאה ממנו[98]·
וישלחהו מעמק חברון· והלא חברון נתונה בהר· שנ׳ ויעלו בנגב
ויבא [צ״ל ויבאו] עד חברון [במדבר יג: כב]· אלא הלך להשלים עצה עמוקה שנתן הקב״ה בינו
ובין הצדיק הקבור בחברון· שנ׳ ויאמר לאברם ידע תדע כי גר
(יהי)ה זרעך וג׳ [בראשית טו: יג][99] ויבא שכמה· מקום מוכן לפרענות· שם קלקלו [ה׳]
(הש)בטים· שם עינו את דינה· ושם נחלקה מלכות בית דוד שנ׳ ויבא [צ״ל וילך]
(ר)חבעם שכמה [ד״ה ב י: א][100]· [37 : 15] וימצאהו איש זה גבריאל שנ׳ והאיש גבריאל [דניאל ט: כא][101]· אמ׳
ר׳ ינאי שלשה מלכים [צ״ל מלאכים] נזדמנו לו שנ׳ וימצאהו איש וישאלהו האיש
ויאמר האיש[102]· [37 : 17] ויאמר האיש נסעו מזה· פשוטו· נסעו מזה המקום
כי שמעתי אומרי׳ נלכה דותינה· שם מקום· ומדרשו נסעו מזה
הסיעו עצמן מן האחוה· שאמרת את אחי אנכי מבקש· ומבקשים
(כנג)דך נכלי דתות שימיתוך בהם[103]· [37 : 18] ויראו אותו מרחוק· ויתנכלו
אותו· חשבו עליו מחשבה רעה[104]· ד״א שיסו בו את הכלבי׳[105]· [37 : 19] איש אל
אחיו שמעון ולוי הם[106]· הלזה· כמו הזה· כעניין מי האיש הלזה [בראשית כד: סה][107]
[37 : 20] ו(א)מ(ר)נו חיה רעה וג׳ [ונאמ׳]· ונאמר[108] ונראה מה יהיו חלומותיו·
(ראו) שיצא בסוף ירבעם מבני יוסף· שישיא עצה לבניהם
לעבוד [ועבידו?] ע״ז שנ׳ ויראו אותו מרחוק שראו דברים רחוקים לעתיד
לכך אמרו לכו ונהרגהו[109]· [37 : 21] וישמע ראובן ויצילהו (מ)ידם· ובמכירתו
היכן היה אלא אותו היום היה זמנו לשמש את אביו· ויצילהו
לכך זכה להמנות בהצלה תחלה שנ׳ את בצר במדבר בארץ
(ה)מישור לראובני [דברים ד: מג][110]· ויאמר לא נכנו נפש· לא נכנו מכת נפש
[37 : 22] למען הציל אותו מידם· התורה העידה על ראובן· שלא אמר
זה אלא למען הציל אותו ולהשיבו אל אביו· אמ׳ אני בכור
וגדול שבכולם לא יתלה הסרחון אלא [בכי׳] בי[111]· ואלו היה יודע
שכתו׳ מעיד עליו כן· לא היה נפרד ממנו אלא היה נוטלו ונושאו
על [כתיב׳] כתיפו אל אביו[112]· [37 : 23] ויפשיטו את כתנתו זה החלוק· את
כתנת הפסים זה שהוסיף לו אביו[113]· [37 : 24] ויקחהו כתי׳ חסר ו׳ו שהיה

VIII (C6.163v)

שמעון לבדו· והיכן פרע לו· במצרים שנ׳ ויקח מאתם את שמעון [בראשית מב: כד][114]

והבור רק· שני בורות היו אחד מלא צרורות ואחד מלא (נחשים) ועקרבי(ם)· ד״א והבור רק· נתרוקן בורו של יעקב כלומ׳ נתרוק(נו) בניו· והם בורו שיצאו מחלציו· ונתרוקנו מדברי תורה בזה המ(עשה) שלא ידעו עונש הדבר הזה וזהו שנ׳ אין בו מים שהתורה אמרה כי ימצא איש גונב נפש מאחיו [...] ומת הגנב ההוא [דברים כד: ז] ואלו מכרו את אחיהם[115]· [37 : 25] וישבו לאכל לחם· אגדה להאכיל לחם לכל באי (עולם·)[116] ארחת ישמעאלים· שיירה של ערביים· ונקראת ארחת על שם הולכי אורח[117]· וגמליהם נושאים נכאת· למה פירש הכתו׳ מש(אם) להודיע מתן שכרם של צדיקים שאין דרכם של ערביים לשאת אלא נפט ועיטרן והקב״ה הזמן לזה הצדיק בשמים שלא ינזק מריח רע· נכאת· כנוס של בשמיו [צ״ל: בשמין] כמו ויראם את כל בית נכותו [צ״ל: נכותה] [מלכים ב כ: יג] בית מרקחת בשמיו· וצרי שרף הנוטף מעצי הקטף והוא נטף האמור בתורה [שמות ל: לד]· ולוט· לוטיתא בלשון חכמים ז״ל [משנה שביעית ז: ו] ופירש שורש עשב

ויש אומרין מאצטיכי· [37 : 26] ויאמר יהודה מה בצע· כתרגו׳ מה ממון נתהני לנא· ויש אומרין מה תועלת כמו מה בצע בדמי [תהלים ל: י]· וכסינו את דמו· ונעלים את מיתתו[118]· [37 : 27] לכו ונמכרנו לישמעאלים· מה ראה יהודה שפתח להם במכירה· אמ׳ להם כנען שחטא נתקלל לעבד· אף זה לכו ונמכרנו לישמעאלים[119]· וישמעו אחיו· וקבילו מיניה כמו וישמע יעקב אל אביו [בראשית כח: ז]· וכן נעשה ונשמע [שמות כד: ז]· לשון קבלת דברים·[120]

[37 : 28] ויעברו אנשים מדיינים סוחרים· מלמד שהיו בשיירה סוחרים הרבה ונמכר כמה פעמים· לישמעאלים· ומהם למדיינים· ומהם למצרים[121]·· ופשוטו אורחת ישמעאלים שהם מדיינים[122]· בעשרים כסף אפשר נער יפה כזה נמכר בעשרים כסף אלא נשתנו פניו וברח ד(מו) מפני הנחשים והעקרבים שהיו בבור ונפחד מהם[123]· אמ׳ הקב״ה אתם מכרתם בכורה של רחל בעשרים כסף יהיה כל אחד מעתה מפריש עשרים מעין בכל שנה שהם מחצית השקל שכל שקל עשרים גרה לכפר על אותו מעשה· ועוד אמ׳ הקב״ה מכרתם בכורה של רחל בחמשה שקלים· יהיה כל בכור מבניכם נפדה בחמש שקלים[124]· [37 : 29] וישב ראובן

IX (C6.95r)

וישב

אל הבור וג׳ ובמכירתו לא היה שם· לפי שהגיע את יומ(ו) וילך לש(מש) את אביו ד״א היה עסוק בשקו ובתעניתו על שבלבל יצוע (אביו) וכשנפנה בא והציץ בבור· [37 : 30] ואני אנה אני בא· אנה אברח (מצערו?) של אבא[125]· ועוד שאמרתי אמצא תרופה למעשה בלהה[126] ואמר (הקב)״ה מעולם לא חטא אדם ועשה תשובה· ואתה פתחת בתשובה (ח)ייך בן בנך מתנבא ועומד ופותח בתשובה· /חייך בן בנך מתנבא (ועומ)ד ופותח בתשובה·/ ואיזהו הושע בן בארי שפתח ואמ׳ שובה (ישראל·) [הושע יד: ב][127] [37 : 31] וישחטו שעיר עזים· לפי שדמו דומה לדם האדם· ולכך (כתיב ש)עיר [...] לחטאת [וכתיב] לכפר עליכם[128]· [במדבר ז: טז, כח: ל] [37 : 32] וישלחו את כתנת הפסים הפיסו (עלי)ה מי יוליכנה אצל אביהם· ועלה הפייס על יהודה[129]· אמ׳ הקב״ה ליהודה אתה אמרת לאביך הכר נא הכתונת בנך וגו׳ חייך שתאמר לך תמר הכר נא למי החותמת והפתילים [בראשית לח: כה][130]· הכתנת בנך· לשון תימה· לכך דבוקה היא לתיבה שאחריה[131]· [37 : 33] ויכירה ויאמר וג׳ אמ׳ רוא(ה) אני ואין יודע מה אני רואה[132]· כתונת בני חיה רעה אכלתהו· נתנצצה בו רוח הקדש שסוף תתגרה כוא [צ״ל: בו?] אשת פוטיפר שהיא חיה רעה· ולמה לא גילה לו הקב״ה הדבר· לפי שהסכימו השבטים והחרימו כל מי שמגלה זה הסוד· ואפי׳ יצחק אביו יודיע היה שהוא בחיים· ולא רצה לגלות ליעקב· אמ׳ הקב״ה לא גלה לו גם אני איני מגלה לו[133]· ד״א חיה רעה אכלתהו· כנגד יהודה רמז· ואמר אותה חיה הגדולה שבחיות שהוא ארייה אכלתהו[134]· [37 : 34] ויקרע יעקב שמלותיו· השבטים גרמו לאביהם לקרוע· ונפרע להם במצרים שנ׳ ויקרעו /יש/ שמלותיו· [צ״ל שמלתם] [בראשית מד: יג] יוסף גרם לשבטים לקרוע· ונפרע (לזרעו) שעמד בן בנו הוא יהושע שקרע ויקרע יהושע וג׳ [יהושע ז: ו]· בנימין גרם לשבטים לקרוע ונפרע לזרעו בשושן הבירה שנ׳ ויקרע מרדכי את בגדיו [אסתר ד: א] מנשה גרם לשבטים לקרוע לכך נקרעה נחלתו חצייה בעבר הירדן וחציה בארץ כנען· וישם שק במתניו· אמ׳ ר׳ איבו לפי שתפש יעקב אבינו אבילות השק תחלה לפיכך אינו זז מבניו עד סוף כל הדורות· אחאב וישם שק על בשרו [מלכים א כא: כז]· יורם וירא (ה)עם והנה השק על בשרו [מלכים ב ו: ל]· מרדכי וילבש שק ואפר [אסתר ד: א]· ומעולם לא שב ריקם[135] ויתאבל על בנו ימים רבים עשרים ושתים שנה· כנגד כ״ב שנה שלא קיים מצוות כבוד [אב] ואם· ואע״פ שיצא כרשותם[136]· [37 : 35] ויקמו כל בניו וכל בנותיו לנחמו והלא לא היה לו כי אם אחת והלואי··

X (C6.95v)

היה קו(ב)רה· אלא אמ׳ ר יהודה תאומות נולדו עם השבטים· ר׳
נחמיה אמ׳ אלו כלותיו שאין אדם נמנע מלקרא לחתנו בנו
ולכלתו בתו[137]· וימאן להתנחם· אמ׳ הרי נפרצה ברית השבטים
כמה יגעתי להעמידם· לפי שהם כסדרו של עולם· י״ב מזלות·
י״ב שעות ביום· י״ב שעות בלילה· י״ב חדשים בשנה· ואשה אחרת
איני יכול לישא· משום הברית של לבן שנ׳ אם תקח נשי׳ על בנותי [בראשית לא: נ][138]·
ד״א וימאן להתנחם לפי שאין אדם מקבל תנחומין על החי שדווקא
על המתים מתנחמין שגזירה היא על המת שישתכח מן הלבי·
אבל על החיים לא נגזרה גזירה[139]· כי ארד אל בני כמו על בני· וכן
אל שאול ואל בית הדמים [שמואל ב כא: א] כולם לשון על· אבל שאולה כפשוטו
ומדרשו שאולה זו גהנם· שהיה בידו סימן מסור מפי הקב״ה
שאם לא ימות אחד מבניו בחייו מובטח לו שאינו רואה גיהנם[140]·
ויבך אותו אביו· זה יצחק שהיה בוכה מפני צרתו של יעקב· אבל
לא היה מתאבל עליו שהיה יודיע שהוא חי[141]· [37 :36] והמדנים מכרו
אותו אל מצרים מכאן שהם ישמעאלים· כמו שנ׳ מיד הישמעאלים
אשר הורידוהו שמה [בראשית לט: א][142]· שר הטבחים· *[שוט]* שוחטי בהמות המלך[143]·
[38:] בעת ההיא וירד יהודה· לא היה צריך לומ׳ כאן אלא

ויהי

ויוסף הורד מצרימה [בראשית לט: א] ולמה הפסיק וסמך פרשה זו
לכאן ללמד שהורידוהו אחיו מגדולתו· כשראו צרת אביהם
שאמרו לו אתה אמרת למוכרו· אלו אמרת להושיבו היינו שומעים
לך ר׳ יוחנן אמ׳ כדי לסמוך הכר להכר [בראשית לז: לב, לח: כה]· ר׳ אליעזר אומ׳ כדי
לסמוך ירידה לירידה[144]· וירד יהודה מאת אחיו· אמרו השבטים·
זה לזה בואו ונפרנס את עצמינו· לשעבר היה אבינו זקוק
להשיאנו· עכשיו הוא עסוק בשקו ובתעניתו· אמרו ליהודה
פרנס עצמך תחלה[145] מיד וירד יהודה מ(את) אחיו· ועל דרך
הפשט כל זה היה קודם מכירת יוסף· ואין מוקדם ומאוחר
בתורה· שהרי יהודה נשא אשה וילדה אשתו ער ואונן· וגדל
ער ונשא אשה ומת וגדל אונן ויבם אשת אחיו ומת· וגדל שלה
ובא יהודה אל תמר וילדה פרץ וזרח· וגדלו ונשאו נשים· ופרץ
הוליד חצרון וחמול כל זה בכ״ב שנים[146]· *[ופרץ הוליד חצרון]* ממכירת

NOTES ON THE HEBREW TEXT

1 The comment occurs in BR. Here, however, the direct object is used with the verb.

2 Although the basic idea of Rebekah's determination is found in various midrashim, the language here is reminiscent rather of the comments of R and RS and, unlike the midrashim, this commentator does not dwell on the disadvantages to her family of her decision.

3 The identification is made in PRE (ch. 16), LT, MG and ST; cp. also R on Gen. xxxv.8.

4 A connection with the blessings given to Abraham is also made by R, JQ, RS, ST and Q.

5 The same reason for Rebekah's temporary infertility is given in BR, LT, ST and YS.

6 The commentary here tallies with BR, LT, MA and YS but does not go as far as R, ST and TNB (vol. I, p. 123) in identifying Hagar with Keturah and referring explicitly to her being brought to Abraham for remarriage. Later comments, however, indicate a sympathy with these latter views rather than with the more critical opinions of RS and IE, given on Gen. xxv.1.

7 That the reference is here to prayer is a well-established piece of exegesis, which occurs in the Targumim and Talmud (BT Ber. 26*b*), is widespread in the midrashim and is preferred by S and R.

8 Such a more literal interpretation is found in the commentaries of IE, B and Q but no mention is made by any of them of the solitary nature of Isaac's stroll.

9 The comment bears greatest similarity to that of YS but cp. also BR and R.

10 The exegetical problem here is the degree of movement and the extent to which it was intentional. From at least as early as BR the exegetes have employed the targumic rendering for clarification of the sense, although N argues that they have not properly understood the Aramaic. The comment here is identical with that of R with the exception of the word *birṣōnā*, which is also found in IE and makes it clear that Rebekah's act was not accidental. Contrast the view of S.

11 The comment occurs in BR and is repeated in the various midrashic anthologies; see LT, MG and YS.

12 Both *pašṭānīm* and *daršānīm* refer to the miraculous events of his journey but the language here used to describe the meeting with Rebekah is a trifle strange. If the text is reliable the stem *zwg* is being used for the more normal *zmn*, while the regular word for prayer has been replaced by a more paitanic expression.

13 See IE, who makes a similar grammatical point.

14 The comment is almost identical with R and is based on BR.

15 See R and PRE (ch. 32).

16 The comment does not tally with those found in the sources consulted.

17 These comments are found in BR and are also included in YS. The sexual application given to the verse in Ecclesiastes is based on the interpretation of *yād* as the *membrum.*

18 The comment does not tally with those found in the sources consulted, but it does occur in BR, R and LT on Gen. iv.25; cp. also TNB, vol. I, p. 20.

19 The comment is very similar to that of R and is based on PRE (ch. 30), TN and BR.

20 The source of this interpretation is BR 39.11, and the comment is once again almost identical with that of R.

21 See BR, R, ST and YS.

22 The consensus of opinion among the commentators and midrashim is that the blessing could not be given because it might include (the children of) Ishmael and Keturah; cp. TJ, MG and ST on Gen. xxv.11, and BR and YS on this verse. R, however, refers to Esau as the source of the problem; cp. Ginzberg, vol. V, p. 266, n. 316.

23 See BR (on the first verse of the chapter), R and ST where the sense is clearer.

24 The same story is related in BT Sanh. 91*a*, BR, LT and YS, but with substantial variations of length, style and vocabulary. This commentary seems to be nearest to BR, but the name of the litigant tallies rather with the other midrashim.

25 The comment is almost identical with that of R; for the form see BR 58.1.

26 The definition given here of 'satisfaction' is similar to that in BR, cited by N, and in LT, MG and ST, with the exception that there it is their future reward and not the Shekhinah that is shown to the righteous.

27 Precisely this interpretation of the Hebrew idiom is one of those cited by IE; cp. also the commentary of B.

28 The motif of Ishmael's repentance is well known in the aggada. It occurs in BT B. Bat. 16*b*, TJ on the previous verse and on verse 17, and a number of times in BR (e.g. 30.4, 38.12 and 59.7), and is cited here by R, MA and YS, and by others on verse 17. Cp. Ginzberg, vol. V, p. 230, n. 114. His correct behaviour in the present context is part of this motif.

29 Whenever a blessing is mentioned the commentators and midrashim address themselves to the problem of its precise nature. Here this commentary follows the suggestion made in BT Soṭa 14*a*, and repeated by R and MG, that the context demands the blessing recited before a mourner. Cp. also BR 81.5 and 82.3.

30 The commentary once again prefers a literal interpretation, identical with that of R and with echoes in ST and Q.

31 The opening and closing parts of this comment are as those of R, but

the reason given for the mention of Ishmael's years is different. His is based on BT Yebam. 64*a* while this commentary prefers to refer back to the repentance of Ishmael, mentioned earlier. Such a reference is indeed made by such works as LT and YS but only as an alternative interpretation after they have presented the one found in the talmudic passage. The attribution to Ḥiyya bar Abba is based on that passage, but the same question is asked in BT Meg. 17*a* and in various midrashim, including BR, and differently attributed. See T-A, pp. 676–7.

32 This definition of the stem is also given by IE as his second suggestion but rejected by him.

33 The connection between the fourth and fifth lines is not clear, and it would appear that a line that contained the other verse cited by R and the first part of the comment found in BR, R, MG, ST and YS has been omitted through homoioteleuton. This has therefore been restored in the text edition.

34 The whole passage is substantially that which occurs in the fourth paragraph of TN on this *sēder*. Cp. also BR, YS and B.

35 The same explanation of the connection between this and the previous *sēder* is given by IE, and the difference in the degree of attention given to Isaac, as opposed to Ishmael, is alluded to by Q. Cp. also R on Gen. xxxvii.1.

36 The basic point that Isaac's facial features were made similar to Abraham's in order to put the latter's paternity beyond question is made in BT B. Meṣ. 87*a* and TJ, and recurs in such diverse sources as MG and B. This commentary most resembles TN and R, and its reference to the similarity of Isaac's piety to that of his father occurs in LT.

37 Having repeated the midrash that Rebekah was no more than three years old when she met Abraham's servant, this commentary, unlike R and YS, who cite it without comment, feels the need to apologize for such a possibility. Others, too, preferred the more rational midrash, which regarded Rebekah as a teenager at this stage; cp. *Sifrē*, Deuteronomy, section 357, ed. L. Finkelstein (Berlin, 1939), p. 429; *Sēder ʿŌlām Rabbā*, ch. 1, ed. A. Neubauer in *Mediaeval Jewish Chronicles*, vol. II (Oxford, 1895), p. 27; the second comment of the *Tōsāpōt* on BT Yebam. 61*b*, and MG.

38 The text of this comment varies only slightly from that found in BR, R, LT, MA, MG and YS.

39 This comment bears a close resemblance to that of LT, but the same idea is expressed in ST and, with more textual variation, in MG.

40 The reference to the Hosea verse is also made, together with a citation of the Arabic cognate, by IE, Q and, if the text is to be trusted, by R, and S offers the same Hebrew 'translation'.

41 The preoccupation with the precise sense of the stem *ʿtr* has a long history among Jewish exegetes and grammarians. BR on this verse records views that understand the basic sense as 'abundant' as in the Aramaic *ʿšr*, 'reverse' as in the Aramaic *ʿtr* meaning 'pitchfork', and 'dig' as in the Hebrew *ḥtr*. There is support for the second view in BT Yebam. 64*a* and Sukk. 14*a* and, among the midrashim, this is the only one cited by MA, MG and ST, while LT also records the third view and YS notes all three. Of the commentators, R, RS and Q are happiest with the sense 'abundant', but B has a clear presentation of all three senses. The medieval Hebrew grammarians such as Ibn Saruq, Ibn Janaḥ and Q refer to two basic senses, 'pray' and 'abundant', while their modern counterparts add a third sense, viz. 'odour', based on Ezek. viii.11. See also the note in T-A and *Aruch Completum*, vol. VI (Vienna 1890), pp. 283–4.

42 The content of the prayer is as that described in BR and followed in LT, MG, ST and YS, while the description of their each standing in a separate corner is formulated as in R.

43 The idea that Isaac waited a certain period of time before requesting divine assistance in the matter of Rebekah's infertility occurs in TJ, PRE (ch. 32) and YS, but there the number of years is given as 22 (see Ginzberg, vol. V, p. 270, n. 7) or 20.

44 The midrash occurs in BT Yebam. 64*a* and is repeated in YS, but this formulation is precisely that of R.

45 See the commentary of JQ, which also refers to TO and the mishnaic passage but is slightly longer and clearer.

46 The comment is very similar to that of IE.

47 The use of this word in the present context is somewhat misleading, since it does not introduce a conclusion reached on the basis of the remark immediately preceding, as is customary, but alternative explanations of the first phrase in verse 22.

48 All three interpretations are offered in BR and recur in LT, MG and YS. The language in which the first is here couched is best paralleled in R and MG.

49 This justification of the terminology here applied to the foetus is precisely that suggested by IE.

50 The idea is found in BR, but the formulation is almost identical with that of R.

51 This aggadic expansion of Rebekah's question into an inquiry of her fellow-women occurs in BR and is repeated not only by the various midrashic works but also by IE and Q.

52 See LT.

53 See R.

54 See LT and ST, presumably based on TJ.

55 That the inquiry was made through Shem in order to accord due

honour to an old man is suggested in BR and widely followed not only in the midrashic but also in the literal commentaries; cp. MG, ST, YS, R, Q and B. Contrast IE, who prefers Abraham or an anonymous prophet, and PT Soṭa 7.1 (21*b*).

56 Both comments closely follow BR in playing on the *Qrē-Kĕtīb* and the similarity of *šny* and *śn*ʾ.

57 This definition, based on the rendering of TO, is also made in BT ʿAbod. Zar. 2*b* and cited by R. Cp. also RS and Q.

58 It is common for the Aggadah to make such claims for those whose attachment to Judaism it particularly wishes to stress; cp. Ginzberg, vol. V, p. 273, n. 26. Here the midrash is based on the 'division' between Esau and Jacob and occurs in many of the exegetical midrashim on the verse.

59 This 'division', rather than the one referred to in the previous note, is that cited by R.

60 The impossibility of a balanced co-existence between the forces of 'Jacob' and 'Esau' is claimed in BT Pesaḥ. 42*b* and Meg. 6*a* and cited here by LT, ST and Q. The formulation is most similar to that of R.

61 As Q points out, it is not clear from the syntax who is the subject, and this lack of clarity provides the opportunity for the midrash. The interpretation of the midrash here offered, namely, that the defective spelling of the verb permits a reading as a *qal* or a *hiphʿīl*, is one possibility. For others, see BR, LT and MG, and the notes of T-A and Buber on these midrashim. See also TJ.

62 This interpretation of the defective spelling is found in BR and in *Midraš Ḥăsērōt Wītērōt* in. S.A. Wertheimer's *Bāttē Midrāšōt*, vol. II (Jerusalem, 1953), p. 241 and is repeated not only in the exegetical midrashim but also by R, Q and B.

63 The passage occurs in BR but, in contrast to MG and YS, this commentary and LT translate the rare Aramaic words of the original into Hebrew. Cp. *Aruch Completum*, vol. VI (n. 41 above), p. 426, and R on verse 26.

64 The idea that Esau chose this world and Jacob the next occurs in LT and BRT. The text placed here in slanted square brackets appears to be misplaced and defective. It belongs to the central part of another midrash, which deals with the various connotations of the word *rīʾšōn*; cp. e.g. BR and YS.

65 It is somewhat strange that the commentary here refers to the grammatical form of the word, with its final *yōd*, much as IE does, and then appears to use the phenomenon as a basis for the midrash about David found in BR and YS and briefly referred to in R, LT and MG. Perhaps he means *sīmān* to refer only to the matter of the colour and not to the grammatical form.

66 Similar interpretations are offered in the Targumim, MG, ST and Q, but the formulation is again most similar to that of R.

67 The formulation is again almost identical with that of R, although a similar point is made in TJ, LT and RS.

68 The *noṭariqon* originates in BR and is repeated in LT, MG, ST and YS. In ST it is specifically defined, as here, as a midrash.

69 The idea that the 'Edomite' hegemony would be replaced by that of Jacob occurs in BR and many other midrashim, but the formulations of this and the next comment are almost identical with those of R.

70 That Abraham survived for the first fifteen years of Jacob's life is also claimed in YS and ST, but LT goes further and notes the part he played in introducing him to 'precepts and statutes'. Here it is 'wisdom and morality' to which he introduced him.

71 The lesson and its parable are borrowed from BR, where the opposite order of presentation is followed. Among the various midrashim that cite this interpretation only TNB and ST have a somewhat similar order, while our text of R is very similar but omits the parable.

72 IE makes precisely this point about the need for a hunter to be especially shrewd and quick-witted.

73 R's comment, which is very similar, is based on BR and TNB; cp. also MA and YS.

74 See BR, repeated in YS.

75 The comment is again almost identical with that of R.

76 The comment is apparently an interpretation of the figure used in BR in order to describe Esau's licentious behaviour, i.e. he made himself as freely available as an open field.

77 The comment is again substantially that of R; cp. also IE and Q.

78 Although BR and many other midrashim, as well as TJ and some of the *pašṭānīm*, refer the phrase to Jacob's outstanding scholarly and religious activities in the academy of Shem and Eber, they do not use this phraseology; cp. *Tōrā Šĕlēmā*, ed. M.M. Kasher, vol. IV (Jerusalem, 1934), p. 1028.

79 See R (whose comments are based on TO), TJ and BR on this verse, and BR on this word in the previous verse.

80 This justification of Rebekah's special love and the interpretation of the participial use are based on BR and recur in LT, ST and YS.

81 See RS here and on verse 23.

82 This meaning of the stem *nzd* is derived from TO and is widely followed in the commentators and midrashim. The assumption is also widely made that the dish was one of lentils (based on verse 34) and was a funeral meal as claimed in BR, TJ and BT B. Bat. 16*b*.

83 This description of Esau's heresy occurs in BR and is repeated in YS and briefly referred to in LT; cp. also TJ.

84 The first interpretation of the word, which is that followed by S, sees it as an epithet for general weariness, while the second, followed here by IE and also in the dictionaries of Ibn Janaḥ and Q, presupposes a more specific link with thirst. Cp. also R and IE on Deut. xxv.18.

85 BT B. Bat. 16*b* and TJ suggest that the number of transgressions committed by Esau was five, but the number differs in the various midrashim. It is interesting that this commentary here defines the method used by the midrashim to arrive at their results.

86 The word is used here in the sense of 'Tannaitic Hebrew'.

87 The comment most closely resembles that of LT, but there are similar comments in BR, R, MA and MG, while TNB and ST have long discussions of the meaning of the stem.

88 The comment is included in the fuller text of R on this verse but occurs in the comments of LT, MA, MG and YS on the previous verse, based on BT B. Bat. 16*b*.

89 LT, like this commentary, specifically asks why the word is mentioned twice. The commentaries and midrashim provide various answers and the one offered here occurs in BR, LT and YS.

90 The same interpretation is offered in R but minus the last two words and with the addition of a reference to the TO at the beginning; cp. also TNB, LT and MA.

91 The comment occurs in LT with a number of textual variations.

92 Cp. S.

93 The literal interpretation preferred here is similar to that of IE; cp. also ST.

94 The point is made in BR, TNB and later midrashim, but the formulation here is almost identical with that of R.

95 Although only the first words of the comment are preserved, it is clearly parallel to that of IE; cp. also *Sēper Ḥăsīdīm*, section 341, ed. R. Margaliot (Jerusalem, 1957), p. 256.

96 The reference is obviously to one of the brothers' various misdemeanours according to the midrashim, but the first few letters are unclear and I have therefore been unable to identify which one.

97 The comment is found in BR, LT and YS but only in LT is it formulated, as here, in the third person. It should also be noted that R has a similar but shorter comment and that the word *mithappĕkīm* used here occurs in the text of BR in MS Vat. Ebr. 30, fo 151*a* (with final *nūn* for final *mēm*).

98 This moral lesson is derived in BR, repeated in LT, MA and MG, and cited by Q. It is intended to explain the concern for the welfare of the sheep.

99 Although this aggadic interpretation of 'the valley of Hebron' occurs in BR, TNB (p. 183) and TJ and is followed by many of the later anthologies, the version used here and in R is that of BT Soṭa 11*a*. Cp. also Q and N.

100 With the exception of the correction, the text is precisely that of R. Similar reference to the unfortunate events that occurred at Shechem is made in BT Sanh. 102*a* and in TN but not in the order adopted by R.

101 The comment is again identical with that of R, based on TN; cp. also MA, MG, PRE (ch. 38), ST, TJ and YS.
102 The text most closely resembles YS; cp. also MA and MG.
103 The comments are substantially those of R with some variations in order and formulation.
104 This paraphrase is found in IE; cp. also N.
105 See BR, LT, MG, ST and YS.
106 On this identification of the brothers involved see TNB (p. 183), TJ, LT and ST and Buber's notes on LT.
107 RS also equates the meanings of these two demonstrative adjectives but argues that the one with *lāmed* is used when the speaker is at a distance from the subject being described; cp. also LT and ST.
108 The simple grammatical point being made is that the *wāw* consecutive is here being used with the imperfect tense but with reference to the future.
109 This midrash is found in BR and LT, but in neither is it made clear, as it is here, that it is based on a chronological interpretation of the word *mērāḥōq*.
110 The midrash on Reuben's absence is included in BR and repeated in LT, MA and YS, while the matter of his reward is found in BR and BT Mak. 10*a* and repeated in LT, MA, MG and YS. The structure and formulation here are most similar to those of LT, with Reuben's comment about his being held responsible as the firstborn, which occurs in many of the midrashim, held back until later.
111 See R, who also cites the midrash from BR here and not earlier.
112 The same point is made in WR 34.8 and cited here by LT, TNB (p. 184) and YS.
113 The comments on Joseph's clothing are almost identical with those of R, the first based on BR and the second similar to the rationalist interpretations of RS, ST and Q.
114 This interpretation of the defective spelling occurs in BR, MA, MG and YS but is as explicit as it is here only in ST. The later *pašṭānīm*, such as B and Q, also make reference to it. Cp. also TNB, introduction, p. 139.
115 It is noteworthy that, unless there has been a case of homoioteleuton, the commentary does not cite the simple midrash that the pit did not contain water but snakes and scorpions (BT Šabb. 22*a* and widely in the commentaries and midrashim) but offers the various interpretations included in BR, in clarified form. Although ST and YS also go further than the simple midrash, neither offers anything as extensive as this.
116 The comment also appears in short form in BR. What is meant is that even their sins benefitted the world, since they led to Joseph's provision of food in time of famine, as is made clear in ST, *Pĕsīqtā Rabbātī* 10.13 and TN on *Kī Tiśśā'*, paragraph 2.
117 The explanation that a caravan is here being referred to is also offered

by R, IE and ST, all based on the rendering of TO. TO and TJ also translate *yišmĕʿʾēlīm* as 'Arabs', and this is followed here and by S but not in the other commentaries mentioned.

118 The whole section varies only to a minor extent from the standard text of R, in which the first midrash concerning the pleasant-smelling materials being ferried by the Ishmaelites originates in BR and *Mekilta* (on *Wayĕhī Bĕšallaḥ*, ed. J.Z. Lauterbach (Philadelphia, 1933), vol. I, p. 235, or eds. H.S. Horovitz and I.A. Rabin (Jerusalem, 1960), p. 106), and the definitions of the Hebrew names for these materials are based on BR 91.11, the talmudic passage cited and Ibn Saruq; cp. also ST and T-A. The alternative explanation offered for the word *bṣʿ* is found in IE.

119 The idea that Judah's intention in suggesting the sale was to find a suitable punishment for Joseph's provocative behaviour towards his brothers is found in BR, MA, MG, ST and YS, but the formulation here is closest to LT.

120 A similar but longer comment on the meaning of the stem, with references to targumic usage, is found in R; cp. also ST.

121 R and ST on this verse and BR, LT, MA, MG, ST and YS on verse 36 explain the discrepancies in the names of the merchants as indicative of numerous sales. They do not, however, make the point that they were all in the same caravan.

122 This more literal interpretation tallies with those of IE and Q; cp. n. 142 below.

123 This explanation of the low price paid for Joseph is offered in TN and MG in more lengthy form.

124 These two midrashim occur, with substantial variation of text, in PT Šeqal. 2.4 (46*d*), PRK Šeqal. 17*b* (ed. B. Mandelbaum, pp. 32–3) and BR 84.18, and are reproduced in YS and partly in MA, MG, LT and ST.

125 The whole section tallies with R with the exception of the first four legible words in the third line. These are borrowed from BR (here and on verse 21 above), which is the source of all but the last comment in the section and the direct reference to Reuben's immorality; for the latter see TJ.

126 The comment that Reuben, instead of finding a penance for his immoral act, now encountered even more trouble, is also made in LT; see also TJ.

127 This text, in common with LT, MA, ST and YS, follows closely the midrash in BR, which claims that Reuben was the first man to repent of his sins; see also *Sifrē*, Deuteronomy, section 31, ed. L. Finkelstein (n. 37 above), p. 52.

128 The similarity of this animal's blood to that of human beings is referred to in TJ and BR and cited by R and many other commentators and midrashim. The formulation here is closest to that of LT.

129 This play on the word *passīm* is widely made in the midrashim on verse 3 but here only in AB 61 (p. 123) and MG.

130 The similarity of the phrase used here to that occurring in Gen. xxviii.25 is used for this interpretation in BR and BT Soṭa 10*b* and widely followed in the midrashim. The formulation here most closely resembles that of YS.

131 The point of the comment is to distinguish the absolute and construct forms of the noun and to argue that here the *hē*' in no way militates against its being the construct case since it is the interrogative particle. R's point on the previous phrase is similar but expressed differently.

132 This statement is attributed to Jacob in BR, MG and YS, but in Aramaic. Here it has been translated into Hebrew.

133 The whole passage tallies with R except that here the description of Potiphar's wife as a *ḥayyā rā*ʿ*ā* is more direct, and an explicit mention of God's partnership in the brothers' oath is avoided. R's sources are BR, PRE (ch. 38), TN and TJ. The variant *nitnaṣĕṣāh* for *niṣnĕṣāh* should also be noted.

134 This allusion to Judah is also claimed by TN (*Wayyiggaš*, section 9), AB 61 (p. 124) and YS; other commentaries and midrashim make reference to it in their comments on Gen. xlix.9.

135 The whole passage derives from BR and is repeated in LT, MG, YS and (partly) ST, the only substantial variant being the omission of a reference to David's wearing of sackcloth (1 Chr. xxi.16) and the addition of the last four words, both as in LT.

136 Many of the midrashim follow BR in identifying this period of time as one of twenty-two years, but the link with Jacob's own failure to honour his parents for this period is more explicitly made by R; see his comments here and on BT Meg. 17*a*. Neither the midrashim nor R add the rider that Jacob had had parental authority for this absence.

137 With the exception that the reference to the Canaanite origins of Jacob's daughters-in-law is omitted, the comment is as that of R, which is based on TNB (p. 182). See also BR, MG, TJ and YS, which have a similar explanation of the occurrence here of 'daughters'.

138 This is a slightly abbreviated version of what appears in TNB (p. 181) and is repeated in YS on the subject of the special significance of the number twelve and Jacob's anguish at the apparent loss of this and the 'death' of Joseph.

139 The idea is found in the addenda to *Masseket Sōpĕrīm*, ed. M. Higger (New York, 1937), p. 368, and BR, and repeated widely in the midrashim, but the formulation here is very similar to that of R.

140 The comments and the style are again substantially those of R, who borrowed the midrash from TN (*Wayyiggaš*, section 9); on the literal meaning of Sheol see also IE.

141 The interpretation that the father here referred to is not Jacob but

Isaac occurs in TJ and is widespread in the midrashim from BR. The formulation is again almost identical with that of R.

142 The view that the different names refer to the same group is expressed here by RS. It is also followed by IE and Q on xxxvii.28 (see n. 122 above) and by MG on xxxix.1.

143 This is precisely the comment of R, who prefers to explain the stem in the sense of 'preparing meat' rather than 'putting to death'; cp. the Targumim and the comments of IE and N on this verse, RS and LT on xxxix.1, and the medieval Hebrew dictionaries s.v. *ṭbḥ*.

144 The commentary here follows R in conflating the midrashim found in TNB (pp. 181 and 183) and in BR but expands the comment by including the statement about ch. xxxix at the beginning and the views of R. Joḥanan and R. Eliezer at the end, all borrowed from BR. Cp. Q and B, who exploit the midrash in similar fashion.

145 The comment about the brothers not having to look after their own matrimonial arrangements occurs substantially in this form in BR and is repeated in MG, ST and YS.

146 The absurdity of establishing the chronology of these events on the basis of where they appear in the pentateuchal narrative is similarly pointed out by IE but in a somewhat less concise fashion. The basic point is that twenty-two years elapsed between the sale of Joseph and the settlement in Goshen and the events described in ch. xxxviii could not possibly be telescoped into such a short period.

Translation of the Hebrew text

I . . . intimating to the girl that she should not go. AND SHE SAID: I SHALL GO of my own free will, unhesitatingly. [xxiv.59] AND HER NURSE: This was Deborah. [xxiv.60] MAY YOU BECOME THE MOTHER OF MILLIONS: May you and your descendants enjoy the blessings promised to Abraham on Mount Moriah in the words I SHALL INDEED MULTIPLY YOUR DESCENDANTS [Gen. xxii.17]. God grant that those descendants come from your line. Nevertheless, Rebekah was not blessed with pregnancy until Isaac had prayed for her, | so that her family would not be able to claim that their prayers had produced results. [xxiv.62] BE'ER LAḤAY RO'I: Isaac had gone there to fetch Hagar, for she had sat down by the well and asked God to heed her plight. [xxiv.63] LĀŚUAḤ IN THE FIELD: That is, 'to pray', as in the verse BEFORE THE LORD HE POURS OUT HIS PRAYER [Psalm cii.1]. Another view is that he was walking alone among the trees [*śīḥīm*]. [xxiv.64] WHEN SHE SAW ISAAC: when she caught that splendid sight of him standing there with his arms stretched out in prayer, she said: 'This must be a great man.' SHE ALIGHTED FROM THE CAMEL: She deliberately let herself down to the ground, | as Targum Onqelos renders it 'and she let herself

down'. [xxiv.65] SHE TOOK THE SCARF AND COVERED HER FACE: Two women, Rebekah and Tamar, covered themselves with a scarf, and both of them gave birth to twins. [xxiv.66] THE SERVANT TOLD ISAAC: He informed him about the miracles that had occurred for him on his journey and also how the encounter with Rebekah had taken place in response to his prayer. [xxiv.67] THE TENT, SARAH HIS MOTHER: That is, the tent of Sarah his mother. Another view is that she took on the role of Sarah his mother. As long as Sarah had been alive a lamp burned in her tent every Friday evening, | there was always blessing in the dough and a cloud [of protection] hovered over the tent. When his mother died these things ceased but with Rebekah's arrival they resumed. ISAAC WAS COMFORTED FOR [THE DEATH OF] HIS MOTHER: It is a fact of life that as long as a man's mother is alive he tends to cling to her, but when she dies, he takes comfort in his wife. Another explanation of ISAAC WAS COMFORTED is that he had almost despaired of finding a woman as worthy and as pious as his mother Sarah when he found Rebekah who was so like her. Therefore ISAAC WAS COMFORTED ETC. [xxv.1] | ABRAHAM MARRIED ANOTHER WOMAN: This is illuminated by the verse [Eccles. xi.6] SOW YOUR SEED IN THE MORNING AND DO NOT REMAIN IDLE IN THE EVENING ETC. R. Eliezer explains: If you have sown early in the season do a late sowing too since you never know which of them will do well. If you have learned Torah in your youth, return to your study in your old age since you never know which lessons will be retained. R. Samuel b. Naḥmani explains: If you had sons in your youth and your wife has died, take another wife in your old age and produce sons, since you never know who will | survive. From whom do you learn this? From Abraham, of whom it is said ABRAHAM MARRIED ANOTHER ETC. Another explanation is that ABRAHAM MARRIED AGAIN at the divine command, as indicated in the [occurrence of the same stem in the] verse THE LORD SPOKE TO ME AGAIN [Isa. viii.5]. Another explanation is that the verb used here alludes to the increased sexual appetite with which God endowed him. WHOSE NAME WAS KETURAH: This was Hagar. Why then is she called Keturah? It is because her actions were as sweet as incense [which is also from the stem *qṭr*]. Another explanation is that she kept herself sexually inviolate [literally 'closed her opening', again from the stem *qṭr*]. No man had had relations with her since the day she left Abraham, in spite of the fact that it is recorded of her that SHE WANDERED ABOUT IN THE
II BEERSHEBA | DESERT [Gen. xxi.14]. [xxv.5] ABRAHAM GAVE EVERYTHING HE HAD TO ISAAC: What kind of blessing was it that God promised him when he said BE A BLESSING [Gen. xii.2]? The meaning appears to be: The blessings are passed on to you for the benefit of whomever you wish; and it was this faculty that Abraham passed on to Isaac. Another view is [that he bequeathed him his] property and [the

right to] burial in the Cave [of Machpelah]. R. Ḥama b. R. Ḥanina states that he gave him no blessing since he foresaw that his issue would include Esau, whose behaviour would become degenerate. All that he gave him was, | literally, a gift, that is, all his possessions. It is like the story of a king who had an orchard, which he leased to a tenant. In it there were two trees, intertwined, one producing a life-saving drug and the other a deadly poison. The tenant said [to himself]: If I water the tree producing the life-saving drug the other tree will also absorb the moisture and will always exist alongside it, but if I do not water it how will it survive? He said [to himself]: I shall not water them at all. Let the owner of the orchard come and do what he wishes. This is what Abraham said: | If I bless Isaac, Esau will be included in the blessing. Let the Dispenser of Blessings come and bless whomever he wishes. This is the reason why God appeared to Isaac after Abraham's death and [himself] blessed him, as the verse states: NOW AFTER THE DEATH OF ABRAHAM GOD BLESSED ISAAC HIS SON [Gen. xxv.11]. [xxv.6] THE SONS OF THE CONCUBINES: He had only one concubine, and this was Hagar. In the time of Alexander of Macedon the Ishmaelites made a case contesting Israel's claim to the birthright. Our rabbis, of blessed memory, asked who would go and argue the case with them. | Gebiha b. Pesisa said: I shall go. If I win, good and well. If not, you can say: 'Why on earth did this nobody represent us?' So he went and represented them. Having been requested by the court to state their claim, the Ishmaelites said: We seek redress from them and we call their Torah as evidence against them for it states: HE SHALL RECOGNIZE THE RIGHTS OF HIS FIRSTBORN, THE SON OF HIS UNLOVED WIFE AND GIVE HIM A DOUBLE PORTION ETC. [Deut. xxi.17]. Ishmael was just such a first-born! Gebihah answered them [with the question]: May a man dispose of his assets during his lifetime in whatever fashion he chooses, or not? They said that he might. Is that so? | (he replied), then it is written in the Torah: ABRAHAM GAVE ALL THAT HE HAD TO ISAAC [Gen. xxv.5]. At this they all slipped away shamefaced. [xxv.7] THE TOTAL YEARS OF ABRAHAM'S LIFE WERE A HUNDRED YEARS, AND SEVENTY YEARS, AND FIVE YEARS: At a hundred he was like a man of seventy, and at seventy like a child of five with regard to sin. [xxv.8] OLD AND CONTENT: This teaches us that God reveals his glory to the righteous at the time of their death and they feel content. HE WAS REJOINED WITH HIS KINSFOLK: As long as the soul plays a part in | bodily functions it is estranged from its source but when it takes leave of the body its honour is restored to its true place. [xxv.9] ISAAC AND ISHMAEL BURIED HIM: This indicates that Ishmael repented. Coming from the desert to pay respect to Abraham, he allowed Isaac to take precedence and played the secondary role. This is what is meant by the HAPPY OLD AGE ascribed to Abraham. [xxv.11] AFTER THE DEATH OF ABRAHAM GOD BLESSED ISAAC: He pronounced over him the

blessing for comforting mourners. [xxv.13] BY THEIR NAMES ACCORD-
III ING TO THEIR BIRTH: | [According to] the order of their birth, one by one. [xxv.17] THESE ARE THE YEARS OF ISHMAEL'S LIFE: R. Ḥiyya b. Abba said: Why are Ishmael's years enumerated? The reason is that he repented during his father's lifetime. It is said of him HE BREATHED HIS LAST and such an expression is used only with reference to the righteous. [xxv.18] HE WANDERED ABOUT NEAR HIS KINSFOLK: It is normal to use this expression *nĕpīlā* of nomads who wander from place to place as in the verse YOU ARE STRAYING OVER TO THE CHALDEANS [Jer. xxxvii.13]. Another explanation is that the stem means 'dwell' as in the verse THE MIDIANITES, AMALEKITES AND ALL THE EASTERN TRIBES WERE STATIONED IN THE VALLEY [Judg. vii.12]. [According to another, midrashic interpretation] the expression *nōpēl* is used here | while an earlier verse [Gen. xvi.12] says [of Ishmael]: HE WILL DWELL [*yiškōn*] NEAR HIS KINSFOLK. As long as Abraham was alive he dwelt [there] but when Abraham died he too passed away. [xxv.19] THIS IS THE STORY OF THE DESCENDANTS OF ABRAHAM'S SON, ISAAC: This exemplifies the scriptural verse GRANDCHILDREN ARE THE CROWN OF OLD AGE AND SONS ARE PROUD OF THEIR FATHERS [Prov. xvii.6]. Ancestral merit is a blessing to the family and worthy grandchildren do credit to their forebears. The first part of this claim is supported by the latter half of the verse cited, while the remainder of the verse | justifies the rest of the claim. Abraham benefited from the merit of Jacob when Nimrod threw him into the fiery furnace. God came down to save him but the ministering angels said: Lord of the World! How can you save this man? Look how many evil men will be among his issue! God replied, I am saving him for the sake of Jacob his grandson. This is what is meant by the verse THEREFORE THIS IS WHAT WAS SAID BY THE LORD, THE GOD OF THE HOUSE OF JACOB WHO SAVED ABRAHAM [Isa. xxix.22]. It was Jacob's merit | that saved Abraham. And where is there an example of ancestral merit blessing members of the family? When Laban pursued Jacob and quarrelled with him, Jacob said: IF NOT FOR THE GOD OF MY FATHER, THE GOD OF ABRAHAM ETC. [Gen. xxxi.42]. It is clear then that Jacob was saved from Laban by the merit of Abraham. There is another interpretation of THIS IS THE STORY OF THE DESCENDANTS OF ABRAHAM'S SON, ISAAC: Once brief mention has been made of Ishmael's descendants, the matter of Isaac's line is taken up and dealt with at length. Since he is mentioned as ISAAC, | ABRAHAM'S SON it was necessary to [remove all doubt about his parentage and] add: ISAAC'S FATHER WAS ABRAHAM, that is, Isaac was physically like his father. The angel responsible for such forms made the facial features of Isaac similar to those of Abraham so that anyone seeing him would acknowledge that Abraham was his father. Furthermore, anyone who saw his good deeds would say that he truly was THE SON OF HIS FATHER, ABRAHAM.

[xxv.20] ISAAC WAS FORTY YEARS OLD ETC.: Some of our rabbis, of blessed memory, made the following calculation: The news of the birth of Rebekah was given to Abraham on his return from Mount Moriah; | Isaac was thirty-seven years old when bound [on the altar for sacrifice], since Sarah was ninety years old when he was born and one hundred and twenty-seven when she died, and her death is recorded in the chapter immediately following the binding; the news of the birth of Isaac's future partner was also given at this time; it therefore turns out that Rebekah was only three years old [in this story]. Nor need one be amazed at the fact that she went to the well and gave the camels water at the age of three; the people of those days were very different from their counterparts of today. DAUGHTER OF BETHUEL, THE ARAMEAN: This [mention of ARAMEAN] is by way of praise for her indicating that, although her
IV father, her brother and | the men of her home town were wicked rogues [*rammāʾē*], she did not learn from their misdeeds but was LIKE A LILY AMONG THE THORNS [Song of Songs ii.2]. AS HIS WIFE: [A wife] suitable for him; it was fitting for such a righteous woman to be married to a righteous man. PADDAN-ARAM: The countryside of Aram [Hos. xii.13]. [xxv.21] ISAAC PLEADED: He prayed continually and fervently until God complied with his wish. [The stem is] the same as that used in the phrase PLEAD WITH THE LORD [Exod. ix.28]. HE RESPONDED TO THE PLEA: He complied with his wish. Another view is that the stem *ʿtr* means 'turning over'. The implement with which one turns over | the grain is called *ʿēter*. The power of the righteous is such that they 'overturn' God's decrees from the harsh to the beneficial. IN RELATION TO HIS WIFE: He stood in one corner and said: Lord of the World, may any children that you may give me be from this righteous woman! She stood in another corner and said: Lord of the World, may any children that you may give me be from this righteous man! FOR SHE WAS BARREN: He prayed for her only after he realized that she was barren, for he had waited | ten years and she had not given birth. HE RESPONDED TO HIS PLEA: His and not hers. The prayer of the righteous child of a righteous father cannot be compared to that of the righteous child of a wicked father. [xxv.22] THE BOYS STRUGGLED: As Targum Onqelos translates it: The boys pushed hard in her womb. [The stem is used] in a similar way [in the Mishnah with reference to] the impurity [contracted through a container being] tightly packed [Ṭohar. 8.2]. Another possible meaning is 'darting' as in the verse DARTING LIKE LIGHTNING [Nahum ii.5]. This indicates that when she passed by entrances to pagan shrines Esau tried to dart free, as the verse has it, THE WICKED CHOOSE IDOLATRY FROM THE WOMB [Psalm lviii.4], but when she passed by the entrance to Shem and Eber's Torah academy | Jacob tried to dart free in the manner expressed by the verse BEFORE I FORMED YOU IN THE WOMB I KNEW YOU WERE MINE, BEFORE YOU CAME INTO THE WORLD I SET YOU APART [Jer. i.5]. Another interpretation

of the use here of the stem *rwṣ* is that it means that each chases after the other to kill him. Alternatively [the use of *noṭariqon* makes possible the explanation that] each permits what the other proscribes. THE BOYS: They are described as such since this is what they ultimately turned out to be. SHE SAID, IF SO: If the suffering of pregnancy is like this WHY WAS I SO desirous of praying to become pregnant. So she went around from house to house | asking the women if they had experienced such distress. SHE WENT TO SEEK THE LORD'S GUIDANCE: She offered a sacrifice. Another interpretation is that she inquired at the academy of Shem and Eber what would become of her and prayed on behalf of her unborn child. The lesson for us is that paying one's respects to the aged is tantamount to greeting the Shekhinah. [xxv.23] THE LORD SAID TO HER: By prophetic mediation, since Shem, Eber and Abraham were still alive and were prophets. TWO NATIONS: [The Hebrew spelling of the latter word alludes to the fact that they would be] TWO LORDS, each | lording it in his own world, each dominating his own kingdom; one would be Hadrian ruling the Gentile world, the other Solomon, ruling Israel. Alternatively [a play may be made on the first Hebrew word of the expression] TWO NATIONS and would refer to the universal hatred which both Esau and Israel would attract. TWO PEOPLES: The word *lĕʾōm* means simply 'kingdom'; as Targum Onqelos translates it, 'one kingdom will be stronger than the other'. PARTING FROM YOUR WOMB: R. Berekiah said: [We learn] from here that Jacob was born circumcised. Alternatively, PARTING FROM YOUR WOMB: One on his way to wickedness, the other to rectitude and integrity. ONE PEOPLE WILL BE STRONGER THAN THE OTHER: One's elevation would mean the other's
V demotion. | THE OLDER WILL THE YOUNGER SERVE: R. Huna said: If Jacob merits it THE OLDER WILL SERVE THE YOUNGER; if not, THE OLDER WILL ENSLAVE THE YOUNGER. [xxv.24] THERE WERE INDEED TWINS IN HER WOMB: [The Hebrew word for TWINS is spelt] without an *ʾāleph* to indicate that while one was upright the other was wicked. In the case of Tamar, however [Gen. xxxviii.27], the word is spelt *plene*, to indicate that they were both upright. [xxv.25] THE FIRST ONE WHO CAME OUT WAS REDDISH: Esau was born first so that all the impurities could be discharged with him. | A parallel may be drawn with the cleansing of a bath-house. Only after the attendant has entered and completed this does he make the facility available to a royal prince. A Roman matron once asked R. Yose why Esau had been born first. He explained that Esau had been conceived from a second sperm and drew an analogy with a tube: 'If you were to place two pearls in a tube and then turn it upside-down, the pearl which you inserted last would come out first [, would it not?]; this is how it was with Jacob, first to be conceived but second to be born.' Another interpretation has it that Esau was born first because he has taken possession of | this, the former world, while Jacob was born after because he is to inherit the world hereafter. REDDISH:

The *yōd* is superfluous as it is in [the Hebrew word for] CRUEL. The use of the word REDDISH alludes to the blood that he was to spill. When Samuel saw that David was REDDISH [1 Sam. xvi.12] he was apprehensive that the lad would be like Esau and spill blood. God, however, assured him that HIS VIEWS AND PERCEPTION WERE FAULTLESS [1 Sam. xvi.12]. Esau had killed at his own whim while David would take life only with the authority of the court of the Sanhedrin. | AS A HAIRY MANTLE ALL OVER: Like a shaggy woollen cloak. THEY CALLED HIM ESAU: All those who saw him styled him 'Esau' because [the Hebrew name alludes to the fact that] the hair on his body was as fully developed as in one of mature years. An[other] midrash [by the use of *noṭariqon*]: [His name was] ESAU because it was of no value to the world that he was created. [xxv.26] AFTERWARDS HIS BROTHER EMERGED WITH HIS HAND GRASPING ESAU'S HEEL: This was an omen that Esau would not succeed in completing his period of rule before Jacob arose and took power from him. HE CALLED HIM JACOB: His father called him Jacob | because of the [Hebrew word for] heel [which has the same stem as the name]. ISAAC WAS SIXTY YEARS OLD: Abraham was [then] one hundred and sixty. He was privileged to see Jacob reach the age of fifteen and provided him with his intellectual and ethical training. [xxv.27] WHEN THE LADS GREW UP: As long as they were small they went to school together and nobody paid close enough attention to them to note their individual characteristics, but when they grew up one went off to the academy of Shem and Eber and the other turned to idolatry. This may be illustrated by the case of the briar and the myrtle. They are indistinguishable | while they grow together but once they go their own ways one produces a scent and the other a thorn. ESAU WAS AN ACCOMPLISHED TRAPPER: Full of guile, for one who hunts game has to be a master of cunning and deceit. According to another explanation, he trapped his father and deceived him. He asked him how one should tithe salt and straw, and his father was given the impression that he was strictly observant. A third interpretation is that he ensnared people with their own remarks [when cross-examining them]. Having [at one stage] elicited the response that they had not stolen or murdered he [later] asked them who had been with them [at the time of the offence]. AN OUTDOOR MAN: A man of leisure, he hunted animals and birds with his bow. Alternatively, [the word *śāde* means that] his behaviour was as little under control as a
VI field | without fencing. BUT JACOB by contrast WAS AN UNSPOILT CHARACTER: He was no expert in all these matters, the adjective *tām* being applied to anyone lacking the ability to beguile. REMAINING INDOORS: In the academy of Shem and Eber. He also found numerous ways of perfecting the inner man and conducted himself within the spirit, not just the letter, of the Law. [xxv.28] ISAAC LOVED ESAU FOR THE GAME IN HIS MOUTH: As Targum Onqelos translates it 'for he had meals from what he had hunted'. Another explanation is that the mouth

was Esau's | and that [Isaac admired the way in which] he trapped people with his mouth. WHILE REBEKAH GREW FONDER OF JACOB: She used to hear him at his Torah studies every day and she developed a special affection for him. This is what is meant by [the use of the participle in the phrase] WHILE REBEKAH GREW FONDER OF JACOB. Another reason for this was that God had said to her THE ELDER WILL SERVE THE YOUNGER. [xxv.29] JACOB PREPARED A BROTH: The word means a cooked dish, in this case made of lentils. AND ESAU CAME HOME FROM HUNTING: He asked what particular significance that dish had for that day and when Jacob told him that it was [a mourner's meal] to mark the death of their grandfather [Abraham], he exclaimed: 'God's judgement has struck | at that [pious] old man! In that case there is no justice and therefore no divine judge!' The divine response is recorded in the scriptural verse [Jer. xxii.10]: WEEP NOT FOR THE DEAD NOR MOURN FOR HIM. RATHER WEEP BITTERLY FOR THE ONE WHO HAS ABANDONED HIS PLACE. WEEP NOT FOR THE DEAD: This refers to Abraham. RATHER WEEP BITTERLY FOR THE ONE WHO HAS ABANDONED HIS PLACE: This refers to Esau who has abandoned his place in the Eternal World. AND HE WAS FAINT: The word means the same as tired. Alternatively, it means that he was thirsty as in the verse MY SOUL THIRSTS FOR YOU AS PARCHED GROUND [Psalm cxliii.6]. We are thus informed that he came in tired, hungry and thirsty. Our rabbis, of blessed memory, stated that on that day he committed five offences. He murdered, committed adultery, stole, practised idolatry and denied God. | They derived all of these from the verse by the method of analogy. [xxv.30] CRAM ME FULL: There are no other occurrences of the stem in the Hebrew Bible, but in the Mishnah there is the statement that ONE MAY OVERFEED A CAMEL [i.e.] by opening its mouth and pouring in food until one has filled its belly when one wishes to take it on a journey involving many days without food [Šabb. 24.3]. Esau thus meant: 'Fill me up with these red lentils the way one does when one crams food [into animals].' Why [is the mourner's meal] of lentils? The reason is that they are round like a wheel and bereavement revolves | like a wheel in the world. Another reason is that just as lentils have no mouth [i.e. cleft] so the mourner may not open his mouth [in greeting]. SOME OF THE RED, THIS RED STUFF: Why is 'red' mentioned twice? The repetition serves to point out [the centrality of that colour for Esau and his history]. Just as the dish of lentils is here called 'red' so Esau, his land and his warriors are all called 'red' [in the Hebrew Bible] and vengeance will one day be taken on him by one dressed in red [Isa. lxiii.1–2]. [xxv.31] HE SAID, SELL ME AS OF TODAY: That is to say, 'Just as today is clear so let your sale to me be completely clear and fully apparent.' Alternatively, 'Just as this day | will depart, never to return, so let your sale be unquestionably conclusive, eternally valid and incontrovertible.' The literal meaning is 'Sell me your birthright today so that I may acquire a double share of my father's possessions.' It was well known that the firstborn took a double share, as indicated in Jacob's statement to Reuben [Gen. xlix.4] YOU ARE UNSTABLE AS WATER AND WILL HAVE NO EXTRA INHERITANCE. Another reason why [Jacob desired] Esau's birthright was because the sacrificial service was then conducted by the firstborn and he thought that such an evildoer was unworthy of offering sacrifices to God. [xxv.32] ESAU SAID, I MAY DIE AT ANY MOMENT: Each day he put himself in danger . . . |

VII [xxxvii.13] but he did not suspect them. Jacob bore these things in mind, and his stomach turned as he thought to himself: 'He knows that his brothers hate him and still he says to me I AM READY.' [xxxvii.14] BRING ME BACK WORD: [We learn from here that one should inquire after the welfare of anything from which one derives benefit.] HE SENT HIM FROM THE DEPTH OF HEBRON: But is Hebron not situated on a hill as indicated in the verse THEY CAME UP BY THE SOUTHERN ROUTE | AND ARRIVED AT HEBRON [Num. xiii.22]? [The word DEPTH is here to be taken metaphorically and means] rather that Joseph went in order to bring about the *deeply* significant prediction that God had made in the context of his agreement with the righteous one buried *in Hebron*; as the verse says: HE SAID TO ABRAHAM, KNOW FOR SURE THAT YOUR DESCENDANTS WILL BE STRANGERS IN ANOTHER COUNTRY [Gen. xv.13]. AND HE ARRIVED AT SHECHEM. A place destined for calamity – it was there that the sons of Jacob went astray, there that Dinah was seduced and there that the Davidic Kingdom was divided, as reported in the passage beginning NOW REHOBOAM WENT TO SHECHEM [2 Chr. x.1]. [xxxvii.15] A MAN FOUND HIM: This was [the angel] Gabriel also [called MAN] in the phrase THE MAN GABRIEL [Dan. ix.21]. | R. Yannai was of the opinion that he encountered three angels as indicated by the [repetition of the word MAN in the] phrases A MAN FOUND HIM, THE MAN ASKED HIM, THE MAN TOLD HIM. [xxxvii.17] THE MAN SAID, THEY HAVE TRAVELLED ON FROM HERE: The literal sense is THEY HAVE TRAVELLED ON FROM THIS place. FOR I HEARD THEM SAY, LET US GO ON TO DOTHAN: The name of a place. A midrashic interpretation of THEY HAVE TRAVELLED ON FROM HERE is that [he told Joseph that] they had travelled far away from brotherly behaviour, and that while he was saying, I AM LOOKING FOR MY BROTHERS, they were looking for cunning devices to use against him and bring about his death. [xxxvii.18] THEY SAW HIM FROM A DISTANCE... AND CONSPIRED | AGAINST HIM: They schemed wickedly against him. Another interpretation is that they set the dogs on him. [xxxvii.19] ONE SAID TO HIS BROTHER: Simeon and Levi were those involved. THAT [DREAMER]: The word has the same sense as the regular demonstrative adjective and is similarly used in the phrase WHO IS THAT MAN? [Gen. xxiv.65]. [xxxvii.20] AND SAY THAT A WILD ANIMAL HAS DEVOURED HIM: The verb means 'and we shall say'.

WE SHALL SEE WHAT WILL BECOME OF HIS DREAMS: They saw that Jeroboam, who would encourage their descendants to embrace idolatry, would ultimately issue from Joseph's line. THEY SAW HIM FROM A DISTANCE therefore means that they saw things in the distant future | and this was the reason that they said: COME, LET US KILL HIM. [xxxvii.21] REUBEN HEARD THIS AND RESCUED HIM FROM THEIR CLUTCHES: Where then was he when they sold Joseph? That day it was his turn to attend upon his father. Since HE RESCUED HIM, Reuben's city of refuge was privileged to be the first of those listed: BEZER ON THE DESERT PLATEAU FOR THE REUBENITES [Deut. iv.43]. LET US NOT STRIKE AT HIS LIFE: Let us not make a fatal attack on him. [xxxvii.22] SO THAT HE COULD RESCUE HIM FROM THEIR CLUTCHES: The Torah stands testimony for Reuben that he said | this only in order to rescue him and restore him to his father. He said to himself: 'I am the firstborn and the leader of them all; the scandal will be associated only with my name.' If only he had known that Scripture would testify in this way on his behalf he would not have left him but would have carried him off on his shoulders to his father. [xxxvii.23] THEY STRIPPED HIM OF HIS ROBE: This refers to his tunic. THE STRIPED ROBE: This refers to the extra one which his father had given him.

'III [xxxvii.24] AND TOOK HIM: [Although read as a plural] the word is spelt without a *wāw* to indicate that it was | Simeon alone who did so. Where was he punished? In Egypt, as it is stated: HE TOOK SIMEON FROM THEM [Gen. xlii.24]. [INTO THE WELL.] THE WELL WAS EMPTY: [The double mention of the word indicates that] there were two wells, one full of pebbles and the other full of snakes and scorpions. According to another explanation THE WELL WAS EMPTY means that Jacob's well was found to be empty, that is to say, his sons who sprang from his loins were empty, devoid of Torah knowledge in this matter, | since they did not know the punishment laid down for such a crime, namely, IF ANYONE IS FOUND TO HAVE KIDNAPPED ONE OF HIS FELLOWS... THAT KIDNAPPER SHALL SUFFER THE DEATH PENALTY [Deut. xxiv.7]. This [lack of Torah knowledge] is alluded to in the phrase THERE WAS NO WATER IN IT [since Torah is midrashically equated with water]. [In spite of the gravity of the crime] these men sold their brother. [xxxvii.25] THEY SETTLED DOWN TO THE EATING OF SOME FOOD: According to one aggadic interpretation, to ensure that all the inhabitants of the world had food to eat. A CARAVAN OF ISHMAELITES: A convoy of Arabs. A caravan is given this [Hebrew] name because [it is composed] of wayfarers [the Hebrew for which is derived from the same stem]. THEIR CAMELS LADEN WITH SPICERY: Why does Scripture specify their cargo? | It is to demonstrate how the righteous receive special privileges. In the normal course of things Arabs carry only naphtha and tar but here God arranged spices so that the righteous Joseph would not suffer from a bad odour. SPICERY: A collec-

tion of spices. The word also occurs in the verse, AND HE SHOWED THEM HIS WHOLE PERFUMERY [2 Kgs xx.13], where it refers to the place where his spices were mixed. BALM: A resin that exudes from the wood of the balsam tree. It is the same as the *nāṭāp* mentioned elsewhere in the Pentateuch [Exod. xxx.34] AND LADANUM: It is known as *lōṭītā* in Mishnaic Hebrew [Šeb. 7.6] and is explained as a vegetable root. | Some say it is to be identified with gum mastic. [xxxvii.26] JUDAH SAID, WHAT VALUE: As Targum Onqelos translates it: What monetary gain shall we enjoy? Some [understand it as non-pecuniary benefit and] translate: What benefit? This is the same sense as in the phrase WHAT BENEFIT IS THERE IN MY DEATH? [Psalm xxx.10]. AND COVER UP HIS BLOOD: And hide his death. [xxxvii.27] LET US GO AND SELL HIM TO THE ISHMAELITES: What logic did Judah see in suggesting to them such a sale? He put the following argument to them: Canaan sinned and was punished with the curse of slavery. Joseph [has] also [behaved badly]; therefore, LET US GO AND SELL HIM TO THE ISHMAELITES. AND HIS BROTHERS LISTENED [TO HIM]: [As Targum Onqelos has it:] They obeyed him. | The same [use of the stem] occurs in the phrases JACOB OBEYED HIS FATHER [Gen. xxviii.7] and WE SHALL DO SO AND OBEY [Exod. xxiv.7]. It means the acceptance of some statement. [xxxvii.28] MIDIANITE MERCHANTS WERE PASSING BY: We are thus informed that there were various [groups of] merchants in the [same] caravan and that he was sold a number of times; [first] to the Ishmaelites, [then] by them to the Midianites and [finally] by them to the Egyptians. The literal sense is that the CONVOY OF ARABS was [in this case] composed of Midianites. FOR TWENTY SILVER PIECES: Is it plausible that a fine young man such as Joseph could be sold for twenty silver pieces? No, it is just that he was so afraid | of the snakes and scorpions in the well that his features changed and he looked anaemic. God said [in reaction to this sale]: 'Now that you have sold Rachel's firstborn for twenty silver pieces every Israelite will have to atone for this deed by making an annual contribution [to the Temple] of twenty *mĕʿāh* coins, that is half a shekel' (since twenty *gērāh* equal one shekel [and a *mĕʿāh* is here regarded as equal to half a *gērāh*]). He also said: 'Since you have sold Rachel's firstborn for five shekels, each one of your firstborn children
IX will have to be redeemed for five shekels.' [xxxvii.29] WHEN REUBEN RETURNED | TO THE WELL ETC.: He was not present during the sale because he was on duty that day and had gone to attend upon his father. Another reason [given for his absence] is that he had been occupied in wearing sackcloth and observing a fast as acts of penance for having sexually interfered with his father's concubine [Bilhah]. As soon as he was free he had come and taken a look into the well. [xxxvii.30] AS FOR ME, WHERE SHALL I GO: Where shall I flee from father's distress? What is more, I had thought that I should find a way of making amends for the Bilhah affair [and not more trouble]. | God responded to this:

'No man is yet on record as having sinned and repented. You are the first to do so. I swear that a descendant of yours will arise as a prophet and be the first to preach repentance.' Whom did he mean? He meant Hosea son of Be'eri, who would first say: REPENT, ISRAEL [Hos. xiv.2]. [xxxvii.31] THEY SLAUGHTERED A GOAT: Because its blood is similar to human blood. It is for this reason that the Torah prescribes A GOAT . . . FOR A SIN-OFFERING [Num. vii.16] TO ATONE FOR YOU [Num. xxviii.30]. [xxxvii.32] THEY SENT THE DICED ROBE: They threw dice | to ascertain who should bring the coat to their father, and Judah turned out to be the unlucky one. God said to Judah: 'You have said to your father PLEASE IDENTIFY THIS ROBE, IS IT YOUR SON'S ETC. I swear that Tamar will [also] say to you: PLEASE IDENTIFY THE SEAL, CORDS [AND STAFF], TO WHOM DO THEY BELONG? [Gen. xxxviii.25]. IS IT THE ROBE OF YOUR SON: This is phrased as a question [and the *hē'* is interrogative]. It is therefore [quite in order to explain the word ROBE as standing] in the construct case in relation to YOUR SON. [xxxvii.33] HE IDENTIFIED IT AND SAID ETC.: I do see but cannot understand what I see. IT IS MY SON'S ROBE. A WILD CREATURE HAS PREYED ON HIM. | A divine revelation came to him and showed him that Potiphar's wife, that is, A WILD CREATURE, would one day entice him. Why did God not reveal the whole truth to him? The reason was that the sons of Jacob had agreed to impose severe sanctions on anyone who revealed the secret [and he had been a party to the agreement]. His father, Isaac, actually knew that Joseph was still alive but did not wish to reveal this to Jacob, and God said: 'If he has not told him, I too shall not tell him.' According to another interpretation A WILD CREATURE HAS PREYED ON HIM contains an allusion to Judah and means that that creature which is | the most powerful of the beasts, the lion [i.e. the lion of Judah] has preyed on him. [xxxvii.34] JACOB RENT HIS CLOTHES: The children of Israel were the cause of such an act of mourning on their father's part and were suitably punished in Egypt; as the verse records: THEY RENT THEIR CLOTHES [Gen. xliv.13]. Joseph was the cause of that act of mourning on their part and was suitably punished when his descendant, Joshua, had to take the same action: JOSHUA RENT [HIS CLOTHES] [Josh. vii.6]. Benjamin was also one of the causes of that same act of mourning on the part of his brothers and his descendant was suitably punished in the capital Susa as indicated in the verse MORDECAI RENT HIS CLOTHES [Esther iv.1]. | Manasseh was another cause of that act of mourning [in accordance with the midrashic identification of the STEWARD in Gen. xliv.1, 4] and his inheritance was therefore split into two halves, one in Transjordan and the other in the land of Canaan. HE PUT SACKCLOTH AROUND HIMSELF: R. Aibo said: Since our forefather Jacob is [recorded as] the first to have used sackcloth as a mourning rite, it is a regular feature of Israelite custom for all time. Of Ahab the verse says: HE PUT SACK-

CLOTH ON HIMSELF [1 Kgs xxi.27]; of Joram it says: THE PEOPLE NOTICED THAT HE HAD PUT SACKCLOTH ON HIMSELF [2 Kgs vi.30]; of Mordecai HE PUT ON SACKCLOTH AND ASHES [Esther iv.1], and their actions were never without effect. | HE MOURNED FOR HIS SON FOR A LONG TIME: For twenty-two years, corresponding to the twenty-two years during which he did not perform the duty of honouring his parents (although he did have their permission to leave home). [xxxvii.35]
X ALL HIS SONS AND DAUGHTERS TRIED TO COMFORT HIM: But he had only one daughter, did he not, and he would rather | have buried her?! R. Judah explained [the discrepancy by suggesting] that twin daughters were born with each of Jacob's sons. According to R. Nehemiah the reference is to his daughters-in-law since a man has no inhibitions about calling his son-in-law his son and his daughter-in-law his daughter. HE REFUSED TO BE COMFORTED: He said: 'God's promise about the twelve tribes is now [apparently] no longer valid. Yet I did make every effort to maintain that number because of the parallels it has in the natural order of things, in the twelve signs of the zodiac, | twelve hours of the day, twelve hours of the night and twelve months of the year. The option of taking another wife is also not open to me because of the pact I made with Laban [when he made me promise] YOU WILL NOT TAKE ANY WIVES IN ADDITION TO MY DAUGHTERS' [Gen. xxxi.50]. Another explanation of why HE REFUSED TO BE COMFORTED is that people will not be consoled for [the disappearance of] the living. They do accept comfort for the dead because it is a fact of life that the dead will gradually be forgotten, but this certainly does not apply to the living. I WILL INDEED GO DOWN FOR MY SON: This means 'on account of my son'. Other examples [of the use of *'el* in the sense of *'al*] are in the verse | FOR SAUL AND FOR HIS BLOOD-STAINED DYNASTY [2 Sam. xxi.1]. In all these cases the word *'el* means 'on account of'. MOURNING TO THE GRAVE: This is the literal meaning while the midrashic explanation identifies *šĕ'ōl* as Gehinnom [i.e. Hell]. Jacob had received a special revelation from God that if none of his sons died during his lifetime this would be tantamount to a promise that he would never see Gehinnom. HIS FATHER WEPT FOR HIM: This refers to Isaac, who wept on account of Jacob's distress but did not join the mourning for him since he knew that he was alive. [xxxvii.36] THE MIDIANITES SOLD | HIM TO THE EGYPTIANS: | This proves that the Midianites are to be identified with the Ishmaelites [in this narrative] since [in a later verse] it says FROM THE ISHMAELITES WHO BROUGHT HIM DOWN THERE [Gen. xxxix.1]. KILLER-IN-CHIEF: [In charge] of the butchers of the royal livestock.

[xxxviii] NOW IT HAPPENED AT THIS TIME THAT JUDAH WENT DOWN: All that required to be reported here was that JOSEPH WAS BROUGHT TO EGYPT [xxxix.1]. Why then is the narrative interrupted and this chapter here inserted? It is to inform us that his brothers brought him down from his high

position. When they saw their father's distress | they said to him: 'You told us to sell him. If you had told us to take him home we should have listened to you.' R. Johanan said [that the reason was] to place two incidents involving [the phrase] PLEASE IDENTIFY [Gen. xxxvii.32 and xxxviii.25] next to each other. R. Eliezer said that it was in order to place the 'descent' [of Judah] next to the 'descent' [of Joseph]. JUDAH LEFT HIS BROTHERS AND WENT DOWN: The brothers discussed the matter and decided that they should now arrange their own lives. Until that time their father had been responsible for arranging marriages for them but his attention was now devoted to his sackcloth and his fasting. They therefore told Judah | that he should be the first to make arrangements for himself. At this JUDAH LEFT HIS BROTHERS AND WENT DOWN. According to the literal meaning of the text, however, this whole episode took place before the sale of Joseph, there being no chronological order in Torah narratives. The story here is that Judah was married and his wife gave birth to Er and Onan. Er grew up, married and died and when Onan had grown up he made a levirate marriage with his brother's widow and he too died. Shelah [their brother] grew up, Judah had relations with Tamar and Tamar gave birth to Perez and Zerah. They grew up and were married and Perez had two sons, Hezron and Hamul. [Is it possible that] all this took place in twenty-two years? From the sale . . .

בְּצֵאת יִשְׂרָאֵל מִמִּצְרָיִם בֵּית יַעֲקֹב מֵעַם לֹעֵז (Psalm cxiv.1)

AVIHAI SHIVTIEL

לד"ר יצחק רוזנטל
בין שיבה לגבורה – ברכה

All the commentaries and translations dealing with this verse that I have checked apparently see little difficulty in explaining or interpreting the combination *mēʿam lōʿēz*.[1] This conviction about the 'simplicity' of meaning of the whole verse is rooted in the impression that it conveys an idea that is, *prima facie*, semantically, syntactically and stylistically uniform and consistent. Semantically, all the components of the verse carry their literal meanings and the sense of the whole verse may consequently be deduced as the simple sum of these components. Syntactically, the verse is to be analysed as an elliptical adverbial clause denoting 'time' in the compound sentence that includes verses 1–2. Stylistically, it is an example of what is well known in poetics as 'synonymous parallelism', the only device that is in fact used in the whole Psalm. Nevertheless, there is no doubt that the combination *mʿm lʿz*, and especially the *hapax legomenon lʿz*, is not all that clear. A distinct lack of lucidity becomes apparent from a close examination of commentaries and translations 'old and new'.

Although it is unanimously agreed that the combination *mʿm lʿz* refers to the Egyptians there are two main trends in interpreting its sense:

(1) a people talking an unintelligible language
(2) a cruel people.

(1A) Dictionaries; e.g.,

(*a*) BDB – ' talk indistinctly, unintelligibly (NH *id.*, in deriv. (לַעַז *foreign language*, לָעוֹז *foreigner*), also *murmur*, *remonstrate;* Syr. ܠܥܙ

1 In fact there are commentaries that have nothing to say about this verse: e.g. David Altschuler (*mṣwdt dwd*), and later commentaries such as S.Z. Pines, *Commentary on the Psalms* (Vienna, 1936).

talk indistinctly; Ar. لغن *distort;* iv. *talk obscurely, ambiguously*); – only Qal *Pt.* ... *a people talking unintelligibly* (‖ מִצְרַיִם)'.

(*b*) L. Koehler–W. Baumgartner, *Lexicon* (Leiden, 1953) – '*speak a foreign language* (*Greek*), *speak ill of* ... לֹעֵז > נוֹעָז ? Js. 33, 19) ... *speaking unintelligibly*'.

(*c*) G. Fohrer, *Hebrew and Aramaic Dictionary of the OT* (Eng. edn, London, 1973) – 'speak incomprehensibly' (*lʿz* is an Aramaism) = *Hebräisches und aramäisches Wörterbuch zum Alten Testament* (Berlin–New York, 1971) – 'unverständlich reden'.[2]

(*d*) J. Herrmann, *Hebräisches Wörterbuch zu den Psalmen* (Giessen, 1924) – *lʿz* – 'barbärisch, unverständl. reden'.

(1B) Translations; e.g.,

(*a*) LXX – βαρβάρου.[3]

(*b*) Hexapla – 'Ex populo barbare loquenti'.

(*c*) Peshitta – '*m' lʿwz*'.

(*d*) Targum – *mēʿammē barbĕrāʾē.*

(*e*) Saadya – אלשעב אללגט (a people articulating sounds that are not clear to the hearer);[4]

Modern translations also follow this tendency as they continue to regard *ʿm lʿz* as 'a people of a strange tongue'. To mention but a few:

(*a*) H. Hupfeld – 'aus einem unverständlich redenden (fremden) Volk'.[5]

(*b*) E.A. Leslie – 'the barbarous-tongued Egyptians'.[6]

(*c*) The New English Bible – 'a people of outlandish speech'.[7]

(1C) Commentaries; e.g.,

(*a*) Rashi – 'a people (speaking) a different language which is not the holy tongue'.[8]

(*b*) Ibn Ezra – '*lʿz* has the same sense as it does in the talmudic expressions *lʿz ʿl bnyh* or *llwʿzwt* [M. Meg. 2.1, BT Qidd. 81*a*, BT Ned. 90*b*].'

(*c*) Qimḥi – 'speaking a different language which is not the

2 See also B.D. Eerdmans, *The Hebrew Book of Psalms* (Leiden, 1947), p. 515.

3 The same word is used by the LXX for *bʿrym* in *ʾnšym bʿrym* in Ezek. xxi.36.

4 Ed. J. Kafiḥ, *Tehillīm ʿim Targūm Ūpērūš* (Jerusalem, 1966), p. 245.

5 *Die Psalmen*, vol. II (Gotha, 1888), p. 507.

6 *The Psalms* (New York–Nashville, 1949), p. 171.

7 *The New English Bible* (Oxford–Cambridge, 1970), p. 714.

8 However, like Saadya, Rashi also connects *ʿm lʿz* with Isa. xxxiii.19 and suggests that *ʿm nwʿz* is in fact *ʿm lʿz* as *l* and *n* are interchangeable as in *lškh* and *nškh* in Neh. xiii.5, 7.

בְּצֵאת יִשְׂרָאֵל מִמִּצְרָיִם בֵּית יַעֲקֹב מֵעַם לֹעֵז *(Psalm* cxiv. *1)* 229

Hebrew language, i.e. they left a people whose language was unintelligible to them, as is said in Deut. xxviii.49 *gwy 'šr (ʿz) l"tšmʿ lšnw'*.

Qimḥi does go on to say that those who were more directly in contact with the Egyptians must have spoken Egyptian even if only with difficulty, while the remainder were sufficiently isolated in Goshen to allow them to retain their native tongue.[9]

(*d*) David Altschuler (*mṣwdt ṣywn*) – 'every national language with the exception of Hebrew is called *lwʿz* and the expression occurs in the phrase *qwryn 'wtm llwʿzwt blʿz* (M. Meg. 2.1)'.

(*e*) Hameiri – 'people speaking a different language which is not Hebrew'.[10]

This tendency continues in modern commentaries as well. To mention but a few:

(*f*) H. Graetz – 'einem frechen Volke'.[11]

(*g*) H. Gunkel – 'stammelnden Volk'; 'unverständlich, barbarisch reden'.[12]

(*h*) C.A. Briggs – 'speaking a language that Israel did not understand'; he refers to Gen. xlii.23; Isa. xxviii.11.[13]

(*i*) E.J. Kissane – 'An alien people', 'a people speaking a strange language'; he refers to Gen. xlii.23.[14]

(*j*) M.Z. Segal – *hmdbr bśph zrh*; cp. Isa. xxxiii.19.[15]

(*k*) W.O.E. Oesterley – '*a people of strange tongue* ... as it would seem to the Israelites who did not understand the Egyptian language'.[16]

(*l*) *The Interpreter's Bible* – 'of strange language', referring to Isa. xxviii.11; xxxiii.19. 'The Egyptian language was unintelligible to the Hebrews', referring to Gen. xlii.23.[17]

(*m*) N.H. Tur-Sinai – 'an epithet for Egypt ... it is quite possible, however, that *ʿm lʿz* was an ancient epithet for Egypt, which only in

9 Ed. A. Darom, *Hapērūš Hašālēm ʿal Tehillīm* (Jerusalem, 1971), p. 257.
10 M. Hameiri (ed. Josephus Cohn), *Libri Psalmorum* (Jerusalem, 1936), p. 228 (based on Codex Vaticanus Ebraicus no. 527).
11 *Kritischer Commentar zu den Psalmen* (Breslau, 1883), p. 598.
12 *Die Psalmen* (Göttingen, 1926), pp. 493, 495.
13 *A Critical and Exegetical Commentary on the Book of Psalms*, vol. ii (Edinburgh, 1907), pp. 390ff.
14 *The Book of Psalms* (Dublin, (1953) 1964), p. 524.
15 In his annotated edition of the Hebrew Bible, *Tehillīm* (Tel-Aviv, 1947; 1960), p. 129.
16 *The Psalms* (London, 1939), pp. 470ff.
17 W.S. McCullough in *The Interpreter's Bible*, vol. iv (New York–Nashville, 1955), p. 603.

later usage was understood to apply to a people speaking an unintelligible foreign language.'[18]

(2A) Commentaries

(*a*) A. Weiser – 'To the psalmist the Exodus from Egypt is essentially the saving act of the God who helped his people and had compassion on their affliction. This is made clear in v.1 where the poet speaks of the Egyptians as of "barbarians". The reason why he regards deliverance from their rule as a specific act of grace is that the burden of foreign rule was felt so much the more strongly as the oppressor spoke a language that was unintelligible to the Israelites.'[19]

(*b*) S.R. Hirsch – 'In Rabbinic Hebrew *l'z* refers to any non-Hebrew language. It is also the equivalent of *l'g* [= mock]. The meaning is, therefore, a people speaking a different language, or the people who mock the Jewish custom and way of life. Either way, it signifies the contrast between the Egyptians and the family of Jacob in spirit and culture.'[20]

(*c*) M. Dahood – 'a barbaric people'. Dahood quotes the traditional explanation of *l'z*, which is based on the Mishnaic Hebrew meaning, but suggests that it is more likely that the poet wanted to emphasize at this point the cruelty of the Egyptians (and not their strange language); the *l* of *l'z* should therefore be regarded as emphatic *l*, and hence the verse should read *'m* (*l*)*'z* meaning strong, cruel, barbaric people, as in Isa. xxv.3 (= *'m'z*) and Lam. iv.3 (= *bt 'my l'kzr*).[21]

It seems from the references quoted that the dictionaries, the translations and the commentaries were all influenced, when handling the root *l'z*, by a comparison with the equivalent roots in other Semitic languages, and in particular by the use of the root *l'z* in Mishnaic Hebrew.[22] Nevertheless, a few of these references show awareness of the deficiencies of the solutions suggested.[23]

18 *Encyclopaedia Biblica*, vol. IV (Jerusalem, 1962), p. 525 (in Hebrew).

19 *The Psalms* (London, 1962), p. 710 = *Die Psalmen*, 5th edn (Gottingen, 1959), *ad loc.*

20 *Die Psalmen* (Frankfurt-am-Main, 1882), vol. II, p. 218 = Hebrew edn (Jerusalem, 1961–2), p. 446.

21 *Psalms*, vol. III (Garden City, N.Y., 1970), p. 134.

22 As Dahood points out, the occurrence of *l'z* in Mishnaic Hebrew 'is sometimes cited as the only linguistic evidence for late composition of the poem' (p. 134).

23 One should not overlook the caution of Saadya and, later, Rashi as attested by their admission of the possibility of an alternative interpretation. See also Dahood's interpretation above.

As to the first interpretation of the compound *'m l'z* i.e. 'a people speaking an unintelligible language', which is, as we have seen, the explanation suggested in the majority of the references cited, it is most unlikely that the Israelites did not understand the Egyptian language.[24] The quotation of Gen. xlii.23 in order to prove that the Israelites did not understand the Egyptian language[25] is misleading since it refers to a period when the Israelites were still in Canaan, so that it was only natural that when Joseph's brothers came to Egypt they needed an interpreter. Also Deut. xxviii.49 is unlikely to refer to Egypt, since the verse speaks of a people from 'far away' and geographically cannot apply to the Egyptians, who had a common border with Israel. Isa. xxviii.11 and xxxiii.19 must also be rejected as incisive proof of the idea allegedly expressed in our verse, since no clear reference to Egypt is made in the two verses quoted.

It is, of course, true that the Greeks as well as the Romans used to call every foreign nation that spoke a different language 'barbarian' (etymologically the term means 'stammerer');[26] still, it is unlikely that, after 400 years in Egypt, the Egyptian language was incomprehensible to the Israelites. For, even if we accept the fact that the Israelites lived separately from the Egyptians, i.e. in the land of Goshen, they could not possibly be separated from rulers who used them as slaves. Are we to assume then that the Egyptians used interpreters all the time that the Hebrews lived in Egypt? Or is there any historical evidence that the Egyptians learnt Hebrew in order to be able to communicate with the Israelites ... ?

Hence, all attempts to prove a degree of Israelite isolation from the Egyptians that would explain the unintelligibility of the Egyptian language[27] are mere speculation. It is quite possible that not all the Israelites were able to read or write the Egyptian language, but there is no doubt that Egyptian was not orally unintelligible to them.

Concerning the second explanation of *'m l'z*, viz. 'a cruel people', it is not surprising that those who favour it exaggerate the severity and cruelty of the Egyptians, citing in evidence the atrocities against

24 Cp. Qimḥi (see above, pp. 228–9).

25 See e.g. Briggs; Kissane; *The Interpreter's Bible;* Oesterley and others (see p. 229).

26 The Arabs likewise used the word *'ajam* (originally meaning 'speaking unintelligibly') for any people foreign to Arabs (see E.W. Lane's dictionary).

27 Cp. e.g. M. Alsheikh's commentary on Psalms, *Sēper Rōmēmōt 'El* (Jesnitz, 1721), p. 105; M.L. Malbim, *Sēper Miqrā'ē Qōdeš*, part 9 (Jerusalem, 1957), p. 437; cp. also the latter part of Qimḥi's comment, already cited above.

the Israelites of which the Hebrew Bible makes them guilty. For such an exaggeration of the strength of the Egyptians makes the superiority of God, who nevertheless defeated them, more evident and impressive.

Nevertheless, if we are to accept this interpretation we still have another problem to overcome: is the *l* in *lʿz* in fact an emphatic *l* (see Dahood, above p. 230), or should it be regarded as the equivalent of *n* (as suggested by Saadya and later by Rashi – see above p. 228)?

Although the second interpretation of *ʿm lʿz* (= *ʿm nwʿz* = 'a cruel people') is not inconceivable, it misses the real point made by the Psalmist, which is surely to describe the position of the Israelites at the time when they left Egypt. For if verse 2 is taken to mean his choice of Judah as 'God's sanctuary and Israel as his dominion', we still need an expression that will explicitly characterize the extreme change that came over the status of the Israelites, viz. their transformation from a humiliated people into a nation proudly accepting God's dominion. *ʿm nwʿz*, therefore, cannot possibly refer to the Israelites. On the other hand, it is unlikely that the poet wishes at this stage to describe the Egyptians as a strong people. Rather, he is anxious to express what Egypt truly means to the Israelites, that is to say, hard work and toil.[28]

It is suggested, therefore, that the phrase *mʿm lʿz* should be emended to *mʿml ʿz* and pointed *mēʿāmāl ʿāz* (= 'from hard toil'), and hence the whole verse should read:

בְּצֵאת יִשְׂרָאֵל מִמִּצְרָיִם בֵּית יַעֲקֹב מֵעָמָל עָז

when Israel went out of Egypt, the House of Jacob from hard toil.

At first sight this reading might seem to be open to the objection that it fails to take due account of the clear distinction between a medial and a final *mem*. When, however, we recall that the distinction was not made until a relatively late stage in the transmission of the text, and that the adoption of such an emendation is sometimes the only way to make sense of a biblical verse,[29] the objection loses its force.

28 Cp. 'I am the LORD thy God, who brought thee out of the land of Egypt, out of the house of slaves (*mibbēt ʿăbādīm*)' (Exod. xx.2).

29 Cp. e.g. Psalm lxxvi.7: מִגַּעֲרָתְךָ אֱלֹהֵי יַעֲקֹב נִרְדָּם וְרֶכֶב וָסוּס, where נרדמו רכב וסוס is the obvious emendation, as suggested by the majority of the commentaries and the translations.

Moreover, the adjective *ʿz* is used in the Bible with both abstract and concrete nouns. Thus, we find *ʾp ʿz*, Gen. xlix.7; *ʿm ʿz*, Num. xiii.28; *gbwl ʿz*, Num. xxi.24; *ʾwyb ʿz*, 2 Sam. xxii.18; *mlk ʿz*, Isa. xix.4; *ʾhbh ʿzh* (*mwt ʿz*?), Song of Songs viii.6; *ḥmh ʿzh*, Prov. xxi.14; *rwḥ ʿzh*, Exod. xiv.21.

Finally, the acceptance of the proposed emendation also provides an example of alliteration (עָמֵל עָז), a poetic device that is found frequently in Hebrew poetry.

Aphrahat and the Jews

J. G. SNAITH

At first sight it is surprising to find Aphrahat arguing against the Jews. One would expect a Christian apologist writing under Persian rule to defend Christianity against the Zoroastrian state religion rather than Judaism, particularly as Shapur II's vicious persecution of the Christians began in A.D. 339, five years before the writing of Aphrahat's second group of homilies (XI–XXII). Yet, whereas the first group (I–X), written in A.D. 336–7, deals with various elements of Christian faith and practice, such as prayer, fasting, humility and resurrection, the second group, written in A.D. 344, concentrates on topics relevant to Judaism, such as circumcision, Passover, Sabbath, messiahship, food laws and even Zionism. When persecution started, Aphrahat turned his attention more specifically towards the Jews and he hardly mentions the persecuting Zoroastrians at all.

For close knowledge of this persecution we must go to the 'Acts of the Persian Martyrs'. It had arisen largely because the Christian conversion of surrounding nations had made Shapur II, the Persian king, feel hemmed in. Armenia had become Christian in A.D. 301, followed by Georgia in 330, and in 311 Constantine had become the first Christian emperor of Rome. This growing Christianization of the Roman Empire coincided with growing rivalry between Persia and Rome over rulership of Mesopotamia. Many must have been frequently irritated by the way in which the boundary of Roman and Persian empires vacillated at this period, and the Syrian Christians had settled right in the disputed area, in a most vulnerable position. That is why Constantine sent his famous but unwise letter commending the care and protection of Persian Christians to Shapur who, with some perspicacity one feels, identified Persian Christians as in league with his enemy and acted accordingly to stamp the religion out. Thus when in A.D. 337 he was defeated by the Romans before Nisibis he imposed a double poll-tax on Christians to finance his war against Rome.

The Catholicos of Seleucia-Ctesiphon, Simon bar Sabbā'ē, refused to collect this increased tax and, although he professed loyalty to the Persian emperor, was martyred in A.D. 341 or 344 (date uncertain). Whether Simon's refusal to collect this war-tax was motivated politically or religiously remains uncertain, but one feature of this martyrdom makes it particularly significant. J. Neusner,[1] in his examination of the Syriac martyrologies, finds no references to Jewish participation in Shapur's persecution of the Christians other than in the deaths of Simon and his sister Tarbo.[2] The accounts of their martyrdoms report that the Jews instigated action and, on these occasions at any rate, took advantage of the new policy to harass Christians. The martyrdoms of Shapur's reign are numerous, but only here do we find Jewish instigation.

It is plain that the Jews were favoured under the Sassanid regime. There were concentrations of Jews in the southern Mesopotamian valley near Nehardea and Sura until the Muslim conquest.[3] The position of Jews had early been improved by Mar Samuel. After A.D. 251 Shapur I had invaded Syria and Asia; Valerian was captured by the Persians, the Orient was lost to Rome and Shapur advanced as far as Caesarea. Several circumstances made Persia a favourable place for Jews to settle. In Palestine the Jews were badly handled under Constantine (even worse under Constantius), and many fled to Persia where Jews were in favour under Shapur II. Jewish talmudic sources (BT Ta'an. 24*b*, Nid. 20*b*) praise Shapur's mother, Ifra Hormizd,[4] as a benefactress of the Jews, but there is no hint in Aphrahat's writings that she incited the Persians to persecute Christians. The Jews in Persia had always to be careful: the Roman Emperor Julian's plans to rebuild the Temple in Jerusalem find no echo in Jewish sources. This indicates, perhaps, that the Jews stood with the Persians and put little trust in Julian's schemes. P.A. Spijkermann thought they hoped for permission to return and rebuild

1 'Babylonian Jewry and Shapur II's Persecution of Christianity from 339–379 A.D.', *HUCA* 43 (1972), 77–99. A general coverage of Judaism in Babylonia may be found in the five volumes of his *History of the Jews in Babylonia* (Leiden, 1965–70) and *Talmudic Judaism in Sasanian Babylonia* (Leiden, 1976).

2 Neusner, *HUCA* 43 (1972), 91–3.

3 A. Lukyn Williams, *Adversus Judaeos* (Cambridge, 1935), pp. 93ff. Among discussions of Christian patristic writers of various countries, he reviews the literature of the Syriac-speaking Church on pp. 93–113, with pp. 95–102 devoted specifically to Aphrahat.

4 J. Neusner, *HUCA* 43 (1972), 93–5.

the Temple under Persian protection.[5] Hopes for return to Jerusalem certainly flourished at this time; Aphrahat devoted a whole homily to this theme, as we shall see below.

Whether or not they supported Persian policy against the Christians, it is clearly the Jews who were favoured and not the Christians. The Christian See of Seleucia-Ctesiphon was surrounded by Jewish settlements under rabbinic leadership, and Jews may well have remained in that area since the Babylonian Exile. Accounts of the origins of the Christian church in this area imply the Jews were not unfriendly: in the *Doctrine of Addai*, Addai, the Christian missionary who reputedly brought Christianity to Edessa, stays in the house of Tobias, a Jew. The religions were closer to each other than either was to Zoroastrianism so that transference from one to the other was probably a considerable possibility. Christianity was under persecution because of political hostility between Persia and Constantinian, Christian Rome, and if Jews were favoured by the Queen Mother, Ifra Hormizd, would not Christians feel temptation or even pressure to convert to Judaism as a 'haven of safety'?[6]

Amid such threats to Christians, Aphrahat seems to have lain low so successfully that, although his writings are well known, his personality is shrouded in mystery. The later Syrian Ephrem enjoyed considerable fame, gathered apocryphal writings as candles attract moths and was reputed to have visited other Church Fathers. Not so Aphrahat. It is uncertain how important a figure he was; some suggest he must have been a bishop of some ecclesiastical standing because of his knowledge of Church affairs. Although he takes great care to date his work exactly, his reputation seems to have been confused with that of Jacob of Nisibis. Certainly, he seems to have emerged from near Mosul in the upper Tigris valley under Persian sovereignty. But, whereas Ephrem was a well-known figure, Aphrahat seems to have remained in obscurity – probably with good reason, considering the persecution going on round him. Indeed, it is surprising that he was permitted to write his homilies without hindrance. But then, of course, they did not attack Persia directly but only debated with the Jews, which was surely not treasonable.

To anyone familiar with Christian patristic literature Aphrahat

5 'Afrahat der persische Weise und der Antisionismus', *Studii Biblici Franciscani, Liber annuus* 5 (1954–5), 198–200.

6 J. Ouellette, 'Aphraate, Qumrân et les Qaraïtes', appendix to J. Neusner, *A History of the Mishnaic Law of Purities*, vol. XV, 'Niddah. Commentary' (Leiden, 1976), pp. 166ff.

seems remote from the wider Christian world. Homily XIX concerning the reconstruction of Jerusalem in the future was written in A.D. 344, seven years after the dedication of the Church of the Holy Sepulchre in Jerusalem, yet he shows no knowledge of it. The Council of Nicaea was in A.D. 325 but, as A. Grillmeier has noted,[7] Aphrahat seems to know nothing of it. M. Simon claims that the canons of Nicaea were not introduced into Persia until A.D. 410,[8] and Grillmeier has not identified any Nicene phrases or statements in his writings (p. 215). Indeed, his rather curious arguments in XVII (785.13–796.7)[9] about the use of the words *'ēl* and *'ĕlōhīm* concerning Moses and others to denote 'the highest honour in the world' are held to reflect pre-Nicene christology. Grillmeier (pp. 214–5) further describes Aphrahat as belonging to an Eastern (Semitic) circle of tradition that enjoyed 'relative autonomy' in comparison with the Greek West and 'virtually no contact at all with the still more distant Latin West'.

This impression of isolation is greatly increased when we look at his style. His Syriac is purely Semitic with none of the Greek and Latin technical terms that creep into Ephrem's work. As F. Gavin pointed out,[10] Aphrahat presents no *a priori* philosophy, seems isolated from the language of christological controversy and speaks in a way closely related to the Jews with no accommodation to any alien medium or Greek philosophical language. Instead of the speculation and classical terms of Christian theology, his writings are soaked in biblical language and quotations. After finding Aphrahat bereft of the expected traditional language of the Christian Fathers it comes as a shock to read that to Robert Murray Aphrahat 'appears almost totally traditional in all that he says'.[11] Perhaps he means 'traditional' here to be understood from the Jewish–Christian standpoint. He certainly uses scriptural quotations a great deal, and the much-quoted phrase 'student of holy scripture' seems more justified than that other phrase, quoted even more frequently, a 'docile pupil of the Jews'. *Specific* references to Jewish rabbinical writings are difficult, if not impossible, to find,[12] but the scriptural

7 *Christ in Christian Tradition*, 2nd edn, vol. I (London–Oxford, 1975), p. 167.
8 *Verus Israel* (Paris, 1964), p. 163.
9 References to Aphrahat's work are to the columns and lines of J. Parisot's edition in *Patrologia Syriaca*, vol. I (Paris, 1894).
10 *Aphraates and the Jews* (Toronto, 1923), pp. 1–3.
11 'Some Rhetorical Patterns in Early Syriac Literature', R.H. Fischer (ed.), *A Tribute to Arthur Vööbus* (Chicago, 1977), p. 110.
12 J. Neusner, *Aphrahat and Judaism* (Leiden, 1971), has an exhaustive analysis.

citations have been counted (1056 from the Old Testament, 564 from the New Testament). The detection of exact citations from the New Testament is difficult because of the uncertainty over which text he is using at any one time. Our ignorance of the exact Syriac wording of Tatian's *Diatessaron* is a considerable handicap, and we are grateful to T. Baarda for his considerable work in examining the problem of quotations from the gospels in Aphrahat's work.[13] This clear preponderance of quotations from the Old Testament over those from the New Testament illustrates his anxiety to debate with the Jews on ground accepted by both parties.

The earlier group of homilies (I–X) are not directed specifically against Jewish practices. In I, II, III and IV, when he is discussing respectively faith, love, fasting and prayer, there is not much material relevant to his views on Judaism, although in I, after summing up the Christian faith in 43.12–20, he concludes the list of good things by saying: 'That is the faith of the Church of God.' He then adds a list of undesirable things from which Christians should separate themselves: 'from observing hours, Sabbaths, new moons, annual feasts, divinations, auguries from birds, Chaldaean astrology and magic and from fornication, from songs and from wicked teaching, all of which are the tools of the Evil One' (44.21–5). To cite normal Jewish observances undistinguished from fornication and astrology, put them on the same level and then sum them all up as 'the tools of the Evil One' seems nothing less than a studied insult to Judaism. Perhaps he deliberately placed this at the end of his introductory homily to prepare the way for the second group, which is more obviously directed against Jewish teaching and practice.

In IV when Aphrahat discusses the second coming of Christ (149.12–16), Christ appears with two distinct companies, Jews and Christians. He claims that this is prefigured in Jacob's return across the Jordan 'with two companies' in Gen. xxxii.10. In these 'two companies' he sees the twofold Church of the Syriac writers, consisting of the *'ammā* ('the people' = the Jews) and the *'ammē* ('the peoples' = the Christians). Thus he finds the twofold Christian Church referred to in the Old Testament.

He seems almost to descend to cheap jibing in v.224.24ff: when discussing the saints of the Most High about to receive the Kingdom of God (Dan. vii.27), he denies that the children of Israel come on the clouds, countering this with a quotation from Jeremiah (vi.30)

13 *The Gospel Quotations of Aphrahat the Persian Sage*, vol. I, 'Aphrahat's Text of the Fourth Gospel, text and appendix' (Amsterdam, 1975).

that says that the Jews were only reprobate silver because the LORD rejected them. He then launches into a passage concerning the vineyard of the LORD and the rejection of the owner of the vineyard, and by v.232.3ff the *'ammā* (Jews) has been replaced by another holy *'ammā* on the basis of Deut. xxxii.21: 'I will rouse their jealousy through a people who are not a people' (*b'am dlā 'am*) – an important passage for his terminology and thought. Murray notes this passage as typical of a Christian midrashic style persisting in isolation from its Jewish cradle[14] – an instance of Aphrahat staying close to the Jews and remaining far from Greek and Latin patristic writers in style as well as in vocabulary and thought-forms.

Earlier in v he began to discuss the ram of Dan. viii.3f (192.24–193.25). Perhaps Aphrahat was wise to keep his distance from the Persian authorities, because in that passage he makes an identification: the arrogant ram of Daniel is identified as the king of Persia, Darius. Darius was not Shapur II, of course, but the implication is obvious. Later (197.21f) he interprets the 'stones of fire' in Ezek. xxviii.14–16 as the sons of Zion, agreeing with Targum Jonathan, which paraphrases the Hebrew as *'ammā qaddīšā*, 'holy people', whereas Theodoret felt strongly against this interpretation, claiming that only angels were intended (Murray, *Symbols*, p. 287). In 208.25–209.24 the children of Esau are referred to as not having a king but a 'senate' (*sic* Gwynn).[15] This clearly denotes the Roman Empire, and the stone cut out in Dan. ii.34 breaks the image in pieces and is claimed to represent the kingdom of the Messiah 'who will bring to nought the kingdom of this world, and will rule for ever and ever' (212.22f). In 232.3f there is a special reference to the Church as in the place of Israel. The gift of sovereignty is traced from Jacob to Esau and remains in Esau's hands until returned to the giver (233.2–15). By the subjugation of Israel to the Gentiles, Christians are shown to be the 'holy people', emancipated from the pressures of this world.[16]

Several features in VI merit attention. In 256.22–4, after speaking of Satan's habitual methods of attack on the faithful, he points out the dangers that may ensue if Christians are enflamed with the

14 *Symbols of Church and Kingdom* (Cambridge, 1975) (hereafter referred to as *Symbols*), p. 98n.

15 J. Gwynn translated into English selected 'Demonstrations of Aphrahat' in the *Select Library of Nicene and Post-Nicene Fathers of the Christian Church*, 2nd Series 13 (Oxford and New York, 1898), pp. 345–412, with a useful introduction in pp. 152–62.

16 Neusner, *Aphrahat and Judaism*, p. 15.

desire of Eve through the instigation of Satan. This proves to be an excuse for a long series of testimonies (see below) on the evils of women, in the course of which we have a very strange passage concerning Exod. iv.24–6, where A. Guillaumont[17] notes some midrashic tradition shared by Ephrem (Commentary *In Exodum* IV, 4). Aphrahat calls Zipporah *mālkat sanyātā* ('a counsellor to shameful acts'). The situation in Exodus is that the LORD met Moses and tried to kill him. No reason for this attack is given in the LXX or Targum Onqelos, but the Targums representing the Palestinian tradition (Pseudo-Jonathan and Neophyti) give a reason: Zipporah explains to the angel that the child had not been circumcised because Jethro would not allow it, in spite of Moses' wish to do so. So Zipporah saved Moses' life by repairing the fault he had committed. Interestingly, in Ephrem's commentary on Exodus, it is not Jethro who opposed circumcision but Zipporah herself, a tradition that fits in with the (rather unfortunate) attitude among the Syriac-speaking Christians to women. Ephrem and Aphrahat here both build on a Palestinian targumic tradition.

In VI we meet with a curious passage concerning the state of the dead (293.2–24). Distinction is made between the *rūḥā napšānāytā*, the 'soulish spirit' (= ψυχή), the spirit of natural life, and the holy spirit in man (= πνεῦμα).[18] The first spirit is received by man from his first birth: 'the first man, Adam, became an animate being' (1 Cor. xv.45); but at the second birth, baptism, he receives the holy spirit. There is a similar division at death: when man dies, the soulish spirit is buried with the body and knows no sensation, whereas the holy spirit flies off to its own nature in Christ (1 Cor. xv.44). The matter is complicated in that Aphrahat does not find in 1 Cor. xv.44 (the body is 'sown as an animal body' (NEB)) the word 'sown', which is in the Greek and the Peshitta, but writes 'the body is buried soulishly [*napšānā'īt*]'. This trichotomy of body, soul and spirit is carried further in VIII (on the 'resurrection of the dead') where he gives a reasonably clear description of this 'sleep of the soul', and in 397.15 claims it as an article of faith. He contrasts the relaxed, unworried sleep and the unquiet, disturbed sleep of two servants, one expecting praise, the other punishment from his master in the morning (396.16–317.14). Gavin shows this belief to

17 'Un Midrashe d'Exode 4. 24–6 chez Aphraate et Ephrem de Nisibe', in Fischer (see n. 11), pp. 89–94.

18 F. Gavin, 'The Sleep of the Soul in the Early Syriac Church', *JAOS* 40 (1920), 103–20.

have been shared by Ephrem. It must have had a longer history than one might expect, as the doctrine was attacked by Origen in the third century and was still held by the later Nestorians. Gavin examines Jewish writings in the last centuries B.C., where the departed are spoken of as asleep, and claims that an early distinction between soul and spirit passed completely into later Judaism. The shadowy existence of the soul in the grave or Sheol was kept separate from the spirit, which returned to God after death. It is interesting to find this lack of precise definition over the death of an individual as early as this, since the definition of the exact moment of death has always been a problem. Gavin's argument that this doctrine came to Aphrahat from Jewish sources is supported by various quotations. Although the later Nestorians seem to have been influenced by Aristotelian sources (which they misunderstood), Aphrahat's position over the sleep of the soul seems to have arisen from Jewish sources and particularly from Pauline teaching, as shown by his quotations from 1 Cor. xv.

With XI we move into the second group of homilies,[19] often called 'controversial' because they were written to persuade the Jews of error or, more likely, to stop Christians defecting to the less persecuted life of a sister religion. The first of these is on circumcision and it is strange that Zipporah's action described in Exod. iv.24–6 is recounted in VI and not here. (Can this be because Aphrahat's 'anti-feminine bias' was more important to him at that moment than circumcision?) The main stance of XI lies in the contempt Jews showed for Christians because they lacked the sign of circumcision. Testimony lists are presented to show that even after circumcision some Jews were condemned by God (468.15–469.14). Various laws and covenants were given to different generations with no stress on the requirement of circumcision in order to be righteous. Indeed, Abraham was the father of faith before circumcision, and even after circumcision he did not observe the Sabbath (XIII.557.15–20). Murray (*Symbols*, pp. 44ff) comments on Aphrahat's liking for Gen. xvii.5 and follows through Paul's exposition in Rom. iv.17. Faith justified several people prior to Abraham without circumcision: Abel, Enoch, Noah, Shem, Japhet and even Melchizedek (XI.473–6), who even blessed Abraham. Gen. xvii is held to show that the Gentiles were called before Israel, Abraham being viewed as

19 A useful summary of, and comment on, this group may be found in O. de Urbina, 'La Controversia di Afraata coi Giudei', *Studia Missionalia* 3 (1947), 85–106.

ancestor and model of proselytes (*Symbols*, p. 205), as the father of *many* nations and not one only.

What purpose has circumcision, then? The rite was imposed on Abraham with the birth of Isaac to set his family apart from the pagans with whom they lived. Lot passed the rite on to other unbelievers. The sons of Ishmael were worshippers of idols, so what good did circumcision do them? When they were isolated in the desert circumcision was not used, but Joshua was ordered to circumcise once more on crossing the Jordan (Josh. v.5f, 477–85), and he in fact entered the promised land uncircumcised (485–8). From this Aphrahat concludes that circumcision of the flesh was intended to set the Israelites apart from the pagans among whom they lived; it was worth nothing spiritually without a change of heart (489–97), and he finds this view confirmed by Jeremiah (cp. ix.25f with iv.4). This new covenant through circumcision of the heart, promised by Jeremiah, is fulfilled in Jesus, and a list of scriptural testimonies contrasting Joshua and Jesus concludes the homily (497–504). Circumcision, and likewise the covenants, were of a temporary nature until the permanent circumcision of the heart and the new covenant in Christ's blood, which were of permanent validity.

In XII, Aphrahat, on the subject of the Passover, seems to move into the attack, and accuses the Jews of misunderstanding it all. Moses celebrated the Passover on 14 Nisan (Exod. xii.3–6) and was ordered to celebrate it in one place, 'the place the LORD thy God shall choose' (Deut. xvi.5). The eating of the Passover by Jews in the Diaspora among Gentiles is, according to Aphrahat, an abuse of Moses' precept. As a result of the Jews' provocative behaviour in celebrating the Passover illegally in the Diaspora, they have been punished (here come some prophetic proof texts), and Moses' words of Deut. xxxii.21 are taken up again: 'I shall provoke them with a people which is not a people, and with a foolish people I shall anger them' (509.27–512.2). Next Aphrahat takes up a text from Jeremiah (xii.7–9), which is very important for him, where the Jews are said to have become 'a coloured bird' (512.17–513.16) (Murray, *Symbols*, pp. 56ff). This many-coloured bird is identified as the *ʿammē*, 'nations', 'Gentiles', as composed of many different nations. The inheritance of the Gentiles is further reinforced by various texts like Isa. ii.2 where 'all the peoples' flow to the mountain of the house of the LORD. The Passover becomes for Aphrahat a type given to the one nation, whereas the real truth (*šrārā*) is given among the nations, i.e. the Gentiles. The 'one house' for the Passover is identified as the collective Church of God. The 'temporal tabernacle' (*maškan zabnā*) is a misunderstanding of the 'tent of meeting' (Hebrew *'ōhel mō'ēd*) (*Symbols*, pp. 70ff, 225), but is taken to indicate a limited span of time for Judaism, whereas the temple of the holy spirit lasts for ever (524.18–525.4). The crossing of the Red Sea, very closely linked with Passover, is a type of Christ's conquest of Sheol (524.6–7) (*Symbols*, pp. 299, 327) and is viewed as a type of baptism.[20] The negative side indicates leaving Satan and his forces, and the positive side is the crossing of the Jordan into the promised land. Indeed, E.J. Duncan (p. 59) cites a fourth-century bishop of Alexandria speaking of the water of the baptismal font as 'Jordan'. The true Passover is to be seen in the Eucharist, but here there are certain differences: Jews celebrate on 14 Nisan, Christians on 15 Nisan; Jews eat unleavened bread with bitter herbs, Christians eat bread without bitterness; Jews escaped from the servitude of Egypt, Christians from the servitude of Satan. Thus Aphrahat denies the Jews the right to celebrate their traditional Passover, because in Christ lies the true Passover in all respects; the Jewish Passover merely points to it in symbols.

Legislation for the Sabbath (XIII) is not a distinctive precept leading to life or death, righteousness or sin, but, as Deut. v.12–14 extends the command to animals, the legislation seeks to ensure proper rest from labour. Enoch, Noah, Isaac and Joseph are deemed just, but not because of the Sabbath law, which did not then exist. The law demonstrates God's care for working men and animals. So Aphrahat follows the thesis that the precept for rest on the Sabbath is primarily hygienic, not moral or compulsory. Abraham and Isaac are cited as people who did not observe the Sabbath, but were counted righteous (557.11–27). In 568.6–569.15 cases are cited where Joshua and the Maccabees flouted the Sabbath without harm (Simon, p. 200). The Sabbath of God (Isa. xxviii.12) was a Sabbath of rest, and this is continued for the good of the people and animals; it has no value for pride or salvation.

Jewish matters are taken up next in XV on the distinction of foods. Whereas the Jews pride themselves on making distinctions between clean and unclean animals, fish and birds, basing themselves on Lev. xi.2f, Jesus taught (Matt. xv.11) that there is no defilement in what *goes in*, but only in what *comes out*. Following this to its logical conclusion, Aphrahat seems rather to enjoy himself describing how

20 See especially E.J. Duncan, *Baptism in the Demonstrations of Aphraates the Persian Sage* (Washington, 1945), pp. 50–60.

food goes through the stomach, and is then divided round the blood supply and various parts of the body until its 'pleasant odour' is changed to a 'stink', its appearance becomes bad and it is cast out in excrement – not pure at all. Aphrahat then tartly observes: 'in these matters is neither sin nor righteousness' (728.1–732.7). He claims that opportunities for discrimination were given by God to stop people from relapsing into idolatry as in Egypt. No such limits were given before the time of Moses. The Egyptians worshipped oxen and calves as gods, abstaining from beef to keep them divine, eating instead fish and pork. It is known that the Hebrews followed Egyptian customs and fell back to calf-worship; hence, to protect them from Egyptian depravities, God gave instructions to Moses concerning food: unclean foods were those holy to the Egyptians, and clean foods were unclean to the Egyptians. They were even ordered to kill calves and sheep for sacrifices (xv.733.20–744.14). Concerning contamination after touching an unclean corpse, Aphrahat confronts the Jews with Samson and the unclean jawbone of an ass and with the unclean ravens bringing food for Elijah (744.15–745.25). He closes the homily by quoting Matt. xi.28–30 to illustrate how Jesus lightened the load to be carried on the yoke, presumably indicating that the weight of observing the Mosaic law is relieved.

XVI ('On Peoples in place of the People') reintroduces the jingle between the Christian *'ammē* and the Jewish *'ammā*, recalling XII.509.27–512.9. The homily is prefaced by a reference to Gen. xvii.5, which Aphrahat refers to the calling of the Gentiles before Israel in the time of Abraham. Gentiles, and not just Jews, are the sons of Abraham (Baarda, pp. 127ff., see n. 13). In 772.4–777.10 he illustrates from texts of the Old Testament that the calling of the Gentile *'ammē* was prior to that of the Jewish *'ammā*. Murray (*Symbols*, pp. 46ff) notes that in 760.9–14 Jacob's blessing occurs with a reading much more messianic than that of the Peshitta, showing a primitively messianic exegesis in common with the Targums (pp. 282–4). Here we see again strongly Jewish features in primitive Christian exegesis.

After homily XVII concerning the Messiah we find in XVIII an ardent discussion of chastity, a subject of great importance for the early Syriac Christians. A whole homily is devoted to this topic, largely to ward off attacks from Jews who believed it was man's duty under God to propagate life.[21] Neusner remarks that Babylon-

21 G. Richter, 'Über die älteste Auseinandersetzung der syrischen Christen mit der Juden', *ZNW* 35 (1936), 102ff.

ian rabbinism was extremely feminist.[22] As virginity was a doctrine so dear to the Syriac-speaking Church, it seems to illustrate Aphrahat's excellent personal commonsense that he should cover the difficulties of sexual temptation with such understanding as in VI.260.13–7: 'Therefore, my brethren, if any who is a monk or a saint [i.e. celibate], who loves a solitary life, yet desires that a woman, bound by a monastic vow like himself, should dwell with him, it would be better in that case to take [to wife] a woman openly and not be made wanton by lust.' Clearly, Aphrahat was not strict to the point of ignoring natural human weaknesses.

Homily XIX may be called anti-Zionist.[23] Aphrahat here completely excludes the possibility that the Jews will be gathered together again as a people. He starts (845.1–849.14) by saying that the Jews were scattered all over the peoples of the world because of their misdeeds. After seventy years in Babylonian captivity Cyrus allowed them to return to Jerusalem, but Aphrahat interestingly anticipates the evidence later discovered in the Murašu documents[24] by stating that not all made use of this permission, many remaining in the Diaspora. Indeed, they left Egypt only under pressure. After detailed description of many texts he then states that just as there were only two Temples for Israel, so there were only two times of salvation: Egypt and Babylon. A close argument on Isa. xi.11 follows (868.19–869.7): the LORD will stretch out his hand a second time to recover the remnant, but no mention is made of a third. There is considerable argument over numbers of years, and he argues at length from Dan. ix.23–7. He claims that Sodom was better than Jerusalem (one wonders how he knew?), and that Sodom had lain destroyed for 2276 years. His arguments look strange today, particularly in view of the existence of modern Israel, but it is noteworthy that the issue takes up a whole homily. It may well be that many of the Jews, favoured by the Persian authorities and bolstered by prophetic promises, were hoping for permission to return from Babylon, and that this prompted Aphrahat to give such special attention to the issue.

Aphrahat rarely uses allegory, always preferring the plain, historical meaning of texts, but in XX (913.15–916.20) we find an allegorical exposition of Isa. xli.18f treated as an allegory of the Church.

22 *History of the Jews in Babylonia*, vol. III (Leiden, 1968), pp. 142–5.
23 Spijkermann (see n. 5), pp. 191–212, discusses this homily in detail.
24 M.D. Coogan, 'Life in the Diaspora: Jews at Nippur in the Fifth Century B.C.', *Biblical Archaeologist* 37 (1974), 6–12, and J.H. Hayes and J.M. Miller (eds.), *Israelite and Judaean History* (London, 1977), pp. 482–5.

His use of the Old Testament is usually more direct than this: he shares with Ephrem an Antiochene approach to exegesis. It is perhaps important to note with Murray (*Symbols*, p. 335) that in 909.23f the words of the angel at the empty tomb of Jesus are quoted in a version that seems closer to the apocryphal Gospel of Peter than to the canonical gospels. This indicates that he did not have an exclusive view of the biblical canon. We noticed previously a reference to the Maccabees, and I suspect that he referred to all the traditions he had collected, including Jewish midrashic collections.

When he comes to tackle persecution in XXI he starts by citing Jewish critics who cunningly cite Matt. xvii.20: 'if you have faith no bigger even than a mustard-seed, you will say to this mountain, "Move from here to there", and it will move: nothing will be impossible for you'. Why, then, the critics ask, does the persecution not cease? If the Christians were true worshippers of God, he would help them. This counters an earlier argument about Sodom and Jerusalem: that is, the Jews mistakenly hope for a rebuilding of Jerusalem (936.6–952.21). Examples are then cited of biblical heroes who were persecuted – Joseph, Moses etc. – and he shows that persecution sometimes works to the advantage of Christians. Western Christians were persecuted by Diocletian, but triumphantly recovered (there is no mention of Constantine). Persian Christians fulfil Christ's words in a similar way.

After treating death (XXII), he deals with the grape cluster (XXIII) and presents a magnificent midrashic compilation including the grape in the cluster of Isa. lxv.8 (the world being preserved because of the righteous), and describes Jesus as the grape being taken from the cluster. As elsewhere when he deals with vine imagery, he combines the Old Testament image of good and bad vines with what he regards as its New Testament equivalents of good and wicked vinedressers and good and bad wine. There are abundant metaphors and parables from which to construct a Jewish-type midrash such as this.

I noted earlier the frequency of Aphrahat's biblical citations: L. Haefeli referred to the Bible as 'a staff upon which he always leans'.[25] It may seem surprising that, although Aphrahat is writing controversial homilies directed to the Jews, he refers to Bible and aggada only, not halaka, even though the rabbinical school of Nisibis was quite close. To speak of his 'immense indebtedness to rabbinic tradition', as does Gavin,[26] goes too far. It seems likely that

25 *Stilmittel bei Afrahat dem persischen Weisen* (Leipzig, 1932), p. 128.
26 *The Jewish Antecedents of the Christian Sacraments* (New York, 1969), p. 105.

the reason for his use of this material was that he wished to fight on ground common to both parties. It is important to note that, although citations from the New Testament do occur, the figures given earlier show that they are far outweighed by citations from the Old Testament, which both Jews and Christians recognize as Scripture.

Many stylistic traits may be attributed to Jewish influence. In XIII.565.7–10 we see an example of the rabbinical exegetical technique known as *qal wāḥōmer*; but here the existence of a more widespread term to define this literary usage ('argument *a fortiori*') shows that there need be no basic dependence on rabbinical techniques here. Towner and Murray have examined his use of scriptural examples and sequences.[27] Here at any rate he uses a mnemonic formula much used by Jews. A good example may be found in I.20.23–21.9, where he uses the seven 'eyes' or 'facets' of the precious stone mentioned in Zech. iii.9 to illustrate the seven operations of the spirit of God, which he then uses Isa. xi.2 to describe: 'a spirit of wisdom and understanding, a spirit of counsel and power, a spirit of knowledge and the fear of the LORD'. Unfortunately, the numbers do not fit. As Towner says (p. 239): 'One is somewhat hard-pressed to bring the count of the attributes of the Spirit in the latter text up to the necessary seven; however, the intention of the teaching to provide substance to the figure in Zech. 3: 9 by means of a numerical analysis of Isa. 11: 1–2 is clear.' In other words, he made use of rabbinic numerical analysis, but it did not work out; however, his use of the literary model is plain enough. Towner further says (p. 241) that we 'are brought to a point at which a rabbinic rhetorical pattern, now taken over by a Christian patristic writer, is applied in its normal rabbinic manner to a sacred literature entirely foreign to the rabbis'.

Murray notes Aphrahat's liking for lists of Old Testament examples, and calls it his 'favourite party piece'.[28] He cites many such lists illustrating the value of prayer, examples of virtue of various kinds, women who made peace; there are examples of people led into sin through women (a long list this), through jealousy and through lust; there are also references to reversals of fortune of various kinds, and saints who were persecuted. Such lists are

27 W.S. Towner, *The Rabbinical 'Enumeration of Scriptural Examples'* (Leiden, 1973), pp. 237–41 and R. Murray, 'Some Rhetorical Patterns in Early Syriac Literature' in Fischer (see n. 11), pp. 109–25.

28 Murray (see n. 27), p. 110.

found in the Bible, of course, and we think immediately of the heroes of faith in Heb. xi.1–xii.2 and Ben Sira's 'Roll of Heroes' in Ecclus. xliv.1–1.21. After the collections of instances Murray traces the love of such sequences in the late Old Testament, Hellenistic Judaism and early Christian prayers, and even in examples of early Christian art in the Via Latina catacombs in Rome. His article continues very usefully along some lines sketched in his *Symbols of Church and Kingdom*, considerably expanding the section 'In Search of Sources'.

Ouellette has done much useful work on Aphrahat's links with Judaism. Following up a remark of Vööbus that there were certain affinities between Aphrahat's homilies and the asceticism that emerged from Qumran, he published a fairly long essay in 1976,[29] part of which he repeated as a tribute to Vööbus himself.[30] He notes various features of these lists important for our purpose: although, for example, Aphrahat uses exegetical procedures used by the rabbis, he shows recognition only of Jewish doctrines found already in Scripture. There is no explicit reference to any single, specified rabbinic tradition, and in xv, when he is writing on food laws, only biblical regulations seem to be known to him. Further, from the fact that he never refers to the Babylonian Jewish authorities, is it not possible to see flaws in the arguments of those who detect in Aphrahat a narrow dependence on the rabbis of his time? In the absence of even a veiled reference to the rabbinic concept of an oral law revealed on the same basis as the written law,[31] the Jews with whom he was in discussion may in fact have been content to observe literally the precepts of religion founded on Scripture alone.[32] S. Funk, F. Gavin and L. Ginzberg list many rabbinic parallels (sometimes with quite inadequate, or non-existent, references),[33] but these remain only *parallels*, and many seem to have arisen through targumim. Ouellette suggests that Vööbus' links with Qumran may have high-lighted the possibility that Aphrahat had links with other kinds of Jews. Was his intelligent Jewish debater a literary figurehead, or may he have derived his information about Judaism from conver-

29 Ouellette (see n. 6), pp. 163–83.

30 'Sens et Portée de l'Argument scriptuaire chez Aphraate' in Fischer (see n. 11), pp. 191–201.

31 J. Neusner, *Aphrahat and Judaism* (see n. 12), pp. 145–7.

32 *Ibid.* pp. 147ff.

33 S. Funk, *Die Haggadischen Elemente in den Homilien des Aphraates, des persischen Weisen* (Vienna, 1891); F. Gavin, *Aphraates and the Jews* (Toronto, 1923); L. Ginzberg, *The Legends of the Jews*, vols. I–VII (Philadelphia, 1909–38).

sation and life with non-rabbinical Jews? Ouellette thinks Aphrahat knew the Jews who were critical of the authority of the Babylonian rabbis and laid the foundations of the later Karaite movement.[34] Certainly, Aphrahat argued with Jews on the basis of the Bible, avoiding rabbinic disputation of *hălākōt* and theological speculation of the Greek sort. He seems to have avoided contact with the rabbinic authorities in Persia in spite of the nearby school at Nisibis, which was strong enough for Neusner to declare 'what Edessa was to Christianity, Nisibis was to Talmudic Judaism'.[35] His contact with Jews was therefore on an unofficial, informal basis, and I suspect that the 'Jewish debater' sums up in his person any number of acquaintances. Surely he was not seeking to convert Jews to Christianity? I think not. That would almost certainly have been dangerous, as Jews were favoured by the Persian authorities. It is much more likely that he was trying to present arguments to Christians who, finding the going tough in persecution, were tempted to move over to Judaism for an easier life. That is why he chooses to fight on common ground without concerning himself much with the dictates of the Babylonian rabbis. In his homilies we have the humble attempt of a pastor of considerable skill and knowledge to debate with Jews on a popular level as far removed from the halakic teaching of the rabbinic schools as from the theological tomes of the Latin and Greek patristic writers. It is this belief in his popular, rather than official or academic, contact with the Jews that leads me to reject Neusner's title *Aphrahat and Judaism* for this article and choose rather the more personal 'Aphrahat and the Jews'.

34 Ouellette (see n. 6), pp. 169ff.

35 *History of the Jews in Babylonia*, vol. I (Leiden, 1965), p. 166 (p. 180 in the revised edition (Leiden, 1969)).

L'homélie du Karaïte Samuel al-Maghribī sur les Dix Commandements

GEORGES VAJDA ז״ל

Le savant que nous honorons par le présent ouvrage a consacré une notable partie de son oeuvre à l'exégèse juive de la Bible. Qu'il veuille accepter en témoignage d'estime et d'amitié la modeste contribution à ce champ d'études que nous présentons ici.

Samuel, fils de Moïse al-Maghribī, *ḥākām* karaïte, et médecin par profession, au Caire, vers 1434, est l'auteur, entre autres ouvrages, de 'Prolégomènes' (*Muqaddimāt*), en judéo-arabe, résumés d'homélies et d'instructions liturgiques rattachées aux sections hebdomadaires du Pentateuque.[1]

Il découle de la nature de l'ouvrage en cause que les sujets traités ne soient ni très amplement exposés ni approfondis. Mais c'est précisément pour cette raison qu'il est une bonne illustration de l'enseignement dispensé au commun des fidèles par un docteur qui a prouvé par ailleurs son savoir et sa compétence dans son 'Code de Lois' (*'al-Muršid*) dont certaines parties ont été éditées mais qui mériterait une publication intégrale et une appréciation critique de la place qu'il tient dans la production juridico-rituelle karaïte et la littérature judéo-arabe.

1 Il suffit de renvoyer ici à M. Steinschneider, *Die arabische Literatur der Juden* (Frankfurt-am-Main, 1902), §199, pp. 250–1, et à l'article de L. Nemoy, *EJ*, vol. xiv, col. 812 (en anglais). Dans un article dans *Kobez Al Jad* 9 (19), pp. 335–50, הערות אחדות על חומר רבני־אגדי ופילוסופי ב״הקדמות״ החכם הקראי רבי שמואל המערבי, nous étudions quelques thèmes aggadiques et philosophiques traités ou mentionnés dans les 'Prolégomènes'. Les textes qui nous occuperont ici sont inédits: ils se trouvent dans les manuscrits Hébreu 298, fols. 231*r*–241*r* et 300, fols. 91*r*–98*v* de la Bibliothèque Nationale de Paris, les seuls qui nous ont été accessibles; pour la liste complète des copies connues voir A. Freimann, *Union Catalog of Hebrew Manuscripts*, vol. ii (New York, 1964), p. 233, no. 5972.

Traduction

La lumière de la Présence (*nūr 'al-šekīnā*) descendit sur le Mont Sinaï;[2] la gloire de Dieu (*'al-Ḥaqq*) se manifesta; l'Envoyé de la Majesté sacrée (*'al-ḥadra 'al-qudsiyya*) se dressa, conforté par la puissance et la providence, entre Dieu et Sa nation. [Saisi] de crainte révérentielle (*hayba*) devant la grandeur (*'aẓama*) suréminente de Dieu – *qui dira les hauts faits du Seigneur*[3] – l'univers se tut.[4] Dieu produisit une voix forte, terrifiante qui sortait du milieu du feu, disant Son essence suréminente (*qā'ilan 'an dhātihi 'l-'aẓīma*).

Je suis YHWH, Ton Dieu

Israël écoutait, l'Envoyé, la paix sur lui, répétait les paroles de Dieu, jusqu'à la fin du discours.[5]

Cette première Parole énonce l'affirmation de l'essence (*dhāt*) du Dieu béni et la profession de son unicité (*waḥdāniyya*). Elle signifie: Je suis Celui qui doit être nécessairement obéi, car tous les existants sont mes créatures. Je suis, peut-on encore paraphraser, Celui que Pharaon avait d'abord ignoré et qu'il a ensuite reconnu.

YHWH, le nom à propos duquel il a été dit (Exod. iii.15): *C'est Mon Nom pour toujours, c'est mon invocation de génération en génération.* C'est à Lui que dans l'avenir l'univers entier rendra obéissance, ainsi qu'il est dit (Zeph. iii.9): *C'est alors que je changerai la lèvre des peuples en une lèvre purifiée [pour que tous invoquent le nom de YHWH, pour qu'ils le servent d'un même effort]*.

Ton Dieu. L'affixe possessif spécifie l'éminence d'Israël. C'est une idée similaire que suggère [la construction possessive] dans (Gen. ix.26) *Dieu de Sem*, à l'exclusion de ses frères, (Exod. iii.6) *Dieu d'Abraham*, à l'exclusion de Tharé, *Dieu d'Isaac*, à l'exclusion d'Ismaël, *Dieu de Jacob*, à l'exclusion d'Esaü, (Exod. xxxii.27) *Dieu*

2 Cette attestation est à joindre au dossier, certainement très incomplet même pour les textes médiévaux, rassemblé dans notre article dans *REJ* 134 (1975), 133–5.

3 Ps. cvi.2, en hébreu dans le texte. 'Suréminent' rend tant bien que mal la clause qui précède la citation hébraïque, littéralement: 'est exalté Celui dont cette grandeur est la grandeur' (*jalla man hādhihi 'l-'aẓama 'aẓamatuh*).

4 Emprunt à *Šĕmōt Rabbā* 29.9: 'L'univers entier se tut et garda le silence, alors que sortit (se fit entendre) la voix *Je suis YHWH ton Dieu*; cf. M. M. Kasher, *Tōrā Šĕlēmā*, vol. XVI, 'Exodus' (New York, 1955), ch. 20, no. 77, p. 20.

5 Ceci semble refléter l'interprétation dans *Mekilta* à Exod. xix.19 et parallèles: ...ניתן כח וגבורה במשה והיה הקב"ה מסייעו בקולו ובנעימה שהיה משה שומע בו היה משמיע את ישראל, interprétation reprise par Rashi.

d'Israël, à l'exclusion des autres. Lui, le Très Haut, (Deut. x.17) *est le Dieu des dieux et le seigneur des seigneurs* et (Gen. xxiv.3) *Dieu des cieux et de la terre.*

Par cette Parole, le Très Haut nous impose la croyance (*iʿtiqād*) en Sa Seigneurie (*rubūbiyya*), ce qui revient à nous représenter et à admettre en notre créance que tous les existants sont Ses créatures et Son oeuvre, qu'Il dispose d'eux souverainement comme un maître de sa propriété, qu'Il connaît toutes les situations des créatures et rien ne Lui échappe. Le principe de la législation révélée est la croyance en la Seigneurie (*'aṣl 'al-tašrīʿ fī' ʿtiqād 'al-rubūbiyya*).

Qui t'ai fait sortir du pays d'Égypte.

Cet énoncé suggère le caractère gracieux (*niʿma*) [de l'intervention divine]. Il suggère aussi l'idée qu'ayant été capable de faire ceci, Il a le pouvoir d'accomplir ce qu'Il leur a promis.

Si les paroles adressées par Dieu [à Israël] commencent par la lettre *'āleph*, c'est parce que le récit de la création a commencé par la lettre *bēt*. Or l'*āleph* précède le *bēt*; il ressort de là que Celui qui s'adresse [maintenant] à Son peuple est antérieur au monde [qu'Il avait créé].[6]

On a également noté que le mot אנכי était formé de quatre lettres parce que l'obéissance due à Dieu a un motif quadruple. Le premier, qu'Il est le Dieu éternel, toujours existant, qu'Il est notre Maître et le Maître de toutes les créatures. Le second, qu'Il a le pouvoir de modifier les situations du serviteur [l'homme]; il est donc nécessaire qu'Il soit obéi, car Il gouverne souverainement le serviteur en vue du bien-être de celui-ci (*mutawallī tadbīr 'al-ʿabd li-yuḥsina 'aḥwālah wayudabbiraha!*). Le troisième, qu'Il nous a honorablement distingués parmi les nations; le quatrième, qu'Il nous a fait sortir de la maison de servitude et nous a rendus libres.[7]

Voilà quelques enseignements que l'on peut dégager de la Première Parole.

6 Les motivations aggadiques de l'emploi des deux lettres en cause, respectivement comme initiales du récit de la création (et de toute la Tora) et des Dix Paroles sont légion; cf. *Tōrā Šēlēmā*, péricope citée, no. 22*sqq*., pp. 7*sqq*. mais le seul texte qui se rapproche quelque peu de ce que nous lisons ici est le no. 41, p. 11, emprunté à la compilation tardive *Mišnat Rabbī 'Ĕlīʿezer*: le récit de la création commence par *bēt*, lettre qui n'est précédée que d'une seule, ce qui nous apprend que l'univers n'a été précédé que de l'Être unique que l'on sait.

7 Pour le *dĕrāš* fondé sur le nombre lettres d'un mot voir *infra*, n. 29. J'ignore la source de l'interprétation précise rapportée ici; le contenu en est banal.

Deuxième Parole

Tu n'auras pas d'autres dieux

En vertu [de ce qu'implique la Première Parole], Il nous interdit d'avoir la [même] croyance à l'égard de tout [autre] objet de culte [concevable]; nous ne devons pas croire qu'ils sont dignes qu'on leur rende culte, nous n'avons pas à les respecter ni à leur attribuer de pouvoir sur quoi que ce soit. Au contraire, ils sont (Jer. xvi.19) *vanité où il n'y a rien qui vaille* (*ibid.* x.5). *Ne les craignez pas, car ils ne font pas de mal et ils ne peuvent non plus faire du bien.* Il n'est permis d'aucune manière de rendre culte en se prosternant à quelque être que ce soit, du plus éminent au plus vil, à ce qui en est issu [= produit naturellement] ou fait de main d'artiste. Et si quelqu'un y était contraint, qu'il se fasse tuer mais ne cède pas, en suivant l'exemple de Hananya, Misael et Azarya – la paix sur eux – qui se laissèrent jeter dans la fournaise ardente plutôt que de se prosterner devant l'idole érigée par Nabuchodonosor, ou de Daniel – la paix sur lui – qui [ayant refusé d'abandonner même temporairement le culte divin pour celui du roi] fut jeté dans la fosse aux lions. Mardochée – la paix sur lui – agit pareillement selon l'interprétation qui considérait le prosternement devant Haman comme un geste d'idolâtrie.[8] Bien au contraire, il faut mépriser dans toute la mesure du possible et traiter outrageusement l'idolâtrie et ceux qui s'y adonnent (Isa. xxx.22): *Tu les disperseras comme des souillures, sors! lui diras-tu;* le verbe *sors* (צא) étant interprété [au sens d' 'excréments'] d'après (Deut. xxiii.14) *tu recouvriras tes excréments.*[9]

En face de Moi

Que la pudeur t'interdise de rendre culte dans le monde à un autre que Moi, comme qui désobéirait au souverain dans son [propre] palais. On peut également expliquer: [ce culte interdit est toujours

8 Traduction *ad sensum*; l'arabe n'est pas très clair (*'alā mā qīla min 'an kāna 'l-gharaḍ bil-sujūd lahu šay' min dhālika*). Le prédicateur karaïte fait ici allusion à un développement aggadique d'Esther iii.2; cf. *Midraš Rabbā in loc.*, et textes parallèles relevés par L. Ginzberg, *The Legends of the Jews*, vol. VI (Philadelphia, 1928), p. 463, n. 100.

9 Le rapprochement *ṣē'*/*ṣō'ā* avec utilisation des deux versets, d'Isaïe et du Deutéronome, est emprunté à l'Aggada, *Tanḥūmā*, *Kī tēṣē'*, 3. (Dans *Pěsīqtā děrab Kāhănā* 13.2, éd. B. Mandelbaum (New York, 1962), vol. I, p. 226, on trouve seulement le rapprochement des deux mots et le verset d'Isaïe; cf. le commentaire de R. David Qimḥi sur ce dernier texte.)

'en face de Moi'], car Je suis omniscient et rien ne demeure caché à ma science.[10]

L'Écriture nous apprend que le Très Haut est 'jaloux' de ce qu'est fait pour autrui de ce qui [ne] revient [qu'] à Lui, et qu'Il punit celui qui agit ainsi jusqu'à la quatrième génération, en exterminant [la postérité du coupable] lorsqu'elle persiste dans la désobéissance[11] en même temps qu'Il conserve Sa faveur pendant des milliers de générations à ceux qui L'aiment, qui Lui obéissent et gardent Ses commandements. L'Écriture le redit à un autre endroit: (Deut. vii.9) [*Dieu*] *garde l'alliance et la grâce jusqu'à mille générations pour ceux qui L'aiment et qui gardent Ses commandements.*

Troisième Parole

Tu ne prononceras pas le nom du Seigneur, ton Dieu, en vain

Il interdit de jurer en vain par Son Nom et de l'évoquer à la légère (*bil-tajzīf*) ou de Lui attribuer ce qui n'est pas vrai: les détails ['divisions', *'aqsām*] seront expliqués plus loin.[12]

L'Écriture dit: *Le Nom Tétragramme*, le Nom suprême (*'al-'a'ẓam*) qu'il faut tenir en vénération; [ce] afin d'avertir que celui qui transgresse délibérément cet interdit est grandement fautif. De plus, c'est le contraire de la vénération [due à Dieu] que d'énoncer à Son sujet ce qui n'est pas vrai ou de Lui attribuer ce qui Lui messied ou de lier à Sa mention ce qui est mensonger et à plus forte raison de se parjurer en L'évoquant – il y a là *profanation du Nom* (חלול השם) [en hébreu dans le texte].[13]

Il ne fait aucune différence que l'on jure par le Nom Tétragramme ou par un autre nom divin, comme Dieu Tout-Puissant (*'Ēl-*

10 Ces deux motifs sont allégués aussi dans le commentaire de Yefet b. 'Elī, *in loc.* (voir la thèse inédite de Ḥaggai Ben-Shammai, *The Doctrines of Religious Thought of Abū Yusūf Ya'qūb al-Qirqisānī and Yefet ben 'Elī* (en hébreu) (Jerusalem, 1977) vol. II, p. 159), mais la ressemblance entre notre passage et celui de Yefet est vague (cf. *infra*, n. 13). L'expression 'désobéir au souverain dans son (propre) palais' a une saveur aggadique; (je ne l'ai cependant pas trouvée relativement au verset en cause): Yefet met en avant le caractère créé de tout ce qui est dans l'univers et la science totale (*'ilm bāligh*) que Dieu en possède.

11 Voir Targum *in loc.* et BT Sanh. 27*b*; cf. *Tōrā Šēlēmā* (*supra*, n. 4), nos. 162–4, p. 43.

12 En gros, la même interprétation dans *Sēper Hammibḥār* d'Aaron ben Joseph (Gozlow-Yevpatoria, 1835), pp. 36–7.

13 Cf. le commentaire de Yefet ben 'Elī, *in loc.* (MS Paris, B.N. Hébreu 281, fol. 46*r*).

Šadday), qualifiant Dieu et Le désignant; dire 'par le Créateur du ciel' ou '[par] le Créateur de l'homme', c'est [également] jurer par Son Nom. C'est pourquoi l'Écriture dit ailleurs (Lev. xix.12): *vous ne jurerez point par Mon Nom par tromperie*, d'une manière absolue.[14]

Il ne fait pas de différence non plus que le serment par le nom de Dieu soit prononcé en hébreu ou en une autre langue. La même règle vaut du serment juré sur tout ce qui est objet de respect [?],[15] la Tora, les Prophètes, le Sanctuaire, les docteurs, les parents.[16]

On distingue deux sortes de serments: serments faux et serments vains (*šeqer*, *šāw'*).[17]

Les premiers sont des formulations verbales énoncées délibérément, qui sont contraires à la vérité: quelqu'un jure qu'il a mangé alors qu'il n'a pas mangé, ou qu'il mangera demain alors qu'il ne le fera pas, ou qu'il n'a pas fait telle chose alors qu'il l'a faite, ou qu'il fera une chose à une certaine condition mais il la fait d'une manière différente.[18]

Le serment est vain quand son objet est futile (*bāṭil*) et frivole (*'abath*), comme jurer que l'homme est femme; dans ce cas, l'objet correspond à une réalité, mais il est le contraire de ce qui en est affirmé; jurer sur ce qui tombe sous le sens et que chaque homme normal sait, est frivole: ainsi, jurer que le soleil est soleil et que l'éléphant est plus grand [*sic*, *'akbar*] que la girafe. Futile est également le serment dont l'objet est contraire à la nature des choses ou à la Loi révélée: ainsi, quand quelqu'un jure qu'il est monté au ciel ou

14 Même précision, rattachée à 'ton Dieu', dans *Keter Tōrā* d'Aaron b. Elie (terminé en 1362), (Gozlow-Yevpatoria, 1866), p. 62*a*; voir aussi Elie b. Moïse Bashyatchi, *'Adderet 'Ēlīyāhū*, 'Inyan Šĕbū'ā (impression d'Odessa, 1870; réimpr. Israël, 1966), chs. 1–2, p. 205*cd*; pour l'exégèse rabbinique, cf. *Sifrā Qĕdōšīm*, ch. 2 (voir *Tōrā Šĕlēmā* (*supra* n. 4), no. 181, pp. 48–9).

15 Traduction incertaine (*bi-dhawı 'l-ḥāqq*) cependant suggérée par ce qui suit (cf. aussi l'énumération plus copieuse dans *'Eškōl hakkōper* (Gozlow-Yevpatoria, 1836), alph. 136, p. 51*bc*; *'Adderet 'Ēlīyāhū* (*supra* n. 14), ch. 2).

16 L'égalité de toutes les langues quant au serment enfreignant les deux versets allégués est soulignée par Qirqisānī, *Kitāb al-Anwār*, éd. L. Nemoy (New York, 1939–43), vi.25.1–2, p. 645; plus brièvement, Yefet, MS cité (cf. n. 13) fol. 46*r*.

17 L'auteur parlant ici en prédicateur simplifie grandement une législation évidemment beaucoup plus élaborée dans le commentaire de Yefet b. 'Elī, les codes tels que les deux cités dans les notes précédentes et aussi dans l' *'Eškōl hakkōper* de Juda Hadasi.

18 Bashyatchi désigne cette espèce de serments par le terme *šĕbū'at biṭṭūy* (*supra*, n. 14; ch. 4, p. 203*c*). Pour la loi rabbinique, voir M. Sebu. 3.1; BT Sebu. 19*b*–20*b*; cf. *Tōrā Šĕlēmā* (*supra*, n. 4), no. 182, p. 49.

qu'il ne mangera pas de pain azyme à la Pâque ou ne jeûnera pas le jour de Kippur.[19]

Toutes ces variétés de serments sont profanation du Nom qui tombent sous la menace de sanctions graves dont l'Écriture prévient en disant: [*le Seigneur*] *ne laissera pas impuni celui qui aura prononcé Son Nom en vain.* Il est d'autres passages scripturaires (Zech. v.4 et viii.16–17) adressés aux gens de la Dispersion, par où l'on voit que Dieu déteste ces comportements.[20]

La multiplication des serments est l'une des pierres d'achoppement (מכשולות) [en hébreu dans le texte] dans l'Exil; les gens y sont habitués dès l'enfance, à cause de la fréquentation des Gentils. C'est pourquoi beaucoup de gens tombent dans le péché de profanation du Nom, la plupart de leurs serments étant frivoles. C'est un des reproches que Jérémie (v.2) lance à ses contemporains: *s'ils disent: par la vie de YHWH, en fait, ils jurent par le mensonge.* Au témoignage du psalmiste (cxliv.8 et 14), c'est un défaut qui caractérise les non-Juifs: *dont la bouche dit des faussetés et dont la droite est une droite mensongère.*

Les gens de bien (*'al-'aḫyār*) habituent, par crainte de jurer, leur langue à des formules inoffensives (*mimmā lā ḍarara fīh*) substituées au serment et quand ils jurent quelque chose de dommageable, [à condition toutefois] qu'il n'entraîne pas le jureur à sa perte, ils sont fidèles à leur parole. C'est ainsi qu'est décrit le juste (Pss. xv.4 et cxix.106): *s'il jure à son détriment, il ne se parjure pas; j'ai fait un serment, je le tiendrai, c'est d'observer les jugements de Ta justice.*[21]

19 Cf. Bashyatchi. Samuel utilise ici, avec des adaptations dont j'ignore si elles lui sont personnelles, une source similaire à celle exploitée par le *Midraš haggādōl*; voir *Tōrā Šĕlēmā* (*supra*, n. 4), no. 183, p. 49; voir également M. Šebu. 3.8 (BT Šebu. 29*a*).

20 La vision de Zacharie, ch. 5, est alléguée par *'Eškōl hakkōper* (*supra*, n. 15), alph. 138, p. 52*bc*, mais dans la perspective des sanctions divines en cas de non-accomplissement des voeux.

21 Nous avons ici, mais en termes assez imprécis, la première des deux interprétations de Ps. xv.4, proposées dans *Kitāb al-Anwār* (*supra*, n. 16), vi.34.4, p. 656; *Eškōl hakkōper* (*supra*, n. 15), alph. 138, p. 52*b*, transpose en hébreu, en l'amplifiant, le texte de Qirqisānī. Aaron ben Elie se réfère à Ps. xxiv.4 ('il ne jure pas pour tromper'), en faisant de l'évitement du serment mensonger l'un des attributs (*'issūr*, dans la terminologie karaïte) du Juste (*ṣaddīq*): *Keter Tōrā* (*supra*, n. 14), p. 62*b*.

Quatrième Parole

Souviens-toi du jour du Sabbat pour le sanctifier

Souviens-toi. Invitation à se remémorer l'obligation déjà imposée lors de l'affaire de la manne (Exod. xvi.23*sqq.*). [D'autre part], il faut se souvenir de ce jour avant son arrivée et se soucier de préparer ce qu'il est possible de préparer à son intention.[22]

Dans la seconde version du Décalogue (Deut. v.12), on lit 'observe' [à la place de 'souviens-toi']; les deux formulations ont valeur obligatoire: il faut observer le Sabbat et l'avoir en mémoire, en s'abstenant de toutes les occupations interdites ce jour-là.

En vertu de la double injonction, 'se souvenir' et 'observer', il faut laisser une marge [*fanā'*, 'espace libre'] au Sabbat, avant et après, en sorte que le temps de l'observance soit inséré entre deux moments neutres [litt. 'choses']: si le ciel est couvert de nuages à la fin de la journée de vendredi, il conviendra d'adopter l'attitude la plus prudente (*yu'ḫadh 'al-'aḥwaṭ*) [autrement dit, il faut se comporter comme si le Sabbat avait déjà débuté].[23]

22 Cf. *Mekilta Baḥōdeš*, éd. J. Z. Lauterbach (Philadelphia, 1933–5), vol. II, pp. 252–3, et les textes apparentés dans *Tōrā Šělēmā* (*supra*, n. 4), no. 220, p. 63. La formulation de notre auteur est cependant trop vague pour qu'on puisse assurer qu'il avait l'un ou l'autre de ces textes à l'esprit. La recommandation de penser au Sabbat comme à un objet précieux, déduite des deux verbes, se trouve dans *'Eškōl hakkōper* (*supra*, n. 15), alph. 145, lettre *mem*, p. 54*d*, mais exprimée, là aussi, de façon vague.

23 L'extension de la vigueur de la loi sabbatique par un 'espace' double, avant le commencement et après la fin du temps sacré, est également prescrite dans le *Muršid* (cf. Nathan Weisz, (*Samuel ben Moses* ...) *Traktat über den Sabbat bei den Karäern* (Pressburg, 1907), pp. 4, 17–18), à titre de 'précaution' (*'istiẓhār*, pour le sens voir R. Dozy, *Supplément aux dictionnaires arabes* (Leiden, 1881), vol. II, p. 87) et en tant qu'impliquée par *zākōr* et *šāmōr*. (Cette règle et sa justification scripturaire ne se trouvent ni chez Qirqisānī (*Kitāb al-Anwār*, (*supra*, n. 22); cf: BT Roš. Haš. 9*a*, Yoma 81*b* voir *Tōrā Šělēmā* (*supra*, n. 4), 145, p. 54*d*), ni dans le passage afférent de *Keter Tōrā* (*supra*, n. 14) pp. 62*b*–63; cf. cependant *Gan 'Ēden* du même auteur (Gozlow-Yevpatoria, 1866), *'Inyan Šabbāt*, ch. 20, p. 37*ab*, mais déduit de *šabbāt šabbātōn*, Exod. xxxi.15 etc.) Elle doit pourtant remonter à une source datant du dixième siècle au moins, à preuve que Yefet, MS cité, fols. 48*v*–49*r*, en fait état, à titre d'opinion qu'il ne prend pas à son compte, d'un docteur anonyme (*ba'ḍ 'al-'ulamā'*) que je ne suis pas en mesure d'identifier. 'Se souvenir' enjoindrait de compter les jours (de la semaine?), de sorte que la connaissance du jour du Sabbat ne se perde pas; 'garder' serait prendre garde (*'iḥtiyāṭ*) 'd'y entrer [avant qu'il commence] et d'en sortir après [qu'il prenne fin], tel que les choses se passent dans la pratique' (*'alā mā huwa mawjūd fī'l-'isti'māl*): on cesse le travail avant, et l'on 'sort du Sabbat' un bon bout de temps (*qiṭ'a wāsi'a*) après le coucher du soleil. Yefet estime, quant à lui, que 'se souvenir' signifie se remémorer que le repos sabbatique avait été ordonné dès la cueillette de la manne (Exod. xvi.22 *sqq.*) ou même institué dès l'achèvement de l'oeuvre de la création, si l'on accepte la thèse selon

Ce précepte est capital (*'aẓīma*); il est un des piliers de la religion et la récompense attachée à son observance est immense (*'aẓīm*). Dieu a garanti la facilité de se procurer la subsistance de ce jour, à preuve (Exod. xvi.22): *Or, au sixième jour, ils ramassaient le double de pain.* Dieu a expressément marqué ce jour comme consacré au culte: *Sabbat, pour le Seigneur, ton Dieu,* tandis qu'Il a institué les six autres pour l'homme qui y accomplit tout ce qu'il a à faire.[24]

Ce jour, Dieu l'institua pour Lui-même, aussi doit-il être employé tout entier aux actes religieux (*yutawaffar fīhā 'alā ṭā'atih*) et à l'évocation de Ses oeuvres, comme le proclame le prophète [*'al-rasūl*, David en l'occurrence, Ps. xcii.2–3]: [*Chant pour le jour du Sabbat.*] *Il est bon de rendre grâce au Seigneur ... d'annoncer Ta grâce dès le matin et Ta fidélité durant les nuits.*

L'Écriture mentionne le Sabbat en trente-six passages dont treize dans le Pentateuque.[25] Chacune de ces mentions apporte un enseignement (*fā'ida*) de plus engageant à l'observance [sabbatique].

C'est grâce au Sabbat que s'était maintenue l'indépendance (*dawla*) [de la nation israélite] et c'est grâce à lui que sera réalisée la délivrance; même le non-Juif qui l'observe est récompensé et jouit du fruit mérité de son oeuvre, alors que (au contraire) celui qui le profane s'exclut de la vie éternelle (חיי העולם הבא) [en hébreu dans texte], se rend passible de la peine de mort dans ce monde et du

---

laquelle les préceptes furent édictés à ce moment (sans doute allusion à une doctrine professée, affirme-t-on, par Benjamin al-Nihāwandī; cf. *Kitāb al-Anwār* (*supra*, n. 16), IV.55.9–57.14, pp. 452–68, trad. *REJ* 120 (1961), 245–56). Nous avons là le correspondant karaïte du principe rabbinique מוסיפין מחול על הקודש (Aaron ben Elie l'allègue du reste (*Gan 'Ēden*, passage cité) que l'on trouve précisément à propos de nos deux versets dans la *Mekilta* (*supra*, n. 22); cf: BT Roš. Haš. 9*a*, Yoma 81*b* voir *Tōrā Šĕlēmā* (*supra*, n. 4), no. 226, p. 65; no. 250, p. 72; no. 255, p. 73).

24 Cf. *Tōrā Šĕlēmā* (*supra*, n. 4), no. 240, p. 69 et no. 246, p. 70, ainsi que les notes complémentaires 14–15, dans le même volume, pp. 242–9: 'faire oeuvre durant six jours' est-il facultatif ou obligatoirement imposé par la Révélation? La remarque de Samuel est trop concise pour que l'on puisse affirmer qu'il a été ou non conscient de ce problème d'exégèse, alors qu'un auteur comme Aaron ben Elie en atteste l'existence chez les Karaïtes et tranche en faveur de la première branche de l'alternative (*Keter Tōrā* (*supra*, n. 14), p. 63*a*).

25 Cf. Weisz (*supra*, n. 23), p. 1 et la note 2 de l'éditeur, p. 23. Les treize mentions faites dans le Pentateuque: Aaron b. Elie, *Gan 'Ēden* (*supra*, n. 23), 'Inyan Šabbāt, ch. 9, p. 28*b*; Bashyatchi ne rapporte, en les numérotant, que onze passages du Pentateuque (*supra*, n. 14, 'Inyan Šabbāt, ch. 3, p. 39*bc*); aucun de ces deux auteurs (et, sous réserve de correction, nul autre que notre Samuel) ne parle de trente-six mentions, nombre trop élevé pour le Pentateuque et trop bas pour l'ensemble de la Bible hébraïque.

châtiment dans l'autre, selon la parole (Exod. xxxi.14): *Qui le profane, de mort il mourra.*[26]

Le Sabbat rappelle deux grands événements: la création (Exod. xxxi.17), *En six jours, le Seigneur a fait les cieux et la terre*, et la sortie d'Égypte (יציאת מצרים) [en hébreu dans le texte], et Dieu a promis la récompense à qui l'observe, le sanctifie et l'honore (Isa. lviii.14): [*Si tu honores le Sabbat*, vs. 13] *alors tu te délecteras en le Seigneur* etc.[27]

Cinquième Parole

Honore ton père et ta mère

Dieu a ordonné d'honorer les deux parents en raison du bien qu'ils ont fait à l'enfant, ce bien venant [juste] après celui que Dieu lui avait fait. Et ils sont les géniteurs [litt. ' racines ', *'uṣūl*] de l'homme [l'individu], qu'ils ont le mérite d'avoir éduqué, traité avec tendresse et bienveillance. Les honorer est un précepte (tant) de la raison (que) de la Révélation; la docilité dont on fait preuve à leur égard soutient la vie bien réglée de l'individu (*'aḥwāl 'al-'insān*).[28] Il faut les respecter et les craindre (Lev. xix.3): *vous craindrez chacun sa mère et son père*, la tournure du verset les mettant à égalité sur ce point. [Le respect qui leur est dû] doit être mêlé de crainte, en raison de la

26 Nous avons condensé le texte qui cite abondamment ici Isa. lvi.1–6; cf. *Muršid* II.12 et 15, ap. Weisz, pp. 18–19/42 *sq.*, 21/47 (*supra*, n. 23). Le double châtiment, ici-bas et dans l'au-delà, est sans doute déduit de la construction infinitif absolu + verbe fléchi, mais je ne connais pas de source à cette exégèse, du moins touchant le verset allégué dans notre passage; la construction similaire *hikkārēt tikkārēt*, de Num. xv.31, est, en revanche, interprétée dans ce sens: *Sifrē Bemidbar*, § 112, éd. H. S. Horovitz (Frankfurt-am-Main, 1917) p. 121, lignes 10–11, BT Sanh. 99*a*. Il convient toutefois de noter que *mōt tāmūt*, de Gen. ii.17, est l'objet d'une exégèse similaire sinon identique (מות | בעולם הזה | תמות בעולם הבא), mais uniquement dans des textes très tardifs, alors qu'on ne trouve rien de tel dans l'Aggada ancienne: *Midraš haggādōl*, éd. M. Margulies, vol. I (Jérusalem, 1947), p. 83, et dans *Tiqqūnē Zōhar* (cf. *Tōrā Šělēmā* (*supra*, n. 4), no. 241, p. 222): *Tiqqūn* 24, éd. R. Margulies (Tel-Aviv, 1948), p. 69*b*; *Tiqqūn* 53, p. 87*b*; (je n'ai rien trouvé aux deux autres endroits indiqués). S'il n'est guère vraisemblable que notre Karaïte se soit inspiré des *Tiqqūnē Zōhar*, il n'est pas exclu qu'il ait utilisé une source également exploitée par le compilateur du *Midraš haggādōl*; nous avons repéré dans les *Muqaddimāt* deux cas analogues: voir les notes 30 et 34 de l'article cité, *supra*, n. 1.

27 L'idée est banale, au reste incluse dans les textes bibliques; cf. *Kitāb al-Anwār* (*supra*, n. 16), XI.27.5, p. 1157; *Gan 'Ēden* (*supra*, n. 23), 'Inyan Šabbāt, ch. 20, p. 36*ab*; *Tōrā Šělēmā* (*supra*, n. 4), no. 274, p. 81; voir aussi Maïmonide, *Guide* II.31; la péricope d'Isaïe est citée dans *Muršid*, ap. Weisz (*supra*, n. 23), pp. 19*sq.*/44*sq.*

28 Ou ' l'ordre social ' (?).

crainte éprouvée devant Dieu et celle de leur malédiction [s'ils sont désobéis].

Le mot hébreu pour 'honore' se compose de trois lettres (*kbd*), car il faut honorer ses père et mère en leur présence, en leur absence et après leur mort. Dans le premier cas, le respect s'exprime en se levant et s'inclinant devant eux, en les installant à une place honorable, en ne s'asseyant pas à leur place, en ne leur coupant pas la parole. En leur absence: parler d'eux courtoisement (*bil-jamīl*). Après leur mort: en invoquant la miséricorde divine lorsqu'on les mentionne. Le détail de tout ceci se trouve dans le [= notre?] commentaire. Notre seigneur Joseph honora son père en sa présence et en son absence. Salomon honora sa mère en se levant et en se prosternant devant elle et en lui faisant avancer un siège, la plaçant à sa droite (1 Kgs ii.19). Dans l'autre rédaction des Dix Paroles (Deut. v.16), l'Écriture ajoute *afin que tes jours se prolongent*, indiquant que le respect des parents est un gage de longévité, tandis que sentence de mort est portée à l'encontre de qui leur manque de respect. Le seigneur Salomon proclame [en effet] (Prov. xxx.17): *L'oeil qui se moque d'un père et méprise l'obéissance due à une mère, les corbeaux du torrent le crèveront et les petits de l'aigle le dévoreront.*[29]

Cette recommandation est la première (de celles) qui intéressent les relations entre les hommes, les précédentes ayant eu trait aux rapports entre Dieu et l'homme.

On dit cependant (aussi) que tout en visant des relations au sein de l'humanité, ce précepte a une attache avec les relations entre l'homme et Dieu parce que le respect des parents est un des droits que Dieu revendique pour Lui-même. Selon cette opinion, les Dix

29 Nous avons déjà rencontré (*supra*, n. 7) un exemple du procédé de *děrāš* fondé sur le nombre des lettres du mot interprété. Le simili-*midrāš* de basse époque *Pěsīqtā Ḥadtā* tire aussi une unterprétation du nombre des letres de KAB(B)ĒD (A. Jellinek, *Bet ha-Midrash*, vol. VI (Vienna, 1877), p. 44, *Tōrā Šělēmā* (*supra* n. 4), no. 305, p. 93), mais il y voit une allusion à l'idée que les deux parents sont associés à Dieu dans la formation de la structure psycho-somatique de l'homme (d'après BT Nid. 31*a*); chose curieuse, Samuel fait ailleurs état de cette idée (voir la note 79 de l'article cité, *supra*, n. 1), mais ne l'évoque pas ici, sinon d'une manière très vague, allusion très brève également dans *Keter Tōrā* (*supra*, n. 14), p. 64*b*, qui cite R. Yēšūaʿ (b. Yehūdā): האבות הם שניים לבן מהבורא. Le reste du du développement rappelle, outre *Kitāb al-Anwār* (*supra*, n. 16), VI.42, pp. 674–5 et IX.19.3, p. 927 et XI.2.6, p. 1119, le *Midraš ʿĂśeret haddibběrōt*, compilation également tardive attribuée à Mōše Haddaršān (cf. *Tōrā Šělēmā* (*supra*, n. 4), no. 318, p. 99); source plus ancienne: BT Qidd. 31*b* (32 dans *Tōrā Šělēmā* (*supra*, n. 4), no. 287, p. 86, est une faute d'impression) (C'est par une distraction que Samuel note ici une différence non-existante entre Exod. xx.12 et Deut. v.16). Le morceau correspondant dans *'Adderet 'Ēlīyāhū* a été traduit par L. Nemoy, *Karaite Anthology* (New Haven, Conn., 1952), pp. 260–3.

Paroles se diviseraient en deux groupes de cinq: le premier rattaché au Créateur, le second à la créature.[30]

Sixième Parole

Tu ne tueras point

Interdiction de mettre à mort les innocents alors que [s'il y a eu meurtre] Dieu a dit (Exod. xxi.23): *âme pour âme*, et Il a prescrit de refuser le prix du sang (Num. xxxv.31): *et vous n'accepterez pas de rançon pour la vie d'un meurtrier.*

Le verbe employé ici se compose de quatre lettres (*trṣḥ*) parce que le meurtre peut être perpétré de quatre manières: directement, par ordre (donnei à autrui), par calomnie (dénonciation), par non-assistance alors qu'on a le pouvoir (de se porter au secours de la victime).[31] L'Écriture se prononce en ce sens (Lev. xix.16): *Ne sois pas indifférent au sang de ton prochain.* Le Sage dit (de son côté) (Prov. xxiv.11): *Délivre ceux que l'on conduit à la mort.*[32]

Septième Parole

Tu ne commettras point l'adultère

Interdiction de la débauche (*fujūr*), c'est-à-dire la fornication (*zinā'*) avec l'épouse d'un [autre] homme, (péché) dont la prohibition absolue a été prononcée dans d'autres passages et qui est moralement mauvais (*qabīḥ*), tant sous le rapport de la raison que celui de la Loi révélée. L'adultère constitue une transgression à plusieurs points de vue: l'un est la confusion des généalogies et l'assomption d'une fausse paternité (*'ilzām 'al-'insān biwalad ghayrih*) et d'autres abus qui en relèvent (*ghayr dhālika min tafnīnih*). Il est contraire à la 'sanctification' (קדוש) [en hébreu dans le texte] que Dieu requiert des Israélites (Lev. xx.7): *Vous vous sanctifierez et vous serez saints.* L'Écriture sanctionne de la peine capitale les adultères (*ibid.* vs. 10):

30 Sans doute comme l'écrit Abraham Ibn Ezra, à Exod. xx.2, parce que les parents sont pour ainsi dire associés de Dieu dans la venue à l'être de l'homme (cf. la note précédente).

31 Interprétation différente du nombre de lettres dans *Pĕsīqtā Ḥadtā* (*supra*, n. 29), pp. 44–5; cf. *Tōrā Šĕlēmā* (*supra*, n. 4) no. 333, p. 103 et la note afférente.

32 C'est une des interprétations traditionnelles juives (Sifrā au verset cité de Lévitique, repris par Rashi). Abraham Ibn Ezra souligne le motif de dénonciation; cf. la remarque dans *Tōrā Šĕlēmā* citée dans la note précédente. Noter que le *Sēper Hammibḥār* (*supra*, n. 12) p. 38*a*, propose des distinctions assez différentes; cf. aussi *Keter Tōrā* (*supra*, n. 14), pp. 64*b*–65*a* et *Gan 'Ēden* (*supra*, n. 23), p. 177*b*.

L'homme qui commet l'adultère avec la femme de son prochain, il sera mis à mort l'homme adultère et la femme adultère. L'Écriture interdit également les unions incestueuses (ערות [עריות] אסורות) [en hébreu dans le texte] et déclare que ce sont là des 'abominations' (תועבות) [en hébreu dans le texte] et menace les transgresseurs de 're-tranchement' (כרת) [en hébreu dans le texte].[33]

Huitième Parole

Tu ne voleras pas

Interdiction du vol: s'approprier secrètement le bien du prochain. La formule de défense est, ici, absolue; ailleurs (Lev. xix.10), l'Écriture emploie le verbe au pluriel.[34]

Le verbe employé ici est formé de quatre lettres (*tgnb*). C'est, a-t-on dit, parce qu'il y a quatre espèces de voleurs: celui qui est tenu de restituer au double, celui qui doit dédommager au quadruple et au quintuple,[35] celui qui est puni de mort – c'est le cas du ravisseur d'un homme afin de le vendre (Exod. xxi.16) – enfin le voleur dont la punition est la honte qu'il ressent (*tasubbuh ḫajalatuh*), celui qui vole des choses comestibles ou buvables, de peu de valeur[?],[36] ainsi qu'il est dit (Prov. vi.30): *on ne méprise pas le voleur quand il vole* (*pour calmer son appétit quand il a faim*).[37]

Le vol est un acte grave [et ses fruits] ne sont pas bénis. L'Écriture compare [le voleur] à la perdrix parce que le résultat de son acte n'est que le péché [avec le déshonneur qui s'ensuit], de même que la perdrix ne tire aucun profit de l'oeuf qu'elle couve pour autrui.[38] [En revanche, à propos de la conduite opposée,] le Sage dit (Prov. xxviii.20): *l'homme loyal a abondance de bénédictions.*

33 Cf. Lev. xviii, xx.17 etc. Samuel illustre ensuite son propos d'extraits de Prov. vi. 32–3, 27–9, 26, cités dans cet ordre. Cf. *'Eškōl hakkōper* (*supra*, n. 15), alph. 276, p. 105*ab*; *Guide des Égarés* III, 49.

34 L'auteur cite simplement le texte, mais il veut dire sans doute que dans le Lévitique, l'interdiction de voler est associée à d'autres espèces d'abus de confiance.

35 Cf. Exod. xxii.1 *sqq.*, xxi.37.

36 Traduction incertaine; le texte porte *'al-ghaniyya*, qui n'est pas en contexte.

37 Sans tenir compte de la suite du verset cité, le prédicateur semble vouloir dire que si, dans le cas mentionné, il n'y a pas de sanction pénale, ni même réprobation publique, le coupable n'est pas fier de ce qu'il a fait. Les exégèses tirées du nombre des lettres de *tgnb* relevées dans *Tōrā Šĕlēmā* (*supra*, n. 4), no. 367 (= *Bet ha-Midrasch* vol. VI, (*supra* n. 29) p. 45) et 367 bis, p. 112, diffèrent plus ou moins de ce qu'on lit ici: la quatrième espèce ne semble pas être, jusqu'à plus ample informé, attestée ailleurs.

38 Allusion à Jer. xvii.11, non cité formellement dans le texte.

Neuvième Parole

Tu ne déposeras pas de faux témoignage contre ton prochain

Interdiction du témoignage mensonger (*kadhib*), selon l'autre version (Deut. v.18[20]), du témoignage à la légère (*juzāf*). D'autres textes concernant [la même transgression]: (Exod. xxiii.2): *Tu ne déposeras pas dans un procès pour dévier* [fausser le jugement]; (Deut. xix.16): *Quand un témoin malveillant se dresse contre un homme*. Le Sage dit (Prov. xix.5): *Le faux témoin ne sera pas tenu pour quitte*. Le faux témoignage est un insigne méfait, car il est cause de perte d'âmes (de vie) et de biens. Il peut [notamment] être accusation d'inciter au culte idolâtre et de fausse prophétie (עבודה זרה et נביא שקר [en hébreu dans le texte]; cp. Deut. xiii.2–19). En revanche, voici comment le Sage s'exprime au sujet du témoin véridique (Prov. xiv.25): *Un témoin véridique sauve des vies.*[39]

Dixième Parole

Tu ne convoiteras pas

Interdiction de l'envie (*ḥasad*), c'est-à-dire le désir qu'éprouve une personne d'avoir ce qui appartient à son prochain; trait de caractère répréhensible au regard de la raison comme de la Loi révélée. Elle englobe chacun des cinq préceptes (מצות) [en hébreu dans le texte] qui intéressent les relations entre les hommes. En effet, quelqu'un peut envier à son prochain sa situation ou sa fonction[40] et cela le conduit à priver ce dernier de la vie comme Achab qui fut la cause de la (mise à) mort de Nabot dont il convoitait le vignoble (1 Kgs xxi) et il transgressa ainsi *Tu ne tueras point*. Ou bien il advient qu'un homme enviant l'épouse d'autrui commette l'adultère avec elle, transgressant ainsi le précepte *Tu ne commettras pas l'adultère*. Or le Sage dit (Prov. vi.25): *Ne désire pas sa beauté dans ton coeur*. Ou encore, il lui porte envie à cause de sa fortune et la lui dérobe, transgressant [ainsi] *Tu ne voleras pas*, ce que fit Akan (Josh.

39 Cette fois-ci, notre Karaïte ne fait pas état, aux fins de déduction exégétique, du nombre des lettres du verbe employé (*tʿnh*); la *Pĕsīqtā Ḥadtā* nous gratifie d'une telle interprétation (*Bet ha-Midrasch*, vol. VI (*supra*, n. 29), p. 45; *Tōrā Šĕlēmā* (*supra*, n. 4), no. 386, p. 117).

40 Le choix des termes employés ici (*martaba, waẓīfa*) n'est pas très heureux parce que le cas allégué concerne la propriété du prochain.

vii.21): *J'en ai eu envie et je les pris.*[41] Enfin l'envie peut porter sur un droit [de propriété] manifeste (? *ḥaqq yatabayyan lahū*) et le coupable en vient à faire une déposition mensongère afin de frustrer sa victime de son droit, transgressant ainsi *Tu ne déposeras pas de faux témoignage contre ton prochain*, comme les vauriens qui, sur l'instigation de Jézabel, témoignèrent [faussement] contre Nabot, en vue de priver celui-ci de sa vigne (1 Kgs xxi.1–16).

Le verbe employé est composé de quatre lettres (*tḥmd*) parce que, dit-on, la convoitise est de quatre sortes, spécifiées dans le verset: l'épouse du prochain, sa maison, son champ et toute autre chose qui peut être sa propriété légitime.[42]

Ainsi donc, ils [les docteurs?] ont fait rentrer sous la rubrique de 'convoitise' l'ensemble des Dix Paroles, ce qui revient à dire: si tu veux être innocent (*ta'taṣim*) des crimes mentionnés, *ne convoite pas* (לא תחמד) [en hébreu dans le texte]. Dieu a clos les Dix Paroles par cette interdiction qui est [si elle est transgressée] à la base de toutes les calamités et vaut [au coupable] la totalité des maux, ici-bas et dans l'au-delà.[43]

[*Postscript*

Sadly, Professor Vajda died while this volume was being printed. We are grateful to Dr P. B. Fenton of the Taylor-Schechter Genizah Research Unit, a former student of Professor Vajda, for his kind assistance with the proof-reading of the above article—*Editors*.]

41 Noter qu'il ne s'agit pas dans le cas allégué d'un larcin commis au détriment du prochain mais d'une appropriation sacrilège.

42 Le texte ne fait que citer les termes scripturaires ('champ' figure seulement dans la rédaction du Deutéronome), mais en les rangeant par ordre d'importance.

43 Pour des considérations similaires sinon identiques, voir les textes alignés dans *Tōrā Šĕlēmā* (*supra*, n. 4), no. 395, p. 120, et no. 408, p. 125, avec les notes afférentes.

דִּבְּרָה תוֹרָה כִּלְשׁוֹן בְּנֵי־אָדָם

J. WEINGREEN

The rabbinic axiom that is the theme of this essay occurs no less than three times in the Babylonian Talmud – in Ber. 31*b*, Sanh. 85*a* and Ned. 3*a*. This statement asserts that the Torah employed ordinary, human language[1] and was evidently meant to be a general, guiding principle in the study of biblical texts. As examples of the application of this principle these three talmudic passages quote the following biblical texts:

(1) In 1 Sam. i.11 we find the expression אִם רָאֹה תִרְאֶה, 'if thou (God) wilt indeed take notice [of the affliction of thy handmaid]'. Here the so-called infinitive absolute (really a verbal noun) placed immediately before the finite verb expresses emphasis. Because the reader is confronted with what, to him, may appear to be a strange arrangement in the Hebrew text, he is told that this is a normal feature in the language.

(2) In Lev. xxii.4 we find the duplication אִישׁ אִישׁ, meaning '*any* person'. It is again pointed out that such duplication of nouns is normal usage in Hebrew.

(3) In Num. vi.2 the cognate verb and noun are used in the phrase לִנְדֹּר נֶדֶר, 'to make a vow'. Once again the student is reminded that this arrangement is the usual practice in Biblical Hebrew and nothing more.

Rashi makes a very pertinent comment on the last of these talmudic examples in asserting: ליכא למדרש מינה כלום, 'one must

1 M. Jastrow, *A Dictionary of the Targumim, the Talmud Babli and Yerushalmi, and the Midrashic Literature* (London and New York, 1903), p. 278, s.v. דָּבַר adds the explanation: 'i.e. uses metaphors and phrases adapted to human understanding'. While this is true, I feel that the axiom refers rather to implications in speech.

not infer any midrashic interpretation from this'. Rashi's apt observation may be applied with equal force to this rabbinic dictum in general, for it indicates the intent of the rabbis in issuing this salutary reminder. It was evidently felt necessary to explain that phenomena in Biblical Hebrew that did not seem to conform to logical thinking were, in fact, nothing more than normal features of the language, and the above biblical quotations were cited as examples. That is to say, there were no hidden concepts involved that could be revealed only by the application of some midrashic rules. Students were to be discouraged from the tendency of over-indulgence in extravagant exposition when faced with what is simply regular usage in Hebrew syntax. While midrashic procedures were indulged in for homiletic or legalistic purposes, there was nevertheless the realization that such interpretations could be inimical to the plain sense of the text and students had to be alerted to this danger.[2]

Another rabbinic dictum that is relevant to the theme of this essay is found in BT Qidd. 49*a*. Though directed specifically to those engaged in the public reading of an Aramaic translation (Targum) of the Hebrew Scriptures in synagogue services,[3] it is of general significance for translators of the biblical text. It is recorded that: ר׳ יהודה אומר המתרגם פסוק כצורתו הרי זה בדאי 'R. Judah said: "anyone who translates a biblical verse [strictly] according to its form [that is, 'literally'] misleads".' This cautionary statement by R. Judah suggests that, because of the sacred nature of the Hebrew text, translators were prone to try to keep to the sequence of the Hebrew words,[4] thereby producing literal renderings, which often did not represent the true sense of the text. He rightly emphasized the importance of presenting the sense of the text, even if this meant a departure from a verbal rendering. Scholars are only too well aware that, in certain instances, literal or verbatim translations

2 A similar warning against the danger of presenting a midrashic interpretation as the sense of a text intended by the writer is given in BT Šabb. 63*a*: אין מקרא יוצא מידי פשוטו, 'a biblical verse can never lose its plain sense' (even though its meaning may be extended by the methods of interpretation). Cp. Jastrow, pp. 832–3.

3 The practice in the public reading of the Torah in synagogue services was שנים מקרא ואחד תרגום, 'the biblical passage [was read] twice and the Targum once' (BT Ber. 8*a*).

4 Such strict adherence to the Hebrew text is seen in the Greek version of Aquila, where violence is often thereby done to the Greek.

may produce ambiguity or a misrepresentation of what the writer intends to convey.

There appears to be a close relationship between these two rabbinic dicta. When taken together and stated in modern terms, their joint import may be formulated as follows: when Biblical Hebrew was a living, spoken language, it manifested characteristics common to living languages. One of these, with which this essay is specifically concerned, is that a word or phrase of which the meaning is not in doubt may be used in a particular context, with the intent not of conveying its simple meaning but of implying a derived meaning indicated by the context, and this may be far removed from its usual sense. Failure to grasp the derived sense required by the context induces difficulties and opens the way for subjective interpretation and comment, as will be illustrated later. When, however, the implied sense, as determined by the context, is grasped, the meaning intended by the writer becomes evident. The purpose of this essay is to demonstrate this phenomenon in Biblical Hebrew and thus to vindicate our rabbinic axiom that the Torah employed ordinary, human language. It will also be shown that rabbinic comments on a few selected biblical texts indicate an understanding of this phenomenon of implied meanings of words, imposed by the contexts in which they appear, as opposed to their plain and basic meanings. Though the comments of the rabbis on these selected texts are couched in midrashic forms, they nevertheless indicate their understanding of this feature in what had been a living language.

The relevance of the phenomenon of implied, derived meanings of words becomes very significant when applied to the class of Hebrew verbs designated as statives. These verbs generally denote states-of-being, which seem to be inactive, but they sometimes assume active meanings when so determined by their contexts. It should be observed that stative verbs are not restricted to intransitives, such as *kābēd*, 'was heavy' and *qāṭōn*, 'was small'. There are quite a number of transitive verbs which, because they indicate states-of-being, may be included under the category of statives. Some such verbs are *zākar*, 'remembered', 'was in a state of remembering', *šākaḥ*, 'forgot', 'was in a state of forgetfulness', *yāda'*, 'knew', 'was in a state of knowing', and *ḥāmad*, 'coveted', 'was in a state of coveting'. In the biblical texts now to be cited it will become apparent that the writer did not mean to convey the plain stative sense but one of active effect or consequence. In other words, samples of what is meant by the axiom that the Torah employed ordinary, human language will be given.

In some instances the derived meanings of words suggest themselves to the reader without any difficulty. Such is the case of the verbs *zākar* and *šākaḥ* in Gen. xl.23. In this chapter, after Joseph has interpreted the dream of the chief butler to mean that he will be reinstated in office by Pharaoh, he begs the exultant butler to bring his case to the notice of Pharaoh and secure his release from prison: וְהִזְכַּרְתַּנִי אֶל־פַּרְעֹה וְהוֹצֵאתַנִי מִן־הַבַּיִת הַזֶּה (verse 14). The narrator tells us, however, that וְלֹא זָכַר שַׂר־הַמַּשְׁקִים אֶת־יוֹסֵף וַיִּשְׁכָּחֵהוּ, 'the chief butler did not remember Joseph, but he forgot him' (verse 23). Clearly this verse does not mean to suggest that the chief butler suffered a lapse of memory. This was a case of deliberate betrayal and abandonment of Joseph. The true sense of this verse is quite obvious, and there is no need for interpretation. That the verb *šākaḥ* in certain contexts is the equivalent of *ʿāzab*, 'abandoned', is made clear by their juxtaposition in Isa. xlix.14, where we read: וַתֹּאמֶר צִיּוֹן עֲזָבַנִי יהוה וַאדֹנָי שְׁכֵחָנִי, 'Zion says "The LORD has forsaken me; my lord has forgotten me."' The parallelism of the verse makes it plain that the two verbs have the same meaning as, indeed, the Targum understood them, by translating שְׁכֵחָנִי as רַחֲקָנִי, 'he has rejected me'. Yet, there are a number of biblical passages in which the derived active sense of effect or consequence indicated by their contexts has not been generally recognized, particularly with stative verbs, and these will now be dealt with.

The simple verb *yādaʿ* generally means 'knew', 'had knowledge', and its nominal form, *daʿat*, is 'knowledge' but, in certain contexts, there is the implied active effect or consequence of having knowledge, producing the derived meaning 'acknowledging', 'giving recognition to'. It is, as mentioned earlier, the context that provides the clue to the derived sense. Dealing first with the noun *daʿat* as it occurs in Hos. iv.1, we read that the prophet declares that God makes a charge (*rīb*) against Israel, in that there is no *'ĕmet*, 'fidelity', *ḥesed*, 'loyalty' or *daʿat 'ĕlōhīm bā'āreṣ*. All the English versions translate this expression as 'there is no knowledge of God in the land'. This literal rendering, having missed the practical implications indicated by the context, has evoked a variety of comments to justify regarding the alleged state of ignorance of God as a misdemeanour.[5] It is surely obvious that, while ignorance of God would be deplored, it would never be considered a state of delinquency on a par with the deliberate abandonment of the virtues of fidelity and loyalty. This Hebrew expression, furthermore, is placed within a context of the criminal acts listed in verse 2: 'oaths . . . are broken, they kill and rob, there is nothing but adultery and licence, one deed of blood[shed] after another' (NEB). The serious charge against Israel is that 'there is no acknowledgement of God in the land' – a negative way of saying that there is a rejection of God in the land, as demonstrated by the people's abandoning of his moral demands and their turning to vice. The Targum, reflecting a rabbinic viewpoint, appears to have recognized the active effect or consequence implied in the prophet's words. Its rendering is וְלֵית דִּמְהַלְכִין בְּדַחַלְתָּא דַּיי בְּאַרְעָא, 'there are none who walk in the fear of the LORD in the land'. This same expression is used also in Hos. vi.6, where God is represented as saying: 'I desire loyalty and not sacrifices, acknowledgement of God [*daʿat ʾĕlōhīm*] rather than burnt offerings.' In contrast to the literal renderings of the English versions, the Targum took this expression in this context to mean וְעָבְדֵי אוֹרַיְתָא דַּיי, 'people practising God's Torah'. Though the targumic renderings of both passages appear in the form of a paraphrase, they nevertheless point to the sense required by the context.

There are two examples of the active effect of the verb *yādaʿ* with a negative, in Exod. i.6 and v.2 in the sense of 'did not acknowledge', that is 'repudiated'. In the former text we read: וַיָּקָם מֶלֶךְ חָדָשׁ עַל־מִצְרָיִם אֲשֶׁר לֹא יָדַע אֶת־יוֹסֵף, of which the general English translation is 'There arose a new king over Egypt who knew not [or, 'nothing of'] Joseph.' Surely it is not suggested that the writer meant to convey the strange information that the new Egyptian king had no knowledge of Joseph's rule before him! What the writer in fact tells us is that the new king did not acknowledge, that is, he repudiated, the legitimacy of Joseph's rule. If, in this passage, there is a veiled reference to the overthrow of the Hyksos regime by the Egyptian Ahmosis, it would be natural for the new, native regime to reject any claim to legitimacy by the

5 E.g. P.R. Ackroyd in H.H. Rowley and M. Black (eds.), *Peake's Commentary on the Bible* (London etc., 1962), p. 607 (532*b*): 'lack of knowledge of God, which means lack of fellowship with God'; also Julius A. Bewer, *The Book of the Twelve Prophets*, vol. I, 'Amos, Hosea and Micah' (New York, 1949), p. 45, 'where the knowledge of God is wanting, the moral sanctions disappear'.

preceding, foreign ruler. In the Babylonian Talmud (ʿErub. 53*a* and Soṭa 11*a*) there is a typical rabbinic discussion of whether the adjective 'new' was to be taken literally or whether it means 'one whose laws were made anew', thereby implying the abrogation of the laws of the overthrown regime. This latter view was adopted by the Targum Onqelos, which rendered this part of the line as דְּלָא מְקַיֵּם גְּזֵרַת יוֹסֵף, 'who did not implement [that is, "who abrogated"] the law of Joseph'. Targum Pseudo-Jonathan, while translating these words correctly as דְּלָא חַכִּים יַת יוֹסֵף, 'who did not recognize Joseph', adds the rabbinic interpretation that וְלָא הֲלִיךְ בְּנִימוּסוֹי, 'he did not follow his laws'. Although the targumic renderings are couched in negative, indefinite language so characteristic of rabbinic comment, one may again see underlying them the practical implications of this phrase in its context as conveying the notion of 'repudiation'.

Our second example, again with the negative, but this time in the first-person singular, is in Exod. v.26. The background is the audience that Moses and Aaron were granted by Pharaoh. These two representatives of the Hebrew slaves present the demand that Pharaoh should permit his slaves to make a journey into the wilderness, in order to fulfil their religious obligations to their God, YHWH, at a pilgrim feast. To this demand Pharaoh replies: 'Who is YHWH that I should let Israel go?' This is followed by the declaration: לֹא יָדַעְתִּי אֶת־יהוה. The RSV translation, 'I do not know the LORD', or the slightly different JB rendering, 'I know nothing of your Yahweh', might, indeed, lend themselves to mean something more than Pharaoh's ignorance of who Israel's God was, but the way would thus be opened to a variety of interpretations. The NEB took this Hebrew expression to mean 'I care nothing for the LORD', but, because this rendering reflects the implicit interpretation that Pharaoh's response was one of arrogance and contempt, the intent of the writer is distorted. If, however, we realize that what Pharaoh's words conveyed to Moses and Aaron was 'I do not acknowledge [the authority of] YHWH', then, according to his own lights, Pharaoh's attitude was perfectly correct and void of any trace of arrogance or contempt. His response contains an implicit reference to the belief current in the ancient Near East that the power and authority of a deity were restricted to a given geographical area, the territory of his adherents. They did not extend beyond these limits except, perhaps, as a consequence of victory in battle over another country. What Pharaoh's statement purported to say was that he knew that YHWH was the God of Israel, and that his authority held sway in the wilderness to which his followers belonged, but that he had no status in Egypt. To paraphrase Pharaoh's statement, what he virtually said was 'who does YHWH think he is to order me to let Israel go? I do not acknowledge YHWH's authority here and I will not let them go.' In the course of a midrashic elaboration of the Hebrew text, Targum Pseudo-Jonathan includes the phrase מִנֵּיהּ לֵית אֲנָא דָּחִיל, 'I do not fear him', that is to say, 'I am not one of his adherents.' Though the publication of this Targum is comparatively late, it often represents an early rabbinic tradition, and is therefore not to be dismissed lightly. In this particular instance there is a recognition of what Pharaoh's words implied.

The commandment: כַּבֵּד אֶת־אָבִיךָ וְאֶת־אִמֶּךָ in the Decalogue (Exod. xx.12 and Deut. v.16) is another case in which there is an active implication of the simple sense of the verb. All the English versions give the translation 'Honour your father and mother', and we are left wondering what duties this positive commandment entails. Commentators seem to give their own version of what compliance with this instruction involves.[6] It is true, of course, that usually this verb simply means the adopting of a respectful stance towards someone. However, one may immediately argue that, since the Decalogue commandments concerned with human relationships are of a protective nature, they involve some form of activity or the avoidance of activity.[7] The talmudic rabbis seem to have been aware of this implication, for they saw in this commandment the obligation to ensure the material wellbeing of parents. In BT Qidd. 32*a* they argued thus: 'It is said "Honour your father and mother" [in the Decalogue] and it is said "Honour the Lord with your wealth" כַּבֵּד אֶת־יהוה מֵהוֹנֶךָ (Prov. iii.9).' Since

6 D.M.G. Stalker, in *Peake's Commentary on the Bible*, p. 228 (193*a*), does indeed mention that 'especially are old and weak parents to be respected and cared for', but the point is that this understanding is inherent in the Hebrew words and not the result of exegesis.

7 One might add that the prohibition לא תחמד in the Decalogue, usually translated 'You shall not covet', is not concerned with illicit emotions. Along with the other prohibitions against murder, adultery and the giving of false evidence, this commandment deals with human relationships and conduct. The sense, not reached by exegesis but by an understanding of the active effect or consequence of coveting, is 'You shall not try to acquire [what belongs to your neighbour].'

the latter text refers to what they describe as חסרון כיס, 'the loss or expenditure of money', so the former text refers to 'the expenditure of money'. Though the presentation of this analogy is in the form of a midrashic exposition, the rabbis, by quoting another text in which the word under scrutiny occurs and where the meaning is made clear by the context, were employing a method of study that commends itself to modern scholars. The renowned commentator Qimḥi makes lavish use of this method, and frequently with profit. We may say then that, in the rabbinic view, this commandment would have been understood in biblical times as ensuring the material wellbeing of parents.

The rabbis went further than merely hinting at the obligation of children towards their parents. In BT Qidd. 31*b* they make a clear distinction between the term *mōrā*', 'fear, reverence', on the one hand (as in the injunction: אִישׁ אִמּוֹ וְאָבִיו תִּירָאוּ, 'everyone shall revere his mother and father' – Lev. xix.3 – referred to in BT Qidd. 30*b*), and the term *kibbūd*, 'honour (given to someone)', on the other hand. The former is said to mean, in conduct, that 'one should not sit or stand in his [father's] place. He should not contradict him nor overrule him.' The latter term, however, involves the practical duties of 'feeding, clothing and assisting [one's parents] in movement'. In spelling out the practical implications of the word *kabbēd* in the context of the Decalogue, the rabbis engaged in a sensible form of exegesis. They were not indulging in a midrashic process designed to read into this commandment a higher ideal not envisaged by the biblical legislator. It seems that they were conscious of the practical effect or consequence derived by the context from this stative-like verb, the basic meaning of which is 'show a respectful attitude towards'.

We cannot do better than follow the rabbinic method of quoting another biblical passage in which the verb *kabbēd* occurs with the implication of giving wealth to someone. In the Balak–Balaam narrative, in Num. xxii.2ff, Balak, king of Moab, sent a delegation to the soothsayer Balaam with the request that he should come to Moab to curse Israel, who were then encamped on the borders of Moab. When Balaam refused to comply, Balak sent another delegation of higher-ranking officials to persuade Balaam to accede to his appeal, and he made him the promise in the words: כַּבֵּד אֲכַבֶּדְךָ מְאֹד (verse 17). The NEB translates this line 'I will confer great honour upon you', while the JB offers 'I will load you with great honours.' Balaam's reply leaves us in no doubt as to what this tempting offer implied. He said: 'If Balak were to offer me all the gold and silver in his house I cannot disobey the command of the Lord, my God, in anything small or great.' Clearly Balak's promise to confer great honour upon Balaam meant, in practical terms, the lavishing of great wealth upon him for his services. Interestingly enough, this was understood by Ibn Ezra, whose comment on this line consists of only one word, *bĕmāmōn*, 'with wealth'.

Comments on biblical texts in the Talmud, the Targumim and the medieval Jewish commentaries reveal an overwhelming tendency towards midrashic interpretation. What has been attempted in this brief essay is to point out that, occasionally, a comment dressed up in a midrashic form may, in fact, conceal the true sense of a text. Though such instances are rare, the fact that they do occur should alert us to the need to study rabbinic commentaries in the expectation that some, at least, might help in the solution of textual difficulties or throw new light on biblical passages. We shall do well, also, to bear in mind the rabbinic axiom that 'the Torah employed ordinary, human language'. In recognizing the validity of this axiom we may be led to a better understanding of the active effect or consequence that is implied in the meanings of some words, usually very simple ones. We should, perhaps, pay more attention to the influence of context on the meaning of words or phrases.

The Origin of the Peshitta Psalter[1]

M.P. WEITZMAN

Our earliest references to the origin of the Peshitta (P) of the Old Testament come from Theodore of Mopsuestia (*c*. A.D. 350–428), who disparaged it as the work of 'some obscure individual' (ἕνα τινὰ ἀφανῆ) of whom nothing was known, and contrasted it with the Septuagint, which had been translated by seventy learned elders and faithfully reflected the original Hebrew.[2] It has been

1 The generosity of the John Goodenday Trust, which enabled me to spend a term at the Hebrew University on this research, is gratefully acknowledged. For valuable discussions and comments I am indebted to more scholars than I can name, but above all to Professors D. Flusser and S. Pines in Jerusalem and Professor R. Loewe and Father R. Murray in London. Professor Donald M. Walter has been kind enough to provide full manuscript collations for the Peshitta Psalter.

2 Migne, *Patrologia Graeca*, vol. LXVI, cols. 437 (commenting on Hab. ii.11), 452f (on Zeph. i.5), 465–8 (on Zeph. iii.1). Though Theodore does not of course use the term Peshitta, he refers explicitly, and disdainfully, in each passage to a translation into Syriac (εἰς τὴν Σύρων [γλῶτταν]). The readings he reports agree with P at Hab. ii.11 (πάσσαλον = *sektā*; MT: *kāpīs*) and Zeph. iii.1 (Ἰωνᾶ = *yawnān*; MT: *hayyōnā*). On Zeph. i.5 (MT: *bĕmalkām*), he cites LXX as κατὰ τοῦ Μελχὸμ, while the Syrians λέγουσι . . . ὅτι Μελχὸμ ἐνταῦθα τὸν βασιλέα βούλεται εἰπεῖν; yet oddly enough the best attested LXX reading is κατὰ τοῦ βασιλέως αὐτῶν, while P (as I was generously informed by the Rev. A. Gelston of Durham) has uniformly *bmalkōm*. Conceivably, Theodore was confused between the two versions, or preserves a P reading that has not survived elsewhere; more probably *bmalkōm* stood in Theodore's P text too, but was popularly interpreted as 'by the king' (contrast the plural λέγουσι with Theodore's insistence on one sole translator of P). In his Psalms Commentary (references are to R. Devreesse, *Le Commentaire de Théodore de Mopsueste sur les Psaumes (I–LXXX)* (Rome, 1939)); much survives in a Latin version only), he introduces six readings by *apud Syros*, ὁ Σύρος λέγει, or the like. These come not from P, with which only one of the six readings agrees, but, it seems, from the Σύρος discussed by F. Field, *Origenis Hexaplorum quae supersunt* (Oxford, 1875), pp. lxxviii–lxxxii. Two are registered as such – at Psalm lx.10 (λεκάνη . . .) and Psalm lxv.11 in Field; the others are at Psalm xvi.2*b*

(footnote 2 continued on next page)

remarked that we today know no more than did Theodore,[3] but this is not quite justified. Differences observed in the translation of different books – notably in the degrees of literalness, influence by the LXX, and distaste for anthropomorphisms – indicate the participation of more than one individual. Again, the Peshitta Pentateuch has been shown, most recently and thoroughly by Y. Maori,[4] to be of Jewish origin. Progress on the remaining books, however, is disappointing, and the long-standing debate whether they are of Jewish or Christian origin continues with no prospect of consensus. The fact that the discussion has been formulated almost entirely in these terms, 'Jewish' versus 'Christian', may itself be responsible for the stalemate, through failure to take account of the diversity that has become increasingly apparent within both Judaism and earliest Christianity.

I

The most recent study on the origin of the Peshitta Psalter was published in 1939 by C. Peters,[5] who was convinced (p. 279) that the need for an Aramaic version of the Psalms had initially produced many different translations, of which the extant Targum represented but one. Peters noted many passages where P agreed with the Targum against the MT (e.g. Psalm ix.2, MT: *'ābad*, P: *'awbedt*, Targum: *hōbadtā*),[6] remarking in particular that P oc-

---

(p. 91, which alone agrees with P), Psalm xvi.3*a* (p. 92), Psalm xxix.6*a* (p. 134) and Psalm xxix.6*b* (p. 134). (It is unlikely that *caddis* at Psalm xxix.8 (p. 134) is a further 'Syrian' reading.) In Psalm xxix.6*b* 'the Syrian' renders *Israhel* where the MT has *wĕširyōn* and the LXX ἠγαπημένος; he and the LXX apparently both read *yĕšūrūn* (cp. LXX on Deut. xxxiii.5), confirming the hypothesis of Field and A. Rahlfs (*Mitteilungen des Septuaginta-Unternehmens*, vol. I, 7 (Berlin, 1915), pp. 404ff) that he translated from the Hebrew. Theodore's references to this version are always respectful.

3 Most recently by S. Jellicoe, *The Septuagint and Modern Study* (Oxford, 1968), p. 247.

4 *The Peshitta Version of the Pentateuch in its Relation to the Sources of Jewish Exegesis* (Hebrew, with English abstract (Jerusalem, 1975)).

5 'Pešiṭta-Psalter und Psalmentargum', *Le Muséon* 52 (1939), 275–96. A. Vogel, 'Studien zum Pešiṭta-Psalter', *Biblica* 32 (1951), 32–56, 198–231, 336–63, 481–502, treats exhaustively the relationship of P to the MT and LXX, but as to its origin he merely observes (p. 485) that the translators were probably Jews or Jewish Christians.

6 Eleven are noted on pp. 277ff, but some fifty were listed by F. Baethgen in *Jahrbücher für protestantische Theologie* 8 (1882), 448.

casionally rendered Hebrew *selā* by *lʿālmīn* or *lʿālam*, just as Targum regularly rendered it *lĕʿālmīn*; he concluded that the Peshitta Psalter was based on another such ancient Jewish Aramaic translation of the Psalms, which had no doubt been extensively revised. Against Peters it may be objected that the Jewish exegesis that he found in P may suffice to demonstrate Jewish influence but not a Jewish origin.[7] That translators should utilize Jewish exegesis, and even a Hebrew original, is equally to be expected in the early history of a Christian community that began – as the Syriac-speaking Church probably did – with a nucleus of converted Jews.[8]

Peters goes on to argue (pp. 283ff) that traces of the Aramaic targum which supposedly underlies P survive in biblical citations in Syriac (and occasionally in Arabic) literature, which preserve freer or more expansive – and therefore 'targumic' – renderings than do the P manuscripts themselves. He begins with a group of citations from works attributed to Ephrem in the *Editio Romana*.[9] The first (*Ed. Rom.* VI.216f) is of Psalm lxxxi.15:[10] *ʿad qallīl gmar*(*w*) *bʿeldbābaw* / *wʿal sānʾaw mahpek hwēt īd*(*y*), which certainly seems a freer translation than P: *ʿad qallīl mawbed hwēt la-bʿeldbābayhōn wʿal sānʾayhōn mahpek hwēt īd* (*y*). The Ephremic work has since been critically edited by E. Beck, who reads the first line: *ʿad qallīl gāmar hwēt leh*.[11] At all events, the fact that the work containing the citation was composed in heptasyllabic lines suffices to explain nearly all the divergences from P, apart from the replacement of *mawbed* by *gāmar*, which could be a lapse of memory. Peters' last example is part of Psalm l.16, where P reads: *lḥaṭṭāyā ʾemar leh ʾalāhā: mā lāk wlaktābē dpuqdānay*. Each strophe in the work in which it is quoted has a central section consisting of one line of six (or seven) syllables, followed by six lines of four

7 Thus Jerome's *Psalterium iuxta Hebraeos* embodies much Jewish exegesis and even renders *selā* by *semper*.

8 See R. Murray, *Symbols of Church and Kingdom* (Cambridge, 1975), pp. 4ff. To the literature there cited add S. Pines, 'The Iranian Name for Christians and the "God-Fearers"', *Proceedings of the Israel Academy of Sciences and Humanities* 2, 7 (1967), 143–52.

9 Probably erroneously. The first work cited was edited in *CSCO*, vol. CCCXI by E. Beck, who denied it to Ephrem (*CSCO*, vol. CCCXII, pp. ixff); the rest, too, are generally considered spurious.

10 Peters also cited verse 14, in the form *ʾelū ʿam*(*y*) *yadʿan*(*y*), which he contrasts with P (*ʾelū ʿam*(*y*) *šamʿan*(*y*)), but as Beck reads *šamʿan*(*y*) in the Ephremic work this divergence vanishes.

11 The word *leh* must refer to the enemy; the construction is awkward.

syllables each.[12] This citation (from *Ed. Rom.* vi.413) comprises almost the whole of such a central section: *dalḥaṭṭāyā lam ʾemar / leh ʾalāhā / dmā lāk mekēl / lmeqrā ktābay / wabpuqdānay / lmethaggāyū* /. The 'targumic expansions' here claimed by Peters are due rather to the demands of metre, and his remaining examples of divergence between Ephremic citations and the P text can all be readily explained through corruption in the *Editio Romana*, lapse of memory, or metrical constraints.

Psalms citations in works undoubtedly by Ephrem[13] in fact agree almost invariably with the P manuscripts, though there are occasional concessions to metre (e.g. at Psalm ii.7, *wlāk yeldet*[14] for P *wʾenā yawmānā īledtāk*), abridgements (e.g. at Psalm lxxxix.10 *wgallaw mšatteq*[15] for P *wadluḥyā dgallaw a*(*n*)*t mšatteq*) and minor slips (e.g. *dṭabbaʿ* for P *wṭarep*[16] at Psalm cxxxvi.15). More interesting is his remark on the Behemoth,[17] viz. that *Dawīd daʿbādē* (the text seems corrupt) states that its pasture is upon a thousand mountains. This reflects an interpretation of Psalm l.10*b* that recurs in rabbinic literature (BT B. Bat. 74*b*; *Leviticus Rabba* 22.7; and elsewhere) but not in P, which has *wabʿīrā dabṭūrē wtawrē*. T. Jansma is probably correct in emending *daʿbādē* to *bʿebrāyā*,[18] in which case Ephrem's citation derives from an authority ('the Hebrew')[19] distinct from P, and there is no ground for supposing that it preserves the text of a Jewish Aramaic translation that underlies P but left no trace here in the P manuscripts. The request that concludes Psalm xcix.8 in P: *prōʿ ʾenōn ʿbādayhōn*,

12 G. Hölscher, *Syrische Verskunst* (Leipzig, 1932), p. 172, no. 70.

13 As listed by Murray (see n. 8 above), pp. 366ff, who relies largely on Beck.

14 *CSCO*, vol. CLXIX, p. 137.

15 *St Éphrem, Commentaire de l'Évangile Concordant*, ed. L. Leloir (Dublin, 1963), 12.8.

16 *CSCO*, vol CLXIX, p. 157.

17 In his Genesis commentary (*CSCO*, vol. CLII, p. 22).

18 *Oriens Christianus* 56 (1972), 60. A gentler emendation might be *dʿebrāyē* 'iuxta Hebraeos', on the analogy of *Dawīd damparršē*, 'David of [i.e. according to] the separated ones', which W.E. Barnes (*The Peshitta Psalter* (Cambridge, 1904), p. li) found in the title of the Psalter in manuscripts as old as the sixth century; he explained the 'separated ones' as the LXX translators, said to have worked in separate cells (*JTS* 2 (1901), 191).

19 This is taken to be the Hebrew text by Jansma, followed by S. Hidal, *Interpretatio Syriaca* (Lund, 1974), p. 71. A likely alternative is the *ʿEbrāyā*, apparently a Jewish interpreter, cited in certain Ephremic commentaries of doubtful authenticity. See J. Perles, *Meletemata Peschittoniana* (Breslau, 1849), pp. 51ff and P. de Lagarde, 'Über den Hebräer Ephraims von Edessa', in his *Orientalia* (Göttingen, 1879–80), vol. II, pp. 43–63.

'reward them [*sc.* Moses, Aaron and Samuel] for their works!', is curiously transformed by Ephrem, who read *'eprō'*, 'I shall reward . . .',[20] and saw here testimony of their resurrection.[21] Apparently the *pr-* with which the imperative began attracted a prosthetic vowel, as in loan-words and foreign names (cp. such spellings as *'prgmṭy'* for πραγματεία,[22] *'prwbws* for Probus, and, at Judg. xii.13, *'pr'twn*, corresponding to LXX^A φρααθων, against MT *pir'ātōn*). At Psalm cxliii.10, *rūḥāk ṭābtā* in Ephrem,[23] where the P manuscripts have *rūḥāk mbassamtā*, may preserve the original reading of P.

Peters found no support for his theory in Aphraates,[24] who almost always quotes (with occasional inaccuracies) the P text familiar from the P manuscripts, though Psalm xxxvii.35 is cited (p. 80) from the LXX.[25] At Psalm cxix.99, where the MT reads *hiśkaltī* and P *sakklayn(y)*, Aphraates (p. 442) has *yelpet*; he may have learnt this from a Jewish contact,[26] or he may preserve the original P reading, the text of the manuscripts being conformed to *sakklayn(y)* elsewhere in the Psalm (verses 34, 125, 144).

Translations into Syriac, or even from Syriac into Arabic, also seemed to Peters worth scanning for citations. Eusebius, *Ecclesiastical History* I.3.14, follows Heb. i.8f in applying Psalm xlv.7f to Christ, anointed with the oil of gladness 'above thy fellows' (MT: *mēḥăbērekā*); the 'fellows', he explains, are 'those who in the past had been more materially anointed as types'. While P at Psalm xlv.8 renders *yattīr men ḥabrayk*, the Syriac translation of the *Ecclesiastical History*[27] has *yattīr men hānōn d'etmšaḥ(w)*, which Peters claims as an 'ancient P variant' (p. 288). More probably, however, the translator, who elsewhere allows himself considerable latitude, shrank from describing mere types of Christ as *ḥabrē* unto him.

20 *CSCO*, vol. CCXL, p. 115. Two manuscripts follow P in *dprw'*, but wrongly, as Ephrem's exegesis shows.
21 R. Meir drew the same lesson from the 'future tense' of *yāšīr* at Exod. xv.1 (BT Sanh. 91*a*, where further proof-texts are adduced).
22 Kindly reported to me by Dr S.P. Brock.
23 *Commentaire de l'Évangile Concordant* 15.9.
24 References are to W. Wright, *The Homilies of Aphraates the Persian Sage* (London and Edinburgh, 1869).
25 See the ingenious explanation by F.C. Burkitt (*JTS* 6 (1905), 289ff).
26 Psalm cxix.99*a*, on which Ben Zoma commented: 'Who is wise? He that learns from all men' (M. 'Abot 4.1), probably became a stock saying.
27 W. Wright and N. McLean, *The Ecclesiastical History of Eusebius in Syriac* (Cambridge, 1898).

The Book of Religion and Empire by Ṭabarī (839–923) is rich in biblical quotations.[28] These depend on P, as A. Mingana noted,[29] but Peters found in many Psalter quotations greater 'targumartige Breite und Freiheit' (p. 292) than in P. Two examples impressed him particularly:

(i) Psalm xlv.5: MT: *wĕtōrĕkā nōrā'ōt yĕmīnekā*, P: *nāmōsāk bdeḥltā dyammīnāk*, Ṭabarī (p. 75): 'for thy law and thy prescriptions are joined (*fa-'inna nāmūsaka wa-šarā'i'aka maqrūnat*) with the majesty of (*bi-haybat*) thy right hand'.

(ii) Psalm lxxii.11: MT: *kol-gōyīm ya'abdūhū*, P: *wkullhōn 'ammē neplḥūnāy(hy)*, Ṭabarī (p. 76): 'and all nations shall serve him with obedience and submissiveness (*bi'l-ṭā'at wa'l-inqiyād*)'.

Such citations, Peters deduced (p. 291), had been translated from a Syriac original that stood closer than the P manuscripts to the targum from which he supposed the Peshitta Psalter derived. He paid scant attention to the possibility that the expansions originated during (or after) the process of translation into Arabic. The latter explanation is proved correct by Ṭabarī's citations of the New Testament, many of which are no less 'targumartig', e.g.:

p. 125 (Matt. iv.19): 'and I shall make you after this day (*ba'da yawmikumā hāḏā*) fishers of men'.

ibid. (Matt. iv.21): 'and he called them to his faith (*'ilā dīnihi*)'.

p. 119 (John xvi.13): 'he [*sc.* the Paraclete] will not say anything of his own accord (*min tilqā'i nafsihi*), but will direct you in all truth (*wa-yasūsukum bi'l-ḥaqq kullihi*), and tell you of events (*bi'l-ḥawādiṯ*) and hidden things (*wa'l-ġuyūb*)'.

Peters also examined Psalms citations in a work of Ibn al-Djawzī (1126–1200),[30] who names his source as Ibn Ḳutayba (828–89). Of the three renderings that seemed to Peters typically targumic (pp. 291ff), two (Psalms xlv.4, lxxii.11) also appear in Ṭabarī,[31] and must go back either to him or to a common (Arabic) source. The third comes from Psalm cxlix.7: *la'ăśōt nĕqāmā baggōyīm*, P: *lme'bad pur'ānā men 'ammē*, Ibn al-Djawzī (p. 49): 'that they may exact vengeance for God upon the nations that serve him not

28 References are to the Arabic text, edited (Manchester, 1923) by A. Mingana, who also translated the work into English (Manchester, 1922).

29 Introduction to the English translation, p. xviii.

30 C. Brockelmann, 'Ibn Ǧauzî's Kitâb al-Wafâ fî faḍâ'il al-Muṣṭafâ nach der Leidener Handschrift untersucht', *Beiträge zur Assyriologie* 3 (1898), 1–59.

31 The texts are identical, except that Ibn al-Djawzī omits 'all' (*kulluhā*) in Psalm lxxii.11.

(*li-yantaqimū 'l-lāh mina 'l-umami 'llaḏīna lā yaʿbudūnahu*)'. Peters' view that this text goes back to an ancient targum is contradicted by the appearance in the same work (p. 50), again with acknowledgment to Ibn Ḳutayba, of a version of John xvi.13 almost identical with that found in Ṭabarī,[32] and of other 'targumartig' citations from the gospels, e.g.:

p. 51 (Matt. xi.14): 'and the Torah and the books of (*wa-kutub*) the prophets follow one another in succession with prophecy and revelation (*tatlū baʿḍuhā baʿḍan bi'l-nubuwwat wa'l-waḥy*) until John came'.

Thus the targum that Peters imagined to underlie the Peshitta Psalter and to survive occasionally in citations proves illusory when one looks into the character of the works from which those citations are drawn.[33] This conclusion runs parallel to that of M.D. Koster, who demonstrates in detail that A. Vööbus' searches in Syriac literature and Arabic translations for 'die alte targumische Grundschicht'[34] supposedly underlying the P Pentateuch are fruitless, and finds P in Exodus to be 'a single translation of the Hebrew basic text into Syriac'.[35]

In Psalms, the character of the translation itself points to the same conclusion. There are idiosyncrasies, such as the persistent rendering of Hebrew root *ḥwš* by *kattar*, 'wait' at Psalms xxii.20, xxxviii.23, xl.14, lv.9, lxx.2, 6, lxxi.12, and cxli.1, the original reading in the last passage surviving in just one manuscript (9*a*1).[36] There are signs of fatigue in the translation of Psalm cxix, with its blocks of eight verses all beginning with the same letter: verse 91

32 Ibn al-Djawzī omits 'anything' and 'all' (*kullihi*), but preserves, after *nafsihi*: 'but he will tell you of what he hears'.

33 In another article ('Arabische Psalmenzitate bei Abū Nuʿaim', *Biblica* 20 (1939), 1–9), Peters found further examples of 'freie Textgestaltung', the origin of which he sought in Jewish targumic tradition, but without claiming that these represent an earlier stage in the development of P than is recoverable through the P manuscripts.

34 A. Vööbus, *Peschitta und Targumim des Pentateuchs* (Stockholm, 1958), p. 107.

35 M.D. Koster, *The Peshiṭta of Exodus* (Assen, 1977), pp. 199–212. In Isaiah the case may be different; cp. L. Delekat, 'Die syrolukianische Übersetzung des Buches Jesaja und das Postulat einer alttestamentlichen Vetus Syra', *ZAW* 69 (1957), 21–54, especially p. 35.

36 This rendering may be due to confusion with the root *ḥšh*, 'be silent, inactive', which comes close to 'wait' at Judg. xviii.9, 2 Kgs vii.9. The only parallel I have found (in any ancient version) is in P on Job xx.2 (MT: *ūbaʿăbūr ḥūšī bī*, P: *wmeṭṭulāt*(*y*) *kattar*(*w*) *lī*). P understands the root *ḥwš* differently at Psalms xc.10, cxix.60.

is omitted, verse 117 is translated a second time in the place of verse 119, verse 148 is repeated after verse 151, and verses 171–2 are transposed. Such features do not suggest the end-product of a thoroughgoing redaction of an ancient Aramaic targum, as Peters supposes, but rather the valiant if erratic efforts of an individual translator.[37]

II

The Peshitta Psalter shows many traits of *prima facie* theological significance. Comparison of these with other literature of the period within which the translation is generally dated – from the second pre-Christian[38] to the second post-Christian century[39] – may reveal something of the background of the translator.

One such trait is the introduction of the idea of election, through the root *gb'*. Hebrew *ḥāsīd* is rendered 'chosen one, elect' in five passages:

(i) Psalm iv.4: 'Know that the LORD has set apart (MT: *hiplā*, P: *praš*) unto himself the chosen one wondrously (P: *btedmortā* – a doublet of *hiplā*)'. As this passage differs from the rest, in that 'elect' is singular, it will be discussed last.

(ii) Psalm xxx.5: 'Sing unto the LORD, O his elect' (MT: *ḥăsīdāw*, P: *gbaw*)'.

(iii) Psalm xxxi.22: 'Blessed be the LORD, who chose unto himself the elect (MT: *hiplī' ḥasdō lī*, P: *dagbā leh gbayā*) in a strong city (MT: *bĕ'īr māṣōr*, P: *baqrītā 'aššīntā*)'. This rendering, no doubt influenced by that of Psalm iv.4, departs from all other versions in taking *hiplī'* in the sense of *hiplā* and reading *ḥăsīdāw*[?] *lō* for *ḥasdō lī*.

37 A division of the labour is perhaps suggested by differences in the rendering of parallel texts (Psalm xiv is parallel to Psalm xliii; Psalm cviii to Psalm lvii.8–12 and Psalm lx.7–14) and by the use of *'ettnīḥ*| six times, for six different Hebrew words, in Psalms xxxv–xxxix, and only twice elsewhere (cvii.29, cxxv.3). It is however possible that an individual, in the course of translating the entire Psalter, suddenly took to *'ettnīḥ* and soon just as suddenly abandoned it. In this essay a single translator will be spoken of; it would make little difference if two or more translators in fact collaborated, since they would have belonged to the same community.

38 F. Wutz, *Die Psalmen* (Munich, 1925), p. xxxix.

39 O. Eissfeldt, *Einleitung in das Alte Testament*, 2nd edn (Tübingen, 1956), p. 852 = *The Old Testament: An Introduction* (Oxford, 1965), p. 699. The translation is to be dated between the LXX Psalter, on which it seems partly dependent, and the Old Syriac Gospels, where it is quoted. The latter are datable to about A.D. 200 (F.C. Burkitt, *Evangelion da-Mepharreshe* (Cambridge, 1904), vol. II, pp. 202ff).

(iv) Psalm xxxii.6: 'Therefore everyone that is chosen by thee (MT: *kol-ḥāsīd*, P: *kul man dagbē lāk*) shall pray to thee at an acceptable time (MT: *lĕʿēt mĕṣōʾ*, P: *bzabnā mqabblā*)'.

(v) Psalm l.5: 'Gather unto him, O his elect (MT: *lī ḥăsīdāy*, P: *lwāteh gbaw*)'.

In its twenty-one other occurrences in Psalms, however, *ḥāsīd* is rendered *zaddīq*, *ḥsē*, *ṭāb* or *mraḥmān*.

The election theme appears in two more passages:

(i) Psalm xlvii.5: 'He has chosen us as his inheritance (MT: *yibḥar-lānū ʾet-naḥălātēnū*, P: *ʾagbayn yartūteh*)'.

(ii) Psalm lxviii.20: 'Blessed be the LORD every day, who has chosen us as his inheritance (MT: *yaʿămos-lānū*, P: *dʾagbayn yartūteh*)'. The root *ʿms* occurs only here in Psalms, and P's rendering, which differs from all others (LXX: κατευοδώσει ἡμῖν, Targum: *ṭĕʿēn lānā* and similarly Aquila, Symmachus and *Psalt. iuxta Heb.*), seems a guess.[40] That the translator, when forced to guess, should have thought of election, seems significant.

Turning to contemporary writings, we first note that the term 'elect', and references to God's 'choosing' Israel, are almost unknown in tannaitic literature.[41] There the word 'elect' (*bāḥīr*) occurs just once, in an obscure and perhaps corrupt passage in Sifre Deut. (§321), which comments on the word *bāḥūr* in Deut. xxxii.25: 'Ye caused me to stretch out my hand against my elect (*bbḥyry*)', and proceeds to adduce Num. xi.28, which includes the word *mibbĕḥūrāw*. The consonantal text does not show whether 'my elect' is singular or plural; perhaps it refers to the Israelites who would one day suffer the punishments earned by the wilderness generation, but Num. xi.28 would then be irrelevant, and the sense is in any case quite uncertain. The critical edition by L. Finkelstein and H.S. Horowitz (Berlin, 1939; reprinted New York, 1969) reports that two manuscripts have the variant *bbḥwr*, which is even less satisfactory. Again, God is said to have 'chosen' Israel in only one passage out of all tannaitic literature, namely *Sifrē* Deut. §312, where Psalm cxxxv.4 is treated as ambiguous:

40 That it was deduced from God's designation of Israel (Isa. xlvi.3) as *ʿămusīm minnī beṭen* (Targum: *rĕḥīmīn mikkol ʿammayyā*) is unlikely.

41 I am most grateful to Prof. Y. Yeivin, of the Academy of the Hebrew Language, Jerusalem, for a copy of the entries on the root *bḥr* in the Academy's computer-generated concordance of the Hebrew of the tannaitic period, prepared for use in the Academy's forthcoming *Historical Dictionary of the Hebrew Language*.

> We do not know whether God chose Israel as his special treasure, or Israel chose God. Therefore Scripture says (Deut. vii.6): the LORD your God chose you. And whence do we know that Jacob likewise chose God? It is also said (Jer. x.16): Not like these is the portion of Jacob, for . . . the LORD of Hosts is his name.[42]

The rabbis' distaste for the expression that God chose Israel is evident also in Targum Onqelos, which may go back to tannaitic times. In every passage that states that God chose (*bāḥar*) Israel (Deut. iv.37, vii.6, 7, x.15, xiv.2), Onqelos says instead that he delighted (*'itrĕʿē*) in them, even though in other contexts the Aramaic root *bḥr* is used both to render its Hebrew cognate (Gen. xiii.11; Exod. xvii.9, xviii.25)[43] and otherwise (Gen. xlix, 16, 17; Num. xxxi.5).

There are admittedly in later literature two references to God's 'choosing' Israel which purport to go back to tannaitic times. PT Yoma 37*a* (on 7.1) reports the text of one of the High Priest's blessings on the Day of Atonement as 'Who has chosen Israel', but as the corresponding Mishnah and the parallel in BT Yoma 70*a* state merely that one of the blessings was 'for (*ʿal*) Israel', the antiquity of the wording of PT is doubtful. Again, *Numbers Rabba* 3.2, in an exposition of Psalm lxv.5 (*'ašrē tibḥar ūtĕqārēb*), tells how a Roman lady complained to the Tanna R. Yose b. Ḥalafta: 'Your God brings near to himself (*mĕqārēb*) whomsoever he pleases.' R. Yose brought her a basket of figs, of which she selected and ate the best, and then retorted: 'You know how to select (*libĕrōr*) but God does not! The one whose deeds he perceives to be good he chooses (*bāḥar*) and brings near (*ūmĕqārēb*) to himself.' Not improbably, however, the word *bāḥar* is an addition, due to the influence of Psalm lxv.5 itself.

Jewish liturgical tradition offers further references to God's 'choosing' Israel, but none is demonstrably tannaitic. The blessing upon the Torah, 'who has chosen us from among all peoples and given us his Torah', first appears in BT Ber. 11*b*, where it is ascribed to R. Hamnuna (mid-third century). The opening of the fourth benediction of the Festival ʿAmidah, 'Thou hast chosen us from all peoples', was recited, according to BT Yoma 87*b*, by ʿUlla b. Rab

42 The passage is discussed in detail by E.E. Urbach, *The Sages* (Eng. edn, Jerusalem, 1975), vol. I, p. 530, and vol. II, pp. 925ff.

43 Though even in contexts unconnected with the election of Israel, *'itrĕʿē* is a far commoner rendering of Hebrew *bḥr*; note especially Gen. vi.2; Deut. xxiii.17, xxx.19.

(*c.* A.D. 330), in whose day it was apparently well known; I. Elbogen considered the text of the benediction largely the work of the Babylonian Amoraim Rab and Samuel (early third century).[44] The many other liturgical references to God's 'choice' of Israel[45] appear to be derived from these two, through a later process whereby certain formulae were imported from one prayer into another.[46] The expression seems to have gained currency only gradually; apart from the citations of the two prayers, the Babylonian Talmud contains but one example (BT Sanh. 104*b*: 'Blessed be he that chose Abraham's seed' – remarkably, in the mouth of a Gentile). All this renders the Targum on Isa. xii.3 particularly intriguing: 'And ye shall receive new teaching (*'ulpan ḥădat*) in joy from the elect of righteousness (*mibbĕḥīrē ṣidqā*).'

In rabbinic Judaism, then,[47] Israel were not called God's elect but (most frequently) his children, or brothers or friends;[48] they are also his servants, and his possession.[49] Nor did the Tannaim lack alternatives to the expression that God chose Israel. Often they speak of his love and compassion for his people;[50] Israel were dear to God, who had shown them mercy though they had no meritorious deeds, and who shared their sorrows and joys.[51] Else-

44 I. Elbogen, *Hattĕpillā bĕyiśrā'ēl* (Hebrew rev. edn of *Der jüdische Gottesdienst . . .* (Tel-Aviv, 1972)), p. 100.

45 S. Baer, *Sēder 'Ăbōdat Yiśrā'ēl* (Rödelheim, 1868), pp. 80f, 198, 219, 226, 240, 335, 366, 391 (cp. also p. 214). The references on pp. 80ff are at the end of the prayer *'Ahăbā rabbā* (cited in BT Ber. 11*b*), which may go back to a Temple liturgy (Elbogen (see n. 44 above), p. 19). One cannot assume, however, that the present wording of these phrases is tannaitic, especially since in three Genizah fragments the prayer concludes quite differently; see J. Mann, 'Genizah Fragments of the Palestinian Order of Service', *HUCA* 2 (1925), 269–338, especially p. 288.

46 J. Heinemann, *Prayer in the Talmud* (Berlin, 1977; Eng. edn of *Prayer in the Period of the Tanna'im and the Amora'im* (Hebrew, Jerusalem, 1964)), pp. 54ff.

47 What follows depends largely on M. Kadushin, 'Aspects of the Rabbinic Concept of Israel', *HUCA* 19 (1945–6), 57–96, and B.W. Helfgott, *The Doctrine of Election in Tannaitic Literature* (New York, 1954). In nn. 48–55, references are to J.Z. Lauterbach's edition of *Mekilta* (Philadelphia, 1933–5) unless otherwise stated. One reference is assigned to each expression, regardless of its frequency.

48 II.21; I.221; III.139. S. Schechter, *Some Aspects of Rabbinic Theology* (London, 1909), pp. 46ff writes: 'There is not a single endearing epithet in the language . . . which is not, according to the Rabbis, applied by the Scriptures to express this intimate relationship between God and his people' – perhaps an exaggeration.

49 III.138; II.75. Many more designations appear on II.80.

50 Tos. Ber. 3.7.

51 II.204, 69, 160.

where they stressed that the Torah was given to Israel and rejected by other nations; Israel accepted God's kingship, and God, to make them worthy, gave them a copious Torah and many commandments.[52] Other expressions are that Israel were designated to be before God from the Creation, that he set his name uniquely (*yiḥēd šĕmō*) upon Israel, that his presence (*šĕkīnā*) rests upon them, that he has no other people, and that God and Israel declare each other's uniqueness.[53] There are references to covenants with Abraham and Israel, but 'the covenant . . . is more presupposed than directly discussed'.[54] Even the most particularist opinions, e.g. that the Gentiles have no share in the World to Come, or indeed in God,[55] do not express election in so many words[56] – despite the centrality of that belief itself.[57]

Outside tannaitic literature, however, the terminology of election is often encountered. At Qumran, the plural of *bḥyr* occurs frequently, nearly always to denote the sect;[58] God is also said to have chosen them.[59] In other works, the term 'elect' (ἐκλεκτός) extends to *all* Israel, or at least to all the righteous in Israel: so Tobit viii.15; Wisd. iii.9;[60] Ecclus. xlvi.1, xlvii.22; rest of Esth. E.21 (τοῦ ἐκλεκτοῦ γένους); Joseph and Aseneth 8.11.[61] Mention of the 'elect' (probably reflecting an Aramaic original *bĕḥīr*[62]) is also common in Enoch, both in the Parables and in other sections (e.g. i.1ff, xciii.2ff); Jubilees i.29, too, speaks of 'all the elect of Israel'.

52 II.99, 234, 238f; M. Mak. 3.16.
53 I.222; III.184; BT Ber. 6*a*; II.69; II.23 (*ʿāśʾanī ʾămīrā waʾănī ʿăśītīw ʾămīrā*).
54 I.33; II.204; E.P. Sanders, *Paul and Palestinian Judaism* (London, 1977), p. 236.
55 Tos. Sanh. 13.2; II.27.
56 The noun *bĕḥīrā*, 'election' is confined to the phrase *bēt habbĕḥīrā*, denoting the Temple, as 'the place which the LORD will choose' (Deut. xii.11 etc.).
57 Kadushin argued that as the phrase 'election of Israel' did not occur in rabbinic literature, it could not be a rabbinic concept ('The Election of Israel in Rabbinic Sources' (in Hebrew), *Proceedings of the Rabbinical Assembly of America* 8 (1941–4), 20–5). In a sense this is a dispute over terms, since Kadushin regards 'Israel' as a central rabbinic concept, but his protest at the use of a term unknown in the sources is not unjustified.
58 1QS 9.14, CD 4.3, 1QH 2.13 etc. 1QM 12.5 (*bḥyry šmym*) is exceptional. See Sanders (n. 54 above), pp. 244ff.
59 1QS 4.22, 11.7; 1QS*b* 3.23 etc.
60 The manuscripts are divided in these two passages.
61 M. Philonenko, in his recent edition (*Joseph et Aséneth* (Leiden, 1968), p. 109), is inclined to date the work shortly before A.D. 115.
62 According to J.T. Milik's reconstructions in *The Books of Enoch: Aramaic Fragments* (Oxford, 1976), pp. 141, 265.

Some have argued that Enoch (the vexed question of the origin of the Parables may be left aside) and Jubilees come from sectarian groups within Israel, who reserved the title 'elect' for themselves,[63] but it is possible that here too the 'elect' are the righteous in Israel, as opposed to heathens and apostates.[64] In the New Testament, the 'elect' are of course the Christians.[65]

Was the title 'elect' in the Peshitta Psalter intended for all righteous Israelites or for some narrower group? What evidence there is favours the latter possibility, though not quite conclusively. One clue is at Psalm cvi.5, where the Psalmist hopes 'to see the prosperity of thy chosen [*bĕḥīrekā*], to rejoice in the joy of thy nation [*gōyekā*]'. P declines to follow the Psalmist in equating the elect with Israel; retaining the former expression, he omits 'thy nation', and renders the second line: 'I shall rejoice in thy joy.'[66] Again, the elect whom 'God chose unto himself in a strong city' (Psalm xxxi.22) sound like a special group; of course the reference to the city is due to the Psalmist, not the translator, but the latter seems to have gone to some trouble to obtain his interpretation of the whole phrase, and could easily have rendered it otherwise had he wished.[67] Finally, the translator's interest in election deserts him in two passages where the historical Israel is clearly meant; at Psalm cv.43, P is the only version to render *bĕḥīrāw* as 'his young men' (*lgaddūdaw*), and at Psalm cxxxv.4, where Israel is called God's *sĕgullā*, P has *lkenšeh* ('his congregation'), which is colourless indeed in comparison with other versions (LXX: περιουσιασμὸν, Symmachus: ἐξαίρετον, Targum: *ḥibbūbeh*) and with the P rendering of *sĕgullā* in the Pentateuch (*ḥabbīb* – Exod. xix.5; Deut. vii.6 etc.).[68] If the 'elect' were in fact a restricted group, it is noteworthy that they took Hebrew *ḥāsīd* to refer to themselves.

63 D. Hill, in *New Testament Studies* 11 (1964–5), 300, regards 'the righteous' in Enoch as 'a special or sectarian group'. J.T. Milik, *Ten Years of Discovery in the Wilderness of Judaea* (London, 1959), p. 32, attributes Jubilees to the Qumran sect. On these questions see Sanders (n. 54 above), pp. 346–87.

64 So Sanders, pp. 361 (Enoch), 380ff (Jubilees).

65 Later the Mandeans often designate themselves *bhiria zidqa*.

66 Unless he was simply baffled by the form *gwyk*.

67 He well knew the meaning 'wonder' for the root *pl'* (Psalms ix.2, lxxvii.12 etc., and even arguably iv.4), and often rendered *ḥāsīd* by *zaddīq* (e.g. Psalm xxxi.24, two verses later).

68 In Psalm lxxviii.31, however, *baḥūrē* is rendered *gbayā*: 'and he laid low ('*abrek*) the elect of Israel'. That one could designate ancient Israel as *gbayā* without believing that all Israel indefinitely remained 'elect' is apparent from Rom. ix–xi.

Perhaps they considered themselves (as the Pharisees and Essenes are widely thought to have been) successors of the *Assidaioi* (1 Macc. ii.42 etc.); on the other hand, *ḥāsīd* is an obvious term for a group to apply to itself, as later happened in medieval Germany and in eighteenth-century Poland and Lithuania.

I now return to the 'chosen one' at Psalm iv.4. At Qumran the singular *bḥyr* has been thought to denote the Teacher of Righteousness (1QpHab 9.12) and the Messiah (1QpHab 5.4; 4QarP and 4QMess ar 1.10), though none of these interpretations is certain.[69] In the Parables of Enoch, the 'chosen one' is the Messiah, though lively debate continues as to whether the work is Jewish or Christian, and when it originated.[70] 'Chosen one' in the New Testament is a title of Christ (ἐκλελεγμένος: Luke ix.35; ἐκλεκτός: Luke xxiii.35; John i.34), and is also applied to individual Christians (ἐκλεκτός: Rom. xvi.13; 2 John 13). There are corresponding possibilities for the 'chosen one' in P: the founder of a Jewish sectarian movement, the (Jewish or Christian) Messiah, or the individual members of the community, each of whom regarded himself as elect and 'wondrously set apart' unto God.

Another significant passage is Psalm xlviii.14, MT: *passĕgū 'armĕnōtehā*, P: *wa'qōr(w) sāḥrātāh*, 'and uproot her [i.e. Jerusalem's] palaces'. This extraordinary rendering[71] transforms verses 13–15, which now read like military commands to besiege (verse 13: *'etkarkūh*, MT: *sōbbū*) and prepare for an assault, 'that ye may tell the last generation that this is our God!' One might suspect that *'qōr(w)* was corrupt, but there is no obvious emendation, and,

69 In 1QpHab 'his elect' (*bḥyrw*) is more probably plural; see A. Dupont-Sommer, '"Élus de Dieu" et "Élu de Dieu" dans le Commentaire d'Habacuc', in Z.V. Togan (ed.), *Proceedings of the Twenty-Second Congress of Orientalists*, vol. II (Leiden, 1957), pp. 568–72. The two Aramaic texts have the singular *bḥyr* but are too fragmentary for confident interpretation; see J.A. Fitzmyer, *Essays on the Semitic Background of the New Testament* (London, 1971), pp. 127–60 (first published in *CBQ* 27 (1965), 348–72), who suggests that the 'chosen one' in both texts is Noah (pp. 158ff).

70 Suggested dates range from the early Maccabean period to *c.* A.D. 270; see M.A. Knibb, 'The Date of the Parables of Enoch: A Critical Review', *New Testament Studies* 25 (1979), 345–59. Knibb's own conclusion is that the Parables are Jewish and may tentatively be dated to the end of the first century A.D. C.L. Mearns, 'Dating the Similitudes of Enoch', *New Testament Studies* 25 (1979), 360–9, prefers 'the late 40s A.D.'.

71 Contrast LXX: καταδιέλεσθε (whence Vulg.: *distribuite*, Syrohex.: *wpalleg(w)*), Symmachus: διαμετρήσατε, another: διαμερίζεσθε, *Psalt. iuxta Heb.*: *separate*. Targum (ed. Lagarde) begins the verse: 'Consider her throngs, reclining (*rĕmēn*) upon her palaces.'

in etymological terms, it is a credible rendering of the root *psg*, which in Rabbinic Hebrew means 'divide', 'cut', and in Jewish Aramaic even 'dismember'.[72] Moreover, it is amply supported by tradition. Arabic daughter-versions have *wa-'qlaʿū*[73] (or *wa-'hdimū*[74]) *quṣūrahā*. Daniel of Ṣalaḥ wrote in A.D. 541–2 that while the 'daughters of Judah' (verse 12) were the 'souls of the believers', the succeeding verses referred to 'Jerusalem, which prepared the cross for the Lord of Glory',[75] and he adduced Christ's prediction concerning the Temple: 'Verily I say unto you, there will not be left here stone upon stone which will not be thrown down.'[76] According to Ishoʿdad of Merv[77] (ninth century) and Barhebraeus[78] (died 1286), the Psalm refers to the invasion in Hezekiah's day, and verses 13–14 recount the Assyrian soldiers' instructions. One must admit that the discord between *ʿqōr(w)* and the preceding verses (1–12), which mirror the love of Jerusalem that pervades the original,[79] is suspicious, but it seems due to the nature of the translation. Where the sense of the original was plain, the translator felt bound to adhere to it, while a crux like *passĕgū* was apt to bring out his own ideas – which might differ sharply from the Psalmist's. The harsh transition resulting in this case would not have dissuaded him, since he knew – and no doubt accepted as one of the mysteries of Scripture – that such transitions did occur.[80]

In the search for a Jewish background, an obvious starting-point is the Qumran sect. Jerusalem was the home of their opponents,[81] whose destruction they anticipated,[82] and the Temple itself was

72 *Lamentations Rabba* 5.6: *hĕwā nāseb leh ūmĕpasseg leh 'ēbārīm 'ēbārīm.*
73 The Qûzhayyensis in Lagarde, *Psalterium Iob Proverbia Arabice* (Göttingen, 1876).
74 Carshuni version in British Library MS Or. 4054.
75 British Library MS Add. 17125, *ad loc.*
76 Matt. xxiv.2; cp. Mark xiii.2 and Luke xxi.6.
77 British Library MS Or. 4524, *ad loc.*
78 *Awṣar Rāzē* on Psalms, ed. Lagarde, *Praetermissorum Libri Duo* (Göttingen, 1879), *ad loc.*
79 E.g. in verses 9 ('God will establish it for ever'), 12 ('Let Mount Zion rejoice and the daughters of Judah exult because of thy judgements, O LORD').
80 E.g. Psalms xxxi.9f, cii.23f.
81 Such as the 'last priests of Jerusalem' (1QpHab 9.4), 'scoffers' (4QpIsa[b], col. ii, 10) and 'seekers of smooth things' (Pap 4QpIsa[c], 11.10f). See J.M. Allegro, 'More Isaiah commentaries from Qumran's fourth cave', *JBL* 77 (1958), 215–21.
82 4QpNah 2.4ff etc.; at 4QpNah 1.3, *trms* may mean that Jerusalem will be trampled.

'polluted'.[83] Even at Qumran, however, 'destroy the palaces of Jerusalem!' seems an unlikely sentiment, as is evident from the *Tanḥūmīm* (e.g. 'contend with kingdoms over the blood of Jerusalem, and see the bodies of Thy priests and none to bury them'),[84] the Hymn to Zion[85] and the Temple Scroll.[86] There may however have been kindred groups who desired the destruction rather than reform of Jerusalem. M. Black's hypothesis of a 'widespread movement of Jewish or para-Jewish non-conformity, characterized by its ascetic or puritanical tendencies and manner of life and its baptizing cult', which included Samaritans as well as the Qumran sect and many inter-related groups,[87] would favour that possibility; within such a movement the enmity that the Samaritans no doubt felt towards Jerusalem might have spread. Jeremiah's use of similar imperatives addressed to the Babylonians (Jer. v.10, vi.6, 9 etc.) suggests another possibility, that P *ʿqōr*(*w*) goes back to one who accepted, albeit with a heavy heart, the inevitability of the fall of Jerusalem in A.D. 70. Thus Josephus reports (*Bellum* VI.5.3) one Jesus son of Ananias, who went about the city from A.D. 62 wailing: 'Woe to Jerusalem!', and BT Yoma 39*b* tells how R. Joḥanan b. Zakkai predicted the destruction of the Temple. Such an exegesis of *passĕgū ʾarmĕnōtehā* might explain the curious paraphrase found in some manuscripts of *Midraš Tĕhillīm*, reported in S. Buber's edition (Wilna, 1891): *qṭʿw bʾrwtyh*, apparently meaning: 'Cut down her citadels.'[88] Buber rejects it as corrupt, preferring *gbhw byrnywtyhm*, 'build high their palaces'.

83 4QFlor 1.5: *hšmw*, with the root *šmm* meaning 'pollute' (Dan. ix.27); so D. Flusser in *Israel Exploration Journal* 9 (1959), 102. Attitudes towards Jerusalem and towards the Temple must be considered together, since, according to Flusser, the Jews in the Second Temple period regarded Jerusalem and the Temple as one entity; cp. Enoch lxxxix.50ff, which depicts Jerusalem as a house and the Temple as its tower. See Flusser, 'Jerusalem in the Literature of the Second Temple' (in Hebrew), *Veʾim Bigvurot* (Festschrift for R. Mass, ed. A. Even-Shoshan *et al.*) (Jerusalem, 1974), pp. 263–94.

84 J.M. Allegro, *Discoveries in the Judaean Desert*, vol. V (Oxford, 1968), p. 60. The *Tanḥūmīm* were composed and not merely preserved by the sect, according to Flusser, 'Pharisees, Sadducees and Essenes in 4QpNah' (in Hebrew), *Essays in Jewish History and Philology in Memory of G. Alon* (Tel-Aviv, 1970), pp. 133–68 (see p. 160).

85 J.A. Sanders, *Discoveries in the Judaean Desert*, vol. IV (Oxford, 1965), p. 86.

86 Cp. especially the references to 'the city in the midst of which I dwell' – 45.13 etc.

87 *The Scrolls and Christian Origins* (London, 1961), ch. 3.

88 *bʾrwtyh* cannot mean 'her wells', which would bear no relation to the MT, but seems to be an aberrant spelling of *bīrōtehā*.

A Christian origin seems more plausible. Denunciations and threats against Jerusalem (Matt. xxiii.37; Luke xxi.24) and the Temple (Matt. xxiv.2, noted by Daniel of Ṣalaḥ, and parallels; John ii.19; Acts vii.48–50) appear from the first, though attitudes varied greatly, and the earliest Christian community daily attended the Temple (Acts ii.46, v.42). Later, Christians regarded the fall of Jerusalem as proof of the rejection of the old Israel.[89] That a Christian translator should have read into the Psalter a prophecy of that event is not incredible.

Next considered are three references which P introduces to the faith of the nations in God:

(i) Psalm xxxv.18: 'and among many nations (MT: *bĕʿam ʿāṣūm*, P: *bʿammē saggīʾē*) I shall sing unto thee'.

(ii) Psalm lxv.6: 'God our saviour, hope of all the ends of the earth and of distant nations (MT: *wĕyām rĕḥōqīm*, P: *wadʿammē raḥīqē*)'.

(iii) Psalm cvii.32: 'Praise him in the assembly of the nations (MT: *biqĕhal ʿām*, P: *bʿedtā d-ʿammē*)'.

The substitution of plural for singular is admittedly very common in the Peshitta Psalter.[90] Most instances, however, stem from the predilection in Hebrew for collective usages, which are rendered by Syriac plurals. Frequent examples are *ʾādām*, *ḥaṭṭāʾt*, *ṣaddīq*, *ṣar*, 'straits', and *tĕhillā*; so even lxxxix.20 ('he spoke in visions to his righteous ones') and cv.33 ('he smote their vine*s* and their fig-tree*s*, and broke the tree*s* (within) their border*s*'). Others occur in similes (xxxiii.7, 'bottle*s*', cii.8, 'roof-top*s*'), or in figurative passages (xxiii.5, 'table*s*', xxxi.16, 'in thy hand*s*'), especially theophanic passages (lxxxiii.16, 'thy whirlwind*s*', xcvii.2, 'cloud*s* and thick mist*s*'), or for other reasons do not substantially affect the sense (xlix.5, 'ear*s*', 'parable*s*', 'riddle*s*'; xci.7, 'thousand*s*', 'myriad*s*').[91] One would be hard pressed to find two dozen cases of meaningful numerical change.

89 Typical are: Justin, *Dialogue* §16.2–4; Tertullian, *Apology* §21, *Adversus Judaeos* §13; Origen, *Contra Celsum* 4.22; Ephrem, *Contra Julianum* 4.18ff.

90 There are some five hundred instances.

91 I leave aside cases where pluralization is incidental to a major departure from the original, whether through choice (lxxxii.1: MT: *ʾēl*, P: *malʾakē*; cvi.28: MT: *baʿal*, P: *ptakrē*) or incomprehension (xlix.15: MT: *mizzĕbul*, P: *men tešbḥāthōn*; lxviii.23: MT: *mibbāšān*, P: *men bēt šennē*), and cases where P's original probably differed from the MT (xxxvi.7: 'thy judgement*s*', with Hebrew manuscripts; lxviii.28: 'their leader*s*', with the LXX).

The passages that pluralize 'nation' therefore seem significant. They contrast with the unrelieved condemnation of the Gentiles at Qumran[92] and in Jubilees, but are consistent with most other forms of Judaism – particularly among Diaspora communities eager for proselytes – and with Christianity.[93]

We now examine two quite different passages. At Psalm ii.12, P has: 'Kiss the son (MT: *naššĕqū bar*, P: *naššeq*(*w*) *brā*)[94] lest he[95] be angry and ye perish from his way (MT: *derek*, P: *men 'urḥeh*).' The interpretation 'kiss the son' appears in no other ancient version, though it was known to Jerome:[96] 'in Hebraeo legitur NESCU BAR, quod interpretari potest, *adorate filium*. Apertissima itaque de Christo prophetia . . .' The references in P to the son, and to his way, certainly suggest a Christian translator. Conceivably, however, the pronominal suffix of *'urḥeh*, though attested by all the manuscripts, is not original, in which case P could be explained as a mechanical word-by-word translation, from which no conclusion could be drawn.

The other passage is Psalm cx.3, where P renders: 'In splendours of holiness, from the womb, of old have I begotten thee, O child (*lāk ṭalyā 'īledtāk*, MT: *lĕkā ṭal yaldūtekā*).' Evidently the translator, baffled by *ṭal*, borrowed *yod* from the succeeding word.[97] This too has a Christian ring,[98] and finds no echo in tannaitic literature, where Psalm cx.1–3 is uniformly applied to Abraham.[99] However, the widely accepted restoration *'m yw*[*ly*]*d* [*'l*] *'*[*t*] *hmšyḥ* at 1QS*a* 2.11f would attest a belief among Jews that God would beget the Messiah, and the silence of the Pharisees reported at

92 Membership was restricted to Israelites, according to 1QS 6.13 (cp. however CD 11.2, 14.4).

93 'The Nation and the Nations' is a major theme of Syriac literature (Murray, n. 8 above, ch. 1).

94 A few witnesses have *'aḥod*(*w*) *mardūtā*, under the influence of the LXX δράξασθε παιδείας.

95 The variant 'lest the LORD be angry' similarly reflects the LXX.

96 *Breviarium in Psalmos*, *ad loc.* (Migne, *Patrologia Latina*, vol. XXVI, col. 827).

97 Vogel (n. 5 above, p. 257) thought *ṭalyā* might be a corruption of *ṭallā* but the P translator is not given to such senseless mechanical renderings.

98 As J. Dathe, *Psalterium Syriacum* (Halle, 1768), p. xxv, pointed out long ago. One writer (probably Jacob of Serug; cp. Beck in *CSCO* 187, p. xii) comments that Christ was no younger than his father, but appeared a child at his 'second birth', so that the Psalmist called him 'the child that was begotten of old'; see *CSCO* 186, p. 207.

99 [H.L. Strack–]P. Billerbeck, *Kommentar zum Neuen Testament* (Munich, 1922–8), vol. IV, pp. 453ff.

Matt. xxii.46 *may* attest the currency of a messianic interpretation of Psalm cx among Jews; conceivably, then, P's rendering could be Jewish.

Questions are also raised by the usage of *pārōqā*, 'saviour', in the Peshitta Psalter. In most P manuscripts,[100] Psalm xvii.7 begins: 'and make thy holy one a wonder and a saviour of those that hope (MT: *haplēh ḥăsādekā mōšīaʿ ḥōsīm*, P: *waʿbedāy*(*hy*) *tedmortā lḥasyāk wpārōqā*)'. This, too, seems a Christian reference; however, the conjunction before *pārōqā* is lacking in some witnesses[101] and may therefore be a Christian addition, in which case *pārōqā* would be vocative and refer to God. It is also remarkable that abstract nouns from the root *yšʿ* (*yešaʿ*, *yĕšūʿā*, *tĕšūʿā*), which occur altogether some eighty times in the Psalter, are rendered by P as *pārōqā* in twenty passages.[102] True, the occasional rendering of an abstract noun by a *nomen agentis* is to be expected, since 'it is not at all uncommon in OT poetry for God to be called by the name of the gift he brings'.[103] However, the number of such treatments of *yešaʿ* etc. in P is far greater than in the Jewish translations, LXX (nine passages)[104] and Targum (three),[105] but about the same as in Jerome's versions. The Vulgate uses *salvator* and *salutaris* four times each,[106] while in eleven other passages *salutare* appears in the genitive, dative or ablative case, in which it is indistinguishable from *salutaris* (e.g. Psalm ix.15: *exultabo in salutari tuo*).[107] *Psalt. iuxta Heb.* employs *salutare* similarly twelve times,[108] *salvator* thrice,[109] and *Iesus* five times.[110] Unlike these Christian versions, however, there is no real indication in the

100 Including the two oldest (6*t*1[ac] and 7*al*).

101 Including 6*t*l[pc] and 9*a*l (on which see n. 36 above).

102 Psalms xviii.47*, xxxvii.39, xlii.6*, 12*, xliii.5*, lxviii.20, lxxxv.5, lxxxix.27*, cxl.8, and all passages in nn. 104–5 below except xxvii.1. (The asterisk is explained in n. 111 below.) P also inserts *pārōqā* at Psalm iv.2 and uses it for *mišʿān* at Psalm xviii.9.

103 J.V. Chamberlain, 'The Functions of God as Messianic titles in the Complete Qumran Isaiah Scroll', *VT* 5 (1955), 366–72; see p. 370. He attributes the variants at Isa. li.5 in 1QIsa[a] to an interpretation of *yešaʿ* as 'saviour'.

104 Psalms xxiv.5, xxv.5, xxvii.1, 9*, lxii.3*, 7*, lxv.6, lxxix.9, xcv.1.

105 Psalms xxxv.3, cxviii.14, 21.

106 *Salvator* at Psalms xxiv.5, xxv.5, xxvii.9, lxii.7; *salutaris* at Psalms lxii.3, lxv.6, lxxix.9, xcv.1.

107 Psalms ix.15, xii.6, xiii.6, xx.6, xxi.6, lxxviii.22 (manuscripts vary), cvi.4, cxxxii.16 – all shared with *Psalt. iuxta Heb.* – and xxxv.9, li.14, cxvi.13.

108 Psalms xxi.2, xxiv.5, xxvii.1, lxix.14, and the eight passages indicated in n. 107 above.

109 Psalms xxv.5, xxvii.9, lxv.6.

110 Psalms li.14, lxxix.9, lxxxv.5, xcv.1, cxlix.4.

twenty P passages that a 'saviour' other than God was intended,[111] and it is, in any case, possible that some occurrences of *pārōqā* are due to Christian revision.[112]

Our 'profile' of the translator concludes with three passages that introduce the doctrine of resurrection:

(i) Psalm xlviii.15: 'He will lead us beyond death (MT: *ʿal-mūt*, P: *lʿel men mawtā*).'

(ii) Psalm xlix.9f: 'endeavour continually that thou mayest live for evermore and not behold corruption (MT: *wĕḥādal lĕʿōlām: wīḥī-ʿōd lānesaḥ lōʾ yirʾeh haššaḥat*, P: *lʾī lʿālam dtēḥē lʿālam ʿālmīn wlā teḥzē ḥbālā*)'.

(iii) Psalm lxxxviii.11ff: 'Behold (P: *hā*, MT: *hă-*), for the dead thou workest miracles . . . and they that are in graves shall declare thy kindness.'

All these features of the translation are consistent with a Christian origin. One cannot, however, rule out some non-rabbinic form of Judaism.

III

It is tempting to suppose that the community that produced the Peshitta Psalter had earlier needed a version of the Pentateuch, and to identify that version with the Peshitta Pentateuch, which may therefore reflect an earlier stage in the community's history.

Maori listed (pp. 67–181) over one hundred renderings in the P Pentateuch in which he detected rabbinic influence. He was surprised to find (p. 288) this influence not particularly marked in legal contexts;[113] if we eliminate instances that are purely aggadic (e.g. Gen. viii.7: 'and it went forth and did not return'), and non-legal elements in legal contexts (e.g. Num. v.28: 'and she will bear a male'), no more than forty of these renderings can be said to deal with halakic matters.[114] Even these, however, demonstrate

111 Apart perhaps from the added conjunction ('my God *and* my saviour') in passages asterisked in notes 102 and 104 above, and in Psalm iv.2.

112 Similarly the translation *ʿedtā* for Hebrew *qāhāl* and *ʿēdā* in favourable contexts only, unlike Psalms xxii.17, xxvi.5 and other passages, where *knuštā* is used, could be due to later interpolation. See G. Johnston, *The Doctrine of the Church in the New Testament* (Cambridge, 1943), pp. 140–3.

113 Nor, Maori adds (n. 4 above), in the poetic sections, though 15 of his 106 passages are drawn from Gen. xlix, the Balaam oracles and Deut. xxxii–xxxiii.

114 Though Maori has adopted what he calls a 'minimalist' methodology (p. xviii), and refrains from inferring rabbinic influence unless other factors can be excluded.

rabbinic influence regarding civil law (e.g. Exod. xxi.19: 'and he shall pay the doctor's fee'), the cultus (e.g. Lev. vi.14: 'he shall bake it soft'), diet (e.g. the names of unclean birds[115] and teeming creatures in Lev. xi), and much else.

A few renderings in P were, however, found to conflict with rabbinic halaka.[116] At Exod. xiii.13 P agrees with Philo (*De spec. leg.* I.135f) and Josephus (*Antiq.* IV.4.4) in prescribing that the firstborn of every (*sc.* unclean) animal be redeemed, while M. Bek. 1.2 limits this duty to the ass. All P manuscripts but one read at Exod. xvi.29: 'Let no man go out of the door of his house (*traʿ bayteh*) on the seventh day', which Maori found paralleled in Karaite sources only; the other manuscript (5*b*1) reads 'out of his boundary' (*tḥūmeh*), which word corresponds to mishnaic *tĕḥūm*, the Sabbath limit. In the light of Koster's study,[117] we may suppose *tḥūmeh* original and perhaps ascribe *traʿ bayteh* to assimilation to Exod. xii.22.[118] Lev. xix.27 is interpreted by P: 'Ye shall not grow long the hair (*lā trabbōn saʿrā*) of your heads', which, Maori notes, resembles the priestly regulation at Ezek. xliv.20. Among adherents of rabbinic Judaism, however, long hair was common in the tannaitic period.[119] Perhaps P condemns excessively long hair, of which the rabbis, too, disapproved;[120] otherwise, a priestly law has been extended to the whole community, which may be a sectarian trait.[121] P at Lev. xxiii.11 designates the time of the presentation of the *ʿŌmer* as *bātar yawmā ʾḥēnā* (MT: *mimmoḥŏrat haššabbāt*), which seems corrupt. Maori supposes (pp. 150ff) that two alternative expressions for 'on the morrow', *bātar yawmā* and

115 Following J.A. Emerton, 'Unclean Birds and the Origin of the Peshitta', *JSS* 7 (1962), 204–11.

116 As opposed to renderings that the rabbis might have found quaint (Lev. xix.26: 'ye shall not eat blood') or even undesirable (Lev. xviii.21: 'do not cast forth thy seed to impregnate a strange woman' – condemned in M. Meg. 4.9, but attested in the school of R. Ishmael (BT Meg. 25*a*) and in Pseudo-Jonathan and Saadya *ad loc.*). At Lev. xi.19, *ṭawsā*, 'peacock', for *ʿăṭallēp* shows merely that the translator was occasionally ill-informed (Emerton, pp. 210ff).

117 *The Peshiṭta of Exodus* (n. 35 above), pp. 177–97 (on the value of 5*b*1).

118 Maori (n. 4 above, p. 284) is aware of this possibility, but is not inclined to follow 5*b*1, which he describes as 'notorious' (p. ii).

119 S. Krauss, *Talmudische Archäologie* (Leipzig, 1910), vol. I, p. 644, n. 830, citing M. Ohol. 3.4, Makš. 1.5.

120 It rendered one *mĕnuwwāl*, 'unkempt' (BT Taʿan. 17*a* etc.).

121 Thus the Qumran sectaries, who designated themselves priests (CD 4.3f), excluded those having bodily defects (CD 15.15f), and the Essenes wore white garments (Josephus, *Bellum*, II.8.3, 5).

lyawmā 'ḥrēnā, have been conflated; the translator intended the morrow of the first day of Passover, but, rather than devise a translation of *haššabbāt* that might fit this sense, he omitted it. However, as *yod* and *nun* look so alike *'ḥrēnā* may be a corruption of *'ḥrāyā*. The counting of the *'Ōmer* was to begin (verse 15) *men bātreh dyawmā*, which would then mean 'on the morrow of' the last day of Passover, as in the Falasha calendar, or perhaps more vaguely 'after' that day, as apparently at Qumran and in Jubilees.[122] Most P manuscripts conclude Deut. xxi.22: 'and he shall be hanged on a tree and be slain' (*wnezdqep 'al qaysā wnetqṭel*), which, as Maori pointed out,[123] departs conspicuously from the MT and rabbinic tradition but agrees with the Temple Scroll, col. 64, lines 8–13. It is, however, worth noting that 9*a*1 whose unique readings elsewhere sometimes appear original,[124] ha the same order as the MT ('he shall be slain and hanged on a tree').

The Judaism of the Peshitta Pentateuch, then, is predominantly rabbinic but embodies some non-rabbinic elements. The religion of the Peshitta Psalter is emphatically different from rabbinic Judaism: the community (probably) regards itself, rather than all Israel, as the elect, and it (arguably) views with equanimity the fall of Jerusalem, though it looks favourably upon the Gentiles. Yet both books form part of the Bible that was cherished by the Syriac-speaking Church, which, it is widely thought, grew out of a Jewish community. The hypothesis may be ventured that the Pentateuch was translated while that community was yet Jewish, and the Psalter when its evangelization was well under way if not complete. How the translations of the other biblical books relate to the Pentateuch and the Psalter remains to be seen. At all events, the Peshitta would seem to have much to tell us of the Judaism from which the community started out, and of the subsequent evolution of their faith.

122 M. Wurmbrand, in *EJ*, vol. VI, col. 1148. Many divergent views on this issue are collected in D.Z. Hoffman's commentary (in Hebrew) on Leviticus (Jerusalem, 1954), pp. 113ff. Cp. also S. Talmon, 'The Calendar Reckoning of the Sect from the Judaean Desert', in C. Rabin and Y. Yadin (eds.), *Aspects of the Dead Sea Scrolls*, 2nd edn (Jerusalem, 1965), pp. 162–99.

123 Maori (see n. 4 above), pp. 171ff; cp. Y. Yadin, *The Temple Scroll*, Hebrew edn (Jerusalem, 1977), vol. I, p. 287.

124 See n. 36 above. Here 9*a*1 is joined by four seventeenth-century manuscripts, as Professor P.A.H. de Boer has kindly informed me.

INDEXES (compiled by Shulamit Reif)

INDEX OF SOURCES

A HEBREW BIBLE
B APOCRYPHA AND PSEUDEPIGRAPHA
C QUMRAN TEXTS
D NEW TESTAMENT AND EARLY CHRISTIAN WRITINGS
E TALMUD
F MIDRASH
G MANUSCRIPTS CITED BY NUMBER

(A) HEBREW BIBLE

(B) APOCRYPHA AND PSEUDEPIGRAPHA

(C) QUMRAN TEXTS

(D) NEW TESTAMENT AND EARLY CHRISTIAN WRITINGS

(E) TALMUD

(F) MIDRASH

(G) MANUSCRIPTS CITED BY NUMBER

INDEX OF PLACES AND ORGANIZATIONS

INDEX OF NAMES

Feldman, L.A., 35n
Fenton, P.B., 265
Field, F., 89, 277–8n
Finkelstein, L., 128, 204 (n. 37), 210 (n. 127), 285
Fischer, R.H., 238n, 241n, 248n, 249n
Fish, T., 6
Fitzmyer, J.A., 290n
Flusser, D., 277n, 292n
Fohrer, G., 228
Forbes, D., 37n, 40n, 47n
Foreiro (Forerus), F., 94–5
Freedman, H., 59n
Freimann, A., 251n
Friedlander, G., 121n, 125n, 191
Friedländer, M., 149n
Funk, S., 59n, 249

Gad, J., 191
Gavin, F., 238, 241–2, 247, 249
Gebhardt, O., 69n
Gelston, A., 277n
Gesenius, W., 95–6
Gibb, H.A.R., 5
Giesebrecht, F., 98
Giḳatilla, Moses, 160n
Ginsburger, M., 119n, 191
Ginzberg, L., 189n, 190n, 191, 202–12 (*passim*), 249, 254n
Gladstone, W.E., 137
Glasson, T.F., 29n
Goetze, Albrecht, 2
Goldschmidt, D., 72
Goldschmidt, L., 57
Gooch, G.P., 36, 42n
Gordon, C.H., 125
Graetz, H., 35–55, 98, 229
Gray, G.B., 95
Gregory VII (Pope), 5
Grelot, P. 121
Grillmeier, A., 238
Guillaumont, A., 241
Gunkel, H., 229
Guttmann, Julius, 3
Gwynn, J., 240n

Hadasi, Juda, 256n, 258n
Haddaršān, Mōše, *see* Mōše Haddaršān
Hadrian, 128, 139
Haefeli, L., 247
Hagar (biblical), 153, 202 (n. 6)
Hakohen, M., 188n
Halévy, J., 98–9
Hameiri, M., 229
Hamnuna, 286
Hannah (biblical), 177
Haran, M., 41n, 43n
Hart, Henry St J., x
Hart, J.H.A., 61n
Hartom, E.S., 99–100
Hasel, G.F., 103, 108, 110
Hayes, John H., 36, 246n
Ḥayyūǧ, Y., 160, 163–5
Heinemann, J., 287n
Helfgott, B.W. 287n
Herford, Robert Travers, 7
Herod (the Great), 130
Herrmann, J., 228
Herzberg, A., 35n
Hesseling, D.C., 66n, 70, 73n
Hezekiah (biblical), 103, 291
Hidal, S., 280n
Higger, M., 211 (n. 139)
Hill, D., 289n
Hirsch, S.R., 230
Hitzig, F., 96, 107
Ḥiyya bar Abba, 204 (n. 31)
Hoenig, S.B., 131
Hoffman, D.Z., 298n
Hölscher, G., 280n
Homer, 126
Hopkins, Simon, 61n
Horovitz, H.S., 128n, 210 (n. 118), 260n, 285
Hupfeld, H., 228
Husain, Zakir, 13
Hvidberg, F., 101–2
Hyksos, 271

Ibn al-Djawzī, 282, 283n
Ibn Ezra, Abraham, 92–3, 98–9, 148–50, 160n, 187–8, 191, 202–12 (*passim*), 228, 262n, 275
Ibn Ezra, Isaac, 148–50
Ibn Gabirol, Solomon, 139–42, 146n, 151–4
Ibn Janaḥ, 205 (n. 41), 207 (n. 84)
Ibn Khaldun, 3
Ibn Ḳutayba, 282–3
Ibn Malka, Nethane'el b. 'Ali, 148
Ibn Saruq, 205 (n. 41), 210 (n. 118)
Ifra Hormizd, 236–7
Isaac (biblical), 149, 202 (n. 8), 204 (n. 35) (n. 36), 205 (n. 43), 212 (n. 141), 243–4
Isaiah (biblical), 103, 114
Ishmael (biblical) and Ishmaelites, 152, 203 (n. 22) (n. 28), 203–4 (n. 31), 204 (n. 35), 210 (n. 118), 243
Ishmael (Rabbi), 297n

GENERAL INDEX

UNIVERSITY OF CAMBRIDGE

ORIENTAL PUBLICATIONS PUBLISHED FOR THE

FACULTY OF ORIENTAL STUDIES

1 *Averroes' Commentary on Plato's Republic*, edited and translated by E. I. J. Rosenthal.
2 *FitzGerald's 'Salaman and Absal'*, edited by A. J. Arberry.
3 *Ihara Saikaku: The Japanese Family Storehouse*, translated and edited by G. W. Sargent.
4 *The Avestan Hymn to Mithra*, edited and translated by Ilya Gershevitch.
5 *The Fusūl al-Madanī of al-Fārābī*, edited and translated by D. M. Dunlop (out of print).
6 *Dun Karm, Poet of Malta*, texts chosen and translated by A. J. Arberry; introduction, notes and glossary by P. Grech.
7 *The Political Writings of Ogyū Sorai*, by J. R. McEwan.
8 *Financial Administration under the T'ang Dynasty*, by D. C. Twitchett.
9 *Neolithic Cattle-Keepers of South India: A Study of the Deccan Ashmounds*, by F. R. Allchin.
10 *The Japanese Enlightenment: A Study of the Writings of Fukuzawa Yukichi*, by Carmen Blacker.
11 *Records of Han Administration*. Vol. I *Historical Assessment*, by M. Loewe.
12 *Records of Han Administration*. Vol. II *Documents*, by M. Loewe.
13 *The Language of Indrajit of Orchā: A Study of Early Braj Bhāsā Prose*, by R. S. McGregor.
14 *Japan's First General Election, 1890*, by R. H. P. Mason.
15 *A Collection of Tales from Uji: A Study and Translation of 'Uji Shūi Monogatari'*, by D. E. Mills.
16 *Studia Semitica*. Vol. I *Jewish Themes*, by E. I. J. Rosenthal.
17 *Studia Semitica*. Vol. II *Islamic Themes*, by E. I. J. Rosenthal.
18 *A Nestorian Collection of Christological Texts*. Vol. I *Syriac Text*, by Luise Abramowski and Alan E. Goodman.
19 *A Nestorian Collection of Christological Texts*. Vol. II *Introduction, Translation, Indexes*, by Luise Abramowski and Alan E. Goodman.
20 *The Syriac Version of the Pseudo-Nonnos Mythological Scholia*, by Sebastian Brock.
21 *Water Rights and Irrigation Practices in Lahj*, by A. M. A. Maktari.
22 *The Commentary of Rabbi David Kimhi on Psalms cxx-cl*, edited and translated by Joshua Baker and Ernest W. Nicholson.
23 *Jalāl al-dīn al-Suyūṭī*. Vol. 1 *Biography and Background*, by E. M. Sartain.
24 *Jalāl al-dīn al-Suyūṭī*. Vol. 2 "*Al-Tahadduth biniʿmat allāh*", Arabic text, by E. M. Sartain.
25 *Origen and the Jews: Studies in Jewish-Christian Relations in Third-Century Palestine*, by N. R. M. de Lange.
26 *The Vīsaladevarāsa: A Restoration of the Text*, by John D. Smith.
27 *Shabbethai Sofer and His Prayer-book*, by Stefan C. Reif.
28 *Mori Ōgai and the Modernization of Japanese Culture*, by Richard John Bowring.
29 *The Rebel Lands: An investigation into the origins of early Mesopotamian mythology*, by J. V. Kinnier Wilson.
30 *Saladin: The Politics of the Holy War*, by Malcolm C. Lyons and David Jackson.
31 *Khotanese Buddhist Texts* (Revised Edition), by H. W. Bailey.
32 *Interpreting the Hebrew Bible: Essays in honour of E. I. J. Rosenthal*, edited by J. A. Emerton and Stefan C. Reif.